# The
# Dictionary of
# Critical Social Sciences

# The Dictionary of Critical Social Sciences

## T. R. Young, Ph.D.
The Red Feather Institute

## Bruce A. Arrigo, Ph.D.
Institute of Psychology, Law, and Public Policy
California School of Professional Psychology–Fresno

Westview Press
A Member of the Perseus Books Group

Copyright © 1999 by Westview Press, A Member of the Perseus Books Group

Published in 1999 in the United States of America by Westview Press, 5500 Central Avenue, Boulder, Colorado 80301-2877, and in the United Kingdom by Westview Press, 12 Hid's Copse Road, Cumnor Hill, Oxford OX2 9JJ

Library of Congress Cataloging-in-Publication Data
Young, T. R.
    The dictionary of critical social sciences / T. R. Young, Bruce A. Arrigo.
        p.  cm.
    ISBN 0-8133-6672-0
    1. Social sciences—Dictionaries.   I. Arrigo, Bruce A.
II. Title.
H41.Y68   1999
300'.3—dc21                                                                99-10750
                                                                                CIP

The paper used in this publication meets the requirements of the American National Standard for Permanence of Paper for Printed Library Materials Z39.48-1984.

10   9   8   7   6   5   4   3   2   1

To everyone who has ever been a student and inquired into the nature of a thing; to everyone who will be a student in search of knowledge, wisdom, and understanding

# Preface

Twenty years have passed since this dictionary's beginnings. Much has changed in both the socialist and the capitalist worlds. In the socialist world, the Soviet Bloc has collapsed to be replaced by a mélange of political economies. Some of these economies are brutal and viciously ethnocentric (e.g., Serbia or the former Yugoslavia). Others are corrupt and indifferent to common need (e.g., what is now Russia). Still others are trying hard to find a decent accommodation to the difficult times in which they exist (e.g., Hungary and Poland). In China, a curious form of capitalism has emerged, about which it is far too early to make judgments. Indeed, in such a sprawling country, judgments usually last but until the next town or province. Cuba has made some accommodations with the new realities, inviting private capital in from Latin American countries but trying to retain some of the gains of the socialist revolution. Castro, now more than seventy, is open to liberation theology and market dynamics more so than in the 1970s when the first editions of the dictionary appeared. Vietnam inches closer to transnational economics. Recently, the country signed a protocol with the United States for official recognition.

The capitalist world is in great turmoil. The globalization of the economy continues apace—a globalization that will transform significant areas and peoples and that will greatly alter existing politics in Europe and North America. Whole cultures will disappear, absorbed in the rush to industrial/urban life. In brief, without the Socialist Bloc to stabilize politics, and in the face of emergent competitors in the third world that destabilize economics, a dramatic swing to the Right has occurred in both Europe and North America. Canada recently elected a very conservative prime minister, and the weak democratic center in the United States is under heavy political stress. The story, in short, is that programs of social justice are difficult to support without profits from the third world, deficit spending, and/or full employment. Each of these suffers immensely.

In spite of dramatic and disturbing changes, most people live and manage to survive. Amidst the billions in India, China, South America, and, indeed, the developed countries, young people fall in love, get married, find work, raise children, attend to some kind of religious impulse, and, more often than one might guess, reach out to support and sustain others in times of trouble or tragedy.

There is also much that gives one hope. Creative thinking and honest reevaluation are prominent in the socialist camp. Liberative and liberation theology continue to endure. Housing is better. Health care is better. Transportation and communication are far better for most people on earth than just a hundred years ago. Infant mortality rates are down, and longevity rates are up. Both are good indicators of the quantity and quality of life in an age. The progressive task is to extend these benefits and to enclose them inside a context of loving compassion—a compassion that might replace the mean and grudging spirit that now distorts so much politics around the world.

Clearly, there is still more to do: Better, more democratic politics are needed; better, more accessible education and health care need development; better, more affordable housing remains a challenge; responsive and responsible economic systems have yet to be instituted; the information superhighway is still a toll road upon which only a few hundred million can travel; art, drama, fiction, and music remain in thrall to ethnic and/or class interests; and racism, sexism, and homophobia endure amidst an insidious climate of support. Science itself remains an arrogant despot that excludes all forms of knowledge other than that which can be simplified and mathematized. Too many children are born and fail to receive the loving, intensive parenting they need; too many elderly die alone, rejected after a lifetime of productive labor; too many women are beaten by too many men made angry and anxious about their essential masculinity. The use of sex and violence to entice children and/or customers remains subversive to the human project.

One can see that a book about words can reveal but a tiny fraction of the incredibly complex social lifeworld around us. Yet words matter. Indeed, without words, social lifeworlds would be impossible. The interesting question is how to make the words move us toward social justice, social peace, and the transcending joy of music, art, drama, literature, and play. This book can help. Twenty years ago, it was a gift given to the world. The nice thing about a gift is that it can be given over and over; the bad thing about a gift is that, for some, it may be hard to accept. A critically inspired dictionary can be difficult to accept, particularly if many of our cherished notions are exposed, questioned, and even abandoned. Of course, this is, in part, what we have done with this glossary. Our aim has been to point out how critical inquiry can signal what work is left to be done if real peace, authentic justice, and true humanity are to flourish.

The first editions of the dictionary emphasized socialist interpretations of many complex and interesting ideas. The first editions, however, were grievously flawed, in that they did not do justice to feminist ideas and gender politics. There were many basic concepts in the sociology of law, religion, philosophy, social psychology, moral development, and political sociology that were, regrettably, not treated. This edition retains its socialist (and critical) edge but is better developed on these matters.

Then, too, postmodern and semiotic paradigms have come along to bemuse and to infuriate those with both modern and premodern sensibilities. Coupled with these perspectives are the revolutionary and wide-sweeping changes wrought by chaos/complexity theory, as developed in the philosophy of science. Taken together, one is left with a very unsettling knowledge process that parallels the disturbing political economics seething and boiling around the world.

Finally, we wish to make clear that this dictionary is written for students—always the student, and for North American students especially. To that end, we sought a balance between those things students are interested in and those things they need to know despite, perhaps, not being inclined to such interest. Our experience teaches us that students are inquisitive about sex and gender relations, crime and justice, sports and the organization of play, religion, and, to their great credit, morality, as well as about the everyday politics of life. We speak directly and critically to these interests in our choice of terms/ideas. Students are also fascinated by money—money more so perhaps than the macroeconomics within which money comes and goes. Where relevant, we tried, as best we could, to relate macroeconomics to the student's condition in life.

*T. R. Young*
*Bruce A. Arrigo*

# Authors' Note

This dictionary is different from others in several ways upon which the student should reflect. First and foremost, the dictionary is not neutral. It includes terms that are central to a critique of alienating social relations and to the creation of life-affirming social interactions. In our elaboration of many entries, we consider questions about race, gender, class, patriarchy, homophobia, and other forms of elitism. Further, a fundamental desire to describe emancipatory avenues by which the drama of life can and does unfold is also pivotal to our investigation. The link between both of these points defines what we mean by the term "critical." Thus, the reader should bear in mind that many of the entries challenge, debunk, unmask, resist, oppose, or reject conventional interpretations in the hope of moving collective understanding in a more pro-social way. Our position is not so much a statement of discontent with knowledge in the social sciences as it is an unflinching fidelity to what it means to engage in critical inquiry.

The dictionary contains references borrowed from and essential to the fields of sociology, philosophy, economics, history, social psychology, political science, criminal justice, anthropology, education, theology, and law. Thus, our critical analysis is spread across the social sciences. The dictionary is also a teaching glossary incorporating key words found in socialist, progressive, radical, humanist, and left-liberal thought. Then, too, it is postmodern, in that it does not treat terms as neutral descriptions of reality but, rather, as part of the process by which realities are called into being. At the same time, the dictionary does not exclude the kind of orderly and predictable social dynamic references so dear to a more traditional and modern scientist.

The dictionary contains not only the ordinary meaning of a word but also the emotional content that celebrates or profanes the thing or deed to which the word speaks. To aid the reader, we have identified "pointers" for most selections. These pointers are in the form of cross references ("Cf.") and/or related terms ("See . . . for more"). The cross references contrast a given entry with other terms in the dictionary. Related or companion terms enhance the meaning(s) of the word/phrase in question. Both the cross references and the references to related terms are designed to tease out or unearth as much of the prevailing sensibility embedded within the expressions/ideas as possible.

Words are also prescriptions for action or proscriptions against behavior. Where necessary and appropriate, we indicate political content as well. The underlying rationale guiding our efforts here is to consider what critical position or paradigm offers the most meaningful statement about the contested character of the particular entry in question. Thus, for example, we draw attention to Marxist, chaos, feminist, postmodern, and semiotic perspectives, among others. Again, selecting which viewpoint to rely upon is dictated by our concern for how best to express the political context of an item in the dictionary.

Throughout the dictionary, we note important luminaries in the social sciences and include some concise biographical or background material on each figure. We also identify several significant journals, magazines, books, occurrences, and organizations and provide explanation and exploration into their meaning. It is impossible to include every notable figure, publication, association, or event; indeed, such inclusiveness would be the source of an entire volume unto itself. Instead, our selection of entries has been guided by our own position on what it means to engage in critical analysis within the social sciences, and those persons, places, and things reflected in this glossary clearly exemplify this attitude.

Finally, we take the position that premodern, modern, and postmodern worldviews are equally valuable to the human project. This perspective will disturb those who work out of one tradition, but the case is compelling. Premodern knowledge processes give us the capacity to believe, to trust, to hope, to sanctify, or to condemn; without them social life would not be possible. Modern science has done much to contribute to the human project in agriculture, transportation, health care, housing, communications, and education. This knowledge continues to provide accurate, timely, useful information and cannot be set aside regardless of the limitations of the truth claims and the politics that shape and pre-shape the quest for valid learning. Postmodern knowledge gives us something impossible in a god-hewn world or in one run by impersonal and eternal laws: an evolving reason and responsibility. The wise student will extricate the best of each approach and apply this learning to the knowledge process and to life itself.

# Acknowledgments

A number of people contributed to the completion of this dictionary in ways that were absolutely indispensable. First and foremost is W. L. Reese. His *Dictionary of Philosophy and Religion* was an invaluable reference that furthered our understanding of many of the important social theorists contained in this text. Dragan Milovanovic provided a patient ear, encouraged us along, and reminded us that the work was important and timely. Sheila Montgomery carefully reviewed and edited the manuscript, making sense out of our ideas regardless of how ill-formed they may have been. Jennifer Santman provided an invaluable final proofing, functioning as our senior copy editor. Over the years, students and colleagues offered commentary, pushing us to do a better job and to make the dictionary relevant. The insight and wisdom of Christopher R. Williams, Lynda Ann Ewen, Martha Gimenez, Elena Bernal, and Richard Kane were especially rewarding and helpful. And, of course, thanks to our families for believing in our work and providing a supportive and loving space within which to work, to thrive, and to learn.

*T. R.Y.*
*B.A.A.*

**A**

**AARP:** The American Association of Retired Persons. This organization was founded to help solve the problems of those elderly often discarded after a lifetime of productive or reproductive labor. AARP is concerned with Social Security, medical care, housing, nutrition, and the well-being of elderly people. With over 40 million members, it is now the biggest membership organization in the United States. Of late, it has expanded its concerns to include children and women's needs. Cf. "Age."

**Abduction:** An alternative to inductive or deductive logic. The process of abduction entails a free play of the imagination or, following the semiotician Charles S. Peirce, a "pure play" of unrestrained thought that represents the locus of novel ideas. Abduction entails both inductive and deductive reasoning processes.

In law, there are three forms of abduction. These include *overcoded, undercoded*, and *creative abduction*. Overcoded abduction (deductive logic) refers to how a given legal premise produces an anticipated or somewhat automatic outcome. For example, if a person deliberately, knowingly, and with malice of forethought kills another individual, then the person is responsible for murder. Undercoded abduction (inductive logic) refers to the selection of the rule of law based upon an available inventory of recognized possibilities. For example, given the previous illustration, a particular jurisdiction may recognize that the person should be tried for first-degree murder, second-degree murder, manslaughter, or some other crime. Creative abduction seeks to identify entirely new and different rules and apply them to legal problems. It accomplishes this task by remaining skeptical about the reasonableness of the existing rules of law. Overcoded and undercoded abduction do not include any built-in skepticism and, instead, accept the wisdom and legitimacy of a given premise unconditionally and nonreflexively. Cf. "Induction" and "Deduction/Deductive Logic." See "Peirce, Charles S." for more.

**Abolitionism:** The elimination of a particular policy, statute, or legal principle. Contemporary examples of abolitionism include the insanity defense, penal incarceration, apartheid. In Scandinavia, for example, the prohibition against the use of certain previously illicit drugs (e.g., marijuana) has been abolished. Historically, the "abolitionist movement" referred to the position taken by those opposed to slavery in the United States.

**Abortion:**   The process by which a pregnancy is terminated, usually within three months of conception. This activity has aroused great debate and much direct social action both to prevent and support it. Abortion opponents argue that every life is sacred and that to abort a fetus is to commit murder. Supporters of abortion believe that such activity is a matter of private concern to be decided in terms of the circumstances in which the mother and/or the father find themselves. Some countries provide abortion on demand at very low fees; other countries forbid it entirely. Some see abortion as a major device for birth control, whereas others see it as a way to avoid collective care for unborn children. See "Birth Control" and "Overpopulation" for more.

**Abuse, Child:**   Critical analysis of child abuse examines the harm (physical, psychological, and/or sexual) inflicted upon a child in the furtherance of one's own economic, social, or psychological power. Child abuse objectifies children (treats them as "things" or "property") and, thus, devalues their existence (undermines their humanity).

**Abuse, Spousal:**   The use of force—displayed physically, psychologically, economically, or sexually—to demean, intimidate, or otherwise harm a marriage partner. In the context of common-law or homosexual relationships, spousal abuse is termed "intimate abuse." The operation and effect of this abuse, however, remain the same. Spousal abuse is about acts of power or the will to harm another. There are many forms of spousal or intimate abuse. See "Macho/Machismo," "Sexism," and "Gender" for more.

**Accenting the Sign:**   In postmodern semiotic terminology, all words, phrases, gestures, and so on within a given system of communication (e.g., sports, law, medicine, gangs) are given preferred meaning. They are accented one way as opposed to another. This is not a problem with codes of speech that are readily available to all people in a society. Thus, the languages of popular culture and commercialism accent words or phrases in ways that are accessible to large constituencies. A problem, however, presents itself with dominant discourse, that is, the speech codes that regulate and control our lives (e.g., law, finance, bureaucracy). The general populace has limited access to "law talk," "corporate talk," "medical talk." In such instances, the meaning of words or phrases are reduced to certain contents. These contents are consistent with maintaining the power of the system's discourse to exclude, to distance, to marginalize, and to alienate. This reduction in meaning is termed *uni-accentuality*. It is the ability of the language system in use to rely upon meanings that affirm the system while invalidating all other interpretations. The result is that we feel left out of the discourse—outsiders seeking access to understanding.

Consider, for example, communicating with physicians regarding the terminal illness of a loved one. The language many doctors use to explain illness does not invite immediate connection; it does not instantly invite shared understanding. We feel frustrated, uncertain, and left out, despite wanting to genuinely understand. According to postmodern semiotics, the aim is to acknowledge how words and phrases are infused with multiple meanings. The goal is to enable users or enactors of dominant and hierarchical grammars to accept and embrace alternative and more complete contents for the words or phrases they use. This explosion in meaning is termed *multi-accentuality*. Multi-accentuality makes possible a reduction in psychic disequilibrium and social disorganization. It promotes richer, fuller relationships between and among citizens who use various grammars. See "Sign" and "Semiotics" for more.

**Act:**   Latin: *agere* = to do. Early philosophers called the Scholastics used the concept "first act" to refer to the form of a thing, whereas "second act" was used to refer to what it did. In Symbolic Interactional theory, George H. Mead used the concept of the act to refer to the basic unit of social meaning. An act is not just behavior but behavior that is used to hang meaning on. The gesture is, for Mead, a physical motion with which one conveys meaning to another person who has learned how to interpret it. See "Act, Philosophy of" for more.

**Act, Philosophy of:**   One of the more important issues in all of social philosophy centers around the following question: To what degree are humans the passive objects of history and/or acting subjects that can plan and fulfill their own destinies? The structuralist answer, in its more deterministic claims, is that single human beings are the object (not the subject) of social forces. The Interaction view, in its most reductionist moments, argues that each individual is the object and agent of his or her own destiny. If a person is rich or poor, it is due to their own merits or failings.

In philosophical terms, an act is only an act when there is insight and the conscious use of material goods to change outcomes. For example, McDonald's claims to sell the same Big Mac in every restaurant in the world and thus defeats both individual action and cultural variety. But are Big Macs really the same in England, Japan, Nicaragua, or Vienna? Do McDonald's clerks do and say things to customers not scripted and rehearsed and sanctioned by supervisors? If so, then not even a corporation as large and powerful as McDonald's can defeat human action. See "Act," "Alienation," "I," "Intentionality," and "Praxis/Practice" for more.

**Acton, Lord (1834–1902):**   Acton's dictum on power is basic to all efforts for social justice: Power tends to corrupt; absolute power corrupts absolutely. T. R. Young offers a complementary dictum: Poverty tends to corrupt; absolute poverty corrupts absolutely. See "Bakunin, Mikhail," "Power," and "Power, Alienation of" for more.

**Actor:**   The more conventional meaning refers to the person who engages and does something with, for, or to something or someone for some purpose or reason. This definition is more akin to Talcott Parson's structural-functional understanding of agency and behavior. A second definition of actor comes from the Symbolic Interactionists and Constructivists, who see the actor as other than passive: more engaged with others, created by social encounters, and living out a drama that contributes to self-identity. A third definition of actor comes from postmodernists, who see the actor (e.g., the person who talks, writes, works, knows, feels) as significantly determined through discourse, or the implicit meanings embedded in language that speak on behalf of the subject/actor. See "Goffman, Erving" for more. Cf. "Performativity."

**Adolescence:**   An age grade composed of young people between 12 and 17. Every society has age grades. Usually they begin with infants, 1–3; children, 4–11; adults, 12–65; aged, 65+. All societies socialize children until puberty and then confer adult status on them in a "rite of passage." Industrial societies extend the socialization process to include mastery of reading, writing, and calculating. Thus, childhood is extended to age 18, and people between 12 and 18 are called adolescents (small adults). High-tech societies extend childhood even further and postpone adult status until 23, 27, 31. See "Age Grades" for more.

**Adorno, Theodor (1903–1969):**   A member of the Frankfurt School, Adorno is credited with developing a critique of philosophy that he defined as a "self-liquidation of idealism." Adorno's critique represents a precursor to much of postmodernism's disillusionment with the idealism of the post-Enlightenment era; namely, that with sufficient reason and rigorous (empirical) examination, the search for underlying Truths are ascertainable.

Adorno articulated a critique of "identity thinking" in which thought and being were said to be inexorably reducible or linked. Instead, he championed a position called "non-identity thinking." Non-identity thinking is significant because it retains and promotes the importance of particularity, heterogeneity, individuality, and difference. These are all cornerstone beliefs embedded in the postmodern assessment of social life, human social behavior, and culture.

In contrast to postmodern theory, Adorno advocated for a strong conception of truth grounded in philosophy and art. Constellations of images, when interpreted, provide cognitive insight and contribute to enhanced social and critical knowledge. See "Frankfurt School," "Habermas, Jürgen," and "Postmodernists/Postmodernism" for more.

**Adventist Religious Groups:**   Adventist religious groups assume that the end of the world is near and that a savior will arrive (advent) to save those who believe. They put away things of the flesh and seek spiritual purity in expectation of the second coming of Christ. The 7th Day Adventists are the best known sect, but periodically new sects appear.

**Advertising:**   An 80 billion dollar per year industry in which market demand is created for products in order to realize profit. Products that are essentially similar to others of the same kind are endowed with special symbolic meaning (e.g., sexuality, power, magic, or status) in order to increase demand and thus expand a market enough to absorb all that is/can be produced. In capitalism, markets are made small, since workers are not paid 100 percent of the value of the goods they produce. Thus, they cannot buy back 100 percent of the product. Further, as capitalism disemploys more people, the market likewise shrinks. Then, too, the quest for profits can lower quality; advertising offers the dramaturgical facsimile of quality or necessity to those who buy time and talent on the mass media. Advertising is directed at market segments based on demographics; often the groups targeted are those who have discretionary income: young, single, working professionals or housewives (who must make a choice between items produced under standardized conditions).
   A major problem generated by the advertising world is the preemption of artistic talent and information media for commercial purposes. A secondary problem is the use of sex, violence, and sports to generate consumers for products otherwise without special merit. See "Market" and "Realization, Problem of" for more. Cf. "Baudrillard, Jean."

**Aesthetics:**   Greek: *aisthesis* = sensation. In philosophy, the term designates ideas about beauty in nature and in cultural products. Premodern and modern sensibilities argued that there were absolute standards for determining that which was beautiful, superb, and excellent. Although these standards were hotly contested in modernist art and literature and, thus, changed depending on historical period, the conviction was that the essential nature of beauty existed and could be retrieved, identified, studied. Postmodernists hold that such definitions are a matter of power and convention and that no "essential" aesthetics exists. In some cultures, heavy women are considered beautiful; in other cultures, slim women are considered beautiful. Generally, women in Western cultures identify the ideological construction of beauty to be profoundly significant for them. Several non-Western cultures link the importance of the construct more particularly to men. See "Philosophy, The Discipline of" for more.

**Aesthetics (Socialist):**   The socialist understanding of all forms of art is not divorced from everyday life nor restricted to an elite in the form of "high culture." In socialist thought, art and society as a totality are reunited. Art is at once an affirmation and a critique of social life. Whereas capitalist art aims to celebrate privatism and consumption, socialist art speaks to questions of solidarity, species-being, and liberated nature. Socialist art is neither decidedly subjective nor objective. It does not tend to freeze social relations. Rather, such art emphasizes the processual character of society and nature. It does not "redeem" the bitter imperfection of life by diversion; it transforms, illuminates, and mobilizes people to action.

**Affect:**   Emotional response. Different societies define different emotional states as appropriate to given social situations. Fear, anger, joy, love, delight, rage, tenderness, sorrow, sympathy, and so on are closely regulated by a society. Failure to feel and express the proper emotional state (affect) is cause for great concern for those charged with socializing youngsters. Capitalist and elitist societies suppress affect since emotion gets in the way of the mass processing of people and, thus, jeopardizes profit and/or control.

**Age:**   One of the more important systems of stratification and differentiation found in all societies involves the chronological age of members. Human infants are dependent upon adults for food, protection, and rich interaction. After this first period of dependency, age grades become increasingly reflective of economic and cultural factors. In sociology, age grades are usually offered in five-year blocs. Taken together, these grades give a picture of birth rates and death rates. As such, they are good indicators of the degree to which social justice is instituted in all other social divisions. Infant mortality rates are especially sensitive to racism, sexism, and class privilege. See "AARP" and "Adolescence" for more.

**Aged, Immiseration of:**   The Marxist theory of the problems besetting the aged focuses upon the dynamics of capitalism. Older workers are less productive, more assertive, and prone to illness. All of these conditions affect costs and profits. The aged (arbitrarily defined as 55+) are encouraged to retire, since capitalists can make more profit on the labor power of the younger, more docile worker. When the aged have nothing to exchange for profit, they are excluded from the various delivery systems in capitalism (e.g., health and medical, food, shelter, clothing, transport, recreation, and education). In a popular democracy such as the United States, the state, responding to voters, provides goods and services to the pauperized aged but in a depersonalized rather than social mode. Thus many of the people who built the roads, bridges, and houses of the current infrastructure and who provided essential services at one stage in their life find themselves miserable as they grow older in the wealthiest country in the history of civilization. See "Immiseration" for more.

**Age Grades:**   A system of allocating status (and tasks) to a series of age cohorts. Each age cohort is initiated into a particular status at the same ceremony, wherein rights and duties are defined. Age grades are destroyed in capitalism as "irrational." It is profitable for the young to work at "adult" jobs for lower pay; and the rationality of the market requires that anything, including child labor, be sold to anyone with the cash in hand. Within capitalism, sex differentiation, ethnic differentiation, and racial distinctions are also irrational. Indeed, much of capitalism's liberalism is anchored by a thinly cloaked, profit-oriented, laissez-faire corporate structure that promotes competitive advantage rather than complete social liberation. Still, capitalism is progressive in this respect. See "Juvenile," "Majority, Age of," and "Sociology of Youth" for more.

**Agency, Human:**   The ability of people to change the institutions in which they live. In both premodern and modern contexts, human agency is absent, minimal, or pathological. In many premodern conceptions of the world, there are gods who know and control every act of every living thing. Hence, little agency is possible. In modern science, "laws" are said to regulate all human behavior: sexual, economic, criminal, or political. In postmodern science, human agency has much more room. In Chaos theory, for example, there are moments when agency is possible and times when it is difficult to change things. Democracy presumes people have both the wit and the ability to change "social laws" to some other pattern. Radical scholarship tries to enhance that capacity. Cf. "Alienation." See "Self-Determination" for more.

**Agitation:**   There are two major purposes of radical politics; both purposes include research and education and fall under the rubric of agitation. The first purpose involves connecting good theory with good organization and good politics. To do this, one takes everyday events of interest for students, workers, women, or minorities and lays them into a structural context together with a plan for remedy. The second purpose involves seeking the moment when progressive politics is possible. Particularly outrageous incidents of gender violence, police brutality, worker insult, or university politics provide a wealth of such opportunities to the radical scholar/activist. It takes wisdom, judgment, and courage to wait or to act. See "Utopia/Utopianism" for more.

**Agnosticism:**   This word literally means without knowledge. It also means without sure and certain knowledge of the existence of a god. Agnosticism arose in the eighteenth century as capitalists and bourgeois philosophers mounted a challenge to the "divine right" of kings to rule. Cf. "Atheism" and "Theology, Postmodern." See "God" and "God, Death of" for more.

**Agrarian Society:**   A vanishing form of social life based upon the labor-intensive production of crops by families and small communities. In 1790, twenty farm families produced enough surplus value to support one city family. In the United States, the Amish, the Hutterites, some few Mormons, and other fragments of agrarian life survive. Now huge industrial farms using capital-intensive production can produce food for thousands. The rural population, driven from the land, gathers as a surplus population in the city and as a reserve army of cheap labor. Without work to pay for food, the surplus population goes hungry while the industrial farm production is shipped abroad to feed the middle classes. In Costa Rica, for example, protein and grain production are up as agribusiness displaces agrarian society while per capita consumption is down. Most of the beef produced in Costa Rica goes to fast food hamburger chains in the United States, such as Burger King, McDonald's, and Arbys.

**Agriculture:**   The process of tending crops and herds for food. There have been several different ways of producing food in human history; hunting and gathering wild plants and animals slowly turned into planting, herding, and harvesting crops. When that happened, new social forms developed; people settled down and built more permanent homes and more permanent relationships. The next big event in agriculture was irrigation (or hydraulic agriculture). It provided enough food to support specialists, and a *division of labor* and *skilled crafts* appeared. The most recent development in agriculture is called agribusiness; the term refers to giant corporate farming that uses capital-intensive production: huge machines, chemicals, and vast fields to grow and harvest crops. Now, genetic engineering and synthetic foods are under development. Again, social organization is affected: Small farms disappear; almost all food is commodified.

**Agriculture, Hydraulic Societies:**   There have been five great hydraulic societies in human history: The first was in Persia along the Tigris and Euphrates rivers; the second was along the Nile in Egypt; the third was along the Ganges in India; the fourth was along the Yellow River in China; and the fifth surrounds what is now called Mexico City. Hydraulic agriculture requires social differentiation (specialization); it does not require social stratification as so many historians argue. Both hydraulic agriculture and social differentiation changed forever the ways in which people live.

**Agrippa:**   Third-century Greek philosopher who laid the basis for a postmodern philosophy of knowledge in five tropes (headings). (1) There is no sure basis for deciding among different philosophical claims. (2) All data are relative to the beholder. (3) Every proof rests upon assumptions that in turn have to be proved, ad infinitum. (4) One cannot trust hypotheses when the truth value of their premises is unknown. (5) There is a vicious circle in which sense data are used to inform reason, which, in turn, is used to establish what is to be taken as data.

**Ahistoricism:**   The term refers to a scientific trick by which a given social form is endowed with the appearance of being part of the eternal and natural order of things. For example, Max Weber's study of bureaucracy ignores the origins, the changes, and the many variations produced by historical conditions. Similarly, the ideas of G.W.F. Hegel and Georg Simmel about Ideal Forms tend to destroy the changing, historical nature of social realities; Hegel and Simmel saw all social issues as purely technical questions, since basic forms are seen as eternal and fixed. Ahistoricism tends to freeze analysis in the present and to reify the status quo. Bureaucracy, gender, class, race, and other social forms thereby cease to be human products and become means of domination or structural force.

**Algorithm:**   The term is used to mean any arithmetic operation using Arabic notations. In Chaos theory, it refers to two or more numerical values, at least one of which is a constant and one of which is a variable. The feedback loop generated by multiplying a constant by a variable produces very complex patterns, some of which cannot be predicted. This fact grounds a postmodern philosophy of science in which the quest for precision and order is decentered to be replaced by a quest for knowledge of the changing mix of order and disorder. See "Cause" for more.

**Alienation:**   The domination of humans by their own products; material, political, and ideological. The separation of humans from their humanity; the interference with the production of authentic culture; the fragmentation of social bonds and community. Any process that reduces people to their animal nature. Liberal definitions of alienation have to do with feelings; socialist definitions have more to do with relations and positions in a social order. In Marxist theory, a variety of terms are used to capture the flavor and variety implicit in the process of alienation: *Trennung* (divorce or separation); *Spaltung* (division or cleavage); *Absonderung* (separation or withdrawal); *Verderben* (spoiled, corrupt); *sich selbst verlieren* (lost to oneself); *auf sich zuruckziehen* (withdrawn into oneself); *ausserlich machen* (externalized); *alle Gattungsbande zerreissen* (ties with others disintegrated); *die Menschenwelt in eine Welt atomisticher Individuen auflosen* (humanity dissolved into fragmented individuals). Taken together these constructs constitute and create the meaning of the term "alienation" *(Entausserung, Entfremung).* (See the work of Meszaros.) Cf. "Agency, Human." See "Act, Philosophy of," "Anomie," and "Theology" for more.

**Alienation, Assumptions of:**   A militant humanism makes the following assumptions: (1) that humans may become dominated by their own social and cultural products; (2) that alienation is the chief source of conflict in society; (3) that there is a hierarchy of forms (economic, ideological, political, and religious); and 4) that in capitalist societies, alienation is produced by an economic system in which people and cultural products are transformed into commodities to be sold for private profit. These assumptions contrast with the pre-Marxian view that alienation involves separation from God; with the Hegelian view that alienation involves failure to understand objective reality; and with the Freudian assumption that alienation involves separation between different parts of the psyche. Each view entails a different solution. Militant humanism involves social revolution. The pre-Marxian view entails an effort to return to a state of grace by hard work, faith, and/or meditation. The Hegelian view advocates modern, order-based science as the solution to alienation. The Freudian approach requires that one come to terms with one's own anxieties and compulsions.

**Alienation, Psychological:**   Most American sociologists reduce alienation to psychological states: feelings of loneliness, powerlessness, hopelessness. For socialist sociology, happy and well-paid workers can be alienated; they can be fired tomorrow; they can lose their pensions overnight; they can be reassigned from friends and family. They must be polite and helpful to those defined as "superior" in the organizational hierarchy of the firm in which they work (see the work of C. Wright Mills). Those at the bottom of a stratification system can live for years with perfect peace of mind: Women, slaves, wage laborers, and migrant workers, for example, are able to fashion both culture and solidarity out of the fragments of wealth they receive (see the work E. P. Thompson).

**Allegory:**   A literary method by which layered meaning is created. An allegory is a fable, a story, an analogy. The allegory creates an opening in which a more tissued dimension for understanding can appear, explode, and scatter. Stories by Han Christian Anderson, the Brothers Grimm, the Greeks, Shakespeare, and so on are common illustrations. In each instance, the narratives represent more than mere stories. They are commentaries on life. In contemporary analysis, allegories are used by critical race theorists, postmodernists, and feminist critics as a way of expanding conventional knowledge on race, gender, identity, the body, agency, and so on.

**Analogy:**   Greek: *ana* = according to; *logos* = reason, ratio. The use of the features of a known thing to explain an unknown thing. Reasoning by analogy is very tricky; usually there are significant differences hidden or set aside by the analogy. Thus a whole society resembles an organism but can also be said to resemble a ship or a machine or an imaginary beast— and each is quite different.

**Analysis:**   Greek: *ana* = throughout; *lyein* = to loose. The breaking down into component parts. Critical theorists question and examine the dynamics of classism, sexism, racism, patriarchy, homophobia, and so on as the underpinnings of much of what we know about social life and of how we engage in human social interaction. These variables tend not to be as closely studied by positivist science, which regards them as separate social conditions mostly detached from the research itself.

**Anarchy:**   Greek: *a* = without; *archos* = head, ruler. A condition in which all efforts of imposed order by a state are regarded as hopelessly oppressive. Vladimir Lenin said that an anarchist is just a bourgeois turned inside out. A more benevolent view holds that social behavior should emerge through free and open interaction among responsible members of a society. Bakunin, Proudhon, Kropotkin are credited with this view on anarchy. In this view all human interaction is uncoerced by power relations. Anarchy assumes the possibility of full socialist consciousness in every adult member of a society. Bourgeois versions substitute elites for the state. Anarchy is often used as a pejorative word to refer to those who would dismantle the forms of privilege and hierarchy.

Marx made the case that capitalism in its pure form is anarchy. Capitalists compete fiercely with each other, and rules are set only to be broken as opportunity for profit comes along: Capitalists try to take markets from each other; they use the state apparatus in one country to exploit capitalists in another country; they neglect essential but low-profit lines of production; and they have no moral foundation other than profit. But see "Capitalism, Advantages of." See also "Corporate Crime" for forms of cooperation. See "Government, Forms of" and "Political Science" for more.

**Androcentricism:**   In (postmodern) feminist theory and praxis, the belief that our knowledge about individuals, the social order, and our interaction with people, places, and things is saturated within a masculine system of comprehension. Thus, the voice of women and their way of knowing is, advertently or inadvertently, relegated to a second-class status. Women are understood through the androcentric standard. This process can be extremely subtle and, thus, detrimental. For example, consider "(his)story," "hu(man)," and "(man)kind"; in each instance, there is no specific inclusion of the feminine. At best, women are understood in their absence or in relation to what male standards define for them. See *"Ecriture feminine"* and "Essentialism" for more.

**Animal Functions:**   Eating, sleeping, dressing, drinking. In general, those activities that keep a person alive physically but not morally. In capitalistic societies, as people become surplus to the productive needs of capitalism, they are increasingly reduced to animal functions.

**Anomia:**   A phrase coined by Émile Durkheim to refer to the psychological feelings produced by anomie: normlessness. A normative order brings security and psychic peace to people. The preceding expression neatly switches attention from the social conditions of alienation to the individual response to that disorder. Those who resist and rebel within racist, sexist, slave, or elitist normative structures suffer from anomia: They are said to be ill, maladjusted, sinful, or poorly socialized.

**Anomie:**   Greek: *a* = without; *nomy* = order. Without order, normlessness. A term used by Émile Durkheim to indicate "the collapse of the normative order." It is a condition of profound disaffiliation with others and with one's environment. The term implies that conformity to norms is natural and normal, that resistance is pathological. Then, too, embedded in the concept is the idea that norms are above and beyond the individuals who are said to organize their behavior in terms of the normative structure. However, there is a Marxist position that the normative structure is a product of transacting humans rather than a "superorganic" thing. To imply, as did Durkheim, that the normative structure is a thing apart from the behavior of people actively engaged in producing situated patterns of behavior through judgment, insight, and mutual purpose is a conservative political act. The political character of the act comes from a misrepresentation of the nature of norms, normative structures, and norming. Norms are not eternally fixed directives for behavior to which all normal people subscribe. Further, they do not collapse apart from the understanding of people that the norms are inadequate to deal with given situations. See "Alienation" and "Durkheim, Émile" for more.

**Anthropocentrism:**   Greek: *antropos* = human being; *kentron* = center. The practice of treating the human species as if it were the center of all values and the measure of all things. Premodernists and most modernists take this position uncritically. Postmodernists point out that 99 percent of the species that have ever lived are now extinct, that one day human beings, too, will evolve into quite different species or destroy themselves and/or their habitat.

**Anthropology:**   The study of people and communities in physical, social, material, and cultural contexts. Anthropologists focus on the origins and evolution of societies, including customs, beliefs, folkways, superstitions, and rituals. Critical anthropology examines such things as the division of labor, the totemic practices, the gendered customs, and the patriarchal codes underscoring various cultures and collectives.

**Anthropomorphism:**   Taking human form. The practice of assigning human characteristics to nonhuman entities (e.g., to gods, animals, plants, or material items). For example, one might treat cars and dogs or cats as though they were capable of human thought or feelings. A comparable process is to attribute inanimate status to humans (objectification). Both anthropomorphism and objectification strip people of their humanity.

**Anti-Foundationalism:**   In postmodern thought, this is a cornerstone to the process by which meaning, truth, and knowledge are understood. Contrary to modernist science, postmodernists contend that there are no essential, structural, or foundational truths because of the intervening variable of language. In other words, even at the level of subatomic events, reality is observer created. These observations always assume the form of a language (i.e., speech). According to postmodernists, because all speech contains implicit values and hidden assumptions, we can never fully grasp or completely retrieve total or foundational certainty about anything. At best, we have approximations uttered from a given point of view, under specified conditions. Cf. "Foundationalism."

**Anti-Semitism:**   Activities, ideas, rhetoric, film, media, and so on that harass and oppress Jews. This usually diverts the discontent of workers from the real sources of economic insecurity and puts the blame on "Jewish bankers" or an alleged plot to take over the world. In turn, Indians, Italians, Poles, African-Americans, Catholics, Muslims, Japanese, Hispanics, and others have been harassed and vilified. See also "Racism," "Sexism," and "Ethnocentrism" for pre-theoretical answers to problems created by the stratification of class, power, and/or social honor. Anti-Semitic and comparable practices divide opposition to power elites.

**Apathy:**   Greek: *a* = without; *pathos* = suffering. Greek and Asian philosophy held apathy to be the most desirable human state. Now it is used to refer to a pervasive disinterest in human life, in the moments of praxis, or in the production of culture. In liberal theory, apathy is a result of ignorance, laziness, or stupidity. The remedy is education, chemotherapy, group therapy, or institutionalization. In the Marxian view, apathy is a product of class inequality, stratified power relations, coercion, and massive communication structures. The solution in socialism is common ownership, control, and use of the means to produce culture; labor intensive socialization; and systematic attention to criticism/self-criticism.

**Apollonian:**   Both Friedrich Nietzsche and Margaret Mead used the word to refer to societies that had, as a central theme, the quest for order, harmony, and moderation. Cf. "Dionysian/Dionysus."

**Apology:**   The term is often used to demystify bourgeois theory, as when one says that a "theory" is an "apology" (justification) for a system rather than a fair description of it or an explanation of how it works. Often theories describe that which exists well enough but fail to consider that there are other and better ways to organize social life. These, too, are apologies even if they are well done.

**Apple, and Temptation to Knowledge:**   A symbol of forbidden things. Adam is said to have been given "the fruit of the tree of knowledge" (an apple; some say orange) and then to have rebelled against his Father and Creator. On one level, this story is a tale that accounts for rebellion, crime, and deviancy in terms of innate evil (on the part of Eve for tempting Adam, and the snake for tempting Eve). On another level, the tale speaks to the responsibility one takes when one learns about one's own self and society.

**Appropriation:**   The practice of defining some part of the wealth produced by the social power of workers as "profit" and using it for private purposes rather than for the common good. Actually, there is no such thing as profit; that is, production always absorbs energy and is a net drain on the larger social and natural system. Profit and, therefore, appropriation are possible only by transferring the costs of production to the workers, to the consumers, to the environment, and/or to the future generation.

**Appropriation, Mechanisms of:**   The means by which the surplus value of labor is directly appropriated and controlled by those who do not produce are varied. These mechanisms include sharecropping, tenancy, tribute, debt servitude, slavery, wage relations, and impressment into work crews. Indirect ways to appropriate labor power and its products include taxes, profits, interest, rents, tithes, tolls, and fees. Mechanisms of appropriation produce unequal social relations (e.g., master to slave, owner to worker). Further, these mechanisms require a political apparatus necessary to enforce and sustain these relations. Finally, such mechanisms entail a financial burden that members of society bear.

**Aquinas, Thomas, St. (1225–1274):**   Aquinas is credited with the most effective grounding of the God concept through reason. He added reason to faith in support of belief in God and incorporated Aristotelian logic into Christendom. Later on, this legitimation of rationality helped protect fledgling modern science from the Inquisition. His five arguments are: (1) The fact of motion in the world implies a first mover, that is, God. (2) There are efficient causes in the world, but the notion of causality implies a first cause, that is, God. (3) All things are contingent and can, presumably, disappear entirely at the same time. Since we cannot get something from nothing (assuming they did or will disappear), there must be something that is non-contingent, absolute, that is, God. (4) In practice, we assume degrees of truth, beauty, goodness, and nobility. Since we have such things in degree, there must be some absolute standard/pattern from which we can make such judgments, that is, God. (5) All things are goal directed; inanimate objects cannot direct themselves toward a goal (think of an arrow); therefore, there must be someone guiding/directing them, that is, God. Cf. "Theology, Postmodern."

Aquinas is important in the sociology of law as well. He specifies four kinds of law: (1) divine law, which is eternal; (2) natural law, which is given to humans via revelation (and now, reason); natural law has two sub-forms: (3) civil law, which can be variable to fit the circumstances of differing societies, and (4) the law of nations, which governs all societies. (See the work of W. L. Reese.)

**Archaeology:**   Greek: *Arche* = that which was in the beginning; *ology* = reason, order. The study of primitive societies and the material artifacts that have survived in order to interpret or predict what social life was like before written history was invented.

**Archetype:**   Greek: primal figures, patterns or forms. For Plato, archetypes were the original or truest forms of things, and "real" things were more or less close copies. Modern phenomenology is dependent upon this assumption. In modern psychology, Jung used the term to refer to basic ways of being human. He set down a whole list of archetypes that reside in every human being and pre-shape behavior by their strength and interplay. Jung held that different cultures supported different archetypes and that mental health depended on societal adjustment to permit a diversity of being.

**Aristocracy:**   Greek: *Aristos* = best; *Kratia* = rule. Those who "owned" the land in feudalism. After conquest by another people, some of the victors remained to claim title to the best land. They also claimed the right to own or to rule the conquered people. The conquerors transformed into an aristocracy after a few generations. Plato called for a political form in which the "best" ruled not on the basis of conquest but on merit. For Plato, merit meant those who had the good of the people at heart and had four capacities to use on their behalf: wisdom, courage, temperance, and justice. The socialist/Marxist view is that these virtues are distributed widely throughout the population and that politics should be democratic in order to draw them out. See "Government, Forms of" and "Political Science" for more.

**Aristotle (384–322 B.C.E.):**   A Greek philosopher, student of Plato, and, later, tutor to Alexander the Great. Aristotle was a leading architect of what is now modern science. He worked in the philosophy of knowledge and in what was then called natural philosophy.

Aristotle believed the primary task of science was to discover the truth value of middle terms upon which depended the truth value of deductions. His view of ethics continues to be adopted by modernist thinkers today; namely, that a virtuous life requires one do the right thing in the right way to the right person at the right time to the right degree. He specified the Golden Mean and gave it a mathematical grounding. Aristotle listed three acceptable forms of government; monarchy, aristocracy, and polity, a sort of constitutional democracy. Three undesirable forms of government were tyranny, oligarchy, and popular democracy. Aristotle set art to work as exploration in what was possible rather than as celebration of that which existed; this view continues to inform emancipatory art. For Aristotle, poetry had the task to conceptualize and verbalize universal truths about life and nature, whereas history dealt with actual events.

Aristotle's contributions to the philosophy of law still survive in the concepts of natural law and positive law. His system of syllogistic logic continues to inform the knowledge process of modernity; however, we know now from Chaos/Complexity theory that the world itself is nonlinear and does not sustain logical derivations, nor does it exclude contrarieties as does Aristotelian logic. (See the work of W. L. Reese.) Cf. "Aristocracy" and "Logic, Syllogistic."

**Art:**   This is the skillful and systematic use of colors, shapes, designs, words, gestures, or other means to craft a particular expressive form or statement of knowledge. Socialist/Marxist theory of art holds that art should grasp the central contradictions and problems of life; make their sources visible; affirm and politicize workers, students, women, and other oppressed minorities. It should be integrated into all aspects of daily life (e.g., food, furnishings, clothing, tools, factories, and housing) rather than confined to a museum or gallery to be viewed once in a while.

**Artificial Intelligence:**   A term used to suggest that a machine can be made to think in such a way that it cannot be distinguished from human thought. A. M. Turning gave proof that a machine could be built that was more complex than the sum of its parts. Today there is much work in artificial intelligence; some chess programs are better than most human chess players.

**Artificial Stupidity:**   A term introduced by T. R. Young in a lecture at the Fielding Institute in 1992. The term refers to societies that have the technical capacity to develop authentic self-knowledge but do not do so for political and economic reasons. Artificially stupid and naturally stupid societies are not the same. Naturally stupid societies do not have the information technology that artificially stupid societies possess and, thus, could not be intelligent even if they tried.

**Asceticism:**   Greek: self-denial. Asceticism informs many religions. It holds that the pathway to knowledge is the denial of the senses and of desires. According to Max Weber, asceticism is a part of the social psychology of religion that leads to capitalism.

**Ascribed Status:**   The standing that is assigned to a person by other people, regardless of the wishes of or the concrete circumstances surrounding the person. Perhaps the most frequently used example of an ascribed status is one's kinship, one's ethnicity, and one's sex. In sexist or racist societies, such an assignment is hostile to praxis and community. In socialist societies, ascribed status is routine. As such, it means that one is able to create culture by virtue of the fact that one is part of a collective apart from merit, sex, race, or other irrelevant characteristics. See "Commune" for more.

**Ashby's Law of Requisite Variety:**   A requirement for an ultra stable system is that, in order to maintain match with its environment (and thus obtain order), it is necessary to have at least one option stored in the system for every change in the environment. Ashby says that only variety (change) can destroy (cope with) variety. Applying this logic to capitalism produces some interesting results. Capitalism is *irrational,* in that it produces irreversible changes in the environment, degrades the environment, and resists change by which to transform the system. See "Deviance" for more.

**Assimilation:**   A process by which one culture is destroyed and another culture is imposed upon a people, usually by force. In the process, the young people of a status group defined as "inferior" adopt the values and norms of the status groups defined as "superior." People do not readily surrender their culture (i.e., their capacity to create a particular form of culture). The current debate surrounding bilingual education (English and Spanish) in primary and secondary public schools, particularly in the southwest region of the United States, addresses the potential destruction of culture, as Hispanics are assimilated into American culture as second-class citizens.

**Atheism:**   Greek: $a$ = without; *theos* = god. Disbelief in gods. The tradition is informed by the work of Anaxagoras, Heraclitus, Feuerbach, and Marx. In humanist thought, atheism denotes the annulment of God and the emergence of theoretical humanism. For Marx, atheism requires one to be authentically concerned with fellowship, community, affirmation, and festivity as human activities rather than as activities that are divinely inspired or that aim at divine worship. In capitalism, atheism can be only a dull resentment of religious hypocrisy or an intellectual doubt about supernatural beings; it then is a negative rather than affirmative act of human relatedness, as in some forms of postmodern theology. See "God," "God, Death of," and "Theology, Postmodern" for more. Cf. "Agnosticism."

**Attitude:**   A predisposition to act based upon internalized values, roles, rules, and/or conditioning. Attitudes are useful in that they provide generalized solutions of action but may be obstacles to judgment and self-determination if rigidly embodied. Some theorists seriously challenge the fact of "attitude," holding that all behavior is situationally produced through transactions. This possibility is not likely in a mass society where there is little opportunity for transactions.

**Attractor:**   In nonlinear theory, an attractor is that region in time-space to which a system tends to go (seems to be attracted). There are five generic attractors in Chaos theory: (1) *a point attractor*—simple systems such as a pendulum can be found at a given point at a given time with great precision; (2) *a limit attractor*—a system cannot exceed the upper and lower values for any given measure (e.g., a thermostat); (3) *a Torus attractor*—a doughnut shaped region in space within which a system can be found. We can't tell just where inside the doughnut the system will be found, but we know that the boundaries of the doughnut set the limits for the movement of the system on selected variables (e.g., think of the norms controlling braking at a stop light. Most people vary around a mean; few come to a full stop; few dash right through); (4) *a butterfly attractor*—a nonlinear state in which the same system, without the addition of any new parts, will suddenly move to two (or more) outcome basins of attraction. Instead of one and only one outcome for a given kind of system, suddenly new patterns emerge. Consider the examples of a drop of water and gender relations. The drop of water may take up two regions in time-space with uncertain paths between these two points. Or, in some conditions, men and women may form two, four, or more marriage forms quite different from traditional relationships; and (5) *deep chaos*—a region of unpredictable patterns; yet even in deep chaos there are regions of order; it is in deep chaos that one finds qualitatively more life forms emerging (e.g., forms of crime, religion, politics, economics, marriage). The factors driving the change to new and more complex dynamics are the text of postmodern science. See "Attractor, Strange," "Butterfly Attractor," and "Chaos Theory"for more.

**Attractor, Strange:**   The concept refers to the behavior of a system. In modern science, systems are supposed to behave with enough precision such that formal, axiomatic, and logical theory can be built. Most complex systems do not behave so predictably. They are strange in terms of the expectations of modern scientists but not in terms of natural occurring dynamics. See "Attractor" for more.

**Augustine, St. (354–430):**   An African theologian who, along with St. Thomas Aquinas, was an architect of modern theology. Augustine held that the pathway to true happiness is self-knowledge. The quest for self-knowledge becomes one for truth, beauty, and goodness; this quest for self-knowledge gives a theologian an endorsement for recourse to philosophy, psychology, and sociology in times when such sciences are seen to be secular and hostile to revealed truth. The quest for self-knowledge also focuses attention upon social relations in this world rather than upon preparation for salvation in a second, spiritual world. Augustine also gave us a utopia: the City of God, which is contrasted with the City of Man. Each person must make a choice between the two; the City of God is exempt from change and collapse; the City of Man is not. In the City of God, church law is superior to civil law. (See the work of W. L Reese.)

**Author:**   In postmodern discourse, any one who does physical, natural, or social science is an "author." This usage derives out of the larger notion that all science is a "text"; that is, a narrative containing many stories that could be generated out of the incredibly complex fabric of natural and social dynamics. See "Writerly (Versus Readerly) Text" for more.

**Authoritarianism:**   A form of government in which one person or a small group controls state power, law, police, military, and other public and semipublic institutions such as school and church. The private sector is usually given over to other authorities, who in turn support the government. Patriarchy thrives in authoritarian societies. See "Police State," "Political Science," "Totalitarianism," "Fascism," and "Elitism" for more.

**Authoritarian Personality:**   A stabilized pattern of learned behavior exhibited by a person who is characteristically intolerant, rigid, and marked by extreme reliance on formal authority. The source of this personality type is found in unequal power systems, beginning with the patriarchal family. Here, people become extremely sensitive and responsive to "higher" authority and insensitive, even brutal, to those in the lower echelons. See "Reich, Wilhelm" for more.

**Authority:**   Many societies allocate more social power to some statuses and require those in "lower" status to comply with the orders, commands, wishes, or expectations of "higher" authority.
   When social power is vested in an office or person, such a person has "authority." Max Weber lists three kinds of authority: *traditional*—that of a parent or priest; *legal-rational*—that of a formal organization with rules and with people to enforce them; *charismatic*—that of a politician, shaman, or entertainer. As Georg Simmel noted, such "power" is always a social product and lasts only as long as the "subordinates" continue to reify the person/office as an "authority." However, when authority is naively reified, people do give up some of their autonomy and allow others to direct their behavior. Both human agency and personal morality are thereby subverted. See "Weber, Max" for more.

**Automation:**   The practice of controlling machines with machines. The transformation from labor-intensive production to capital-intensive production. Up until 1960, most of the time automation replaced unskilled workers. Now automation threatens to replace lower level white-collar workers. IBM, Xerox, Apple, and other hi-tech industries are developing computer chips to process words, sounds, images, and even reality. As "artificial intelligence" systems are designed, secretaries, teachers, professors, postal workers, and others who use words become surplus to corporate needs. Automation in capitalist societies increases production and prices while eliminating wage workers. Without work, demand falls and the surplus population grows. Socialism and communism distribute on the basis of need and merit. In these systems, crisis is not necessary.

**Autonomy:**   Greek: self-regulation. An autonomous person has principles that s/he uses in organizing responses to events in everyday life. An autonomous city or nation makes its own laws and directs its own affairs. In Marxian theory, autonomy is one of the moments of *praxis* mediated by other important factors. Lawrence Kohlberg argued that the principled individual was more moral than one who based judgments upon utilitarian notions of reward and punishment.

**Away(s):**   Standard methods of avoiding involvement in a given social occasion. Usually such involvement is pointless, exploitative, or demeaning. Thus, people have cause to remain away and to feign interest. Examples include daydreaming, shielded mockery, doodling, spacing-out, and boundary collusion by subsets of persons.

**Axiology:**   Greek: *axios* = value. Theories of value. See "Deontology" for more.

**Axiom:**   Greek: *axioun* = to think worthy. The word refers to unprovable but necessary assumptions in a set of theoretical propositions based on axioms. Agrippa refused to accept axioms without proof and doubted that all such "worthy" assumptions could be grounded. Postmodern philosophy of knowledge takes his view. See "Agrippa" for more.

**Back Stage:** A term used by Erving Goffman to make the point that in a dramaturgical society there is much hidden from the view of those who are caught up in social institutions. In conflict-ridden societies, teams rehearse performances back stage and then offer the dramaturgical facsimile of service, quality, or honest agency to those who are in the audience (front stage). In markets, politics, religion, and education, such hidden routines invalidate most of the assumptions of Symbolic Interaction theory about how symbols are shared and call forth the same responses and feelings in all parties to such interaction. See "Goffman, Erving" for more.

**Bacon, Francis (1561–1626):** Bacon was an English philosopher who gave us an appreciation of the new science of systematic empirical study and mathematical analysis that now is center point of the knowledge process in higher education. In the *New Atlantis,* he also wrote of an ideal society made possible by wise use of science. He thought science would banish the "four idols" that contaminated human understanding: idols of the tribes (gods); idols of the cave (see "Plato"); idols of the market; and idols of theater (bad theory, see "Theory"). He specified the use of operational definitions and gave us basic research designs or "tables." He ranked the sciences from logic to metaphysics. His goal was the Great Instauration, the installation of human beings as masters of the natural and social world; as such he was important to the Enlightenment. (See the work of W. L. Reese.) See "Enlightenment, The" for more.

**Bakunin, Mikhail (1814–1876):** A Russian philosopher and leading anarchist. His argument was that privilege depraves both heart and intellect; therefore all hierarchy should be dismantled. The only laws one need obey are natural laws; indeed one must obey them since they are his/her "true" nature. Bakunin held that neither patriotism, law, religion, nor morality should keep one back from destroying political and economic privilege. One can accept the first dictum without accepting the others. (See the work of W. L. Reese.) Cf. "Acton, Lord."

**Balance of Payments:**   The flow of wealth from one country to another, measured by dollars, francs, pounds, yen, or shillings. There are many ways this flow occurs, including trade, foreign investment, duties on goods, loans, and interests on loans by international banks. When a U.S. company builds a factory (invests) in Brazil, it has to spend money in that country, hiring workers and buying raw materials. Once that factory is operating, money flows back to the United States in the form of profits. Military operations and foreign aid also involve major dollar flows. The difference between the number of dollars that flow into and out of the United States is the balance of payments, a major indicator of the international strength and power of the U.S. economy. The United States maintains a balance of payment deficit, since large corporations continue to move their factories to poorer nations where cheap labor, cheap materials, and new markets are found. In order to keep workers from organizing (and thus reducing class struggle), the United States uses a huge military apparatus to stop socialist liberation movements and to train, install, and support military dictatorships, which then guarantee law and order (labor peace). All this activity increases deficits in the balance of payments.

**Balance of Trade:**   If you go buy a Volkswagen, you pay for it in dollars at your local dealer. Most of these dollars go back to the German firm that produced the car; dollars flow from the United States to Germany. The dollar value of all U.S. made goods sold abroad (exports) minus the dollar value of all foreign made goods sold in the United States (imports) is the balance of trade. This balance indicates how effectively U.S. firms are competing with their foreign rivals. When balance of trade is positive for a nation, its factories are busy and the surplus population small. When the balance of trade is negative, the surplus population grows, welfare and other costs go up, and the state has a fiscal crisis. Further, a negative trade balance produces too many people on welfare and too few workers left to pay taxes. The workers' tax contributions support welfare and help pay the costs of production that capitalism transfers to the state.

**Banditry, Social:**   A form of pre-theoretical rebellion in which particular nobles or capitalists were the target of violence or theft. The bandit would steal from, kidnap, or murder rich and/or famous persons and share the wealth with kin and friends. Banditry tends to disappear as social justice increases. Robin Hood and Pretty Boy Floyd are among the better known bandits. Many view Jesse and Frank James as social bandits, since they robbed the banks that were thought to be robbing the worker and farmer.

**Barbarism:**   In socialist writing, the term refers to an "advanced" society in which technology is used as an instrument of domination. Barbaric societies exist when the masses are controlled by external rules, rewards, and systems that are established by managers on behalf of some elite. When people are stripped of social relations (relations that require mutual participation in the collective construction of culture and cultural products), then they are barbarians.

**Barthes, Roland (1915–1980):**    Barthes was one of the architects of the French poststructural movement, along with Michel Foucault, Julia Kristeva, Jacques Derrida, and Jean-François Lyotard. Barthes emphasized the role that language plays in understanding mass culture and cultural theory. In this context, he examined fashion, advertising, and art. See "Poststructuralism" for more. Cf. "Structuralism."

Barthes developed a literary critique of interpreting texts through his use of semiology and, more generally, sign theory. He critically examined the way in which mass mediated culture idealized and mythologized reality such that new forms of propaganda were conspicuously consumed. He also advanced the "writerly versus readerly" approach to decoding a text. This approach deemphasized the centrality of the author as the locus for understanding, intent, and meaning. Instead, he stressed the process of interpretation in which meaning explodes and scatters. See "Semiotics," "Sign," and "Writerly (Versus Readerly) Text" for more. Cf. "Readerly (Versus Writerly) Text."

**Base:**    According to Karl Marx, the means and the relations of production of material culture are found in the economic base. The tools, factories, techniques, and lines of commodity production form one part of the base. The way the producers of value relate to each other and to those who do not produce value form the other part of the base. In slavery, the relationship includes slave and master. In feudalism, the relationship includes lord and serf. In capitalism, the relationship encompasses worker and owner. In socialism, the relationship is between worker and state. In communism, the relationship is between worker and worker. In capitalism, there is a tendency to improve the means of production and to destroy the relations of production. Cf. "Superstructure" for more.

**Baseball:**    A North American game adapted from the English game cricket. A functional analysis would claim that baseball tends to reproduce the social dynamics of competitive capitalism, a dynamics limited to rules that make any given game fairly free from bias. One should note that baseball teaches young people the morality of team work within a larger competitive structure. It also provides a forum for and a stimulus to elegant physical activity, as do sports in general. See "Football, Ideology of" for more.

**Base Communities:**    Nuns, priests, preachers, and ministers who orient their ministry to liberation theology, helping peasants, workers, and/or minorities to form strong and mutually supportive communities. In base communities worship extends beyond spiritual existence to encompass all of daily life. The idea is to create an approximation of the heavenly city/community here on earth by opposing and dismantling new and old structures of domination. See "Praxis, Christian" for more.

**Bastard:**   A child born out of wedlock in certain social formations. Bastardy arises only in those tribes or states that permit the private holding of land, real estate, or other property. Given the idea of private property, the question arises: Who is to inherit it? At that point the paternity of the issue becomes important. (Maternity is usually known.) Only those born within the marriage form are legally entitled to protection, resources, and inheritance. In many societies, any child born to a female who is herself a member of a clan, tribe, or family is, by such birth, a full member of that group. Thus children are never bastards; rather, the legal system of a political economy creates the category. See "Natural Child" for more.

**Baudrillard, Jean (1929– ):**   Professor of sociology at the University of Nanterre in France from the 1960s to 1987. Baudrillard is regarded as a major proponent of postmodern thought as it relates to cultural theory, communication studies, art, and social life. Baudrillard offers the most radically nihilistic and pessimistic postmodern framework of any of the other contemporary social theorists. Cf. "Deleuze, Gilles," "Derrida, Jacques," "Foucault, Michel," and "Guattari, Félix"

Early in Baudrillard's career, he attempted to integrate the political economy of Marxian thought with structuralism and semiotic theory, emphasizing advance monopoly capitalism and conspicuous consumer consumption. In this context, Baudrillard advanced the proposition that everyday life is commodified such that objects (consumer goods) represent signs. This produces a "hypercivilization; that is, a new technical order that dominates the human subject. Baudrillard eventually distanced himself from Marx and neo-Marxian analysis. In his works, *For a Critique of the Political Economy of the Sign* and *The Mirror of Production*, Baudrillard demonstrates that a Marxian-informed social theory inadequately accounts for the condition of contemporary society. Baudrillard argues that in a mass mediated culture where everything is a sign (simulacra)—that is, where everything is a representation of the "real"—the artificial and the "counterfeit" lose meaning because there is no reality upon which they are based. Thus, image and form devour the real, but since reality does not exist nothing is left but simulations of the real, or a hyperreal existence. See "Advertising," "Cyberspace," Hyperreality," "Simulacrum," and "Simulation" for more. Cf. "Postmodern, Affirmative."

**Beauvoir, Simone de (1908–1986):**   Beauvoir was a French feminist author and philosopher. She argued that patriarchal systems produce gender effects that marginalize the status of women. In particular she demonstrated how the masculine register is defined as the norm and how the feminine is defined as the absence of the norm. The feminine was designated by Beauvoir as "Other."

The Otherness of women was, for Beauvoir, an integral dimension of being human. She traced this alienating identity for women to their bodies, especially their reproductive capacities. She drew support for her thesis from the division of labor in which women were relegated to producing children and caring for them. See "Existentialism" for more.

**Behavior:**   Old English: *be* = about; *habban* = to hold. The word means "to take oneself in hand" or to "comport oneself with dignity" and thus refers to activity informed by conscious reflective will. It has come to mean all activity of all organisms including plants.

**Behaviorism:**   A term in psychology that holds that the proper study of behavior is actual conduct rather than mental tests, opinions, drives, needs, desires, or other Freudian or mentalist concepts. J. B. Watson and the Russian Ivan Pavlov are credited with this form of psychology. The sociology student should note that it eliminates socialization, roles, relationships, norms, interaction, and human will from the study of behavior. Cf. "Emotion, Sociology of."

**Behavior Modification:**   A political technique by which the principles of psychology are used to eliminate behavior that is embarrassing, awkward, or irritating to others. By circumventing the self-system and by eliminating interaction, behavioral modification can enable a small cadre of psychologists to manage the behavior of a mass of consumers, prisoners, students, patients, or others. Since authentic therapy is labor-intensive, behavioral modification is an inexpensive way for the state to solve the problems of an unruly surplus population, including displaced workers, the homeless, frail elderly, and juvenile delinquents.

Other critics question whether behavior modification works effectively, if at all. They draw attention to the fact that, after time, human conduct initially regarded as unacceptable and then exposed to repeated behavior modification techniques resurfaces. Essentially, the argument is that it is not so easy to "unlearn" existing problematic or otherwise socially unacceptable behavior. Further, it is not easy to "learn" new, socially sanctioned behavior, particularly when it is not consistent with how a person understands and experiences everyday life. For example: think about how difficult it is to stop smoking, "get off" of drugs, financially succeed in the face of intergenerational poverty, or genuinely understand human suffering and misery when wealth and privilege surround you.

**Belief:**   A mental act by which a social fact comes into being. Many sociologists and anthropologists treat "beliefs" as something that ignorant and superstitious folk embody, whereas civilized and educated people embrace "true facts." The latter position assumes that social facts exist apart from intending, wanting, hoping, believing human beings.

**Bentham, Jeremy (1748–1832):**    Bentham is the founder of *Utilitarianism*, which set pleasure (rather than salvation and spiritual purity) as the goal of life. Pleasure for each required the greatest good for the greatest number of persons. There are seven ways to measure pleasure: intensity, duration, certainty, propinquity, fecundity, purity, and the number of persons to which it extends. Bentham is used widely to justify accumulation of private wealth and to locate the quest for happiness in the marketplace rather than in the church, the academy, the polity, or the family. (See the work of W. L. Reese.)

One of the most significant and visionary of social policy ideas developed by Bentham was "Panopticon Hill." During the late eighteenth century, in the midst of the early Industrial Revolution, concern spread throughout England as the problem of the poor became substantial. Bentham's response was to establish relief through national, self-sustaining "houses of industry." These facilities were agrarian houses of refuge: caregiving dwellings where the poor, the infirm, and the helpless could congregate and thrive. The aim was to enable society's victims to rediscover their natural abilities through education and training. Cf. "Panopticism," "Punishment," and "Utility/Utilitarianism."

**Berkeley, George (1685–1753):**    Berkeley was an Irish philosopher and bishop who contributed to an early postmodern philosophy of science. He argued, with Locke, that all ideas originate in sense data; we have no direct evidence of such abstract categories as space, time, color, volume, or quality. A thing exists only if it is perceived; *esse est percipi*. He went on to disagree with Locke that one can use reason to get from specific sense data to abstract categories without imagination and faith. Berkeley was interested in showing that God was necessary to ground such concepts. (See the work of W. L. Reese.)

**Birth Control:**    The concept refers both to the technology with which birth rates are increased or decreased, as well as to the larger moral question about these practices. This is especially the case with abortion. For moralists, the only acceptable form of birth control is abstinence from sexual intercourse. Some proponents of birth control contend that by decreasing the number of poor, ethnic children in society the problems of a surplus population will be reduced. These advocates do not endorse the same policy for rich, white, male children. One can see the sexism, racism, and classism implied in this view. The socialist position is that concern should rest with attempts to increase the quality and quantity of life for all people rather than with attempts to solve the problems of poverty and ethnocentrism through a stratified birth control policy. See also "Abortion," "Over-population," and "Population Theory" for more.

**Biological Reductionism:**    The practice of explaining all human behavior in terms of purely biological processes: genes, instincts, hormones, and pre-programmed brain activity. Stratification, sexual dominance, territoriality, acquisition, and conflict are said to be basic biological behaviors. Actually, we do not know just how much social behavior is grounded firmly in biology, nor do we know when and how biology is mediated by society. The interactions may be so complex that only loose generalizations are possible. See "Reductionism" for more.

**Blanqui, Louis (1805–1881):**    A French socialist who gave Marx and socialism several concepts, including class struggle, proletarian revolution, dictatorship of the proletariat, and the idea that socialists should form a small, secret group to engineer the overthrow of capitalism.

**Bloc Formation:**    Several factors contribute to large, multinational blocs and describe their composition. First, bloc formations produce strength to compete with the more powerful nations. For example, Japan, Germany and the United States are economically and politically stronger than African, Asian, and Latin American nation-states. Thus, these nation-states must cooperate if they are to compete/resist the more potent ones. Second, the rich capitalist nations have a common interest in suppressing liberation movements and guaranteeing the free movement of goods and profits around the world. Third, cultural factors such as language, religion, and colonial status bind people across national boundaries. Bloc formations are likely to be the largest, most visible, and most active sociopolitical units in the twenty-first century.

**Blocs, Economic:**    A coalition of several nation-states pursuing common goals and establishing common rights and obligations for those residing within the bloc. There are three competing views on how the global economy works. The first view claims that there are some 160 sovereign nation-states that compete freely among themselves. The second view argues that there is a capitalist world order in which the "Group of Seven" is at the top and poorer nations are arranged in layers below it. The third view argues that nations are aligned into larger economic systems called blocs. The European Common Market and the North American Free Trade Association are examples of more developed economic blocs. Within the twenty-first century we might well see several such blocs competing for markets, raw materials, and for rights to deep sea or outer space resources.

**Boas, George (1891–1980):**    An American philosopher who helped fashion a postmodern philosophy. He held: (1) Humans try to impose order and logic on the world and fail, since time subverts the effort to prove basic terms. (2) There are no universals; humans create and impose them and, when they fail, discard them. (3) There are no individuals, but individual persons and things are the basic metaphors out of which we build explanations. (4) The idea of a cause is a metaphor built upon myths. Mechanistic, deterministic, and teleological causal models are expanded far beyond what is warranted. (5) Some abstract terms become "emblems" that guide the knowledge process: Nature, truth, beauty, law, order, and cosmos are human inventions treated as ontologically prior to human thought and action. (6) Dividing history into periods (including premodern, modern, and postmodern) is to build myths that leave residues in all thought processes. Even those who work in the history of ideas carry a distorted philosophy of history. Boas's contribution to philosophy and postmodern thought is that as long as we accept our own hand in what we make or say, we do not reify history, nature, causality, or the individual as something beyond our own social and cultural work. (See the work of W. L. Reese.)

**Bodhisattva:**   Sanskrit: *boddhi* = wisdom, *sattva* = existence. A bodhisattva is, in Mahayana Buddhism, one whose essence is compassion. A guiding symbol on both popular and learned levels, a bodhisattva embodies basic Buddhist values of practical wisdom (*prajna*) and love (*karuna*) and has chosen a life-vocation of beneficial action toward all beings in order that their suffering, whether physical or mental, be ended. A bodhisattva can be anyone, a layperson or monk, who begins to postpone individual satisfaction in order to work for the welfare of others in the world. Their lives, in turn, are free for similarly attentive contributions in their own situations.

**Bolsheviks:**   It refers to the party of Vladimir Lenin and, later, Joseph Stalin. It means "majority." Great expectations were made for the Bolsheviks prior to and in the wake of the Russian Revolution. Prior to the Revolution, Bolsheviks competed for political and economic power with their counterpart, the Mensheviks. The Mensheviks represented the more conservative political element in the country, controlling, at the time, much of its infrastructure. As the more liberal political entity, Bolsheviks were opposed to Menshevik control. Indeed, the Bolsheviks were the impetus behind the Revolution. The events of the late 1880s, however, saw the heirs of the Bolsheviks rejected by the masses that the party purported to serve. Considerable gains were made under the Bolsheviks, but severe problems—including inflexibility, corruption, elitism, and the cult of the individual—discredited them.

**Bourgeois Democracy:**   A form of government in which political power is in the hands of those who have the time and money to do political work. This usually means business persons, lawyers, doctors, and the idle rich who have sufficient guaranteed income and sufficient release time to do the basic groundwork in choosing candidates and policies. The product of such lawmakers tends to support capitalism.

**Bourgeoisie:**   Old English: *burg*; Old French: *burgeis; bourges* = dwelling; by extension, those who live in town: craftspeople, merchants, officials, and so on. The bourgeoisie include that sector of a society that, by one rationale or another, expropriates part of the surplus value produced by the proletariat (i.e., workers). The term carries strong and often negative emotional content in the writings of the Left. Cf. "Marx, Karl" and "Proletariat."

**Bourgeois Revolution:**   A political revolution in which the rights of the individual to pursue private goals and to accumulate property are guaranteed. A series of bourgeois revolutions, from the English Revolution in 1688 to the American Revolution in 1775, replaced feudalism with capitalism.

**Bourgeois Society:**   A society in which exchange relationships replace social relationships, cultural items (e.g., sex, drugs, food, loyalty, sports) become commodities exchanged for profit, and private profit is the central test of production.

**Bridgman, P. W. (1882–1963):**   Bridgman is noted for his concept of "operationalism." All concepts in science are defined by the operations one uses in finding the value/measure of a thing. The concept of length or weight or opinion is identical with the operations one uses to measure, weigh, or elicit opinions. One can see the grounding of postmodern philosophy of science in this view. Plato and most modern scientists would hold that length, weight, or truth are natural categories existing before measurement; measurement can only approximate real values/attributes.

**Brothel:**   A place used for male or female prostitution.

**Buddhism, Hinayana:**   The early form of Buddhism stressed the inevitability of suffering in this world. In order to end suffering, one must put away the "shells of existence" and unite with the infinite (nirvana). Cf. "Buddhism, Mahayana."

**Buddhism, Mahayana:**   A later and more popular form of Buddhism in which a bodhisattva can help bring social justice and moderate suffering in this world. The bodhisattva postpones his/her approach to nirvana in order to share wisdom with others in this life. In Mahayana Buddhism, everyone can become a bodhisattva by passing through nine stages: delight; purity; intelligence; leaving behind ignorance and evil passion; grasping essences; producing that which is needed for social justice; saintly innocence; practical knowledge; and, finally, embodiment of love and compassion. This form of Buddhism is compatible with liberation theology in Christianity. (See the work of W. L. Reese.) See "Bodhisattva" and "Theology, Liberation" for more. Cf. "Buddhism, Hinayana."

**Buggery:**    A British term for anal intercourse with males or females. Said to be a sexual perversion.

**Bureaucracy:**    French: *bureau* = writing desk and, later, drawer. It has come to mean any work requiring the keeping of files and, later, a form of social organization in which order, rationality, and hierarchy represent key elements. In more general terms, the word refers to a way of organizing social life such that an elite can control the behavior of a large mass of people by means of a staff (or cadre). Vladimir Lenin said that a bureaucracy was first a military (i.e., police) apparatus and then a judicial apparatus, and that it corrupts from above and below. It is also an apparatus that locates moral agency in the hands of a few. Marked by formal and uniform application of rules, bureaucracies are supposed to be "rational" instruments by which the goals determined by an elite may be achieved. Bureaucratic organization typifies modern industrial corporations, military organizations, and a managed society. See "McDonaldization of Society" for more.

**Bureaucratic Socialism:**    A distorted form of socialism in which the state holds title to the means of production. As in capitalism, part of the production is extracted by law or by force, but unlike capitalism, the surplus is invested in improving the basic health, housing, food, transport, and military delivery systems. A part of the surplus is also used to provide the ruling elite with class privileges. The USSR was the prototype of bureaucratic socialism.

**Buridan's Ass:**    A dilemma attributed to John Buridan (1295–1356) that involves a starving ass unable to decide which of two bales of hay to eat. Think of radicals on the Right and Left who fail their quest for social justice by an inability to see the strengths in each other's work.

**Butterfly Attractor:**    In Chaos theory, an attractor refers to the movement tendencies of a dynamic system. A dynamic system can be composed of neurological events such as the design of brain wave activity during bouts of dissociation, of natural occurrences such as the pattern of waves washing up a coastal shore line, and of social phenomena such as the configuration of discourse during a victim/offender mediation session. An attractor tends to have a more or less stable geometric design and, thus, is said to be attracted to that shape. The butterfly attractor is the most celebrated form. Given a series of inputs (stimuli), a system can behave in two ways simultaneously. Over time, this movement can be plotted. The mapping of this movement assumes the shape of a butterfly's wings. The plotting reflects a great deal of indeterminacy and uncertainty for how the system behaves at the local, situational, or micro-level of analysis. However, at the global, systemic, macro-level of analysis, a pattern does emerge. See "Attractor" and "Chaos Theory" for more.

# C

**Cadre:** A central core of workers who activate and direct the activities of a larger mass. A bureaucratic organization (school, military, hospital, agency, business) has a paid set of workers who process people as isolated individuals or as faceless blocs through the routines of the system. In elitist societies, the expectation is that the cadre and the mass are in a permanent relationship since the point of the bureaucracy is to control workers, customers, patients, students, or prisoners and, thus, to reproduce class, status, honor, or social power. A socialist revolution establishes cadres to organize the poor and the powerless. In the latter instance, the cadre is supposed to arrange for those conditions in which collectives become unnecessary. See "Vanguard/Vanguardism" for more.

**Calvin, John (1509–1564):** French theologian who laid the basis for the Protestant ethic and the spirit of capitalism (Max Weber). Calvin's argument was: (1) God is the absolute cause of everything. (2) God ordains all that happens to people. (3) Humans were pure but fell from grace; even so part of God remains in each person. What remains is not enough for salvation. (4) Therefore Christ is necessary to salvation. (5) There is a two-fold scheme: Some are destined to salvation; some to damnation. (6) All people are equal before God. (See the work of W. L. Reese.)

Assumption 5 above is central to the idea that great wealth is a blessing of God, since assumption 2 holds that God ordains all. Assumption 6 grounds a thoroughgoing individualism and rejection of authority other than the Bible.

**Camp:** A verb meaning to enjoy cultural items rather than to celebrate them or to condemn them. As social conditions change, values that have been considered for a long time as certain and unquestionable begin to be considered doubtful, false, or harmful. The strong, silent, decisive cowboy in the cinema now looks strange. Films like *Midnight Cowboy* and *Blazing Saddles* camp on the John Wayne genre. The new Showtime cable series *Sherman Oaks* camps on the American family. For example, the son, who is white, speaks, thinks, and acts as if he was an oppressed black youth. Thus, the series neither celebrates racism nor condemns it but, instead, plays around with it. The father, a plastic surgeon, camps on the status-conscious consumerism of successful medical doctors. Again, there is neither celebration nor condemnation of this behavior.

**Campanella, Tomasso (1588–1639):**   Campanella, following Plato, set forth a Utopia called City of the Sun. In it people hold property in common and there is a class of philosopher/guardians as well as a state program of eugenics. The City of the Sun is infused by the love of God and rejects evil in personal and social relations. A forerunner of liberation theology. (See the work of W. L. Reese.)

**Canon/Canon Law:**   Greek: *kanon* = rule or rod. In Latin, the term came to mean those writings that were authoritative for a given religion. Canon law is the most authoritative law of the Roman Catholic Church. For centuries it served as a basis for justice and rulings about crime, property, marriage, and contracts. Gregory XIII had canon law codified in 1582. Based on Deuteronomy and other books of the Old and New Testaments, it still informs legal proceedings via secular legal codes that are based on it.

**Capital:**   This term has two different meanings: (1) manufactured physical objects—machines, equipment, buildings, and so on—that are used in the production process, or money available to buy these objects; (2) a relationship that gives a near-monopoly over money and machinery to a small group of people (capitalists) who are able to hire other people to work for them in order to make more money. Capitalism is a social relationship; most people have to work for somebody else in order to survive. In the United States, about 12 percent of the people are capitalists and live off of the surplus value of labor, whereas 58 percent sell their labor power. The rest live on the wages of paid workers, go on welfare, or hustle and steal. Capital in the first sense (physical objects) is necessary for production in every economic system. However, capital in the second sense (the ability of the owners of those physical objects to hire others to work for them) is unique to one particular system. According to Marx, capital is "dead labor that like a vampire only lives by sucking the blood from living labor."

**Capital, Accumulation of:**   The transformation of surplus value into machines and technology to produce more goods and services with fewer and fewer workers. All economic systems need to accumulate and improve capital goods; only capitalism tries, as well, to disemploy more and more people in the process. Marxists, socialists, and communists, as well as liberal economists, hold that part of surplus value should be set aside for essential but low-profit services: child care, health care, teaching, elder care, the environment, and so on. Capitalists tend to argue that capital accumulation should a) follow demand and b) be invested in the goods and services that yield the highest profit rates.

**Capital, Accumulation Crisis of:**   This idea refers to the problem of securing profits as the number of workers needed in capital-intensive production declines (and markets for mass-produced goods decline). Capitalism must either find new markets overseas or sell the "surplus" production to the state to give away to those who can't find work. The first solution requires a "warfare state" and the second a "welfare state." Both solutions require high taxes and/or deficit spending and, thus, contribute to a crisis in political legitimacy.

**Capital, Constant:**   This form of capital refers to machines, raw materials, buildings, tools, fuel, and other physical objects to which labor (variable capital) is added and from which all wealth comes. It is called constant capital, since, unlike variable capital (labor power), its value does not change in the production process beyond the wear and tear of producing wealth.

**Capital, Organic Composition of:**   This concept refers to the ratio of workers to machines. The more machines and fewer workers, the higher the organic composition of capital. Some lines of production are capital-intensive (they use very few workers); some are labor-intensive (they use few machines). Nursing, teaching, parenting, playing, and religious activities are labor-intensive. Mining, farming, milling, machining, transporting, and accounting are much more capital intensive. A good and decent society tries to keep a balance between capital and labor such that there is full employment in pro-social lines of production.

**Capital, Variable:**   That part of capital used to purchase the labor power of workers. It is called variable capital because labor power produces more than enough value to replace itself and more surplus value. Labor power also varies over time. Whereas workers get tired, sick, angry, or hurt, machines do not. The value workers can produce therefore varies much more so than that of machines. The costs of labor can go up or down more rapidly than the cost of capital goods, since capital goods come from other capitalists who have more power to control prices than do workers.

*Capital (Das Kapital:* **1867):**   A three-volume set in which Karl Marx went outside the capitalist paradigm to criticize it as an economic system. The text's basic thesis is that capitalism is a dynamic system that (a) destroys community, (b) converts praxis into alienated labor, and (c)"contains internal contradictions which tend to produce crises." Basically, capitalism is a system of capital accumulation for private purposes. This feature puts it into conflict with the human interest in production for social purposes. The major internal contradiction is that as capitalism succeeds, it has less use for workers. This means there is no one to exploit, since unemployed workers can't buy.

In the good years of capitalism, there was some doubt about the validity of Marxian analysis. War, new technology, and Keynesian policies kept the system growing. Recent developments tend to confirm the instability of capitalism as a system of production. For the United States, loss of markets to Germany, Japan, and socialist liberation movements have produced a crisis centered now in the state sector. The state covers much of the costs of capitalism at present in the United States. As deficit spending, taxes, and other federal revenue sources are exhausted and as welfare and military costs increase, production overhead must be shifted back to the private sector or political legitimacy is lost. Either the crisis is in the state sector or the private sector. Whatever the case, inflation and unemployment increase and more and more sectors of the population grow uneasy. There are two likely outcomes, fascism or socialism.

**Capital-Intensive Production:**    The use of machinery to produce food, shelter, clothing, electronics, automobiles, or other commodities. Workers cost a lot of money; wages, pensions, vacations, health insurance. Machines don't. Workers get ill, get angry, go on strike, criticize management, and quit. Machines don't.

**Capitalism:**    A system that separates workers from any true property rights. The means by which workers produce culture (through their labor) is not assigned equivalent value consistent with the product of their labor. Instead, through capitalism, there are artificial equivalents, and the most significant equalizer is money (e.g., a dozen apples = $2.00). See "Exchange-Value" and "Value (Use-)" for more.

Capitalism transforms the social means of subsistence (i.e., work) into capital on the one hand and the immediate producers into wage laborers on the other hand. Most of the time, capitalism is defined as the private ownership of the means of production, but that definition does not encompass the great harm done to humanity by the system. By claiming all (or most) of the means to produce culture as private property, a small class of owners preempts material culture for their own comfort while denying the vast majority the means to subsistence as well as the means to produce ideological culture when they are not working. See "Necessary Labor" for more.

**Capitalism, Advantages of:**    There are many aspects of capitalism most congenial to the human project: It is the most productive economic system in history; it is the most flexible; it is the most innovative. It also responds to human desire and personal preference; it requires an honest and unflinching knowledge process; it often requires merit; and it tends to destroy the ancient structures of oppression when it cannot use them. Cf. "Anarchy."

**Capitalism, Disadvantages of:**    Marx argued that there were laws within the everyday workings of capitalism that would create misery and lead to the destruction of the system. These laws include: (1) the tendency of the rate of profit to fall; (2) the tendency of large firms to buy out or destroy small firms; (3) the tendency to transform all goods and services into commodities; (4) the tendency to transfer (externalize) costs of production to workers, consumers, or the environment; (5) the tendency to disemploy workers (surplus labor force) in favor of machines and capital intensive production; (6) the tendency to dominate the political process; (7) the tendency to control the production of ideological culture (art, science, music, literature, and religion); (8) the tendency toward economic imperialism; (9) the tendency to abandon low-profit but essential lines of production (the Law of Uneven Development); and (10) the tendency toward revolution.

**Capitalism, Economic Laws of:**   There are three "laws" that capitalist economists say are the heart of all economics: (1) the law of supply and demand; (2) the law of marginal utility; and (3) the law of diminishing returns. These are all valid enough within the logic of capitalism. Cf. "Capitalism."

**Capitalism, Fiscal Costs of:**   It cost the United States about $250 billion to keep capitalism as a form of production in 1990. Corporate profits were about $213 billion; interest costs were $23.5 billion; excessive salaries of top executives were about $12.5 billion more. Depreciation allowances came to about $108.3 billion in 1988, and part of this allowance transferred to owners since it was not all spent to replace worn-out capital. URPE estimates that altogether in some combination of profits, interests, and rents the capitalist class takes a 19 percent cut of national income, even though it does nothing in return. (Managers get paid to manage; brokers and money managers get paid to invest.) In addition to these direct fiscal costs, the worker also pays taxes to support a military apparatus that protects the overseas markets of American capitalists, to support the surplus population on welfare, and to support the policing of the surplus population (members of which steal a lot when they can't find work and so hustle the worker and each other). These calculations do not count the social costs of capitalism measured in human misery and despair rather than dollars and profits.

**Capitalism, People's:**   An economic system in which a large portion of the wealth is shared widely in society or is held by a democratic state on behalf of all the people. In this system, democratic freedoms, market dynamics, and private property are retained. The state does not represent the interests of the capitalist class but, rather, the general interest (including future generations). Social democracies try to approximate this economic form (e.g., England, France, Germany, Sweden, Italy, Australia, Canada, and New Zealand). Many Marxists argue that the basic conflicts remain and will reassert themselves when times get bad. See "Kondratieff Cycles" for more.

**Capitalism, Reproduction of:**   The capitalist system must be continuously reproduced. This is accomplished by two general means: the reproduction of private/elitist ownership and the management of dissent via ideological hegemony and/or outright repression. The ideological process starts in school and college, where capitalist ideas are celebrated and socialist ideas are distorted or ignored. The state plays a large role in reproducing capitalism through laws that establish the right to appropriate part of the value of labor by non-workers and through public policy that subsidizes almost all of the "costs" of capitalism. What is required for the continuation of capitalism is a legal system that permits the "free" trade of commodities, where "free" means that a necessary social good is withheld unless a seller can make a profit. The state also commits many crimes against rebellious workers and political opposition in the name of law and order. In order to increase profits, obtain raw materials, destroy competition, or control markets, capitalist corporations commit many crimes that are unpoliced, uncharged, untried, and uncounted. Many, if not most, military ventures of the United States have no design other than to penetrate and protect markets, provide cheap labor, and guarantee capitalism's access to low cost raw materials.

Feminists point out that women are charged to reproduce the labor power of their working husbands by providing unpaid domestic service and by rearing/socializing the next generation of compliant workers. They also reproduce capital by "super" exploitation; they are paid 30, 40, 60, or 90 percent of what males get for the same work. Then, too, women reproduce the status system while at work via gender-based norms and as the victims of sexual harassment.

**Capitalism, Social Costs of:**   In addition to a 19 percent bite out of the value of the wealth produced by the working class, capitalism also costs much in the way of human misery. Capitalism withholds the basic necessities of life unless one has something to exchange (so the capitalist can make a profit). Capitalism also systematically degrades work while trying to enlarge the surplus value of labor. Further, part of the wealth produced by labor is turned into repressive structures: law, police, prisons, psychiatry, and "public relations." But the conversion of culture and of social relationships into commodities cheapens and destroys a society. Capitalist relations reproduced in the family, the school, in medicine, and in sports turn human beings themselves into commodities to be bought and sold.

**Capitalism, Stages of:**   The periods of capitalist development differ according to the ways in which the value of labor is appropriated by those who own and/or control the means of production. The first stage was mercantile capitalism, which emerged on a large scale in Venice and Genoa in the thirteenth century. It culminated in the English empire in the nineteenth century. The second stage was industrial capitalism, as factory cities replaced independent commodity production at home by artisans. This stage began around 1730 in England with the factory system and remained dominant until the twentieth century, by which time finance capitalism began to displace industrial capitalism as the major means of extracting surplus value. Capitalism in the United States claims about 23 percent of the GNP, and of that amount 13 percent is rent or profit and 10 percent is interest. Most corporations, such as Sears or Wards or Master-Charge, now prefer to sell credit (finance capitalism) rather than merchandise (industrial capitalism) because credit has lower capital costs and higher returns.

**Capitalism, Theory of Its Collapse:**    Marx laid out the dynamics by which capitalism will bring on its own demise. In brief, Marx said that capitalism brings into being productive forces that it cannot control and that will burst under the constraints placed on it by capitalism. Capitalism creates a huge productive apparatus, and, at the same time, it creates a surplus population by replacing workers with machines. It generates demand for products, and, at the same time, it withholds products in order to get higher prices. It cheapens labor, and, at the same time, it requires that one labor in order to purchase goods. It brings together industrial armies that then constitute a threat to property relations. It must create waste even as raw materials come into short supply. It must argue for freedom in the marketplace while growing more bureaucratic in the factory and office. It must disempower its employees even as they become better educated. It must eliminate other capitalists and thus erode its own power base. These and other factors create the objective conditions by which social revolution is more likely. Even without a communist conspiracy or social reformers ("do-gooders," "bleeding-hearts," and "eggheads"), capitalism outlives its usefulness. The problems of capitalism lie within the system not outside it.

**Capitalist World System/New World Order:**    Often called the New World Order, this phrase refers to a model of global economics in which some 1000 huge multinational firms produce and distribute goods across national borders. When one looks more closely, one can see a hierarchy of nations in which these firms are located. At the top is the Group of Seven; then there is a layer of NICs (newly industrial states), including Korea, Taiwan, Hong Kong, Singapore, and Malaysia; below them are semi-feudal states, including most of the Islamic nations and the more industrial African, Latin American, and Asian nations; at the bottom are some 20 economically depressed nations unable to compete on the world market. See "Dependency Theory" for more.

**Capital Logic:**    A version of Marxist analysis. Capital logic (similar to the commodity-exchange principle) is based on Marx's work in Volume 1 of *Capital* (1867). Commodities are merchandise (e.g., produce, appliances, automobiles). Following the logic of capital, products are transformed

when sold. All commodities possess intrinsic value. This natural value includes the amount of work and time it takes to harvest or make the commodity and the satisfaction one experiences having harvested or made the
product. When a commodity enters the marketplace, the intrinsic *use-value*
is replaced with an equivalent *exchange-value*. For example one loaf of
bread = $1.05; a Chevrolet Camaro = $20,000; an elite athlete for the Atlanta
Braves baseball team = $3,000,000 per year. As capital logic proponents re-
mind us, the problem with this process is that money becomes the ultimate
arbiter of value. Money masks and conceals the differential amounts of
labor required to make products. These things disappear in the marketplace. They are brought under the neutralizing form of money. The concrete dimension of existence and experience is replaced with the abstract.
The qualitative aspects of human social interaction are substituted with
quantitative ratios. The realities of work, leisure, ritual, celebration, and so
on are replaced by their suggested monetary forms or equivalents. See
"Exchange-Value" and "Value Use-)" for more.

**Capital Punishment:**    Execution by the state. There are several crimes
that are classified as "capital" offenses (i.e., they carry the death penalty).
The most common of these include murder, kidnapping, treason. The Federal Crime Control Act also made several drug-related felonies capital offenses. The United States reinstated capital punishment in 1973. It is the
only advanced, industrial country of its kind to retain this form of punishment.

Several critics contend that the death penalty is a mechanism of racial
discrimination. When controlling for representation within the general
population, the disproportionate number of serious felony convictions for
people of color substantially increases their likelihood to receive capital
punishment sentences as compared with their white counterparts.

The means used by the state to kill prisoners are many: shooting and
hanging are uncommon; cyanide gas, electrocution, and injection with a
lethal dose of poison are preferred.

**Career/Careerist:**    Latin: *carraria* = carriage road; French: *carere* = race
course. Now used to refer to any one who is on the "fast track" in a job or
occupation. A careerist is one who uses a social position for private advantage. Usually by catering to superiors or looking away from other's
misdeeds, the careerist succeeds by protecting his/her position.

**Carrier's Case:**    A famous legal case in which a carrier stole part of the
cargo he was carrying and was then sued by the merchant owner. At issue
here were matters of conversion and possession. In a landmark decision, a
British court ruled that the merchant had legal standing to come before it
for redress of grievance. Thus the wrong was against the state rather than
against the owner of the goods. It was the beginning of a legal system in

which a wrong against a capitalist became a wrong against the entire state. The state consequently became a partisan on behalf of owners. Workers and customers had no such legal standing until the twentieth century.

**Cartel:**   A group of firms or countries that jointly decide on prices and output. By coordinating actions, they can be certain not to compete and do away each other's profits. Cartels have existed for well over a century. The Organization of Petroleum Exporting Countries (OPEC) is now using a tactic that large and powerful firms (including oil companies) have used for generations. There are six companies in a cartel that meet regularly and control the prices of grains and breakfast cereals. Cartels of nations that supply raw materials or coffee, cotton, sugar, or cocoa are a threat to capitalist nations because they fuel inflation and squeeze profits. The U.S. State Department spends a lot of its time on behalf of capitalism to control cartels in undeveloped nations. Little effort is made to control U.S. cartels abroad. This is because the business of American foreign policy is business.

**Case Law:**   Those cases in law that serve as bases for making legal judgments. Opposed to statutory law, which is law passed by a law-making body. Usually case law embodies age-old norms and sanctions; statutory law embodies the interests of that elite in power at the time.

**Caste:**   A system of social differentiation and stratification in which one set of persons are defined as inferior or superior in some important respect. Life chances and life courses are determined at birth in societies organized by caste. Capitalism tends to replace caste systems with class systems.

**Casuistry:**   Latin: *casus* = case. The doctrine of resolving issues of right versus wrong or problems of conscience by appealing to holy books, scriptures, or religious texts. The use of biblical law, sayings, convention, or cases to judge/interpret present questions of ethical behavior. For example, one might say, "No casuistry will persuade me that your cruelty is a kindness that can be justified by appeal to the teachings of Christ." Today, casuistry is often regarded as an unsystematic and unsophisticated line of argumentation. It tends to be invoked by religious professionals to explain social, psychological, and interpersonal dilemmas.

**Cause:**   Latin: *causa*. The antecedent of an effect. Aristotle identified four categories: efficient, material, final, and formal cause. Hume gave the term its modern sense: the constant conjunction of events. Kant laid the foundation for a postmodern view of cause when he held that cause was an a priori category used uncritically by those who sought to explain something. Chaos theory replaces the idea of cause with the idea of feedback, of which there are three forms. See "Algorithm" for more.

**Caveat emptor:**   Latin: let the buyer beware (of the possibility the goods may be stolen, the components damaged or faulty, the ingredients poisonous, or the prices fixed in conspiracy).

**Central (Economic) Planning:**   An economic system in which the state manages the economy through periodic plans, usually five-year plans. Such plans used to call for the economy to: a) change rapidly to industrial production; b) improve neglected lines of production; c) reemploy the surplus labor force; d) redistribute wealth to housing, hospitals, schools, roads, highways, dams, irrigation systems, electric power plants, and other "infrastructure" needs. Although rightly claiming many achievements in many socialist countries, central planning still has several flaws: (1) it is too inflexible; (2) it promotes white-collar crime as well as a "black market"; (3) it obstructs more democratic forms of production and puts quantity before quality.

**Central Executive Committees:**   Almost all socialist and/or communist parties have central committees that run things in the interim between Congresses of the People. Too often, the congresses are pushed aside and all social power remains in the hands of an elite rather than in the hands of a people working toward a democratic communism.

**Central Intelligence Agency (CIA):**   A large branch of the U.S. government whose operations are mostly classified and clandestine. It is concerned with espionage, counter-espionage, and, in its counter-revolutionary activities, the safeguarding of capitalism/free-market dynamics in third world countries. Like the KGB of the former USSR, it has become a law and a government unto itself. For example, it profits from the drug trade by obtaining funds to engage in activities not approved and funded by the U.S. Congress.

**Centralism, Democratic.**   A fraudulent facsimile of democracy in which a central committee makes all the relevant policy decisions while party members are expected to carry them out in the name of democratic centralism. In the former USSR, the Central Committee of the Communist Party had effective control of the government; the people's congresses were little more than rubber stamps. See "Vanguard/Vanguardism" for more.

**Certainty:**   Latin: *cernere* = to decide. There are three quests for certainty in social science. One quest is for logical certainty; there are many forms of logic, chief among them is syllogistic logic. Logical certainty may have little to do with empirical truth. The second quest is for certainty about present and future states/behaviors of real systems; this is the task of empirical research and statistical inference. The third quest is for psychological certainty; what to believe and how to be confident that what one believes is close to the truth.

**Certiorari, Writ of:**   The name of the legal process by which evidence is reexamined by an appeals court to make certain that a judgment is supported by that evidence. Most of the time, appeals courts look only at technical questions; if new evidence is found, such writs can be made.

**Chance:**   Latin, *cadere* = to fall. In Greek mythology, the fall of sticks or stones was thought to be a result of the will of the gods; chance serves as a pathway to knowledge in many religions; one who benefits from gambling is thought to be favored by the gods. In modern science, chance is reduced to the work of unknown and perhaps unknowable variables. A great deal of mischief ensues when causality is attributed to chance. Chaos theory offers a systematic way to better understand unexpected outcomes, accidents, and nonlinear transformations. See "Chaos Theory" for more.

**Chaos Theory:**   A body of knowledge about the changing mix of order and disorder in natural and social systems. Modern, Newtonian science gives preference to order and stability; Chaos theory tends to support the idea that some disorder is essential to all complex, adaptive systems and that change is continuous with the human experience. Chaos theory provides an elegant empirical support for both dialectic theory and for postmodern concern with variety, surprise, contrariety, and difference.

In Chaos theory, existing structures have a fractal and temporary geometry; there is a secession of dynamical states; with each bifurcation, more complex dynamics develop, causality is looser, and prediction is less possible. According to Chaos theorists, all living creatures and societies require some disorder to survive. Innovation, creativity, flexibility, and revolution are everyday words we use to make this point. If there is too much order, systems will die. If there is too much disorder systems will not behave as expected. See "Attractor," "Fractal/Fractal Geometry," "Dialectic," "Dissipative Structure," "Far-From-Equilibrium Conditions," "Linear/Linearity," "Mysticism," "Nonlinear Dynamics," "Prediction," "Routine Activities, Theory of," "Science, Postmodern," "Solution," "Statistical Significance," "Structure," "Truth," "Ultrastability," and "Wave Theory" for more.

**Charisma:**   Greek: full of grace. One who embodies charismatic authority embodies the highest values and hopes of a given culture. Charisma is a social product; one does not have charisma apart from a set of followers who "believe" in her/him.

Max Weber lists charisma as one of three forms of authority; of the three, charisma has the most potential for dramatic social change. Jesus, Mohammed, Hitler, Martin Luther King, and the Ayatollah Khomeini were able to arouse great loyalty and make dramatic social changes.

**Charity:**   Latin: *caritas* = dear. Christian love and care for the poor and oppressed (1 Corinthians 13). Charities (e.g., United Way, March of Dimes,
Red Cross, as well as cancer, heart, or lung drives) engage in collective,
healing actions in order to help restore people, given the state's increasing
inability to adequately assist its own citizen with health, mental health,
and social service needs.

Socialist Marxists point out that one effect of capitalism is the increasing
number of citizens in the workforce who succumb to some form of injury
on the job. Because the capitalist system does not always provide full
health care coverage for its employees, charities are assigned the task of
taking care of these workers.

The word often carries negative emotional content, since both giver and
receiver lack the compassion and grace embodied in the religious meaning.

**Child Savers:**   A social movement begun around 1850 to keep children in
school, out of adult prisons, and to prevent them from competing with
adult men for jobs as the surplus population grew. Throughout the 1800s,
several judicial and policing measures were instituted in order to "save"
the children from the brutalizing effects of the criminal justice system. See
*"Parens patriae"* for more.

**Chiliasm/Chiliastic:**   Greek: *chiliiad* = thousand. Chiliasticism is the belief
that the world will end in the year 1000, 2000, or some multiple of the
1000th year after the birth of Christ. See "Millennium" for more.

**Chomsky, Noam (1928– ):**   An American linguist known for his work on
language and grammar. Chomsky holds that there are genetically based
structures in human beings that give rise and pre-shape speech acts. He is
an articulate critic of capitalism and of the role of the United States in serving the global interests of transnational corporations with both military
and ideological weapons. Chomsky works with Z magazine, Edward Her-
man, Holly Sklar, and many other progressive scholars, as well as with the
South End Press. Z magazine and South End Press are mainstays of radical, transforming consciousness in the United States.

**Christ, Jesus (4 B.C.E.–29 A.D.):**   Founder of one of the first world religions that set belief, faith, and good works as tests for status rather than
birth in particular tribes. Christianity has many progressive moments; people are to live with purity of heart, compassion for others, and to form supportive communities; they are to search for peace and justice in this life in
order to gain salvation for eternity. One is to "turn the other cheek" to violence and hate. One is to forgive those who do harm (rather than to pursue vengeance and technical punitive justice). Christ helped to change the
angry, tribal God of the Old Testament into the universal loving God of the

New Testament. His teachings ground liberation theology. Jesus is the Greek transliteration of the Hebrew name Joshua.

**Christian Right:**   Made up formally of organizations like the Christian Coalition and the Moral Majority. The Christian right represents a growing constituency of people in the United States (many of whom are in the South and the Midwest) who believe that political and social action must be driven by ethical, moral principles first. The Christian right believes in teaching the biblical version of creation only, promotes school prayer, rejects homosexuality, and supports political leaders who endorse strong Christian/religious values. The Christian right is responsible for such television personalities as Jim and Tammy Fay Bakker, Jerry Falwell, Oral Roberts, as well as for spawning associations such as the 700 Club. The Christian right is often criticized for its conservative, patriarchal, sexist, and homophobic viewpoints. Cf. "Theology, Postmodern."

**Chronophone:**   One who sees time as linear and/or as a natural construct apart from the conceptions and interests of human beings. Postmodernists tend to reject such a view. See "Derrida, Jacques" for more.

**Church:**   A formal way of organizing the religious experience in which a small cadre of professional clerics (called priests or ministers) can regulate the life of a mass of people. Membership is proclaimed de facto by birth or residence and everyone is expected to give allegiance. Cf. "Sect" for more.

**Civil Inattention:**   A norm of mass market societies that requires one carefully avoid interaction with others physically present. If the others are part of a social base, then civility would be required. If others are nonpersons, then one can be uncivilly inattentive (i.e., one can stare, push, look through, speak through, or talk about others in their presence). Black persons are often the subject of uncivil inattention in the North and the South, as are dwarfs, cripples, celebrities, and strangers. The norm of civil inattention, when observed and along with the other social conditions that destroy social relatedness, produces a mass society. Sometimes privacy is basic to the adoption of the norm of civil inattention.

**Civilization:**   Greek: a primitive; French: *civilis* = of or belonging to the citizens. A concept used to refer to a specific stage in the cultural evolution of a particular people within a geographic area. Some civilizations are marked by formal social relations that are highly impersonal and extremely rational.

Mills and Coleridge contrasted civilization with culture and imbued the first with positive emotional content and the latter with negative emotional content, as in savage, primitive, barbarian. Spengler distinguished between traditional community and civilization. The latter was the highest form of social life. The elements of civilization include a separation of private and public life; the primacy of civil law in public affairs; the right to privacy in business, home, and personal relationships; and respect for difference and variety.

**Civil Society:**   A social order in which the rights of egoistic, atomistic individuals are proclaimed. A system (not really a society) in which the bonds between people are those of physical survival, safety, and preservation of private property. Civil society contrasts with community, where bonds are social.

Many critical scholars have commented on the meaning of the civil society. See "Gramsci, Antonio," "Lukács, Georg," and "Marx, Karl" for more.

**Class:**   Class is one of five great systems of domination that affect patterns of health, housing, self-esteem, religion, education, recreation, and politics. It is based upon one's relationship to the means of production and distribution.

For Marxists, a class consists of people who have the same role in the process of production. The two basic classes under capitalism are the capitalist (or ruling) class—called the *bourgeoisie,* those who own and control all productive processes—and the working class—called the *proletariat,* those who lack that control and have to sell their labor for wages. Bankers, major corporate stockholders, top managers, and absentee landlords belong to the capitalist class. Factory and construction workers, police, secretaries, hospital workers, teachers, and many others belong to the working class. There are also other classes, such as the middle class of self-employed people (farmers, store owners, poets, brokers, lawyers, doctors).

The Marxist definition of class is different from that used by many sociologists, who use terms like middle class to refer to level of income rather than relationship to the process of production. Many workers do have incomes comparable to middle-level functionaries in the United States. However, since the workers do not own the means of production, their position in terms of wages could quickly change. As factories move overseas, as inflation increases, and as taxes increase, the difference in wealth between capitalists and workers becomes more visible.

**Class Action Suit:**   A legal procedure in which a number of persons harmed by a company or an agency come together to petition a court for remedy. This legal action is important in controlling corporate crime and/or unconstitutional action by a local governing body. Corporate conservatives try to limit eligibility for class action status. Advocates for those who are harmed try to expand it.

**Class Collaboration:**   When elements of the working class or the intelligentsia cooperate with owners or with the state, they are said to "class collaborate." Liberals claim that class collaboration produces qualitatively different and more humane economic systems. Many orthodox communists, however, despise class collaboration. According to them, it is better for workers to remain independent and work for the common good than to cooperate with capitalists in the exploitation of unorganized workers, third world countries, and weaker firms.

**Class Conflict:**   In class organized societies, there are several conflicts of interest between workers and owners. First and foremost, some of the surplus value of labor produced by workers is appropriated and claimed by capitalists. Second, there is the question of how the labor process is to be organized; capitalists want workers to be excluded from management decisions over how fast workers work, when they work, where they work, and with whom they work. Third, there is the question of what is to be produced; some workers don't like to produce unsafe toys, foods with dangerous additives, weapons of death, or low quality goods. Indeed, some religions prohibit this kind of labor. However, as long as a lot of workers have access to sufficient material wealth and the time to create ideological culture, and as long as the instruments of coercion are in the hands of an elite, the conflict of interests is contained.

When capitalism faces an accumulation crisis, however, appropriation of surplus value increases and the capacity of people to create culture is threatened. At this point, class conflict transforms into class struggle. Usually the class struggle is over wages and working conditions, but success here is short-lived. The Marxist position is that the objective of the class struggle is to reclaim ownership of the means of producing culture rather than to gain an increase in wages with which to purchase culture. Some hold that the class struggle is to be seen in absentee rates, turnover rates, wildcat strikes, petty sabotage, shoddy workmanship, grievance rates, quarrels, and drug and alcohol use at work. But such things are more privatized conflict than organized struggle. See "Class Struggle" for more.

**Class Consciousness:**   An awareness of one's own class interests, a rejection of the interests of other classes, and a readiness to use political means to realize one's class interests. Most people identify themselves as middle class even if they don't get paid much and even if they can be fired tomorrow with no warning. Many people go to college and learn they are better, more successful than are "common laborers" and, thus, try to distance themselves from their brothers and sisters who work at unskilled jobs. Workers, too, look down upon the underclass, and, thus, the "working class" is fragmented into sectors with little interest in class struggle.

Capitalists, too, have different interests but tend to unite in the face of class opposition. Those who produce raw materials have to sell them to industrial capitalists. There is always conflict there. Merchants have to buy from industrialists. There is conflict there as well. Both merchants and industrialists need to borrow money from finance capitalists; so there are more conflicts of interest. Then, too, all those in the same line compete with each other. Big business tends to destroy small business, as, for example, when WalMart comes in and takes customers away from small shops and stores; or when McDonald's comes in and takes customers away from small restaurants.

**Class Consciousness, Theory of:**   Marx's theory of class consciousness holds that industrialism and the factory system bring thousands of workers together in the same place. While together, they begin to realize their own social power and see more clearly the conflict between workers and owners. Vladimir Lenin said that workers are not truly class conscious until they respond to all cases of tyranny, oppression, violence, and abuse, no matter who is affected.

**Class Structure:**   In advanced capitalism, the three significant strata are the capitalist class (1.5 percent of the adult population); the working class (73.5 percent); and the surplus population (25 percent and growing, relative to the working class). Allied with the capitalist class are professionals, middle management, and bureaucrats (18.5 percent), who, possessing only their labor power to sell, still support their employers politically and ideologically because they get higher wages, higher status, and, often, a share in profits. Separated from the unskilled workers (30 percent) are the skilled workers (15 percent) and the technical workers (10 percent) who are organized on occupational lines rather than class lines. Then there is the reserve army (composed mostly of minorities, women, and young people, 15 percent). The class struggle is to forge class alliance now in order to advance theoretically informed class conflict later. See "Underclass" for more.

**Class Struggle:**   A struggle over who controls the labor process. It arises between strata in any exploitative society, since each class has different and incompatible differences. The struggle is over a) who owns the means of production; b) the uses to which they are put; c) the labor process itself; and d) how "surplus value" is to be divided. Class struggle on the part of the capitalists involves price fixing, black listing, union busting, bribery, preselection of candidates for public office, pollution, disinvestment, and cartels. Class struggle by workers includes strikes, sit-ins, general work stoppages, unionization, support of political candidates, and sometimes rebellion. Sabotage, theft, falsification of time cards, and acts of petty rebellion are also tools occasionally used. Consumers, too, sometimes engage in class struggle with boycotts, bans, pickets, shoplifting, and political activity. For the socialist, class struggle does not mean the replacement of one elite by another but, rather, the end of class relationships. See "Class Conflict" for more.

**Client State:**   This term refers to a situation in which the government of a small country works in the interest of another country. Consider how the

United States subverts the political process of independent countries. Latin American governments get arms, easy credit, and military advisers from the United States to help maintain oligarchy/elitism. The CIA has many such politicians directly on its payroll. For example, former Panamanian President Manuel Noriega was on its payroll, as are foreign dignitaries and/or other high-level political figures.

**Closed Shop:** A factory, mill, mine, office, or other place of employment in which all workers are required by terms of a labor contract to belong to and contribute dues to a union that then bargains on behalf of all workers. Such agreements can include requirements that only union members be hired or that newly hired persons join the union within a specified time.

**Code:** In semiotic terminology, all communication—whether spoken or nonspoken, whether verbal, nonverbal, or extra-verbal—is conveyed through a specialized language (e.g., lawyers use "legalese"; athletes use the terminology of their particular sport). Thus, all forms of communication are systems of communication or "sign systems." The words and phrases of the sign system are loaded with specialized meaning. These meanings are unique to the code in use and must be interpreted from within the grammar of the code if proper understanding and sense making are to occur between the sender and receiver of the "coded" message. Postmodernists examine and "decode" the implicit meanings communicated between senders and receivers of messages. See "Semiotics" and "Sign" for more.

**Coercion:** The use of social, economic, physical, or moral power to force a person to do that which s/he does not want to do. One of the major disadvantages of a stratification system is that it gives some persons social and economic power to force those in lower social echelons to provide services to which the persons in a higher echelon are not otherwise entitled. The use of social power by a boss to solicit sexual favors or bribes are cases in point. One should note the class bias in coercion: Older, rich males have money to use to coerce; young minority males in the underclass have only physical power to coerce. Both kinds of coercion are to be feared and carefully regulated in pursuit of a praxis society.

***Cogito ergo sum:*** Latin: "I think therefore I exist." It has also been translated as "I think therefore I am." There are two meanings that René Descartes may have had in mind when he set forth this proposition. The first is the well-known breakthrough in epistemology: I think therefore someone such as I must exist in order to do the thinking. The act of thought implies a thinker. The second is the larger task of mapping out reliable knowledge: One exists in a significant way by thinking on his/her own rather than by accepting as truth what others say. See "Descartes, René" for more.

**Cognitive Capacities:**   The capacities of perception, awareness, imagination, reason, judgment, purpose, evaluation, and reevaluation by which people organize their own behavior with insight and understanding. A praxis society is one in which cognitive capacities are encouraged. See "Consciousness" and "IQ" for more.

**Cohort:**   A set of persons born within the same five-year period. One can follow the life cycles of a given cohort and discover the larger patterns that shape and pre-shape human behavior. Cohort analysis is a powerful tool in macro-social psychological work.

**Collective:**   In socialist usage, a collective is a tightly knit group of people who produce something of social value for others. Socialist collectives try to be self-governing, self-supporting, and mutually supportive. Although not related by kinship, a collective has many of the characteristics of an extended family: intimacy, trust, accessibility, responsibility for each other, and warmth. This definition sharply contrasts with standard American sociological usages in which a collective is defined as a cadre of unrelated others acting spontaneously in much the same fashion (e.g., a street mob).

**Collective Bargaining:**   The direct negotiation between workers and owners of a company. This bargaining usually centers around three key questions: share in profits, job security, and the labor process in the factory, mill, or mine. The larger needs of society are usually not of immediate concern in collective bargaining. Often one set of workers do well while unorganized groups continue to have hard times. See "Compromise, The Great" for more.

**Collective Behavior:**   In conventional sociological terms, the term refers to mass response to a "problem" in life not adequately handled by existing solutions within the system. Most conservative theorists denounce collective behavior as some kind of mass hysteria, lunacy, craze, or mindless imitation. Each instance of collective behavior should be studied on its own terms. Rosa Luxemburg held that people usually do things that make sense to them at the time, even if theorists do not understand why.

**Collective Conscience:**   A term developed by the French sociologist Émile Durkheim. Societies are characterized by a degree of uniformity. This uniformity is evident in daily practices such as work and leisure. Collective conscience refers to the totality of social likenesses or shared attitudes, beliefs, customs, thoughts, and sentiments a society embodies. According to Durkheim, all functional (mechanical or organic) societies demand a certain degree of uniformity from their members. Thus, the collective conscience is found in every culture. See "Division of Labor" and "Durkheim, Émile" for more.

**Colony:**   A poor or weak country that is occupied by the military and/or police forces of a more powerful country. England, France, Germany, Italy, and Japan all had colonies until just after World War II. After that time, colonialism was replaced by economic imperialism and client states.

**Comenius, John Amos (1592–1671):**   A Moravian educator and pastor who held that students should take part in their own education; that subject matters should be connected; that language should be taught through conversation and cooperative work; that universal education was a prelude to social reform and social justice. See "Education, Revolutionary" for more.

**Commodification:**   The practice of converting use-value into exchange-value. For Marxists, commodification is an important idea. To illustrate, think about food. It has a use-value (to satisfy hunger) but its exchange-value (the cost of purchasing the food) may be set so high that people may starve even when there is a lot of it. The same is true for any essential good or service once it has been commodified. Then, too, as Marx noted, all that is sacred can be commodified; sex, friendship, child care, even religion can be marketed. See "Property" and "Sacred/Profane" for more.

**Commodity:**   The transformation of a good or service from its meaning as a support for social relationships to a meaning of private profit. Food, sex, housing, medicine, and transport could be used to create and affirm social relationships (as is the case in a family) or for profit (as is the case in capitalism).

**Commodity Fetishism:**   In Marxist analysis, the entire process by which major economic transformations take place in the value of a given commodity or product. When the use-value of a certain item is transformed into an exchange-value, there is an artificial transformation from quality to quantity, from concrete to abstract, from content to form. When a loaf of bread is valued at $1.05, the inherent value that went into making the loaf of bread and the intrinsic goodness the baker experienced for having made it are equated with a ratio of exchange. This process, when applied to various commodities, represents their fetishism. Today, we speak of the same process in relation to the value of one's labor. For example, we define the worth of a person based on what they produce. An elite football player is valued at $5,000,000 per year, whereas a nurse is valued at $40,000 per annum, and a preschool teacher is valued at $20,000 per year. See "Capital Logic" for more.

**Common Law:**   Those laws set forth by royal courts in the three centuries after the Norman Conquest in 1066. The content of common law predates the Normans. The French did not impose French law (derived from Roman law) on England, but they did try to centralize and regularize the administration of law. Henry II (who ruled from 1154–1189) sent judges around to the shires, and slowly a body of law developed (now called common law) to replace multiplicities of local laws. In England there is a distinction between local law and the law binding on all people (or the law common to all). Civil law (Roman law) is also common to all people, including Britons when England was occupied by the Romans, but the codes are different in many ways.

The United States uses law from British common law, Roman civil law, Christian law (Deuteronomy), Justinian's code, the Mosaic code of the Israelites, and the code of Hammurabi when considering questions of crime, punishment, and social justice.

**Common-Law Marriage:**   A marriage without a formal wedding. Such marriages are recognized as valid in law when a) two people have been living together for a given period of time (usually six months) and b) when they announce themselves as husband and wife in public. Common-law marriages have many legal consequences for property rights, inheritance rights, pension and support rights. Children born to such marriages are often considered bastards. See "Marriage" for more.

**Commune:**   In Marxist/socialist theory a commune is the most human and humane form of social life. The means of production are owned by the whole community, and food, shelter, health care, education, and recreation are shared on the basis of social status rather than on the basis of wages, profits, dividends, rents, or other nonsocial grounds. Governance is by direct participation of all adult members. In the former USSR, communal life was mandatory until 1931. Extensive agricultural- and industrial-based communes exist in China.

In the modern United States, a commune is an attempt on the part of young people to form an extended primary group in which middle-class values of property and commodity are avoided. Communes can be exploitative of women (e.g., David Koresh and the Branch Davidians). Some communes try to avoid elitist, sexist, or other harmful practices. The term comes from the medieval towns in France, which demanded and practiced local self-government. This was the beginning of the end of feudalism and of the rise of capitalism. In these communes and in the Paris Commune, Marx saw the promise of communism. See "Ascribed Status" for more.

**Communication:**   The process by which people, through the use of symbols, construct a shared frame of meaning, line of understanding, or social lifeworld. Communication is not merely the use of symbols by which one person influences another, as defined in many texts but, rather, a remarkable process by which people can bond, share, or otherwise connect with one another with amazing accuracy. Communication, then, is a tangible source of solidarity among people.

**Communism:**   Latin: *communis* = common, universal, public. Communism is now chiefly understood to be an economic system as described by Marx and a great many other critics of capitalism. For Marx, communism entailed the appropriation of human nature through and for people. It was a return of people to a state of humaneness (i.e., sociability), as well as a system that promoted and enhanced the natural and dialectical unity of individual and society. Communism represents a non-alienating, humane, and decent society. It is not to be confused with bureaucratic socialism, which existed in some eastern European states. In advanced communism, the means of production are held in common; that is, what is produced, who produces it, and how it is produced is a matter of collective discourse and decision. Further, advanced communism means that any surplus value (profit) is allocated to serve collective rather than private needs. See "Government, Forms of," "Necessary Labor," "Socialism," and "Socialism, Bureaucratic" for more.

**Communism, Idea of:**   A society without the structures of domination that now debase and degrade so many people. *Primitive communism* is marked by production and distribution for use (rather than for profit) and by a low-tech means of production. *Advanced communism* has both an energy efficient and effective means of production as well as a system of distribution based mostly on need but also on merit. It uses surplus value in capital-intensive production to provide for labor-intensive lines of production (e.g., child care, health care, government, and policing). Surplus value is also used for public goods: parks, art forms, roads, bridges, the environment, water, sewage, and so on.

Chinese policy is to set income in a ratio of 4 to 1; four parts based upon need, one part based upon merit. In advanced monopoly capital systems such as the United States, managers of big corporations have an income 500 times greater than that of the average worker (in Germany the ratio is about 350 to 1; in Japan about 90 to 1), even though the needs of the managers and the workers are roughly equal.

**Communism, Movement of:**   A loose coalition of socialists, Marxists, and other radicals bent on the overthrow of any society organized in such a way that the mode of production of culture alienates people from self, from nature, and from each other. In capitalist countries, the movement has a bad name for a number of reasons: It puts aside national loyalty in favor of working-class unity across state boundaries; it is largely negative in its criticism of a society; its rhetoric is sometimes strident and contrived; it is supported by repressive socialist regimes; and counter-intelligence operations in capitalist societies plant false evidence, whereupon members of the movement often discredit each other. See "Vanguard/Vanguardism" for more.

**Communism, Primitive/Communalism:**   An economic formation in which all persons share on the basis of kinship and/or social status, but one in which there is a simple technology and division of labor. As Thomas Hobbes said, in these societies life is often ugly, brutal, nasty, and short.

**Communist Manifesto:**   A document distributed in London in 1848 by the Communist League. It linked theory and revolutionary action by providing a brief overview of the social sources of human misery and suggested a plan of action to eliminate those sources. It was drafted by Karl Marx and Friedrich Engels. In brief, the *Manifesto* reviews the history of oppression, lists the positive and negative aspects of capitalism, and concludes with a call for the workers of the world to unite and throw off the economic and political chains that reduce their humanity. By comparison, the Declaration of Independence attributed social evil to a single person (George II) and grounded the reasons for action on supernatural law. Both documents have moved many to revolution since their inceptions.

**Community:**   In a community, all persons have social standing. Standing entails the right and responsibility to produce culture in its manifold forms. A person shares community with another when the person cannot disengage from his/her social relationship with the other. A good test for the existence of community is to see if one person is able to ignore another's troubles; if so, then the two don't share community. In the West, community is understood in terms of geography. In socialist countries, community is understood in terms of the solidarity of social relations. The German term for the concept is *Gemeinschaft*. To say that an organization or society has community is to say that it is non-alienating and is somehow in tune with the conditions by which individuals create themselves as human beings. See *"Gemeinschaft"* and *"Society"* for more.

**Community Policing:**   The practice of locating the police function broadly in society rather than in a special force appointed by and under the control of local elites. In Cuba, members of the Committee for the Defense of the Republic (CDR) police an area of a few square blocks, participate in hearings on minor crimes, and provide support for families of victims and offenders. They also give support to offenders after they complete their sentence. In the United States, the "neighborhood watch" phenomenon embodies the idea. Such community-based policing efforts are effective in reducing crime and challenge the racist, sexist, and ethnic hegemony of the police force. Further, the community-oriented patrol officer is trained to meet the changing needs of the area s/he patrols.

**Comparable Worth:**   A feminist demand that people who perform the same work with the same training should receive the same wages. The effect is to eliminate sexist, racist, and ethnic bias when setting wages and salaries in a society. Profits can be increased by using ancient systems of social honor to pay lower wages to those in the lower strata.

**Competence:**   A legal term regarding the ability or right of a person to testify or to claim protection of the law. Children are usually held to be incompetent. In some countries, women are incompetent in legal terms. The mentally ill, the developmentally disabled, and members of some political groups are held to be incompetent in many legal proceedings. See "Person" for more.

**Competition:**   The process by which individuals or groups are stimulated to produce more or perform better by contesting against each other. Competition cannot exist except within an overall framework of cooperation in which competition is restricted to some small margin of human endeavor. It is often used to increase the surplus value of labor and, by extension, profit margins. Studies suggest that people produce more and enjoy work more under conditions of friendly cooperation. However, friendly competition adds interest and zest to work. Friendly competition may be just another form of cooperation. For Marx, competition is the process in capitalism by which small business is eliminated by monopoly corporations. Cuba uses emulation rather than competition to improve art, craft, skill, and innovation.

**Competitive Sector:**   That sector of the economic institution characterized by many undercapitalized companies with low wages, poor working conditions, transient labor, small work forces, arbitrary discipline, and little opportunity to advance. Consisting of small businesses supplied by the monopoly sector, this sector involves about one third of the work force and is a market share to huge corporations such as WalMart or McDonald's.

**Compromise, The Great:**   After a century of class struggle, American workers and owners came to an uneasy labor peace after the devastation of World War II. Good wages, safe working conditions, health care plans, good pensions, and paid vacations were put in place for most large corporations and many smaller ones. This compromise ended when a series of decertification elections and take-backs occurred as the United States lost its semi-monopoly in the world capitalist system to Japan, Germany, and the "NICs." The compromise crumbled when President Reagan attacked the Air Controllers' Union in the early 1980s. See "Collective Bargaining" for more.

**Computer Crime:**   The use of a computer to violate any of the rights of intellectual and financial property owned by a firm. Computer crimes can be civil (e.g., copyright violations) or criminal (e.g., stealing classified government documents) offenses. The critical position is that the dissemination or flow of information should be mostly free. It is difficult to control the flow of information, especially when it is broadcast over a mass electronic medium such as a computer network. Anyone with the right equipment can intercept the electromagnetic waves that carry the information. Computer "hackers" are especially adept at breaking into the data banks of universities, banks, insurance companies, and public agencies that (1) use computers; (2) use existing phone lines; and (3) use simple codes to regulate access to the data. However, most computer crime (approximately 80 percent) is perpetrated by persons working within a given organization.

With the right software, a good computer can try millions of combinations of letters and numbers to find the access key to a program. Computer crime is a growth industry. One of the most common forms is the appropriation of a software program without paying the company that owns its copyright.

**Comte, Auguste (1798–1857):**   French philosopher and founder of positivism. Positivism is a science in which nothing is said to be knowable unless it is retrievable and studied as a physical fact through various tests of observation. Comte was interested in such facts—and their interrelatedness—as they operated in society.

He is credited with first coining the word "sociology." In his work *Positive Philosophy*, Comte systematically argued that all other social sciences (e.g., political economy, social psychology) are ancillary to sociology. Comte divided sociology into two broad areas: statics and dynamics. He defined the former as society in a state of order, stability, and equilibrium. Today, we refer to this dimension of society as its structure. He defined the latter as society in a state of progress, particularly in its laws, institutions, and conditions. Today, we refer to this dimension of society as its process. Comte was uniquely interested in the dynamic patterning of society. For Comte, both progress and evolution were identical because both were rooted in a developmental and fluid process.

Auguste Comte also was a prophetic thinker. He outlined a unique utopia of positivism, systematically described in his second major work, *Positive Polity*. In this treatise, Comte preached the virtues of a positivist society in both its structure and process. Cf. "Humanism." See "Positivism" for more.

**Concentration:**   A measure of the control firms wield over a market; it tells what fraction of sales are controlled by the largest firms. The more concentrated a market, the more control a few individual firms exert over the level of profits and prices. In the U.S. cigarette market, the top four firms account for 80 percent of the sales. Similar levels of concentration exist in other markets: autos, food retail, beer, sugar, cereals, electronics, chemicals, pharmaceuticals, steel, and many, many more. Price, as a market control, is replaced with advertising, bribery, credit cards, and long-term contracts.

**Condensation:**   A psychological process developed through the dream analysis work of Sigmund Freud. In explaining dreams and their underlying psychic meaning, Freud found that the words/phrases people used to explain their dreams often represented a compression or amalgamation of other words and phrases. These words/phrases were linked to images that appeared during the dream stage of one's unconscious longing. This compression often revealed unstated beliefs or feelings that, when expressed through the activity of condensation during the analysis, revealed more about what the person was experiencing through his/her unconscious images. Examples of condensation include the compression of sex + satisfactory = sexifactory, as in "I found her testimony sexifactory"; credible + critical = critible, as in "The principal felt that the student's comments were critible"; and reliable + laughable = relaughable, as in "The congregation believed that the pastor's sermon was relaughable." In each instance, when the condensation is examined, something more is disclosed about what the person who speaks is up to. Cf. "Displacement." See "Dream Work" and "Freud, Sigmund" for more.

**Conditioning:**    Denotes the learning process by which some stimulus becomes linked with some behavior in such a way that the stimulus will cause the behavior to occur. People use conditioning to help break bad habits or phobias; corporations use it to control workers or customers; states use it to control students, prisoners, patients, or those who resist and rebel. Conditioning defeats cognitive processes and replaces interaction with determinism as the relevant causal model. See "Operant Conditioning" for more.

**Condorcet, Jean (1743–1794):**    Condorcet was a French philosopher who helped turn social science and politics toward quantification. He called for a "social mathematics." He calculated that a congress of 300 would be wrong less than once in a billion times if they used the three-quarter vote to pass laws. Condorcet supported the French Revolution and died in prison for that support. (See the work of W. L. Reese.)

**Confession:**    In common law (English law), a voluntary statement that one is guilty of violating a legal specification. In some religions (particularly Catholicism), confession is an element of the sacrament of penance. Confessing one's sins to a priest is a necessary condition for absolution.

**Conflict Methodology:**    A method of inquiry that serves the human interest in change and renewal. Conflict theory employs conflict methodology to reduce the conflict in favor of those who are oppressed or excluded. The knowledge required to emancipate humans from alienating social forms is often withheld by a class or a bureaucratic elite. Under such circumstances, a partisan stance is required by a social scientist. Participatory research, action research, standpoint methodology, and the new "incorporative" research of M. Wardell and A. Zajicek all affirm the perspective of those at the bottom of the social hierarchy and try to empower them and democratize the organizations studied. See "Consensus Methodology" and "Eleventh Thesis" for more.

**Conflict Situations:**   Adam Schaff speaks of two different kinds of conflict situations in connection to the question of human freedom. The first involves a choice between different systems of values (e.g., a choice between a conservative versus a more revolutionary value system). This choice instantly restricts further choices and fulfills a larger freedom (i.e., political enlightenment). The second situation of conflict is common to all value systems, since a choice of any kind comes into conflict with other values and no moral code can prescribe an answer for every contingency within a system of values. Life is too rich and full of conflicting values, changing conditions, and personal differences to permit a coherent and predictable moral code. In this sense, every person is "doomed to freedom" (i.e., has to face the fact that s/he must make choices). This realization of being "doomed to freedom" is the beginning of wisdom and the end of innocence.

**Conflict Theory:**   A term that includes a wide variety of perspectives. Essentially, conflict theory holds that not all structures in a society are helpful or necessary to a harmonious existence. Society is said to be held together by conflict. For example, class, race, and gender relations point to "structures of domination." This domination exists when groups with higher levels of money, status, and power control and/or regulate collectives with lower levels of money, status, and power. Cf. "Consensus Theory" and "Functionalism."
  G.W.F. Hegel, Karl Marx, Charles Darwin, Max Weber, and others looked at the sweep of history and identified systematic efforts to exploit/degrade people on the one hand and rising opposition to such forms of domination on the other hand. As Hegel describes, "History is a slaughter bench for the happiness of people." See "Marxism" for more.

**Conglomerate:**   Large firms that buy businesses making and selling all sorts of unrelated items. A conglomeration allows one company to control a large part of several different markets. This control increases the conglomerate's ability to set whatever prices it wants. Conglomeration is the most active process found in capitalism today. A conglomerate helps in an accumulation crisis: It helps befuddle government lawyers who sue a company for some crime, and it helps lower corporate taxes in a number of ways.

**Consciousness:**   Ways of thinking, feeling, and acting, usually involving some degree of awareness and intentionality. See "Cognitive Capacities" and "IQ" for more.

**Consciousness Industry:**   The organized flow of information in mass society is such that the human interests in praxis and community are defeated while the content of the media is such that capitalist and/or elitist relations are reproduced. The characteristics of the system include: (1) the repressive use of the media; (2) centrally controlled programming; (3) immobilization of isolated individuals; (4) one transmitter, many receivers; (5) depoliticization of content; (6) passive consumer emphasis; (7) production by specialists; (8) control by capitalists or bureaucrats. These conditions obtain in the United States where "leaks" create some slippage with political legitimacy.

**Consensus Methodology:**   A method of inquiry by which information necessary for the prediction, control, and reproduction of modern society is assumed. Research goals are set in cooperation with those at the top of the social hierarchies where the research occurs. This type of science tends to reproduce existing social forms irrespective of alienation and coercion. Since consensus methodology claims to be value-free it becomes the amoral research instrument of whoever has the power or the price. To define a scientific procedure as value-free is a quick way to turn it into a commodity for sale to the highest bidder. Cf. "Conflict Methodology."

**Consensus Theory:**   The view that all structures in society are useful and necessary; that most well adjusted persons in society share values and norms; that those who do not are either deviants or subversives in need of sanctioning. Among the structures viewed as "functionally necessary" are class, gender, race, occupational, and national (modernized nations) divisions. See "Durkheim, Émile" for more. Cf. "Conflict Theory" and "Sociology, Emancipatory."

**Consent:**   Free, willing, and explicit agreement to an action by a legally competent person. A legal term required in a number of circumstances: the making of a contract, a marriage, or, in the case of criminal law, sexual activity between an adult and a young person. The age of consent varies; in rural societies it is usually set at age 13 or 14; in industrial societies, it is usually set at age 16 or 18. See "Sociology of Youth" for more.

**Conservatism:**   An ideology that opposes change from an existing social paradigm. There are many things in any society worthy of conserving; however, sometimes this ideology also insists that any change within the social paradigm be under the direction of an elite or governing body. For example, capitalists do not oppose radical change. Change within the paradigm is often referred to as "the sociology of development" and is engineered by contract research.

**Consideration:**   In law, an act, promise, or forbearance by one party to a contract made in order to purchase an act, promise, or forbearance from another party. Without consideration, such promises are not valid in modern law. Promises are, of course, binding in premodern law where a promise was a person's bond.

**Conspiracy:**   An agreement between two or more persons to do something that is a crime. The agreement itself is a crime even if the planned offense does not occur. It is a crime even if the offense planned is impossible (e. g., to murder someone already dead). It is one of the few crimes for thought or thinking.

Usually conspiracy laws are used against political opposition, but, of late, they have been used against organized crime.

**Constitution:**   The rules and regulations by which a state is governed. They regulate the relationship between the state and the individual as well as between individuals under the jurisdiction of the state. Modern states have written constitutions; the most admired of which is that of the United States. The United Kingdom does not have a written constitution but, instead, uses common law. Constitutions are important, but social life is so complex that it is impossible to cover every exigency with laws. Thus, wisdom and judgment must inform every legal and moral case.

**Constitutive Theory:**   Blends key insights found in Symbolic Interactionism, phenomenology, and labeling sociology, along with Marxist political-economy rationales and postmodern social thought.

Constitutive theory recognizes that people struggle to identify reality for themselves in the lifeworld. The person is a "subject in process;" that is, not a passive receptacle of ideologies, as in Marx's instrumental economic determinism. The constitutive approach attempts to show how institutional expressions of society (e.g., law, the family, education, poverty) are key elements in a subject's construction of reality. For example, education both constitutes social relations and is constituted in turn by a subject's use of the educational process. Thus, education, and all institutional expressions of the social order, both compose and are composed by others in everyday social encounters and social constructions of reality. Determining which comes first (i.e., the institutional formation causing social relations or the subject's reliance upon the institutional formation as directing social relations) is precisely where constitutive theory positions itself.

In a broader context, the sociology of constitutive knowledge amply illustrates this point. Meaning is neither entirely separate from a subject's experience of given phenomena nor entirely dependent upon the subject's directed glance of attention upon identifiable phenomena. Rather, meaning is the result of an interdependence. Meaning is therefore in flux, contingent, local, positional, and, thus, resides between autonomy and dependence.

Constitutive theory further argues that the problem plaguing reality is language. Discourse is a medium that furthers the voice of some and represses the voice of many. Consider the constitutive dimension of a civil commitment tribunal. Persons involuntarily hospitalized for psychiatric treatment demonstrate that they no longer are a danger to themselves and/or to others when appealing to that very clinicolegal system responsible for their present confinement. In order to be released, psychiatric citizens must employ only those speech patterns and those coherent thought sequences consistent with medicolegal wellness. By adopting this discourse, mental health system users re-legitimize and further concretize the power of medicolegal discourse to linguistically (and therefore socially) regulate their lives. If they resist the discourse, these citizens must succumb to the power of the system to return them to institutional confinement. The manifestation of this constitutive problem is the essence of linguistic oppression. See "Lacan's Four Discourses" and "Superstructure" for more.

**Consumerism:**    An attempt to modify the most outrageous excesses of commodity capitalism by guarding the consumer against fraud, shoddy products, poisonous or otherwise dangerous foods, toys, medicines, and tools. Led by such admirable people as Ralph Nader, consumerism has two flaws: (1) It is merely a reform of capitalism rather than an end to it, and (2) it implicitly assumes that private consumption is the central reason for human existence.

**Consummation (of a Marriage):**    A legal term that holds that a marriage is not valid in law unless there is a sexual act; the sexual act is defined as penetration of the vagina by the penis. If one partner refuses to consummate the marriage, it can be annulled. In some patriarchal societies, rape is considered consummation, and the male may claim the woman as wife.

**Contract:**    A legally binding agreement. The requirements for a binding contract are: (1) an offer and an acceptance; (2) consideration; (3) informed consent; (4) capacity to fulfill; (5) conformity to law (agreements to commit crimes are not binding); and (6) an act on the part of one of two parties involved. Contracts may be oral, written, implied from conduct, or implicit in a relationship (as in common-law marriage). Contracts may be set aside in case of fraud, incompetency (e.g., underage), or other good cause.

**Contradiction:**    In logic, one of the three laws of thought; it holds that the same thing cannot belong and not belong to the same class of things; cannot be and not be at the same time. The new sciences of Chaos and Complexity refute the claim; an event can belong to two quite different solutions at the same time and, with fractal geometry, can be and not be depending upon the scale of observation. Think of an atom: At one level of observation it is a solid unitary event; at another, it is a loose assemblage of particles.

In Marxian economics, the term is used to point to the problems that capitalism creates as a mode of production. The major issues (or contradictions) of capitalism include: (1) great poverty in the midst of affluence; (2) technical rationality without substantive reason; (3) an emphasis upon ability in an elitist system; (4) fewer and fewer capitalists as wealth is concentrated in the hands of fewer and fewer; and (5) a tendency to run down when there is still a lot of labor, land, capital, and human need. Crime is endemic to capitalism, as is resistance and revolution.

**Controlled Drugs:** Chemicals that are to be used internally and that carry some danger to the person. There are two kinds: (1) prescription drugs (which should be monitored by a competent doctor) and (2) street drugs (often the same as prescription drugs). Drugs have always been used as psychogens: alcohol, marijuana, peyote, hashish, tobacco, opium, cocaine, and so on. They are prohibited for three main reasons: (1) They interfere with societal expectations about roles and role performance (e.g., drunken workers, parents, ball players, pilots); (2) they are used as pathways to the holy in forbidden religions (e.g., peyote, marijuana, opium); and (3) they are dangerous to the short- and long-term health of a person (e.g., tobacco and alcohol). Cf. "Corruption, Theory of."

**Control Theory:** A theory put forward by Travis Hirschi that claims that crime occurs when social controls (e.g., attachment to others, commitment to ideals, involvement in tasks, and belief in shared values) are weak. The theory ignores or does not account for crime that occurs within well-organized, highly controlled social groups, including most political crime, most organized crime, most corporate crime, and a lot of street crime. This theory provides ideological support for more control rather than for more social justice as a way to reduce real crime rates.

**Cooling Out:** A term developed by Erving Goffman that indicates the routines by which unwanted persons are removed from social interaction.

**Cooperation:** The process by which individuals organize each other's consciousness: ways of acting, feeling, and thinking. Cooperation focused in on the production of the various forms of culture is social power. Neither culture nor society nor self as a form of culture can be created without cooperation.

**Cooperatives:** A system of non-profit marketing (within a larger system of capitalism) that aims to provide food and other goods at low cost and within some sort of community. Co-ops may solve the problems of those who join them, but they don't help solve the larger contradictions of capitalism—especially that of adequate resources for the surplus population. Then, too, co-ops must work within a capitalist system. Thus, by buying and selling to private corporations, they help reproduce capitalist relations. Cf. "Market Socialism."

**Co-Parenting:**   The socialization of child(ren) is shared by several adults—in socialist theory, by men and women equally. Most societies in history vested the parenting process in several persons; usually aunts, older sisters, and female friends of the mother. Sometimes boys are sequestered, and the parenting is given over to older males alone or older males within small groups. Whatever the case, young children need as much loving parenting as they can get; ideally, the whole community would help in the parenting process. See "Kibbutz" for more.

**Copyright:**   A right that extends to all people, especially used by authors, playwrights, artists, publishers, or composers in order to benefit from a work for a period of time. Usually, this period of time is twenty-eight years. Copyright protection exists from the moment of original expression. However, the right is formally given/acknowledged by the state upon the filing of a claim.

Copyright laws are enforceable when an audience is limited or a medium is mechanical. In an electronic age, copyrights are difficult to police since everyone with the right equipment can intercept transmissions and copy them without paying a fee to the holder of the copyright; software programs, television broadcasts, and music on radio are copied by millions in the United States without payment of required fees. Generally, property rights to intellectual materials are difficult to enforce. However, copyright protections can be enforced both legally and normatively.

Students and professors often copy protected materials to use in class without payment. This practice is based on the "fair use" doctrine. See "Patent" for more.

**Core:**   A term used to refer to the structure of imperialism. The core imperialist countries were European. The colonial countries were called the "periphery." These peripheral countries were the colonies of England, France, Germany, and Italy. The core imperialism of the United States extends to Africa, Latin America, Asia, and islands in the Pacific.

**Corporate Crime:**   The antisocial activity of corporations to increase profit or reduce costs: adulteration of food, unsafe products, bribery, avoiding taxes, subverting the political process, and so on. Corporate crime is far more prevalent and involves larger amounts of money than petty unorganized crime (burglary, robbery, extortion, embezzlement, etc.). The average street crime garners about $150; the average white-collar crime over $100,000. Corporate crime runs into the millions and sometimes hundreds of millions. Corporate crime is seldom policed, reported, or punished. See "Anarchy," "Interest," and "Part I Offenses" for more.

**Corporate Liberalism:**   A strategy of management, mass media persuasion, and welfare benefits (subsidized by the state) as a solution to the problems of capitalism (e.g., its surplus population, political unrest, consumerism, inflation, and unemployment). In foreign affairs, peaceful coexistence with the socialist states and harmony within the capitalist states are desired in order to protect the operations of the multinational corporations. Sometimes identified with eastern finance capitalism (the Yankees) in contrast with southern/western oil/real estate/weapons industry capitalism (the Cowboys).

**Corporation:**   A body chartered by the state and consisting of a formal agreement or contract among people joined in a common purpose to hold property, make contracts, and share profits. It has the added virtue that, as a legal entity, it enables the people who own the stock to avoid the responsibility for any harm done to the larger society.

**Corporativism:**   An economic variety of capitalism in which a weak state helps achieve the integration of workers, capitalists, farmers, and other class fragments into a "corporate" whole. It is a bit different from fascism, in that the state is not as central to the process. Japan is the current embodiment of corporativism in the capitalist world. Singapore is a high-tech version of corporativism. See "Fascism" for more.

**Corruption, Theory of:**   There are four general rules through which a society maintains a social monopoly on items and behaviors used to reproduce that society:

1. Some supplies and activities are defined as sacred and used to create dramas of the holy in which persons, roles, and institutions are sanctified. Among the supplies are special clothing, psychogenic drugs (beer, wine, marijuana, etc.), special foods, and special tools. Among the activities are sexual acts, music, gambling, pain/violence, as well as eating and drinking. The rule is that these are required; one must do these things and/or use these things even if unpleasant.
2. The nonsocial, purely personal use of such items and events is forbidden. Pejorative terms are used to discourage such use (e.g., perversion, pathology, addiction, depravity).
3. Those psychogens and ecstatic activities used by other cultures to create different dramas of the holy are also forbidden and defined as deviancy, depravity, and degrading.
4. Activities that tend to subvert age, class, gender, or other social differentiations/stratifications are also defined as deviant or pathological.

See "Controlled Drugs," "Deviance," "Gambling," "Medicalization," and "Perversion" for more.

**Costs (Socially Necessary):**    The costs of producing the material base of a society. These include the cost of capital goods (factories, railroads, etc.), of reproducing a healthy labor force, of the extraction of raw materials, as well as the cost of repairing any damage to the environment upon which all life ultimately depends. The concept is of interest since it enables an analyst to subtract the socially necessary costs (SNCs) from the gross national product and get the surplus value produced. Once we know surplus value, we can see how it is used (misused) and can judge that society. In the United States, there are many socially unnecessary costs that restrict the use we make of surplus. Among these unnecessary costs are (a) profits; (b) selling costs; (c) legal services; (d) surplus employee compensation; (e) bribes, political donations, and such. (See the work of Baran and Sweezy.)

**Counter-Memorializing:**    A postmodern concept that denies the underlying reality of scientific truth, including the truth of social science. It rejects impersonal and eternal foundations of standards, morals, or inquiry. Claims of origins and endings are also questioned.

**Coup d'etat:**    French: blow to the head. A phrase meaning an attempt to take over state power by a small group. Sometimes called a "palace revolution," it does not involve the people generally and often replaces one elite with another.

**Courage:**    Latin: *cor* = heart. One of the four cardinal virtues in Greek social philosophy. The other three were inseparable: wisdom, justice, and temperance. It refers to one's internal fortitude or fundamental capacity to confront bravely and fearlessly an opposing force. This force can be physical (e.g., warring nations), interpersonal (e.g., domestic violence), and intrapsychic (e.g., confronting one's own demons).

**Court:**    An agency of the state authorized by law to judge matters in dispute; criminal, civil, and family disputes are the most common.

**Court, Kangaroo:**    An informal court constituted by those who have been offended and who judge degree of guilt and inflict penalties on the spot.

**Court-Martial:**    A legally constituted hearing convened within the military to try offenses committed by armed services personnel. It consists of serving officers (not enlisted persons) acting as judges (there is no jury) and a judge advocate advising on points of law. Offenses and penalties are listed in the Unified Code of Military Justice, last revised in 1966. Since that time, many constitutional protections have been given accused persons.

**Court of Last Resort:**    In state cases, the governor is the court after which no further appeal is possible. In federal cases, it is the president. In both instances, the appeal is for clemency; that is, a request that the verdict be set aside and the convicted felon be released due to some extraordinary circumstances.

**Creationism:** The belief that God creates a soul for every new human being. It extends to the claim that God created the whole universe as well as each form of animal and plant life in a single creative period, usually set at seven days. Creationism is opposed to theories of organic evolution and to abortion. Abortion is a sin since it destroys a living soul precious to the Christian God. There is a story that Lucifer took some 30,000 angels with him when he was cast out of heaven and that heavenly peace depends upon the return of this number of souls. To abort a fetus is said to delay that event. Cf. "Evolution, Social."

**Creativity:** As a moment of praxis, creativity involves thought and action located in history (i.e., produced uniquely in the situation at hand by insightful humans). In contrast to behavior that is identical to that of other persons at other times (thus producing a social lifeworld in which prediction and control are possible), praxis requires unpredictable behavior and, at the same time, delight in its aptness and originality. It is not restricted to poetry, painting, or marginal cultural endeavors. Creativity should be central to work, religion, sports, and love.

**Credit:** The purchase of commodities to be paid over months and years. Credit has a given rate of interest. Credit is important to capitalism. Credit creates a mass market; it postpones downturns in an economic cycle; it may help a country get out of a depression; and it is extremely profitable (since there is little investment of capital or labor). See "Keynesian Economics" for more.

**Crime:** Sanskrit: *Karma* = that which a person is responsible for as opposed to that over which a person has no control. In American criminology, crime is defined as: (1) a violation of a legal specification, (2) enacted by a competent law-making body, (3) involving both culpable intent and (4) overt action that (5) carries a specific penalty. This definition safely confines the kind of behavior subject to policing to that which is defined as illegal, behavior often under control of an elite.

In socialist theory, a crime is that which tends to destroy community or detract from human dignity. In addition to murder and rape, the most serious crimes in socialist theory are: elitist ownership or control of the means to produce human culture; appropriation of the surplus value of labor for and only for private use; objectification of other humans; and counter-revolutionary activity. Reductionist theories of crime demand that the individual change, whereas the socialist theory of crime requires radical social change, intensive socialization to instill a socialist consciousness, primary group (commune, brigade) control, and incorruptible policing. See "Demonization," *"Nullum crimen sine lege,"* "Pre-Theoretical," and "Rebellion" for more.

**Crime, Female:**   Historically, little attention was given to female criminality or juvenile girl delinquency. Critical scholars argue that this was a function of the patriarchal (male-dominated) system of crime and justice. The last twenty years, however, have witnessed substantial new knowledge on the origins, causes, and consequences of female crime.

The crimes women are likely to commit are mostly economic offenses, including shop-lifting, writing bad checks, prostitution, and embezzlement. Recent studies, though, link female criminality to drug-related offenses, as opposed to the more traditional "feminine" offenses. Cf. "Crime, Male."

**Crime, Forms and Theory of:**   There are five kinds of crime promoted in capitalism as a system: (1) *street crime*—involving theft, burglary, arson, robbery, murder, and kidnapping (see "Rape" separately). Street crime increases as the surplus population increases and as welfare systems become depersonalized. Marxian theory holds that most street crime is the forcible reunification of production and distribution by the underclass and underemployed; (2) *corporate crime*—acts committed in order to enlarge market share, lower costs, or increase profit rates. Corporate crime involves conspiracy to fix prices, the use of dangerous ingredients, the sale of dangerous toys and medicines, violation of labor laws, pollution, and tax evasion. It increases as profits fall, demand slackens, competition increases, or public laws lower profit; (3) *organized crime* (the "rackets")—activities producing and distributing sex, gaming, alcohol, drugs, and other supplies traditionally used for solidarity purposes. Organized crime commodifies sacred supplies; (4) *white-collar crime*—it involves betrayal in a position of trust. White-collar crime increases as the middle class attempts to build a retirement portfolio, maintain an upper-middle-class lifestyle, and/or when employees come to resent working conditions; and (5) *political crime*—crime committed by the state or against the state. State crime increases for two reasons: (a) to help the capitalist class realize profits at home or overseas, and (b) as legitimacy is lost and the state moves to repress criticism and oppress critics. Crimes against the state increase when oppression is endemic and when institutional politics do not work. When migration is difficult or when underground structures are heavily policed, direct political action increases.

**Crime, Male:**   Most crimes are committed by males. Violent crimes are predominantly male perpetrated because patriarchy requires males to be controlling and dominating. In the absence of social or economic power, males often use physical power on each other or upon women in order to command compliance. See "Macho/Machismo" for more.

**Crime, Social Location of:**   Each kind of crime is found in a different part of society and is policed differently. Street crime is located mostly in the underclass (mostly poor males, white and black). Corporate crime is located mostly in the upper class (mostly white males). White-collar crime is committed in the professional and managerial classes for the most part. Organized crime is organized by white males in the middle or upper classes, whereas employees usually come from the underclass and customers from every social class. Political crime is usually committed by the state or by small groups opposed to the state. Cf. "Crime, Forms and Theory of."

**Crimes Without Victims:**   Legally prohibited actions that involve no unwilling or complaining party (e.g., drug sales, public intoxication, and prostitution). Often injury occurs slowly and is hard to link closely to the acts in question. The phrase is often used to promote the privatized use of drugs and sex through decriminalization.

**Criminal Injury:**   Any act involving the use of force against a competent person: rape, assault, poisoning, and destruction of property endangering one's life. Note that in most instances it is not a crime to kill, rape, beat, or mutilate non-persons. In some instances, parents may beat children; husbands may beat wives; members of one ethnic group may rape, plunder, or murder another without penalty of law. War itself is organized injury without criminal status.

**Criminalization/De-criminalization:**   Many acts that are not permitted within a system of norms are defined as sin in premodern sensibility. In modern times, they have been defined as crime rather than sin, as science displaces religion in the explanation of human behavior. Of late, such behaviors have been redefined as illness rather than as sinful or criminal. Postmodern scholarship treats both the prison and the mental institution as social control tactics that reproduce stratified cultural formations. See "Sanctification/De-sanctification" for more.

**Criminal Justice:**   A state-initiated and state-supported effort to rationalize the mechanisms of social control in order to solve the problems of advanced capitalism, which include an unruly surplus population, political dissent, monopoly, and inflation. Most criminal justice systems are based upon pain and degradation. Utilitarianism teaches that human beings organize their behavior on pain and pleasure rather than upon norms and mores. In fact, what is defined as painful and pleasurable vary considerably across cultures.

Initiated under the Johnson Administration, the criminal justice program in the United States socializes the costs of solving the problems of capitalism, but it does not socialize the profits of capitalism. The criminal justice program strengthens the larger system, which produces crime in the first place. See "Social Control, Parallel Systems of" for more. Cf. "Social Justice."

**Criminal Law:**   A set of laws that define what is and what is not subject to punishment and incarceration. Criminal law is greatly influenced by class, gender, and race dynamics. Some critics contend that the criminal law is a social construction that effectively ensures the standing (economic, social, and political) of those already in power. Consider, for example, the acquittal of O. J. Simpson in the double-murder criminal trial.

French radicals of the nineteenth century (e.g., Anatole France) had a saying: "The law in all its majesty forbids equally the rich and the poor from sleeping under bridges."

**Criminology:**   Literally the study of crime. There are many dimensions to the study of crime, including its origins, causes, and consequences, to name just a few. Criminologists address both macro- and micro-level explanatory and/or predictive analyses when examining specific crimes (e.g., white-collar, street) or when interpreting crime per se.

The study of crime can be divided into several prominent schools of thought. These include the following: (1) classical criminological theories; (2) psychological and biological approaches; (3) sociological models; (4) subcultural explanations; (5) control theories; and (6) social process theories.

Critical criminology emphasizes Marxist-based and post-Marxist-based explanatory models. Some variations of critical criminology include: (1) discourse analysis; (2) socialist feminist; (3) anarchist; (4) constitutive; (5) critical race theory. See "Rational Choice, Theory of" and "Routine Activities, Theory of" for more.

**Criminology, Radical:**   A Marxist-based approach to the theory of crime and crime prevention. It has several assumptions: (1) considerable political influence determines which behavior is defined as a legal wrong; (2) the causes of crimes are largely related to the social loss of community and the obstacles to species-being; and (3) reduction in antisocial behavior requires social change rather than individual therapy or punishment. The United States has the highest crime rate in the world, the largest surplus population, the greatest wealth, and the least community. These factors are not unrelated. In the United States, radical criminology was located at the University of California at Berkeley until the approach fell in disrepute with the university administration as politically dangerous.

**Crisis Theory:**   Marxian crisis theory has two parts: The first part says crises are generated by the separation of creative processes into two phases, production and consumption. This separation occurs since, in capitalism, production is not for direct use but, rather, for exchange/profit. The crisis occurs when production increases at the same time consumption decreases. When there is surplus production and when people are in need without the means to buy these "surplus" goods, trouble comes. The second part of the theory holds that crisis is a rational mechanism for the reactivation of the economy. There are several ways to solve the crisis, involving the "forcible reunification" of production and distribution. This means either customers pay what is demanded or that suppliers sell even when they cannot stay in business on these terms. Reunification is further achieved through welfare, war, crime, or other political action. A third aspect of crisis theory generalizes the theory to encompass both capitalism and bureaucratic socialism by emphasizing the separation of formal rationality from human purpose.

**Critical Legal Studies:**   A movement in law that rejects the formalism, linear syllogistic reasoning, impartiality, objectivity, and value-neutrality that is presumed to govern legal reasoning and decisionmaking. The Critical Legal Studies (CLS) movement began in the 1970s. Essentially the movement argues that legal texts (e.g., case law, legislative statutes, appellate decisions) convey implicit messages embedded in the discourse that is used. These underlying messages represent hidden values and unstated assumptions that can be traced to the interests of certain groups. These hidden values and assumptions help to establish a belief system or citizen consciousness regarding the rule of law and its power in society. CLS commentators investigate these matters because of their interest in the notion of legitimacy. They argue that one of law's functions is to affirm domination by powerful elites. CLS scholars seek to unveil the values and assumptions embedded in the law as a way of identifying the sexist, ageist, racist, and classist dimensions of legal thought and the legal system. In this way, CLS commentators conclude that law is nothing more than the privileging of certain ideologies over and against other ideologies.

In order to accomplish their objective of exposing the law, CLS commentators engage in a "trashing" or deconstructive technique. In essence, they study the words that are used in a legal text and attempt to identify the competing factions of meaning embedded within them. They then establish which meanings are privileged and which ones are not. Finally, CLS scholars link the values and/or assumptions that are esteemed in the discourse to the perspective of those who benefit from the legal narrative in question. CLS commentators are interested in establishing a legal discourse that is more sensitive to the multiple points of view reflected in society's heterogeneity. See "Critical Race Theory" for more.

**Critical Race Theory:**   This is a movement that began in the late 1970s. Critical Race Theory (CRT) is an extension of the Critical Legal Studies (CLS) movement. The main difference is that CRT proponents seek to identify, through a narrative method, how legal texts represent a point of view that excludes non-white perspectives. This exclusion has had profound and harmful effects for people of color in legal decisionmaking. See "Critical Legal Studies" for more. See "Feminism, Black" and "Womanism" for more.

**Critical Social Science:**   A series of distinctive approaches to investigating social phenomena that uniquely examine questions of marginalization, victimization, alienation, and de-legitimation for women, racial/ethnic minorities, the poor, gay/lesbian citizens, the elderly, the disabled, and other underrepresented and undervalued constituencies. Critical Social Science encompasses Marxist, left-liberal, feminist, postmodern, humanist, socialist, and radical traditions. See "Authors' Note" to this volume for more.

**Critical Theory:**   An approach to the study of society in which human interests shape and guide the research enterprise, from the formation of analytic categories to the quest for accurate, relevant, timely, sensible information. Critical theory has an overt political goal: that of a rational and decent society. By contrast, structural-functional theory asserts itself to be value-free, when in fact its analytic categories and research foci are controlled by its sponsors. The transfer of the political responsibility for the use of science from the producer to the user simply masks its politics and, at the same time, exculpates the scientists from any responsibility for his/her product.
  Jürgen Habermas identifies three kinds of knowledge necessary to critical research: positive knowledge, hermeneutic knowledge, and emancipatory knowledge. Critical theory is associated with the Frankfurt School. Cf. "Frankfurt School" and "Habermas, Jürgen." See "Methodology, Theory of" for more.

**Criticism/Self-criticism:**   A process by which obstacles to community and praxis are made visible by open self-reflection within a collective and then are eliminated by collective action in a supportive and collegial atmosphere. Criticism can be used to self-correct the policies and practices of a party, of a state, of an agency, or of an individual. Developed and practiced in communist countries, criticism often became a system of elitist control. When well done, it can be helpful to a rational and humane society.

**Cruel and Unusual Punishment:**   Prisoners are protected from many practices formerly used in American prisons and/or issued by judges. These include public whipping, hanging, branding, removal of offending organs (hands, tongues, and other appendages), drawing and quartering, as well as caging in public display. This protection from cruel and unusual punishment is a guarantee secured through the Eighth Amendment of the U.S. Constitution.

**Cult of the Leader:**   When people invest great authority and power in the person of a single individual, they help form such a cult. Often, leaders surround themselves with people who are paid one way or another by promoting the infallibility of the leader. This happens in politics, religion, business, and military systems. The needs and interests of single persons then become more important than the collective needs of a community, congregation, or company.

**Cult of the Self:**   A Marxian phrase used to denote the lonely, mistrustful, solitary philosophy of privatized individuality that develops in capitalism or in other elitist systems such as the military, the bureaucracy, or the nobility.

**Cultural Conflict:**   Often there is conflict between different cultural groups over the essentials of life: raw materials, land, water, governance, jobs, and social status/honor. Sometimes this conflict is complicated by class conflict as well. Racism explodes into violence when problems exist in capitalist societies (e.g., the L.A. riots of 1992). As jobs become scarce, men grow angry when women demand affirmative action to eliminate job preference for men. When times are bad, Serbs claim the right to jobs, land, and resources from Croats or from Bosnians; Christians become bigoted and refuse the right to Jews or Muslims to live in peace in the same territory, or vice versa. Today, the various private militias in the United States are made up of white, lower-class men who previously had many privileges (e.g., racism, patriarchy, job security, social honor) but now have lost them through the Civil Rights Movement, the women's movement, and the flight of capital to third world countries where wages are much, much lower. These men do not develop a structural analysis to explain their troubles and thus are thrown back to conspiracy theories that blame the government, "uppity" women, inferior Blacks and Jews, or "eggheads" rather than the capitalist class. They join with other reactionary class fragments to support right-wing, white racist, and sexist agendas, thereby fueling the culture conflict. See "Cultural Lag" for more.

**Cultural Diffusion:**   The spread or dispersion of artifacts, beliefs, or patterns of behavior from one culture to another. The diffusion of political or ideological culture usually involves coercion and violence.

**Cultural Lag:**   The difference between the appearance of a given kind of technology and of the social institutions that arise in response to that technology. Cultural lag theory is often used to explain why people resist and rebel against modern approaches to work, school, church, or play. The theory deflects attention from racism, class conflict, gender oppression, and ethnic struggles for independence from colonial masters. Sometimes it is used by liberals to condemn conservative positions that oppose the growth of the state, transnational corporations, or the intrusion into family or religious matters. See "Cultural Conflict" for more.

**Cultural Relativism:**   The idea that a culture must be evaluated by its own standards and not by those of another culture. Historically, this is a rather new and "liberal" idea. Conservative societies tend to reject the idea in favor of their own ethnocentric beliefs. Some humanist philosophies (e.g., Christian, Marxist) also reject the idea of cultural relativism in favor of the view that there are common ingredients in all human experiences and that thus it is possible to judge another society as oppressive or not. Cf. "Ethnocentrism."

**Cultural Revolution:**   In China, an attempt to integrate technicians and managers with the workers in order to eliminate the division of labor into mental versus physical labor. The thought is that the production of culture requires that unity. Hence, there is cultural revolution. See "Mao Tse-Tung" for more.

**Culture:**   Latin: *colore* = to cultivate. The word has come to mean all the art, science, religion, social forms, and values that inform or are part of a social lifeworld. It has the meaning of elitist values and standards of art, music, and theater. In socialism, using Mao Tse-Tung's types, culture in the sociological sense may be conceived of as the material, ideological, and political products of humans. The active production of culture is the sine qua non of human existence. The view of culture as that which has been produced by humans is a political act, since it confuses the material objects with the active labor of people who create culture in the moment of using those material items in creative ways. The view of culture as upper-class art, music, science, and recreation is also political, in that it tends to degrade other classes and the culture they need to produce in order to become humans. The standard definition of culture is that culture is all those things developed and used by a society. This misses the essential meaning of culture as something that exists only in the act of people creatively using material items to create a social lifeworld.

   The concept of culture replaced the concepts of instinct, of gods, and of "blood" to explain why people behave as they do. As such, it is fundamental to all humanist philosophies.

**Culture (of Resistance):**   A term coined by Mina Caulfield to indicate those social structures in a colonial society that oppose, neutralize, and/or destroy the efforts of colonists to impose a capitalist culture upon occupied lands. These structures also protect socialist modes of production. Caulfield analyzed life in the West Indies, Africa, Appalachia, South America, and other colonized areas. She identified many social structures that resisted economic and cultural oppression. The family structure was central among these.

**Custody:**   A legal term defining who may restrict the physical movement of a person. In family law, legal parents have custody of a child and may forbid the child or command the child to do certain things. In criminal law, courts take custody of the accused and, if found guilty, transfer custody to a jail or prison. In military law, soldiers can take custody of opposing soldiers and hold them in ways compatible with the Geneva Convention on War Prisoners.

**Custody of a Child:**   In divorce proceedings, if there is no agreement between parents, courts have legal authority to decide custody.

Many children suffer from custody disputes between parents who may use the children to punish each other. In any event, children of broken homes have serious difficulties knowing who to trust and defer to for guidance, council, and command. Courts take custody of children whose health and welfare is held to be endangered in the home. Significant harm is done to children when left in an abusive or neglectful home environment or when placed in a series of inadequate foster homes.

**Custom:**   Latin: *con* = with; *suere* = to make one's own. Thus a custom is that which has become a habit. In sociology, a custom is a set of institutionalized responses to everyday contingencies. Montesquieu used the term to refer to the role of folkways in shaping human behavior. This perspective gave macro-social psychology its impetus. William Bagehot spoke of the "cake of custom" as an obstacle to social progress.

**Cybernetics:**   Greek: *cybernetes* = steersman. The term was given to the science of control and guidance in the late 1940s by Norbert Weiner in his work on guided missiles. Some critically apply it to the control of societies (e.g., Jean Baudrillard). A cybernetic system has three basic parts: (1) a monitoring system; (2) a decisionmaking apparatus that gauges the gap between goal and present status; and (3) an effector apparatus to change course.

**Cyberspace:**   The illusion of time-space created by computer technology. Thus, those who join a network dwell in cyberspace rather than in "real" time-space; that is, in really existing groups, facts, or events. All of the natural categories of time, space, weight, quality, quantity, and so on disappear in cyberspace; a whole new way of being/doing is required for such space.

Cyberspace includes a variety of computer/modem-mediated communication methods, including Bulletin Board Systems (BBSs), home pages, discussion groups, Internet electronic mail, and public access systems where people meet, shop, fall in love, and so on. Real-time interaction, such as on-line "chat/talk" or IRC (Inter-relay chat) allows simultaneous interaction between numerous people.

In the sociology of knowledge, cyberspace is a metaphor for the compression of reality and illusion, so that such concepts as meaning, truth, identity, and so on are mere simulations of the real mediated by language (simulacra). See "Baudrillard, Jean," "Hyperspace," "Mass Media," "Value, Postmodern View of" for more.

# D

**Darwin, Charles (1809–1882):**   An English scientist generally credited with the theory of evolution. From 1831 to 1836 Darwin traveled around the world on the *Beagle*, a British ship, and collected the data that led to his theory. Darwin published his book *The Origin of Species* in 1859, and *The Descent of Man* in 1871; they remain sources of great debate, since they attribute the appearance of human beings to natural rather than supernatural events. In brief, Darwin took Thomas Malthus's idea of population checks and went on to argue that competition for food and for sexual partners gave some individuals and species a better chance at survival than others, since there are small or large differences between every individual and every species. Together, these differences make for a *natural selection* rather than a divine creativity. A. R. Wallace made the same argument a year earlier and might well have been credited with the theory had not Darwin published his work. See "Evolution" and "Survival of the Fittest" for more.

**Data:**   Latin: that which is given. One collects data and analyzes them in order to confirm or reject a hypothesis. The term thus refers to a set of observations from nature (physical or social) that are independent of the interests and cognitive processes of the scientist. There is no such independence in the Marxian philosophy of science nor in most postmodern philosophies of science. See "Hypothesis" and "Science, Postmodern" for more.

**Days of Grace:**   A legal term setting the amount of time after default on a debt in which payment must be made before remedy is permitted. It varies from three days to three months.

**Death of God:**   A nineteenth century claim made by Friedrich Nietzsche, and in the twentieth century by Jean-Paul Sartre, that belief in God is impossible for a person educated in modern science. Modernists thus dismiss the God concept or identify it with natural and social laws. Postmodern theology holds that God is a social construct and is destroyed when believers cease to believe and to act upon the teachings of that particular God concept. There is a radical American theology (Thomas Altizer, William Hamilton) that, in 1966, proposed a religious sensibility without the God concept.

**Death of the Subject:**    A key point delineated by skeptical postmodernists such as Jacques Derrida and Jean Baudrillard. Nihilistic or skeptical postmodernists argue that since there are no essentially retrievable and structurally knowable realities, then the subject, too, does not exist per se. According to negative or nihilistic postmodernists, the subject disappears into oblivion. It is negated as a unifying presence and is, at best, incomplete, fragmented, decentered.

**Death Penalty:**    See "Capital Punishment."

**Decentered Subject:**    This is a reference to the philosophy of the person (subjectivity) developed by the psychoanalyst Jacques Lacan. Lacan argues that people long for identity fulfillment through discourse. Lacanian subjectivity challenges the mainstream (modernist) Cartesian notion of subjectivity, which states that individual subjects are purposeful, rational, stable, and active. Thus, as autonomous, self-aware individuals, we are at the center of all human affairs and determiners of all human events. This position is contained in Descartes' famous dictum: *cogito ergo sum*. Lacan argues that the subject is decentered; that is, the plenary or unitary "I" is divided or slashed ($). For Lacan, individual actors submit to and are situated in a floating stream of signifying practices (i.e., meaning processes) located within the unconscious. These practices preliminarily "accent" the desiring subject's linguistic reality, resulting in the articulation of a specialized code conveying preferred meanings. Thus, following Lacan, individual subjects are more determined than determining, more unstable than stable, and more disunified than unified, because discourse and all that it implies speaks *through* the subject. See "Floating Signifiers," "Lacan, Jacques," and "Subjectivity" for more.

**Decentering:**    A postmodern objective: the result of reexamining truth claims of, say, patriarchy, stratification, or truth itself and showing the human hand and human agenda that brought the claim, theory, or practice to the forefront and celebrates it as eternally valid and objectively existent.

**Decertification:**    A process by which the right of a union to represent a group of workers and to bargain for them is ended. This is done through formal elections, usually sponsored by the company and facilitated by the government. Workers have a hard choice: Vote to decertify or see the company move the factory to southern states or foreign countries.

**Decidability:**    One of three characteristics of a hypothesis or theory; the other two being completeness and consistency. Decidability depends upon the existence of a method of proof with a finite number of steps: no method, unlimited steps; no proof, no knowledge. This is why Agrippa held that sure and certain knowledge was impossible. Cf. "Prediction."

**Decode:**   In semiotic terminology, the process of interpreting a coded message by relying upon the linguistic coordinates or the signs of the specialized discourse in use. Thus in legal discourse, for example, in order to more fully understand the specialized meaning of "willingly," "*mens rea*," "wrongfulness," "the reasonable man standard," or "negligence," one must rely upon the grammar, code, and sign system of lawspeak (i.e., legalese). See "Sign" and "Trope" for more.

**Deconstruction:**   Also known as "trashing." Deconstruction refers to a postmodern method of discourse analysis in which the warring factions of meaning communicated through a text (all phenomenon and events are texts) are identified, examined, and carefully studied. Typically a deconstructive critique endeavors to point out the classist, racist, sexist, ageist, and other so-called oppressive dimensions of speech. Thus, situated in and communicated through the grammar (i.e., the words) of a given code are a constellation of unconscious values (implicit assumptions) about individuals, events, and the social order. Deconstructionists believe in the importance of "unpacking" the layered dimensions of speech in order to appreciate the unconscious intent behind words, particularly when that intent invalidates, de-legitimizes, or otherwise devalues specific individuals or a class of citizens. See "Derrida, Jacques" for more.

**Deduction/Deductive Logic:**   Latin: *de* = from; *ducere* = to lead, to draw out. In logic, a deduction is a conclusion that follows from two or more given assumptions, which, if true, make the conclusion true. In social science, a deduction is a conclusion from the logical implications of a theory; thus one deducts a hypothesis and collects data in order to confirm or deny the truth of it. See "Peirce, Charles S." for more. Cf. "Abduction" and "Induction."

**De facto:**   Latin: that which exists as a matter of fact rather than as a matter of legal right (de jure). Often de facto existence creates de jure rights, as in the case of residence, employment, or marriage. Cf. "De jure."

**Defection of the Intelligentsia:**   The phrase brings into consideration the question of how those who produce art, science, music, drama, literature, and religion can be pried away (defect) from the support of capitalism and/or elitist ideologies and recruited to socialist endeavor. Regis Debray held that acts of terrorism would "debourgeoisify" the intelligentsia by emphasizing how precarious the capitalist order is. Mao Tse-Tung insisted on close contact between workers and the intelligentsia, whereas Karl Marx insisted on the unity of physical and mental labor in the individual so that the intelligentsia would not develop as a separate stratum and create an ideology by which to bolster capitalism.

**Deficit Spending:**   The government spends a huge amount of money on war, airports, dams, highways, unemployment checks, education, and many other things. When the government spends more than it collects in taxes, this is called "running a deficit." Deficit spending must be financed by borrowing. The U.S. government currently spends more than 10 percent of its budget on interest payments on the national debt, which has resulted from its past deficit spending. The national debt is about $3 trillion (1996) and growing fast. It is the price a nation pays to keep capitalism going. See "Keynesian Economics" for more.

**Definition:**   Latin: *finire* = to limit. In formal logic, that which is to be defined is called the *definiendum*, while that which is used to define a term is called the *definiens*. Lexical definitions follow common usage. Stipulative definitions are new terms made up from old stable language or mathematics. Definitions can be made by analogy, by example, or by noting differences between two things.

All definitions are both a poetics and a politics; that is, there is always something more or something other conveyed through a definition (poetics), yet all definitions are an anchoring of meaning, a type of closure, in which certain views are privileged over others (politics). This reading of definition is consistent with postmodernism. Postmodern philosophy of knowledge holds that all concepts and categories of nature and society are convenient tags to put on some slice of an incredibly complex and interconnected reality of interest at the moment. These tags are helpful but tend to freeze the knowledge process and defeat imagination and change.

**Definition of the Situation:**   The first step in the construction of social reality is the definition (collectively) of what kind of social event is going to be produced: a wedding, a party, a funeral, a meeting, and so on. The definition must be shared, or at least not challenged, by all present. This shared definition is accomplished by symbolic interaction. Social reality has no facticity apart from the collective definition and the collective performance of it. A pattern of observable behavior defined as a class or as a chess move is, in the consequence, a social fact. It is not enough simply to define something as real; compliance with a publicly known set of standards is also required.

**Degradation Routines:**   Every social institution has a ritual by which unwanted people are removed: The criminal justice system degrades people in a courtroom trial in which they are stripped of social standing; divorce is used to remove people from a marriage; court-martials strip officers of rank; decertification turns a doctor into a non-doctor; disbarment proceedings removes the social identity of "lawyer" from the self-system of those so processed; schools expel students; and some religions excommunicate people. Degradation routines are the reverse of rites of passage in which people are allocated social identities that then are supposed to organize their behavior in spite of wants, needs, desires, or other psychological imperatives. See "Mobility, Downward" for more.

**Deism:**   A term introduced by the Socians, who wanted to distance themselves both from atheists and from those who believed in a personal God. In deism, the God concept refers to an original creator/creating force that set a clock-like universe in motion and that no longer intervenes in its workings. Thus both science and reason are pathways to knowledge, rather than to ecstasy, meditation, revelation, or inspiration. The latter were major pathways to knowledge in premodern sociology of knowledge.

**De jure:**   Latin: that which exists as a matter of legal right. De jure existence often confers a legal right, as in the case of common-law marriage or the possession and use of property after a period of years. Cf. "De facto."

**Deleuze, Gilles (1925–1995):**   Professor of philosophy who, together with Félix Guattari, advanced a substantial postmodern critique of thought, writing, psychoanalysis, capitalism, subjectivity, and politics. See "Guattari, Félix" for more.

Deleuze was originally known for his philosophical investigations of such luminaries as Benedict Spinoza, Immanuel Kant, and Friedrich Nietzsche. For example, in *Nietzsche and Philosophy* Deleuze embraced Nietzsche's polemical dismissal of dialectical thought, contending that it is nothing more than a totalizing, nihilistic, and reductionistic system of reasoning. In its place, Deleuze, consistent with Nietzsche, called for a theory of difference rooted in multiple and contingent ideas of truth and becoming.

Deleuze and Guattari are credited with substantially challenging and debunking many icons of modernity, including such notions as unity, hierarchy, and identity, while affirming alternative convictions such as disunity, difference, and plurality. Their most influential works include *Anti-Oedipus* and *A Thousand Plateaus*.

*Anti-Oedipus* is a Foucauldian-inspired renouncement of modernity, especially the manner in which, through capitalism, it quashes alternative desires. The work critically centers on capitalism, the family, and psychoanalysis. Indeed, Deleuze and Guattari call for a micro-politics of desire, one that overcomes the territorialization of modern (read capitalistic) modes of expression. Central to their critique is the re-validation of repressed voices and silenced ways of being. This re-validation is essential to establishing transformative and liberating possibilities for the schizo-subject; that is, the new human condition grounded in multiplicity, difference, and decenteredness.

In *A Thousand Plateaus* Deleuze and Guattari return to the problems inherent in capitalism and schizophrenia. They develop the concept of the "rhizome": a term that signifies the deterritorialization movement, in which unities, dichotomies, and totalities are uprooted and differences, heterogeneities, and multiplicities are established. Rhizomatics is a form of "nomadic thought" in which lines of escape and flight are key to affirmatively transforming the control that systems and bureaucracies exercise over one's life. "There is no social system that does not leak in all directions." This leakage or spillage is key to transcending "state thought." *A Thousand Plateaus* is chiefly concerned with extending the analysis developed in *Anti-Oedipus* as an application of their postmodern models to the rhizomatic condition of natural, social, and personal reality. See "Baudrillard, Jean," "Guattari, Félix," and "Lyotard, Jean-François" for more.

**Delinquency:**   The behavior of young people defined as criminal by a lawmaking body and ruled as such by a judge in court. Generally young people are not held to the same standards of responsibility as are adults. On the other hand, they are required to obey the rules of home and school or else be labeled "delinquent." Young people became a special category around 1850 when both laws and social control systems were set up to address them as a group. The changing labor market required children to stay in school and learn skills appropriate to industrial capitalism; hence, the legal system began to create a new age grade, the "adolescent." See "Adolescent," "Age Grades," *"Parens patriae,"* and "Status Crimes" for more.

**Demagogue:**   One who is able to lead other people by virtue of his/her persuasive powers. Often a negative term applied to people who appeal to greed, patriotism, or ethnic superiority; the term is also used by elitists to discredit democracy and those who oppose power, privilege, and inequality.

**Democracy:**   Greek: *demos* = the people; *kratein* = to rule. Rule of the people. Not to be confused with republican forms of governance. Bernard Barber has set forth the elements of a strong democracy: open discussion, direct voting on significant issues, and policy formation in all realms of social life (economics, education, religion). Democracy is a central principle in socialist thought. However, in socialist theory, the sphere in which the people are to rule is not limited to political life, "wherein the masses are permitted to decide which of the ruling class will govern." The socialist position is that people rule in the arenas where decisions count (i.e., in economic and in cultural spheres as well). For both Karl Marx and Vladimir Lenin, parliamentary democracy was a place for talk, whereas decisions that shape the course of history are made in private by elites. The thrust of democratic socialism is to make those decisions in the public sphere with maximum participation. Bureaucratic socialism is thus un-Marxist. See "Government, Forms of," "Political Science," and "Republican, As a Form of Government" for more.

**Democratic Self-Management:**   A form of work in which the workers decide upon all the major issues of production and the distribution of profits. In both socialist and capitalist societies, some firms are owned and/or operated by workers. They decide upon managerial staff, hiring, work schedule and working conditions on the floor, investment and dividends, wages, bonuses and fringe benefits such as vacations, health care, and pensions. Cf. "Fordism" and "Z Theory."

**Demographic Transition Theory:**   Under this theory, populations go through three stages: a preindustrial stage, in which both the birth rate and mortality rate are high; an early industrialization stage, in which the birth rate is high and mortality declines (therefore there is a "population explosion"); and a mature industrialization stage, in which both the birth rate and the mortality rate are low. The theory sees population change as related to the process of industrialization and its concomitant social changes. Cf. "Overpopulation."

**Demography:**   The science that charts the characteristics of a population in a given region. Age, sex, gender, class, and education are considered to be demographic variables.

**Demonization:**   The social practice of treating someone or some people as if s/he or they were demons, monsters, devils, or the source of all bad things. Most capitalists demonize communists; many communists demonize capitalists; most racists demonize minority groups; some minority groups demonize Anglos; some women demonize men, whereas many men blame women for their own troubles. The Marxist/socialist position is that the enemy is to be found in alienated social relationships rather than in people as such. It is true enough that there are thoroughly despicable people, but most people work within social institutions that embody social values to which they were socialized as children. See "Alienation," "Crime," "Patriarchy," "Profanation," "Racism," "Reification," and "Sexism" for more.

**Deontology:**   Greek: *deon* = necessity. The study of ethics and of theories of social obligations or duties. See "Axiology" for more.

**Dependency Theory:**   A theory of colonial imperialism that informs anti-American sentiment in Latin America and elsewhere. The theory asserts that capitalist imperialism distorts local economics, creates a surplus population, and is often an effort to substitute foreign exploitation with that of local capitalists. A country becomes dependent upon the United States, Germany, England, or Japan by selling cash crops or natural resources and dependent upon the same countries for food and luxury goods. The developed capitalist countries set terms that benefit multinational corporations and banks and give "aid," subsidized by workers in capitalist countries, to repair some of the social ills (e.g., hunger). At the same time, coffee, cocoa, tea, beef, or other foods are exported to capitalist countries. See "Capitalist World System/New World Order" for more.

**Dependent Variable:**   A social fact said to be caused by some prior, independent factor(s).

According to Chaos theory, the notion of a dependent variable, like a magician's wand, takes one's attention from the possibility that causality, rather than being determined externally, may be composed of complex, interactive feedback loops that change continuously within the dynamics of a social system. Loose systems of causality are pushed aside in search of tight connections between two, three, or four variables.

**Depoliticization:**   The process of reducing the range of questions that are to be settled by collective and public discourse. Questions of foreign policy, employment policy, crime, education, and science are treated as resolved. Depoliticization transforms ongoing debate and collective decisionmaking into technical management. Citizen input is extinguished. Cf. "Politicization."

**Depression:**   A depression is a downturn in the demand for goods, the demand for labor power, and the demand for investment capital itself. Depressions are part of the ups and downs of capitalism. Of the five great economic systems in history, capitalism is the only one with such cycles; in other economic systems, hard times are the result of natural calamity, not the everyday working of the economy. There are three economic cycles that have been identified: Kondratieff cycles (which come in thirty- to fifty-year cycles), Kutznets curves (15-year cycles), and two- to five-year mini-cycles. In bad times, workers are laid off; they cannot buy goods and services; factories close; and the economic process grinds to a halt. Capitalists blame depressions on organized workers, on government interference, and on "unfair" competition by "foreigners" (other capitalists). Workers blame depressions on the government, and the government blames the previous administration. Capitalism causes depressions: Since workers do not get paid 100 percent of the value of goods they produce, they cannot buy all of it back. The "surplus" piles up, factories shut down, and the depression worsens. See "Expansion" and "Kondratieff Cycles" for more.

**Dereification:**   The process by which social reality is dismantled. A process by which the naive and trusting acceptance of a given social form is brought into question. The process by which faith is lost and people get discouraged and turn away from existing systems of religion, gender relations, economics, or politics. The Mormon experience is a classic case of dereification: Whole groups of people otherwise committed to traditional forms of marriage, economics, and religion walked away from these to found a new social lifeworld, first in Missouri, then in Utah. These events tend to support the idea of nonlinearity in social affairs, as well as to give testimony to the role of human agency within larger historical processes.

**Derrida, Jacques:**   Architect of French deconstructionist philosophy. Derrida's contributions to deconstructionism include a number of important postmodern concepts:

1. *Reversal of hierarchies:* Any value position (e.g., man, good, objective) takes on its valuation in relation to some other oppositional value (e.g., woman, evil, subjective). A text, however, can be read so as to reveal such power relations and reverse them through "discoursing" about them.

2. *Metaphysics of presence:* Related to the reversal of hierarchies is Derrida's "presence of the absence." What this means is that in every binary opposition, the value that is dominant/privileged is present. The value that is subordinate is "absent." The oppositional value of "beauty" is "ugly." The value "beauty" is dominant and therefore privileged. We automatically assign positive value to persons identified as beautiful. The oppositional value "ugly" is subordinated and, therefore, repressed.

3. *Differance:* *Differance* (with an "a") implies both the activity of differing and of deferring. All hierarchies include words that are different from each other (e.g., male versus female, heterosexual versus homosexual, white versus black). In addition, however, each defers to the other in the sense of implying the opposite term. We cannot understand what it means to be white without understanding what it means to be black (and vice versa). There is a mutual deferential interdependence.

4. *Trace:* Hidden within each term of a hierarchy, is the trace of the other. The trace is what maintains the relationship between the two terms. In order to deconstruct the hierarchy, one must identify the trace that maintains the ascendancy of the privileged, dominant term as a presence. This is the activity of making visible the hidden. Revealing the hidden trace (women, minority, gay, poor) makes possible the decentering of the dominant term (men, WASP, straight, wealthy).

See "Baudrillard, Jean," "Chronophone," "Deconstruction," "Difference," "Habermas, Jürgen," "Logocentric," and "Phonocentric" for more.

**Descartes, René (1596–1650):** Descartes is one of the more important architects of modern science. A French philosopher and mathematician, Descartes was both rationalist and empiricist; a difficult combination to sustain in a world marked by nonlinear dynamics. Descartes is well-known for his formula for the possibility of knowledge, as against pure skepticism; he offered as evidence of that possibility the saying, *cogito ergo sum,* by which he meant that there was at least one unassailable proposition that can stand against doubt: I think, therefore there must be a thinker who thinks, namely, me. Therefore I exist.

Descartes wrote extensively on the God concept; in short, such a Being exists and is infinite, eternal, immutable, and independent of all that He creates. Descartes' main contribution to mathematics is analytic geometry, which charts the movement of events in time-space, or in what is called *Cartesian space*. The new science of chaos uses Cartesian space extensively to chart the changing mixture of order and disorder in the behavior of complex and fractal systems. (See the work of W. L. Reese.) Cf. "Pascal, Blaise." See "Cogito ergo sum" for more.

**Desire:**   Old French: *de* = of; *sirer* = to wish. In French postmodern terminology, desire (French = *desir*) is always and already communicated in and through language. All speech is saturated with certain longings, aspirations, needs, fears, passions, and beliefs. The French psychoanalyst Jacques Lacan argued that desire was at the core of our being. When articulated, however, Lacan maintained that desire could never be fully described. We can never completely capture in speech—in words and sentences—the essence of our very existence without leaving something or some trace of it behind. When describing why we love someone our words are filled with desire. Often, however, we find that we do not do our love justice; that is, the words themselves are inadequate to communicate how we feel. We have the same experience with art, poetry, the pleasure of a sunset, or the play of little children. Thus for Lacan, *desir* was illusive yet polymorphous, elusive yet omnipresent. See "Lacan, Jacques" and "Topology" for more.

**Deskilling:**   The subdivision of labor into ever more simple tasks. The idea is that wages can be reduced, production increased, and quality improved with this division and subdivision of labor. See "Z Theory."

**Deskilling of America:**   The practice of moving high-paying, skilled jobs overseas, leaving U.S. workers to take low-paying, service jobs. Owners can take advantage of both economic and status inequality by moving jobs to countries with a large unemployed labor force.

**Determinism:**   The philosophical position that phenomena are best explained in terms of the events that have immediately proceeded them: rigid cause and effect. This idea assumes social significance when it is applied to the behavior of individuals, for if a person and the brain are rigidly bound by cause and effect, how can that person be "free" to do what s/he wants? The argument runs that what one wants and will do are rigidly determined by prior considerations. It is further claimed that one's behavior could be accurately predicted if only enough information were available. The logical conclusion to this idea is that a human is merely a complicated machine.

When determinism is applied in this manner to the realm of psychology, it is called "behaviorism." B. F. Skinner is the foremost behaviorist in the United States. Behaviorism is antithetical to the convictions of humanists, Marxists, and fundamentalist Christians. The alternative view is that human beings think and act with judgment and insight. In this mode, causality is weak or absent; reflective social interaction produces social facts. See "Chaos Theory" for more.

**Developing Countries:**   About 120 nations in the world have systems of production and distribution organized by a low-tech base (economy) and strong social ties. These countries are said to be underdeveloped. The term implies that capitalists and capitalist societies can solve three problems by controlling the politics of the country: cheaper labor, cheaper raw materials, and expanded markets for manufactured goods.

Developing countries experience problems of crime, class inequality, juvenile delinquency, suicide, prostitution, and drug use.

**Development/Underdevelopment:**   Theories of progress assume that a society becomes developed when it: (1) industrializes; (2) commodifies all goods and services and exchanges them in a market; (3) discards all traditional stratifications in favor of class stratification; and (4) replaces social status (kinship, ethnicity, race, or gender) with money as a nexus for the exchange of goods and services. Societies that do not accept these changes are said to be underdeveloped. See "Modernization Theory."

**Deviance:**   Nonconformity with existing/traditional social norms. This nonconformity is often said to be pathological when it challenges power and privilege; it is said to be innovative or creative when it is approved by the gatekeepers of morality. All societies in a changing environment require deviance adequate enough to reduce mismatch between system and environment. Deviance is a negative asset when the environment is stable but can be a positive asset when the environment is irreversibly changing, depending of course on the nature of the variation. See "Ashby's Law of Requisite Variety" and "Corruption, Theory of" for more.

**Deviance, Primary:**   A term used by Charles Lemert to refer to those deviant acts that do not redefine the self or become a matter of public image. See "Labeling Theory" for more.

**Deviant:**   Someone who is noticeably different from the average within some dimension of social behavior. As it applies to behavior, that which is generally considered to be beyond the tolerance limits of the community.

**Dewey, John (1859–1952):**   American philosopher/educator who taught at Michigan, Chicago, Minnesota, and Columbia. Dewey is known for his work in progressive education; he started an experimental school in Chicago. Dewey argued that education should have no fixed syllabi or standard objectives but should fit itself to the different and changing needs of students; experimentation is encouraged; and the future is more important than the past. In his philosophy of knowledge, Dewey argued that research begins in situations that are troubled, ambiguous, and full of conflict. One does not look for order but for solutions congenial to democracy and empowerment. The quest is not for truth so much as for transformation of troubled, conflicted situations. Dewey's contributions are linked to postmodern education and to postmodern philosophy of science. See "Pragmatism" for more.

**Dialectic:**    Greek: *dialektos* = discourse, debate. In everyday life, dialectic refers to a dynamic tension within a given system and the process by which change occurs on the basis of that tension and resultant conflict. In Marxian thought, a dialectic has (1) a thesis; (2) an antithesis; and (3) a synthesis (when the dialectic has run its course). A dialectic is said to arise since all *a* implies *not a*. Thus, the notion of a class system implies its negation. Cf. "Feedback."

In orthodox Marxist views, dialectics are raised to a science of the general laws of society and knowledge (after Friedrich Engels). In this formulation, the three forms of the dialectic are: (1) struggle and unity of opposites; (2) the transition of quantity into quality; and (3) the negation of a prior negation. An example of the first form of a dialectic would be class struggle between workers and owners, out of which a new, more humane economic system might/will arise. Of the second form, an example might be the transformation of water into steam with a small quantitative rise in temperature; and for the third form, a good example might be when capitalism (a negative) is destroyed by revolution (another negation).

The concept of the dialectic is hostile to the linearity that is at the core of modern science. As such, it is a better explanation for how complex systems work. The rise of Chaos theory gives dramatic empirical support and much sharper focus to the concept of the dialectic. See "Chaos Theory" for more.

**Dialectic Materialism:**    The view espoused by Karl Marx, Friedrich Engels, and Vladimir Lenin that revolutionary change comes as a result of contradictions in the concretely existing modes of production rather than as a result of supernatural or mystical phenomena. The idea of *telos* (fate) is pushed aside as well. Natural stage theory, historical cycles, and metaphysical causes are rejected in favor of human action and activity as explanations for changes in the nature of a society. For Marx, each economic system may have tendencies that can be seen, but they should not be taken to be inevitable.

**Dialogical Pedagogy:**    A critically informed position developed by the educator and social philosopher Paulo Freire. Dialogical pedagogy refers to the active engagement with the voice of the oppressed when constructing mechanisms for revolutionary change. Dialogical pedagogy is a method and attitude for reclaiming the way of knowing embodied by the disenfranchised masses. In essence, Freire argued that conventional mechanisms for expression denied the perspective of disempowered groups such that there was a "culture of silence." Freire analyzed the process of speaking true words, or how to break free from the constraints of standard speech. For him, dialogical pedagogy simultaneously embraced action and reflection, which were always in a dialectical relationship. True words, then, were necessarily steeped in praxis. The word was work. In the act of speaking, if either action and reflection were missing, then, according to Freire, transformative possibilities were likely thwarted. To speak a true word is to meaningfully change the world. Postmodernists utilize the insights of Freire in their articulation of "Replacement Discourses" and "Transpraxis." See both for more information. See also "Pedagogy."

**Dictatorship:**   The rule of one small group over an entire society by force. Often, the word is used as if one person or one small party were the dictatorship. Such a view is decidedly un-Marxist; it takes a lot of people to support dictators and reproduce dictatorships. If a lot of people were not direct beneficiaries of Nazi, Italian, Spanish, Argentinean, or Nicaraguan dictatorships, such dictatorships would disappear. There can be no leaders without willing followers (Georg Simmel). Force and ideological hegemony play a part in dictatorships; however the objective interests of a lot of people are served by dictatorships. See "Great Man Theory (of History)" and "Political Science" for more.

**Dictatorship of the Proletariat:**   Control over the production of political and economic policy by a party elite in the name of the workers. Orthodox socialists argue for an intermediate stage in which state control of production replaces capitalist/elitist control. This stands in sharp contrast to the ideas of Rosa Luxemburg, who argued that mass democracy should set policy from the beginning. Centralized control, although un-Marxist if permanent, is said to be necessary until the false consciousness of workers is repaired and the last vestiges of bourgeois mentality are gone. Since the Marxist position is that consciousness grows out of concrete social relationships in the production of culture, any such dictatorship must be short-lived and closely constrained, else socialist consciousness is aborted. Careerism and sycophancy develop along with self-glorification and the cult of the individual and/or elitism.

**Dictionary:**   A book that defines words. A good dictionary tries to present the more common usages of a word since, in every society, words mean different things to people in different social positions. For example: "Rape" as a concept is used differently, almost casually, by men; women see it in a different way. All dictionaries are political, in that the definitions given first place are those that make the most sense to the writer in a given social lifeworld. All dictionaries thus reproduce that world by setting the understanding of a thing as fixed and beyond argument. A good dictionary is admittedly political and admits its politics.

**Differance:**   See "Derrida, Jacques."

**Difference:**   A way to establish an idea or truth claim by its positive and negative references to other texts. The meaning of a text thus recedes in history and/or is circular. See "Derrida, Jacques" for more.

**Differential Association:**   A "theory" of crime. It borrows heavily from social learning theory and holds that criminal behavior is learned much like anything else. Criminal behavior is learned based upon one's close, ongoing relationships. The greater the intensity, type, duration, frequency, and quality of one's associations that support rather than reject antisocial behavior, the more likely it is that one will adopt criminal rather than law-abiding behavioral patterns.

Differential association is less a theory of crime and more a theory of social behavior. It emphasizes the learned character of antisocial conduct.

**Differentiation:**   A division of labor based upon race, gender, ethnicity, merit, or age. Not to be confused with "stratification." There may well be some important advantages to social differentiation by merit, age, interest, ethnicity, and/or religion. This variety tends to increase both skill and productivity; it offers a reservoir of ideas and ways of life that serve well in times of economic, climatic, or social change. The division of labor on the basis of race, gender, religion, or ethnicity also may carry with it great harm to the overall capacity of a society. It is in this understanding of the division of labor that wisdom and judgment as well as kindness and compassion need full range. See "Stratification" for more.

**Diminishing Returns, Law of:**   A theory from Thomas Malthus that holds that productivity decreases with the addition of more and more workers. If one worker can produce ten pins per day, ten workers might produce 100 per day, but twenty workers might produce fewer. This idea was used to diminish the value of workers and to point to the problems of capitalists who hired "too many" workers. Marx pointed out that improvements in technology rendered this law invalid.

**Dinks:**   Double income, no kids. This acronym refers to married couples who form loose unions in order to enhance their lifestyle. They do so by sharing household and recreational expenses while refusing to have kids or, if they have them, refusing to support them. See "Yuppie," "Monks," "Swinks," and "Wonk/Wonks" for more. All are popular terms used by young people to refer to those who avoid traditional gender relations and marriage forms. See also "Extended Family."

**Dionysian/Dionysus:**   Dionysus was the Greek god of wine and nature. His name is given to a philosophy of life that sets passion, joy, and rare good spirits as its center point. Cf. "Apollonian."

**Disaster:**   Premodern sensibility explained large, unexpected events that adversely affected a society as messages from the spiritual world, acts of God, or divine retribution for sin. Modern theory defines a disaster as a natural calamity in which large numbers of persons are injured and/or property destroyed. Postmodern scholarship explains a disaster as some large scale event that destroys people and property and that is undesirable. Events that destroy people and property but that are desired are not defined as disaster. For example, consider war, environmental pollution, poverty, child abuse, and so on. These are defined as personal crimes, accidents, or are not noticed. (See the work of M. Ephraim.)

**Disciplinary Society:**   See "Foucault, Michel" and "Panopticism."

**Discourse:**   A special kind of interaction in which "validity claims" are checked out. Most of the time, people just talk together about the practical matters at hand. But sometimes that which is taken for granted is called into question. Jürgen Habermas identifies four validity claims about discourse that may result in distorted communication and that need to be examined more closely. In postmodern work all that is written or spoken is seen as discourse; claims of objectivity and impartiality are presumed to be political tactics that remove truth claims (about gender, race, class, or reality) from discourse. See "Paralogic" for more.

**Discrimination:**   The practice of treating a group of people as if they were somehow inferior in some important way: usually race, class, gender, religion, or ethnic origin. Sometimes discrimination is confused with "prejudice," which refers to psychological states rather than actual behavior. The two are often closely connected, but it is possible to discriminate against people without conscious prejudice. See "Institutional Racism" for more.

**Discursive Formations:**   This is a key concept developed in the writings of Michel Foucault. Foucault never identified himself within the Marxist, semiotic, or postmodern camps; however, several of his epigones situate his work squarely within the postmodern tradition. Foucault was concerned with the manifestation of power communicated through language. To speak of discursive formations is to refer to the normalizing and depathologizing effects that social formations (e.g., law, sexuality, mental illness) exercise in the lives of people. Foucault encouraged active resistance to all discursive formations, alleging that they produced system-sustaining social control, citizen alienation, and a disciplinary society. According to Foucault any systematic, sedimented constitution of reality possesses the capacity to wield tremendous influence in our lives. This influence represents a specialized knowledge that includes no (or little) room for dissension, difference, or alternative knowledge forms. Thus as power/knowledge, discursive formations privilege certain ways of knowing and certain claims to truth while ensuring the continued silencing of repressed (oppositional) voices. See "Foucault, Michel" and "Panopticism" for more.

**Disemployment:** Capitalism is the only economic system in which there is a systematic elimination of workers, either by replacement by machines (to increase profits) or during a depression (in order to control costs). Capitalist economists say that a 5 percent disemployment rate is necessary in order to keep wages down and profits up. If there were full employment, profits would fall, capitalists would fail, and the economy would collapse. Harrison and Bluestone estimate that over 3 million high-paying jobs have moved overseas and that more than half of the new jobs pay below the poverty line. Cf. "Full Employment." See "Fiscal Crisis" and "Unemployment" for more.

**Disengagement Theory:** The view that all connections between persons and social roles are affirmed or withdrawn within social rituals. The more common social processes that disengage a person from a role include: divorce from marriage; defrocking from a ministry; disbarment from the practice of law; decertification from medical practice; dismissal from the military via court-martial. It is the final rite of passage after which one has lost all rights to embody a social role. Some include funerals as disengagement routines, since the person concerned is treated as no longer a member of a social group; some societies hold funerals for living persons to make the point.

**Displacement:** Developed through the dream analysis work of Sigmund Freud. Displacement refers to the transferring of negative thoughts, feelings, and impulses from one person, who is perceived as potentially harmful or dangerous, to another person, who is perceived as potentially kind and safe. For example, when a student athlete gets yelled at by a coach, rather than talking back to the coach the student athlete vents his/her frustration onto a sibling or parent. Similar to condensation, this process is often unconscious and pre-thematic. Displacement provides clues to one's unconscious longings. When correctly deciphered, it can unlock important information regarding one's behavior. See "Dream Work" and "Freud, Sigmund" for more. Cf. "Condensation."

**Dissipative Structure:** In Chaos theory, the more normal circumstance in which society and its dynamic systems exist is a state of *far-from-equilibrium* conditions. These conditions make it possible for a variety of perspectives and a multitude of logics to thrive in which dissipative structures abound. Dissipative structures refer to the condition or state in which a given system behaves. Dissipative structures tend toward spontaneous self-organization. They simultaneously gravitate toward order (structure) and disorder (dissipation). Dissipative structures are in a perpetual state of becoming, transforming, emerging. Thus, they overcome equilibrium or static conditions. Dissipative structures are open to flux, chance, spontaneity, randomness, unpredictability. Bureaucracies (e.g., the criminal justice system, the mental health system, the social welfare system) are excellent illustration of what dissipative structures are not. Bureaucracies promote rigid, tight control and limited, status quo conditions. Such things as intentional communities, housing co-ops for the homeless, and peer-directed rehabilitation facilities for the chemically addicted are examples of systems that behave in a more dynamic, fluid fashion and in which dissipative structures are more likely to prevail. See "Chaos Theory" and "Far-From-Equilibrium Conditions" for more.

**Dividends:**   That portion of expropriated surplus value (profits) given to stockholders in permanent payment for investment. If dividends go to a few, there are many problems surrounding the concentration of wealth. If workers can invest part of their wages in stocks, they become owners, once or twice removed. See "Rent" for more.

**Divine Right (of Kings):**   The view that all authority is vested in a king who gets that right from God. If so, all rebellion is sinful. Few people seriously argue for this right now, but the larger point remains: If God does exist and does have a plan (patriarchy, stratification, etc.) or a chosen people, then opposition to such inequalities is both evil and wrong. Cf. "Theology, Liberation."

**Division of Labor:**   A concept relevant to the writings of the French social thinker, Émile Durkheim. Durkheim's first major work was titled, *The Division of Labor in Society* (1893). In this text, originally Durkheim's doctoral thesis, he studied the processes of social change or evolution involved in industrialization. Durkheim was interested in the transformation of societies from those that were simple and primitive ("mechanical") to those that were more complex and differentiated ("organic"). In simple societies there was little division of labor. In more advanced societies there was greater division of labor. Understanding this division of labor (e.g., its organization, routinization, duration) provided insight into how societies, whether mechanical or organic, experienced solidarity. According to Durkheim, more advanced societies have a highly specialized division of labor. Although Durkheim held that the division of labor promotes solidarity, Marx held that it destroys solidarity. As a scheme to divide up tasks the division of labor may be useful; as a scheme to exclude people from human agency and praxis, it is harmful.

In contemporary society, when different people do different things in the production process, there is a division of labor. Think of the construction of a house: One person can do everything or can hire different people to do the carpentry, plumbing, wiring, masonry, or painting. A society constitutes itself as a human society by the creation of culture. Any division of labor that eliminates or restricts people in the production of material, ideological, or political culture as a complex unity subverts the human condition. For example, capitalism assigns manual labor to the worker, the production of ideological culture to the manager, and the production of political culture to an elite. In advanced capitalism, there is also a geographical division of labor. In the electronics industry, the "brain" inhabits the laboratories around Boston and San Diego, whereas the "hands" are in Taiwan, Korea, Haiti, El Salvador, South Korea, Malaysia, Hong Kong, and Spain. See "Collective Conscience," "Durkheim, Émile," "Solidarity, Mechanical," and "Solidarity, Organic" for more.

**Dogma/Dogmatism:** Greek: decree. The word applies to all policies and practices held to be beyond dispute. When one is absolutely sure that s/he is right and all others are wrong for all time, one is said to be dogmatic. Cf. "Eclectic/Eclecticism."

**Double Bind:** The notion of a double bind refers to a condition that occurs during the construction of a social occasion when one party receives inconsistent or contradictory information from the other party or parties. The best examples involve actual contradictions, such as when someone says one thing verbally, while indicating the opposite with their body talk. A person who is in a double bind has a difficult time deciding how to act toward the source of the contradictory information.

**Dracon/Draconian:** Dracon was a Greek king who established a unified legal code in the seventh century B.C.; the code did not distinguish between degrees of severity. Thus when laws are harsh for small crimes, they are said to be "draconian."

**Dramaturgical Analysis:** The use of the concepts and processes found in the world of theater and cinema to discuss how social reality is constructed. The political question to be raised is whether dramaturgy is simply a helpful approach to teach people about society (Erving Goffman) or an ideology used by people to pursue private goals such as profit, manipulation, and management. The radical perspective is that such an approach arises in a society in which social relationships warrant it. See "Goffman, Erving" for more.

**Dramaturgical Society:** A society in which the technology of theater is used to manage the masses via electronic media and with the aid of the sciences of sociology and psychology. The world of make-believe enters the world of serious discourse as an alien and dominating force. In politics, a cadre of hired specialists (marketing and advertising experts) now use dramaturgy to generate a public for a candidate or an issue. This practice converts politics from a cultural item into a commodity to be purchased by the highest bidder. The same is true in sports, medicine, religion, and other activities that used to be cultural activities (see the work of T. R. Young and John Massey). Dramaturgy could be used to celebrate, illuminate, or politicize rather than alienate people from the political and economic questions that affect their lives. See "Goffman, Erving" and "Radical Theater/Cinema" for more.

**Dramaturgy:**   Greek: *draein* = to act, to do; *ergein* = to work. A term introduced by Erving Goffman as a key to understanding advanced monopoly capitalism and the widespread practice of using devices from the world of make-believe in order to create convincing and profitable impressions among unknown others. Cf. "Goffman, Erving." See "Impression Management" for more.

**Dream Work:**   In significant part, the work of Sigmund Freud entailed the analysis of dreams. In his dream work investigations, Freud found that dreams represent a text, a narrative with their own structure, meaning, and coherence. A dream embodies unconscious images and exists much like a puzzle; that is, it needs to be deciphered or decoded for its meaning and relevance to the one who experiences it. As Freud discovered, the presence of condensation and displacement are found at the most basic level of a dream. Condensation refers to the compression of thoughts, feelings, and impulses represented in an unconscious image or series of images. When these images are spoken, they sound almost nonsensical. For example, "He treated me *famillionairely*." The compression of familiar + millionaire. Displacement refers to the ability of our desires and longings to attach themselves, again unconsciously through images, to different aspects of a dream. For example, when describing a dream, one moment we are flying as if we possess wings, the next instance we are walking on top of water, and in the third instance we speak several different languages. These descriptions might reveal something about our ego identity and our sense of self-worth, accomplishment, and esteem. These psychic processes, when examined, represent clues to better understanding the untold story that remains concealed and dormant deep within the unconscious, giving rise to the dream. See "Condensation," "Displacement," and "Freud, Sigmund" for more.

**Dühring, Eugen (1833–1901):**   German economist who held that matter is the sole reality; that morality is based upon compassion and sympathy; that pain helps define pleasure; and that capitalism should be modified not eliminated. Karl Marx and Friedrich Engels attacked the latter point. (See the work of W. L. Reese.)

**Durkheim, Émile (1858–1917):**   Durkheim made many contributions to the study of society, including suicide, the division of labor, solidarity and religion, sociological method, the idea of "social facts." He was the first French academic sociologist, assuming the appointment in 1887 at Bordeaux. He held the first chair in sociology (and education) in 1902 at the Sorbonne in Paris.

Durkheim's intellectual pursuits focused on the problem of order and the study of sociological method. He said that the God concept was a false reification (collective representation) of the power of groups to shape the behavior of members and of religion as a solution to the problem of solidarity (how to hold people together when they have conflicting interests); he argued that suicide increases when society falls apart (anomie) and that there were other ways to get solidarity rather than by religion. He spoke of mechanical (religion) solidarity and organic solidarity as different ways to bind people together. Organic solidarity was supposed to emerge out of a complex and functionally interdependent division of labor.

The socialist response to Durkheim is to question the ways in which the labor process is to be organized, the degree to which order takes precedence over social justice, and alternative ways to get solidarity. See "Anomie," "Collective Conscience," "Division of Labor," "Function/Functionalism," "Functional Interchange," "Organic Theory of Social Organization," "Solidarity, Mechanical," and "Weber, Max" for more.

**Duty:**   Latin: *debere* = to owe. Our word "debt" comes from the same root. Stoicism as a social philosophy sets duty as the center point of ethical behavior; one is to do one's duty even if it conflicts with notions of good or with cherished values.

**Dyad:**   Greek: *duos* = two. In sociology, the smallest unit of observation and interaction. Sociology begins with dyads rather than with single individuals outside of a status role. Think of the impossibility of studying the mother without the child or the failings of a student without looking at faults of the professor.

# E

**Echelon:** An arbitrarily defined level or stratum in a table of bureaucratic organization that is held accountable to levels defined as superior to it. Persons in an echelon have roughly equivalent duties, rewards, and responsibilities. The use of echelons is an efficient but scarcely human way to establish control of many by few. It is a formal type of stratification that ignores earlier forms of privilege (e.g., racism, sexism, religious bigotry, or ethnocentrism) and claims to be modern and progressive.

**Eclectic/Eclecticism:** An eclectic is one who sees validity in a lot of ideas/theories or differing points of view. There are many who scorn eclectics as weak minded, ignorant, vacillating, and/or moral cowards. Cf. "Dogma/Dogmatism."

**Ecology:** The study of the patterned ways in which organisms distribute themselves in time and space with reference to other organisms and to inorganic aspects of the territorially limited environment. Ecology is of interest to socialism insofar as capitalism tends to destroy ecosystems by exploiting raw materials and dumping toxins to protect profits.

**Economic Determinism:** The view that economic events determine, shape, and influence all social forms. In orthodox Marxian terms, the base determines the superstructure. Thus, capitalist relations shape art, science, religion, and other forms of ideological culture. These forms in turn tend to reflect and reproduce capitalist relations. See "Economics" and "Marx, Early" for more.

**Economic Formations:** There are five economic systems in human history. (1) *Primitive communism*—for most of history, people lived in bands and tribes and shared food and labor. In this system the technology and division of labor was simple. (2) *Slavery*—interspersed in such economies was a certain slavery in which people were captured through predatory warfare. Slavery grew to be an industry in itself in the sixteenth, seventeenth, and eighteenth centuries. (3) *Feudalism*—the conquerors in predatory warfare often extracted tribute from conquered villages. Some of the conquerors remained behind to collect on behalf of the others. Rome and Greece, for example, became imperial systems based on warfare. (4) *Agricultural systems*—settled agrarian economies developed about 10,000 years ago and, about 4,000 years ago, hydraulic societies developed near river systems to irrigate crops. The surplus food permitted a great division of labor and, most say, complex stratification systems; (5) *Industrial capitalism*—developed in the eighteenth century to upset all prior economic arrangements. Feudalism, slavery, and primitive communism were pushed aside as capitalists replaced kings, and workers replaced serfs, peasants, and slaves. There are two other economic systems that have had little success: *Bureaucratic socialism* had limited success early on but collapsed in its rigidity and inability to improve the means of production; *advanced communism* has yet to be instituted. Cf. "Market Socialism."

**Economic Forms, Parallel:**   Wage labor is the only way those who do not own capital can reunite production and distribution. However, there are many parallel economic systems in every capitalist society. Indeed, most goods and services produced in the United States are available through these other systems. The more important economic systems that parallel and, thus, moderate capitalism include: (1) The family system continues to be a very active economic system; most goods bought in the marketplace are later redistributed on the basis of status within kinship systems. Many goods and services are produced and distributed within the family system on the basis of status rather than profit. (2) The social welfare system of the state, which redistributes tax dollars to rich and poor alike. (3) Private charities (e.g., Red Cross, Good Will, the Community Chest) as well as private foundations give away billions to rich and poor alike. (4) Crime is a large economic system in the United States. Wide-ranging estimates indicate that corporate crime, street crime, white-collar crime, and organized crime make up an economic system worth from 8 to 25 percent of the gross national product. (5) A "gray" market (barter system), in which friends, neighbors, and other people exchange labor instead of cash in order to avoid taxation, also exists. See "Economics," "Friendship," "Labor Power," and "Wage Labor" for more.

**Economic Imperialism:**   The use of state power by multinational corporations to ensure cheap and docile labor, access to natural resources, and easy entry into the markets of weaker, poorer countries. Japan, Germany, and the United States are the major nations involved in this practice. See "Economics" for more.

**Economics:**   The division of the social sciences concerned with the management of wealth and capital. There are various forms of economic practice, emphasizing different philosophical traditions. See "Economic Forms, Parallel" for more. Cf. "Economic Determinism" and "Economic Imperialism."

**Economics, Demand-Side:**   The view that the best way to prevent economic depressions or to get out of them is to make sure that capitalists get high enough profits, such that they can invest in new factories, outlets, and products. Cf. "Economics, Supply-Side."

**Economics, Supply-Side:**   The view that depressions are best handled by increasing wages or decreasing taxes of ordinary citizens in order that they may buy products and services and thus stimulate the economy. Cf. "Economics, Demand-Side."

**Economism:**   A term that helps warn against the tendency to turn social revolution into bread-and-butter issues, as trade unions often do. This tendency may leave capitalist relations intact, as in American worker movements, or minimize the Marxian emphasis upon worker self-management, praxis, and community, as in the former Soviet Union.

*Écriture féminine:*   In French postmodern feminist theory, the question is whether it is even possible to cultivate a language or a way of knowing free from the misogynous trappings of masculine culture and malespeak. This question is part of an important enterprise. Establishing such a grammar would open the door to new vistas of meaning, different expressions of truth, and alternative ways of knowing. However, some postmodern feminists have considered whether the question itself might not be cloaked in the logic of masculine thought. After all, developing such a code distances women from men in an essentialistic, singularly driven, precise way. According to several postmodern feminists, this is precisely the way men understand social phenomena, human relations, and feminine consciousness. Thus, on the one hand, such a grammar is needed for furthering our understanding of women; but, on the other hand, the process of producing such a code would further legitimize the power of masculine consciousness in the lives of women. See "Androcentricism," "Irigaray, Luce," "Kristeva, Julia," "Phallogocentrism," and "Voice/Voices" for more.

**Ecstasy:**   Greek: *ex* = out; *histanai* = to stand. In premodern knowledge processes, ecstasy was one of the major pathways to truth. One put one's own concerns aside and entered into a state of rapture in which divine truth was revealed. In modern thinking, ecstasy is understood as a form of madness to be treated by psychiatry. Many postmodern religions return to ecstasy as a valid source of insight and enlightenment, especially feminist religions.

**Education:**   Latin: *e* = from; *ducere* = draw out. To draw out of young people the knowledge that lays dormant in them. Socrates assumed that people were born with all the knowledge of the gods but that birth was so traumatic that there was a forgetting. The role of the teacher was to draw out that knowledge. In the United States the educational system has complex effects. On the one hand, it is one of the most egalitarian and open systems in the world. On the other hand, it still tracks people into class, race, and gender systems of inequality. American education is torn between efforts to keep costs down and to teach each student effectively. The recent trend is toward larger classes, less equality, more technical instruction, and outcome-based learning. Cf. "Inculcate."

**Education, Revolutionary:**   A form of education in which cognitive, emotional, and political capacities are developed and critical use of them encouraged in and out of the classroom within a framework of community. The line between teacher and pupil is eliminated; cooperation rather than competition marks the progress of the class. See "Freire, Paulo" for more.

**Education, Technical:**   The prevailing form of education in the United States is one in which strong and well-designed business and industrial systems are the subject of lectures, workshops, and seminars, rather than self-systems, social systems, or cultural systems. One can look at the catalog of any major university to observe the degree to which the technical/rational interest is served at the expense of the hermeneutic or critical interest.

**Egalitarian (Society):**   Equality in social arrangements. A society based on the principle that all are entitled to equal treatment and rights in the society. The point of an egalitarian society is not that everyone is treated exactly alike (as in a massive bureaucratic system), but rather that everyone is accorded full status as a human being to produce culture. There can be different roles and different rewards in such societies, but no one is excluded by reason of birth.

**Ego:**   Latin: *ego* = I. Used in Freudian psychology, the ego is seen to be the mediator between the id (unconscious desire and instincts for life or for death) and the superego (the moral regulator of behavior). The id is the source of the pleasure principle (not just genital sex), and the ego embodies the reality principle. The superego develops from society, and its demands are for sacrifice of self and "primitive impulses" (the wish for pleasure or for peace; the death wish). Father is representative of society, and his demands thus become hated objects in the unconscious. Mother embodies the pleasure principle and thus is the object of incestuous desire. The aim of Freudian psychiatry is to strengthen the ego and improve its capacity to control/channel the impulses of the id and to mediate the demands of father/society, while transferring desire from mother to more mature sexual relationships.

**Eidetic:**   Plato used the term to refer to the "essence of a thing." Edmund Husserl used it to refer to the natural categories of thought and perception into which human beings fit sense data. In Husserlian phenomenology, one sets aside (brackets) all particular aspects of a thing so that its essence will "shine forth." Postmodern phenomenology sets aside both eidos and eidetic reduction as human devices rather than intrinsic essences of a thing.

**Einstein, Albert (1879–1955):**   In three short years, Einstein published four articles that changed the field of physics; his work on light, gravity, and philosophy of science continues to find confirmation. He developed the notion of absolute time/space and thereby helped solve several problems in physics. The new view is that findings are valid only within a special inertial system. Einstein accepted the God concept as the orderly harmony found in nature. He was a pacifist and wrote President Roosevelt urging research that led to the atomic bomb and nuclear energy. He argued for a Jewish nation in Palestine, for socialism, as well as for an international political order dedicated to peace and social justice. Feminists point out that his wife was a mathematician (he failed math in school) and did the math that supported many of his more formulaic postulates. Einstein did not list her as coauthor and left her for another woman. (See the work of W. L. Reese.)

**Electra Complex:**   The hidden desire, according to Sigmund Freud, of a girl to replace her mother as the wife and lover of the father. Named after Electra—a tragic figure in Greek literature who convinced her brother Orestes to kill their mother, Clytemnestra, and her lover, Aegisthus. Freud used a play by Sophocles to generate this pathology, peculiar to women and the source of illegitimate children. The girl selects an undesirable boy to father a child, which she then symbolically offers to her father as proof of her own desirable sexuality. Cf. "Oedipal Complex."

**Eleventh Thesis:**   Philosophers have only interpreted the world in various ways; the point is to change it. This is Karl Marx's comment on the role of depoliticized science, religion, and politics. Vladimir Lenin, too, said that one best understands social reality when one participates in the building and rebuilding of it. See "Conflict Methodology" for more.

**Elite:**   French: *élire* = elect. Early on, the elect/elite referred to those selected by God to manage on His behalf the affairs of the world. Now it refers to a set of persons who control policy and practices in a stratified system, or a group privileged on the basis of wealth, race, gender, or position in a bureaucracy or formal organization. Thus, the term carries pejorative content with those on the Left. See "Stewardship" for more.

**Elitism:**   The belief that the masses are not fit for the creation of political and ideological culture but are only too well suited for the production of material culture. The elite then claim a large part of the material production as their due for producing ideological and political culture. In the United States, 50 percent of the people claim 90 percent of the wealth produced. Those engaged in the production of ideological culture (sometimes called professionals—doctors, lawyers, sports figures, professors, judges, actors) and those engaged in the production of political culture (managers, politicians, wardens, psychiatrists, administrators, public relations and advertising executives) claim salaries many times greater than those who produce material culture. This disparity declines a bit if the workers are organized and bargain. See "Authoritarianism" for more.

**Emancipation:**   A transformation of society such that individuals are liberated to create various forms of human culture: art, science, music, religion, and the process of self-creation as human beings. Not to be confused with political emancipation in which people may vote once in a while and, between times, assign their own social power to the state. The socialist vision is that there is/should be an interactively rich and informationally rich discussion and debate prior to direct votes on social policy questions. See "Political Emancipation" for more.

**Emancipation of the Senses:**   The origin of the radical impulse in the thought of Karl Marx was his understanding that human freedom is rooted in the human sensibility. The senses do not just "receive" what is given to them; instead, they transform, interpret, form, and discover that which exists or may exist. In a society based on alienated, divided labor, people perceive things as they are given by bosses and managers, made by owners and elites, and used by the existing society. In a repressive society, new emancipatory forms are forbidden. Breaking out of this prison requires breaking away from alienated society and once again emancipating the senses of each adult person to interpret, transform, and discover. See "Praxis/Practice" and "Sexuality" for more.

**Emancipatory Science:**   A system of research and critique by which the human interests in change and renewal toward a rational and decent society are served. Emancipatory science is always in dialectic conflict with existing social forms and is served by conflict methodology.

**Embourgeoisiement:**   The thesis that workers are gradually becoming middle class, in that they earn more and live the middle-class lifestyle. Workers living this lifestyle overlook the loss of their control over the means of production and confuse possession of consumer goods with ownership of productive property. An example of the thesis would be employing the better paid workers of first world countries while ignoring exploitation and oppression of third world countries. The comforts and securities of the former are based upon the conditions of the latter. See "Proletarianization" and "Immiseration" for more.

**Emergence Theory:**   The assumption that the whole is greater than the sum of the parts. Thus, the characteristics of a sugar molecule cannot be understood in terms of a complete knowledge of the attributes of the included atoms taken one at a time. In social terms, self, society, and culture are emergent in that individuals acting alone cannot produce these items. Social power is social in that it emerges from the coordinated labor of many. Hence, social power cannot be the "property" of one except by force or fraud. See "Psychology" for more.

**Eminent Domain:**   The right of the state to take property for the general good. The thought is that there is a higher law of property that gives private persons temporary use and benefits of property for a lifetime. These rights can be set aside by the claim that land belongs to (is in the domain of) the larger community.

**Emotion, Sociology of:**   A branch of sociology that makes visible the ways in which positive or negative feeling or thinking is buried in words, social roles, social processes, or social groups. The discipline assumes that most if not all emotional responses are pre-shaped and given form within a sociocultural complex; anger, hate, jealousy, love, compassion, indifference, and disgust are all equally encouraged, elicited, forbidden, or required in social life. This position sharply contrasts with the assumption that emotions are natural responses arising from purely physical or psychological processes. See "Behaviorism" for more.

**Empathy:**   Greek: *empeiria* = experienced with or skilled at. The term refers to the capacity of one person to know and to respond to the pain or problems of another person.

**Empirical Investigation:**   The method of acquiring primary knowledge by direct sensory observation and experimentation in order to test hypotheses. The method works well with simple dynamics of physical phenomena but has only limited utility with complex systems, especially those founded upon meaning, intention, and purpose.

**Empiricism:**   Greek: *empeiria* = experienced in; skilled at. In modern science, the philosophical position that "real knowledge" is gained through measurement and observation. It takes the view that if something exists or is true, you can measure it. A problem arises when quantity is made the focus of attention at the expense of quality. Empiricism tends to freeze all of history in present findings. Empiricism also leads one to suppose that social relations are controlled by external and eternal laws of nature made visible by statistics. This view minimizes the role of judgment, intent, and human activity in producing society. The radical position is that three methodologies are necessary to a rational and decent society. Empiricism (also called positivism) is informed by the human interest in prediction and control. Marxists argue that hermeneutics and emancipatory science are also necessary. See "Knowledge, Sociology of/Process of" for more.

**Empowerment:**   This is an affirmative philosophy of social living that is extremely person-centered. Acts of empowerment entail the validation of individuals, despite their frailties, shortcomings, or vulnerabilities. The empowerment movement is designed to encourage poor, disenfranchised, oppressed, and marginalized groups (e.g., the homeless, the welfare dependent, the mentally ill, survivors of abuse, AIDS victims) to reclaim their dignity. Empowerment movements maintain that all people have a right to actively and meaningfully contribute to setting the social, economic, and political agenda in their own communities and in society, regardless of their income or social standing.

**Enclosure Acts:**   In Europe, Africa, Asia, Latin America, and elsewhere, the land of serfs and common lands were enclosed by the nobility in order to change to commercial farming (e.g., sheep, wheat, sugar, tea, coffee, bananas, cocaine, wine grapes, and beef cattle). Serfs and peasants were forced off the land and into towns and cities where they had to sell their labor power to whoever would hire them. Some of their children turned to petty crime, prostitution, and domestic service. Others migrated to the Americas, Australia, or New Zealand to take by force the land from hunting and gathering peoples. Enclosures produced new ways of social life and a whole new set of problems never before seen in human history. Prior to enclosure acts, property ownership was related to title or to one's control of land by force. Enclosure acts further legitimized the power of the nobility to regulate commerce at the expense of the peasantry. See "Farming, Modern" for more.

**Encoding:**   The process of assigning meaning to a particular sign or a particular sign system. For example: the phrase "the mentally ill" is a sign. It can be interpreted (i.e., encoded) in one of several ways. In the language of psychiatric medicine such a person is often understood as "in need of treatment," or "diseased." In the language of mental health consumerism such a person is often defined as "differently abled," or as "a user of psychiatric services." Depending upon the code through which one intends to convey meaning, a particular encoded regard for the sign "the mentally ill" will result. See "Semiotics" for more.

**End of Ideology:**   The thesis that all the political questions of a good society have been worked out and all that remains is to set up the technical means by which to handle social problems. This view tends to freeze society in one historical moment and preempts all future history while eliminating human beings from the production of political culture. The thesis was developed by Daniel Bell, a liberal theorist. With the collapse of bureaucratic socialism, many in the West believe that all economic history has ended and that all that is left to do is to extend capitalism to other parts of the world. Chaos/Complexity theory teaches us that history never ends; that is, it never repeats itself with the precision required by "modern" science.

**Endogamy:**   A marriage norm that restricts marriage partners to those in the same ethnic group. Most forms of intimacy occur within the same class, race, ethnic, or religious groupings. The current trend, however, is to more open marriage/intimacy norms. Cf. "Exogamy."

**Engels, Friedrich (1820–1895):**   A wealthy German industrialist and a friend and colleague of Karl Marx. Together Engels and Marx wrote the *Communist Manifesto*. Born to manufacturing wealth, Engels first entered the military but resigned the next year. He used his wealth to help the working-class movement and, over the years, became an economist, historian, philosopher, and revolutionary. He gave the Marx family considerable financial help and took responsibility for the natural child of a maid fathered by Marx. After Marx's death, Engels continued the struggle for social justice. He is credited with collaboration on *The Holy Family*, the *German Ideology*, *Anti-Dühring*, and *Origin of the Family*, among other of Marx's works. (See the work of W. L. Reese.)

**Enlightenment, The:**   A period in eighteenth century Europe characterized by a faith in the ability of science to enlighten human beings by the discovery of all the laws of nature and society. It used a slogan from Immanuel Kant, "Dare to know," and inspired the works of Locke, Racine, Molière, Bach, and Rembrandt. It remains the center point of the modern science knowledge process, pushing aside both premodern and postmodern knowledge processes. Hegel and many others assumed that precise knowledge about nature and society was possible, that rational, linear methodology was essential to the discovery of such laws, and that such rationality would be found in the state guided by scientists. The God concept was reduced to that of a creative and indifferent watchmaker who used very precise tools to build the cosmos but no longer interfered in it.

The premodern critique is that faith, belief, trust, hope, and inspiration were foundational to the knowledge process and that a divine spirit still watches, judges, and intervenes in order to reward and punish. The postmodern critique is that rationality and linearity are greatly overused and that human beings pick and choose the problems to research, the concepts to sort with, the findings to apply, and the truths to turn into public policy. All this and more makes the knowledge process more political than enlightening.

**Entelechy:**   Greek: *en* = in, inside; *telos* = actuality, reality; *enchein* = to have, to hold. The word refers to the Aristotelian idea that inside a thing is the tendency to realize its complete and perfect nature. An axiom of modern, rationalist phenomenology, it assumes that social categories are natural and that there is a tendency for each to change in such a direction so as to achieve perfection. The idea that there is some natural destiny toward which all persons, things, and societies tend.

This view can be contrasted with the humanist belief that human beings increasingly have choices to make about how best to organize family, religious, economic, and political life. In humanistic thought nothing at all is pre-decided. See "Phenomenology" and "Phenomenology, Postmodern" for more.

**Entrepreneur:**   One who seizes opportunities as they come along. In capitalism, an entrepreneur is one who invests capital and hires workers to create a new product or service.

**Entropy:**   Disorder, random arrangement, probability, noise, or chaos. There are a lot of ways to refer to entropy, depending upon the phenomena studied. The term, however, simply means that nothing has any relationship to anything else. In sociology, a mass society embodies the sense of unrelatedness specified by the term. Social relationships are fragmented; solidarity is low; and each is alone or in small groups with his/her own problems of survival.

**Epicureanism:**   A school of social philosophy founded in Athens in the year 306 B.C. by Epicurus. The school stressed the atomic theory of matter, direct empirical observation as the source of knowledge, and trust in one's senses to judge facts. It laid the groundwork for modern philosophies of science and social policy. Souls and minds are seen as swiftly moving atoms; perception is possible by grasping the outline (*eidola*) of complex bodies. Epicurus taught that there must be a God since we are receiving outlines of the divine all the time, especially in dreams. The goal of life, he taught, was happiness as much as knowledge. (Happiness is *ataraxia,* or a state of pleasure enjoyed in tranquillity.) Prudence is a guide for happiness: "We cannot live in pleasure without living wisely and nobly and righteously." In popular culture, Epicureanism means a life of indulgence and often carries negative content.

**Epiphenomena:**   Greek: *epi* = side; *phainomenon* = appearance. The idea that some features of a thing observed are accidental or trivial and can be safely ignored. There is an epistemological trick here that allows one to set a category or establish a truth by conveniently ignoring that which does not fit. For example, in Boyle's Law, the actual behavior of billions of gas molecules is set aside for an average value of temperature, pressure, and volume. This allows one to derive precise predictions although the actual behavior of such molecules is unpredictable.

In behaviorist psychology, the mind is said to be an epiphenomena, and thus drives, motives, needs, desires, anxieties, expectations, obligations, duties, norms, values, opinions, and other mental factors and processes are set aside when explaining human behavior.

**Epistemological Category:**    An idea or thought category that has no facticity or realness in and of itself. Chaos/Complexity theory teaches us that there is a deep and often loose connection between all systems at all levels of system dynamics. To mark boundaries between these connected systems is a political act, which, though convenient, distorts the reality such boundaries propose to clarify.

**Epistemology:**    The study of how reliable knowledge is possible. Premodernists claim that only an intellect such as that of a God can know everything. Modernists claim that the world is fully knowable. Postmodernists claim that although much can be known, there remain uncertainties and surprises that are beyond the scope of the most powerful theory or research technology. Chaos theory provides a grounding for the latter view.

The Marxist position is that human knowledge is actively created by human beings engaged in producing culture. In such a process, humans reify epistemological categories (categories of thought) into ontological categories (categories of really existing things). According to Marx, self, social relations, social institutions, and other cultural facts are known (reliably) in the act of creating them by intending, trusting, insightful humans. This view differs from the position that knowledge about nature and society is completely independent of human consciousness and interaction. This is one of the most interesting and challenging parts of the politics of science.

Feminists also critique the constitution of knowledge. They argue that all sense-making claims are saturated within a masculine logic. This logic excludes, marginalizes, or otherwise silences women's ways of knowing. Thus, all (male-centered) epistemology must be carefully examined and deconstructed. All hidden gender biases in the knowledge process must be exposed and then reconstituted consistent with multiple feminine epistemological standpoints. See "Phallogocentrism" and "Philosophy, The Discipline of" for more.

**EPM:**    *The Economic and Philosophic Manuscripts of 1844.* They contain much of the humanist/democratic thrust of Karl Marx's work. They were rediscovered and published only in 1932. By 1932, social and cultural factors worked to establish Marxism as merely a dogmatic, economic, and materialist doctrine. EPM created a revolution in Marxism that infused it with a humanism and concern for the individual as an active/potential creator of a decent society. This polemic of Marxist humanism continues to be the central point at dispute between the "structuralist" and the "praxis" wings of Marxism.

**Epoché:** Greek: to suspend judgment. Pyrrho used the word as a solution to the problem of knowledge: One simply suspended judgment and found *ataraxia* (pleasure/tranquillity). Edmund Husserl used it in his modernist phenomenology in order to engage in the process of reducing understanding of a thing to its essence. He called this process eidetic reduction.

**Equilibrium Conditions:** In modernist approaches to science, reason, knowledge, and truth, there is a search for essential stability, order, permanence, certainty. This modernist search produces equilibrium conditions, closure, and stasis. According to postmodernists, equilibrium conditions give the illusion of complete understanding in which the subject (the individual) is in total control of what happens. Equilibrium conditions are said to be illusory because this condition ignores the more messy, fragmented, and incomprehensible dimensions of human existence. Cf. "Far-From-Equilibrium Conditions."

**Equity:** Latin: equality. In English law, that part of law that sought substantive justice more so than technical judgments. It began as an appeal to the king for justice. Usually advised by a priest, the king set aside rational but unfair judgments in favor of a higher form of justice. Equity in U.S. law places the responsibility for higher justice in appellate courts, but juries can refuse to follow a judge's instructions in the interest of such justice through "jury nullification."

**Equity, Maxims of:** There are many maxims that inform the quest for social justice. Among the more memorable and useful are: (1) Equity will not suffer a wrong without a remedy. (2) Equity follows the law unless there is good reason not to. (3) Equity looks at intent rather than form. (4) Prior equity takes precedent over other equities. (5) S/he who seeks equity must do equity. (6) S/he who seeks equity must come with clean hands. (7) Equity does not assist inequity.

**Equivalence Principle:** A logic derived from the commodity exchange and commodity fetishism principles as developed by Karl Marx. The equivalence principle posits that commodities are artificially equated and that these ratios mask and conceal the intrinsic value of each (e.g., a pound of butter = a basket of apples). The "value" for each is more fundamentally related to the labor invested to produce the commodities and the emotional investment the laborer places in their production. See "Marx, Karl" for more.

**Erotic/Eroticism:** Greek: *eros* = love. Today, any art, music, or literature that facilitates mutually rewarding and enjoyable sexual relationships. Erotic art is fulfilling to the human project when it is used to affirm sensuality and sexual passion expressed in a mutually rewarding and enjoyable relationship. Cf. "Pornography."

**Eschatology:**   Greek: *eschatos* = last things; *logos* = study of. A Jewish and early Christian theology that held that God would send another savior at the end of 1000 years. At that time, there would be a last judgment, and people would either be saved or condemned to one of the circles of hell. More optimistic views of these last things include a time of peace and social justice for all. See "Millennium" for more.

**Essentialism:**   This concept is particularly relevant for postmodern feminism. Essentialism refers to the possibility of establishing a feminine voice and way of knowing free from masculine understandings of the world. French postmodern feminists have termed this an *ecriture feminine*. The philosophical works of Luce Irigaray and Julia Kristeva, for example, have been especially helpful in describing the significance of this grammar and also the problems associated with it. Briefly, the tension is as follows. On the one hand, identifying how women experience and come to know the world around them requires a reliance on language. Clearly, it is important to develop a code through which this knowledge can be voiced and disseminated. This language would necessarily (essentially) exist in the absence of the masculine/androcentric standard, otherwise it would not embody the essential identities of women. On the other hand, this very activity of singling out one, unifying, and totalizing voice to represent the collective conscience of diverse women is itself how "malespeak" functions. Thus, the dilemma of establishing a replacement grammar that is simultaneously for, by, and about women must not proceed in an essentialistic (masculine) way. How to do this remains a challenge for postmodern feminists. See "Androcentricism" and "*Ecriture feminine*" for more. Cf. "Gilligan, Carol", "Irigaray, Luce," and "Kristeva, Julia" for more.

**Estate System:**   Estate = standing; social honor. A system of stratification in which one group owns the land and other groups must give both labor and harvest to them. The feudal system had four estates.

**Ethics:**   Greek: *ethikos* = custom or usage. In philosophy, the study of that which is right and good to do. One can talk about a set of rules with which to guide behavior or about the larger human interests that guide the selection of these rules. Premodern philosophies tend to use the Word of God (as interpreted by a priesthood) as the source of ethical behavior. Christians tend to argue that one should do unto others what one would have them do unto oneself. Modern utilitarians argue that the greatest good for the greatest number of people sets the stage for the determination of ethical behavior. Immanuel Kant argued that the moral imperative is that which one should do as a universal law. Nihilist postmodern thought argues that all ethics serve special interests and cannot be universalized. Affirmative postmodern thought tends to accept that there are transcendent rules for all human behavior across all societies but that these have to be flexible and often accommodating to contradictory lines of behavior. This flexibility and accommodation raises major questions for all good and decent people to ask and answer in their own lives. See "Philosophy, The Discipline of" for more.

**Ethnic:**   (1) The social and cultural traits of immigrants (and possibly their descendants) to the United States. The word is often associated with lower-middle class and upper-lower class persons who are generally Catholic descendants of immigrants from southern and eastern Europe, plus many of Irish descent. Those Italian-Americans who are discernibly of Italian descent are, for example, an ethnic group. (2) That cultural complex that makes a group unique in history irrespective of biological heritage. Often confused with race.

**Ethnicity:**   A person's discernible ethnic background. Not necessarily the same as nationality. There are some 3,000 to 4,000 discernible cultural/ethnic orientations. Today the political question is how to honor such diversity without the hierarchy or exploitation so often seen. A second political question is whether ethnicity is biologically or culturally determined. Most Marxists hold that one's ethnic background is a cultural rather than a biological fact.

**Ethnocentrism:**   The belief that the values, practices, and general social setup of one's own native culture are superior to all others. This view tends to justify exploitation by more militant societies. See "Anti-Semitism" for more. Cf. "Cultural Relativism."

**Ethnomethodology:**   Literally, folk methods: The study of the folk methods used to construct social reality. According to Harold Garfinkel, just as grammar deals with the rules with which language is used to create meaning, ethnomethodology attempts to clarify the rules of social interaction used to create meaning by interacting people. Ethnomethodological research stands in contrast to that which holds that the regularities found in human behavior arise from genes, instincts, physiology, or purely psychological processes.

**Ethos:**   The special character of a society. "To be French means one thing, to be German another, and to be American means scarcely anything at all." As a society becomes a mass society, it loses the capacity to create culture and thereby loses any special character.

**Euclid/Euclidean Geometry:**   Euclid (third century B.C.) was a Greek mathematician and the founder of Euclidean geometry, which specified three dimensions and clear boundaries as well as precise mathematical relationships between these aspects of space and the things within it. For three centuries Euclidean algebra was taught as the major pathway to understand the features of real objects or systems. It was thought that all non-Euclidean geometries were merely imaginary games. Today there is considerable evidence that nature does not fit Euclidean geometry. B. Mandelbrot developed his fractal geometry of nature and developed a method to quantify fractal forms. String theory in physics suggests there may be as many as twenty-six dimensions in nature. Postmodern philosophers of science say that such dimensions are a feature of our ways of looking at nature and society.

**Eugenics:**   A term coined by Sir Francis Galton in 1883. Eugenics is the science (and art) of perfecting a certain species (including the human species) based on principles of genetics and inheritance. The scientific aim of eugenics is to achieve a desirable combination of physical and mental traits in the offspring of a given species.

Eugenics came under considerable disrepute during the 1930s, particularly in Adolph Hitler's Nazi Germany. Hitler was keenly interested in creating a "master Aryan race" and relied on eugenics as a scientific justification to exterminate millions of Jewish people throughout Europe. Today, eugenics is linked to cloning, test-tube babies, and genome research. The scientific community is criticized for manufacturing "ideal" life-forms. In the case of artificial insemination, a couple that is unable to conceive on its own can select what kind of surrogate will match their physical and mental trait needs for a "perfect" child. Further criticism of eugenics is linked to the possible termination of life for persons who do not measure up to these ideal life-forms. Persons with physical and mental disabilities, the elderly, and others braving life-altering disease raise staunch resistance to the widespread practice of eugenics. See "Social Darwinism" for more.

**Evil:**   Anglo-Saxon: *yel* = the opposite and opponent of good. In many religions evil is an equal force at war with good. In Buddhism, evil comes from desire; the solution to evil is to eliminate desire for wealth, status, and power. Martin Luther King located evil in class and racist structures, as do most people in liberation theology. The postmodern view is that evil is a human category/label and is a product of social relations.

**Evolution, Organic:**   A theory and body of facts that supports the idea that living organisms evolved from the simple to the complex via competition, a struggle for survival, survival of the fittest, and chance changes in genetic patterns, making survival for some more likely. Charles Darwin is credited with the first systematic statement and extensive research to support the theory. There are many skips, jumps, twists, and reversals in plant, animal, and human evolution that lead some to suppose a God created each species and continues to create new species. A revision of Darwin called "punctuated equilibrium" explains these jumps empirically rather than theologically. More generally, Chaos theory can be used to explain many of these sudden, inexplicable changes; this does not mean that all miracles and mysteries can be explained scientifically; there is always room for doubt, wonder, and poetic genius. See "Darwin, Charles" for more.

**Evolution, Social:**   Generally, a view that society is changing for the better as a consequence of the struggle for survival in which the best (fittest) social forms survive. There are many well-known generalizations about the direction of evolution. These include the transition from religious to scientific societies (Auguste Comte); of social relations from status to contract (Sir Henry Maine); of human bonds from mechanical to organic solidarity (Émile Durkheim); the transition from traditional to legal-rational authority (Max Weber); from sacred to secular social life (Howard Becker); from community to society (Frederich Tonnies); from the simple to the complex (Herbert Spencer); and from trial and error in social evolution to scientific self-control of society (Ward). There is little evidence that things are getting better and certainly no assurance that things get better all by themselves. See "Social Darwinism" for more. Cf. "Creationism."

**Exchange Rate:**   Every country in the world has its own kind of money: in the United States, dollars; in Japan, yen. When companies from different countries trade with each other, they expect to be paid in their own country's currency. Weyerhauser Corporation does not particularly want to receive yen for the sale of its logs in Japan. Lumberjacks in Oregon have to be paid in dollars; yen would not do them much good. Thus, international bankers are constantly exchanging one country's money for another's. The rate at which they are traded is called the exchange rate. When the number of yen that $1 will buy falls, the dollar is not worth as much as it once was. This means that imports from Japan are now more expensive, whereas exports from the United States are cheaper. The United States used to be in a favored position in the exchange process, but other capitalist countries forced a new method of exchange. This added to the fiscal crisis in the United States, since profits fall even as production increases.

**Exchange-Ratio:**   See "Capital Logic," "Commodity Fetishism," and "Marx, Karl."

**Exchange-Value:** See "Value (Exchange-)."

**Exclusionary Rule:**   Refers to evidence that cannot be used and is inadmissible at the trial of a defendant. A legal term that considers the ways in which evidence against a person was collected. The Fourth Amendment to the U.S. Constitution forbids illegal seizures and searches and provides that people are to be secure in their homes from the state.

**Existentialism:**   Founded by Søren Kierkegaard (1813–1855). Existentialism sees people in a state of profound tension, always haunted by a sense of sin and their betrayal of their God. The outlook is pessimistic: At best individuals can come to terms with their God, and failing that, they lose God and face *le Neant*: nothingness. Modern existentialism (after Jean-Paul Sartre) connects human anguish to a poorly designed social lifeworld but retains an interest in the intense personal struggle of (wo)man (an element structuralists often neglect in a one-sided concentration on class and political struggle). However, structuralists charge existentialists with giving too much freedom and personal responsibility to one's fate. Cf. "Beauvoir, Simone de" and "Sartre, Jean-Paul." See "Freedom" for more.

**Exogamy:**   Greek: *exo* = out, outside; *gamy* = mate, mating. A social norm that requires that one marry or mate outside one's clan, tribe, or sib. Cf. "Endogamy."

**Expansion:**   Firms produce only in order to make money. In periods of prosperity, when it is easy for them to do just that, the economy expands; firms hire more workers because it is a profitable thing to do. More people in jobs means that more is produced; if all the increased product is sold, more income is generated. Expansion means that output, income, and sales are growing. During periods of extended expansion the bargaining power of labor rises because jobs are not so scarce. But, as capital-intensive production increases, fewer workers are needed and expansion slows down, since demand drops. Then, too, workers do not get paid 100 percent of the exchange-value since they earn only the value of their labor (which can be low, given an army of surplus workers). The state often intervenes with deficit spending to renew the expansion cycle. As long as capitalism can expand with new products or new markets it can survive. However, expansion means using up natural resources faster (e.g., water, land, minerals). See "Depression," "Keynesian Economics," and "Kondratieff Cycles" for more.

**Exploitation:**   This term refers to (1) the process by which wealth is taken from the people who produce it and (2) the more general process by which the capacity to produce culture is impaired by claims of private ownership of the means to produce both material wealth and culture. An example of the first concept is farm workers who do not get enough capital when working for Del Monte. An example of the second concept is the use of mass media to merchandise commodities instead of relying on public discourse.

**Exploitation, Super:**   Wages below the level for the reproduction of labor power. Each set of workers needs enough to reproduce itself; that is, to get ready to work the next day, week, and year. The amount of work needed to do this is called "necessary labor." See "Labor, Surplus," "Necessary Labor," and "Rent" for more.

**Expropriation:**   Socialist economic theory holds that most rich people get rich by expropriating the surplus value of the labor of the working class. This means they take the wealth that is produced by one class and use it to support a nice lifestyle for another class. Both force and ideologies are used to justify expropriation. There are three ways to expropriate: interest, rent, and dividends. Sometimes corporations fix prices or bribe politicians to increase the rate of expropriation. Marx argued that the expropriators must be expropriated. Cubans expropriated the land and factories that were abandoned after the 1959 revolution; Sandinistas expropriated the farms and firms left when the bourgeoisie fled to Brazil and Miami after the 1979 revolution. Sometimes liberal states expropriate wealth via taxation. Criminals expropriate through force or fraud. White-collar criminals steal from corporations using the knowledge they have to take bribes. See "Corporate Crime" for more.

**Externalization:**   The process by which humans attribute their essential properties to a God through worship or attribute their hopes and dreams to another person through charisma. At the same time, the evils (faults) in a social system are denied by projecting them on to a devil, witch, or scapegoat.

# F

**Fabianism:** A socialist movement advocating a slow, peaceful, and parliamentary road to socialism. It was founded in England in 1884 and gets its name from the Fabian Society (after a cautious Roman general, Quintus Fabius). Its most famous members are George Bernard Shaw, Sidney and Beatrice Webb, G.D.H. Cole, and H. G. Wells. The society founded the London School of Economics and helped found the Labour Party. The Labour party looked beyond the immediate wage/work process interests of workers to help institute many social justice programs: free education, health care, housing allowances, and pensions for all citizens.

**Face Rights:** The right of a person to enter into the construction of a given social occasion. Sometimes a ticket gives face rights; sometimes a complicated rite of passage is required. In mass societies face rights are obliterated as impersonal routines are instituted.

**Facticity:** The degree to which a given social event is real. Facticity of social phenomena (and perhaps physical events also) varies from 0 to 1; from sheer fantasy to hard, palpable thingness. The facticity of an event depends upon a number of factors, chief among which is the adequacy of the reification process. Social occasions are assembled and dismantled routinely in everyday life, and so the facticity of social reality varies.

**Factors in Production:** Land, labor, and capital goods, sometimes entrepreneurship. In capitalist economics, each factor is entitled to its share: rent for land; wages/salaries for workers; interest and dividends for capital; and royalties/fees for entrepreneurs. Socialists regard labor as the sole creator of wealth; these categories are seen to be inventions to justify expropriation. Capital is thus wealth created by previous workers; land is a gift of nature that does not have value until worked by labor.

**Faith:** Latin: *fidere* = to trust. In religion, faith involves a commitment to the God figure. Further, this concept is often used to denote a particular set of beliefs (e.g., one is a member of a "faith"). This second meaning is often used in modern thought to dismiss the importance of spiritual and religious sensibility that underlies all symbolic interaction and all group behavior, irrespective of other beliefs.

Most hold that reason and faith are incompatible. Modern philosophy of knowledge sets faith aside in favor of reason and logic as a means for determining that which should be believed. Postmodern theologians and social psychologists see faith as one of the many social psychological capacities central to the process by which affirmative social relations and social facts are constituted. Faith, hope, belief, and suspension of doubt are all necessary to such social constructions.

**Faith, Social Psychology of:**   One of the basic social psychological capacities developed in premodern knowledge processes and inculcated in early childhood. The capacity to believe, to trust, and to have faith in things unseen is basic to all self-fulfilling prophecies by which social realities are constructed.

**Fallacies (of Thinking):**   Latin: *fallacia* = trick, deceit, fraud. Those who place logic at the center of the truth process also raise logical fallacies to the center of the falsification process: if illogical, then wrong. In both premodern and postmodern knowledge processes, inconsistent and illogical truth claims can be valid insofar as (1) faith, hope, belief, and trust are involved in the construction of social life (see "Self-Fulfilling Prophecy" for more) and (2) insofar as complex dynamical regimes produce nonlinear behavior of natural and social systems (see "Chaos Theory" for more).

However, there remain many tricks of speech and thought used to deceive and to defraud people; it is worth learning about these:

1.  The Fallacy of Amphiboly: the use of words in such a way that more than one interpretation is possible, as in: I'll pay you *soon*. The word, soon, has many interpretations; it could mean later today, next week, or next month.
2.  The Fallacy of Accent: the practice of shifting the emphasis of a key word to render it trivial during an argument in order to win the argument. I am a *good* teacher (Dr. Smith is a poor teacher, I am better than he; therefore I am a good teacher). The meaning of "good" shifts from an absolute quality referring to all teachers to a particular quality referring to a conveniently low standard of teaching.
3.  The Fallacy of Equivocation: selection of a different meaning of the same word in order to confuse an opponent: Think of the word "bad" and how many different meanings it offers in a argument.
4.  The Fallacy of Composition: the practice of attributing the property of a part to the whole, as in: She got a *bad grade*; therefore she is a *bad student*. (Some people who get bad grades may well be

poor students, but one might be a good student and have been ill, have had to work during the review session, or have been verbally abused by the teacher at some time during the test.)

5. The Fallacy of Division: the practice of attributing the property of the whole to that of all its parts: Blue people average higher scores on IQ tests than Green people; I am Blue; therefore I am smarter and more deserving than all Green people.

6. The Fallacy of Slanting: the use of positive or negative words to win an argument, as in: Men are assertive; women are pushy.

7. The Fallacy of Reification: the practice of treating something variable and complex as if it were one and only one kind of reality: All workers are lazy; all women are passive; all politicians are crooked; all lawyers are dishonest.

8. The Fallacy of Personification: the practice of treating an inanimate thing or animal as if it were a human being, as in: "Don't Mess with Mother Nature"; or, "I Love My Jaguar."

9. Appeal to Force: the use of force or bribery to persuade, as in: Vote the way I say, and all my top employees will donate to your campaign fund.

10. Poisoning the Well: the use of a minor fault or flaw of a person to discredit the argument on a different issue, as in: Detective Smith is a racist; therefore my client is innocent.

11. Appeal to Pity, Mercy, Compassion: He is a war hero; therefore we should elect him Senator.

12. Appeal from Authority (*ipse dixit*): Johnny Cash drinks Folger's coffee; therefore you should drink Folger's.

13. Appeal from Association (*post hoc ergo propter hoc*): the use of a false cause to justify one's action, as in: the children of teenage mothers get welfare; therefore to prevent teenage pregnancy, we should deny these children welfare.

14. Stacking the Deck: the practice of putting the answer in the question, as in: When will you give up your evil ways? It presupposes that one's ways are indeed evil and by definition should be given up.

15. Binary Logic (thinking in "black and white"): the practice of giving only two alternatives to a complex question that might call for an entirely new option, as in: Either you are a communist or you are a loyal American.

16. Argument from Ignorance: the practice of using that which is not known to prove that something else must therefore be true, as in: God must exist since no one can prove S/he doesn't exist.

17. Hasty (Over) Generalization: the practice of making a conclusion based upon inadequate observation: No one has ever climbed this mountain; therefore no one will ever climb this mountain.

18. Argument from Analogy: the use of the attributes on one thing to explain the working of another thing, as in: All life is jungle warfare; eat or be eaten; or: All life is a game; there are winners and losers; or: A factory is a complex machine; workers are merely exchangeable parts.

19. The Fallacy of the Undistributed Middle Term: One changes the first term in a logical argument to make it the middle term and then distributes it incorrectly, as in: All dogs are mammals; all cats are mammals; therefore all dogs are cats. It should be: All female animals with breast milk are mammals; dog and cat females have breast milk; therefore dogs and cats are mammals.

20. The Fallacy of the Middle Term: the use of a hidden fourth term to generate a faulty final term, as in: The end of all life is to achieve perfection; death is the end of all life; therefore death is the final perfection. Notice the ambiguity of the word "end"; it was used in the first term to mean "objective"; it was changed in the middle term to mean "termination." But you knew that.

21. The Fallacy of the Major Term: the practice of using the first term in a way that goes beyond its reach, as in: All good students get good grades; no bad students get good grades; he got a bad grade; therefore he is a bad student. See number 4 above.

22. Circular Argument (vicious circle; begging the question; catch 22; *petitio principii*): He must be guilty, since he is in prison (being in prison is used as proof of guilt). He must be deserving, since he has been rewarded with great wealth (being rewarded is used as proof of merit of reward).

23. The Fallacy of the Minor Term: the practice of relating the last term in an argument to the first term in a way that goes beyond the premise of the major term, as in: All fraternity men drink too much; all fraternity men are in college; therefore all college men drink too much.

24. The Fallacy of Denying the Antecedent: the practice of denying the minor term in order to deny the major term, as in: When it rains, all streets get wet; it has not rained; therefore the streets are not wet. You know that there are other reasons streets could be wet; the fact that they are wet does not invalidate the assumption in the first (major term).

25. The Fallacy of Logical Thought: the practice of using logic to judge behavior of complex systems: All major terms may be valid, and all due respect may be given to sound reasoning, but still some minor terms might be contrary to the major term. A small change in tax rates may produce a big and unpredictable change in corporate crime; a big change in poverty may produce a small change in crime. In nonlinear dynamics, all rational connections are contingent upon dynamical regime and upon region in an

outcome basin, so logic and rational thinking lose their ability to serve the knowledge process.

(See the work of W. L. Reese.) See "Logic, Syllogistic" and "Non sequitur" for more.

**False Consciousness:** The inability to identify and act in one's own interest. Marx's assumption was that the class controlling the means of production controlled the production of ideas. The ruling class produces ideas that justify its own existence. Because they are powerless, the subjugated class readily embraces this set of false ideas about what is and what must be. Thus, they embrace as true and necessary their own subjugation. See "Mystification" for more.

**Family:** A social form in which several important human services/needs are met: intimacy, discipline, affection, and the reproduction of labor power. In a family system of reproducing labor power, one generation provides a new generation with all the food, shelter, clothing, health care, socialization, and recreation required to turn them into decent human beings. There are other ways to reproduce labor. Costs could be charged to the firms that benefit from the production of labor power, but that would severely limit profits. There have been some 3000 to 4000 different family forms in human history; the patriarchal nuclear family is but one. See "Marriage" for more.

**Family, Disorganization of:** There are several factors in capitalism that tend to disorganize families: (1) the capitalist philosophy of individualism and self-interest; (2) the conversion of social relationships into cash commodity; (3) the need for cheap labor; (4) the use of the family as an instrument to reproduce the labor force; (5) the use of the spouse as an unpaid worker; (6) the use of advertising to turn children into demanding consumers; (7) the division of labor into paid male work and unpaid women's work; (8) the destruction of the family as a productive unit; (9) the conversion of the family as a productive unit into a unit of consumption; and (10) the inability of parents to socialize children as the state controls the educational process and converts it from moral to technical training. Then, too, advanced (semi-) monopoly capitalism moves workers and capital around the world to take advantage of short-term profit opportunity. This tends to destroy the family system, as men migrate in search of work and as whole communities deteriorate when capitalists move jobs to cheap labor states and countries.

**Family, Extended:** A family system in which three or more generations have intensive social rights and obligations. Often two or more generations work and live together. Extended families are disappearing. See "Family, Disorganization of " for more.

A type of family organization often found in traditional or folk societies in which several generations and a broad collection of blood- and marriage-related kin live together in a single dwelling or a close collection of dwellings. In recent times, a "family" is often a collectivity of unrelated persons who take brother/sisterhood seriously. Types of family organization have exploded in the past fifty years.

The critical position draws attention to capitalism. Capitalism can erode the ability of people to live in extended families, and market considerations can force people to migrate, looking for jobs and/or safe haven. Commodification and materialism also impact social relationships in the family since people may not want to share with children, brothers, parents, or other kin. See "Dinks," "Monks," "Swinks," and "Yuppies" for more.

**Family Violence:**   In radical family theory, family violence has several major sources: patriarchy, bureaucracy, and/or capitalism. Each stratifies power. In patriarchy, men are given the moral right to beat women and children into compliance. In capitalism and/or bureaucratic socialism, those men who have been socialized to patriarchy have no social realm in which to exercise their "masculinity" other than in the home and/or fights and brawls in bars and sports events. When things go badly at work, some males resort to violence within the family.

**Far-From-Equilibrium Conditions:**   The opposite of equilibrium conditions. In Chaos theory, the more natural state in which a system behaves is through orderly disorder or nonlinear dynamics. In other words, order, predictability, stasis, control, precision, and so on are some aspects of human social interaction and system behavior. However, there are also random, spontaneous, serendipitous, and uncertain conditions that need to be accounted for in understanding the activity of people and the evolution of events. Far-from-equilibrium conditions account for the mixture of predictable unpredictability. Far-from-equilibrium conditions present an openness and responsiveness to the more irregular, unexplainable, inconsistent facets of social life. See "Chaos Theory" and "Dissipative Structure" for more. Cf. "Equilibrium Conditions."

**Farming, Modern:**   Modern farming is a high-tech, capital-intensive system of food production. Free farmers (peasants) are replaced by hired labor—often migrants—while monoculture replaces the biologically diverse ecology of small farming. New technologies are replacing these giant farms: hydroponics (plants grown in a greenhouse and placed in a liquid bath); genetic engineering (genes from one plant or animal put inside the seed or eggs of another); and synthetic foods (foods made directly out of chemicals in a factory). All these changes eliminate the family farm, the small towns that serve them, and a way of life in which people grow their own food. See "Enclosure Acts" and "Peasant" for more.

**Fascism:**    Latin: *fascis* = bundle. A bundle of rods (signifying unity of the people) was a symbol of the authority of Roman magistrates. It now refers to a form of government in which state power is used to reproduce elite privilege based upon class, race, religious, or ethnic inequality. It is marked by nationalism, authoritarianism, totalitarianism, and militarism. The fascist state has two main activities: suppression of dissent at home (usually by force and propaganda), and exploitation of minorities or other countries to ensure loyalty from the masses at home. Usually based in the small business strata and supported by the underclass in its desperation, fascism gathers into its hands the entire state apparatus (e.g., the army, universities, schools, the press, networks, and worker organizations). Although workers, small business, and the surplus population expect to benefit from state power (and thus support fascism), big business typically thrives by increasing its share of surplus value. In this scenario, inflation runs wild as the state tries to maintain legitimacy either by coercion or by appeals to patriotism and nationalism. Deficit spending has been used extensively in the late twentieth century to preserve legitimacy.

Germany, Italy, and Spain were the first modern states to try fascism. As Leon Trotsky once proclaimed: "Out of human dust, fascism unites and arms the scattered masses. It gives the petty bourgeois the illusion of an independent force. It begins to imagine it will really command the state." See "Authoritarianism," "Corporativism," "Government, Forms of," "Mussolini, Benito," and "Police State" for more.

**Fascism, Techno-:**    The use of computers and other electronic devices to monitor the behavior of workers, customers, voters, students, and petty criminals. These range from software that counts the number/time/topics of employees who use the computer, to electronic "dogs" that sniff out all sorts of forbidden chemicals. Soon every automobile will come with a chip so that police can monitor speed and location and fix their own location via communication satellites. See "Social Control" for more.

**Federal Bureau of Investigation (FBI):**    The FBI is a federal police force. It deals with crimes of high visibility and with those crimes that tend to target the rich and powerful (e.g., bank robberies, kidnapping, rebellion, and revolution). In the 1960s, the FBI ran five "Cointel" (counterintelligence) programs: antiwar, antisocialist, antifeminist, anti-civil rights, and antistudent power movements were targeted. Their leaders were arrested, and their members were illegally harassed. Martin Luther King was a particular target. Under its first and long-time director, J. Edgar Hoover, the FBI ran many illegal operations against socialists, feminists, workers, and civil rights workers (e.g., burglary, wiretapping, anonymous letters to family and newspapers, as well as the spotting of leaders for "Red Squads" and "Swat Teams" of local police who then used violence to destabilize progressive politics). Of late, under new directors, it is less racist, sexist, and class biased. Recently it hired 500 more agents to work on corporate and white-collar crime.

**Feedback:**  In the new science of chaos, feedback loops replace the notion of causality. There are three kinds of feedback loops most important to a postmodern philosophy of science. The first is *positive feedback,* which tends to expand the boundaries of a system until it is so open that one can no longer discern boundary. For example, think of the screech on a sound system in which two microphones feed sound back and forth to each other. The second is *negative feedback,* which tends to eliminate the system. For example, if pain were a feedback response every time one made a racist comment, sooner or later one would stop. The third kind of feedback is *nonlinear;* it is important since structure can be maintained (stabilized) in a changing environment. Nonlinear feedback alternates between positive and negative without any clear pattern. For example, in social terms, mercy, compassion, love, and forgiveness are nonlinear feedback loops. These contrast with rational applications of sanctions for norm violations or crimes. Cf. "Feedback."

**Fem-Crits:**  A group of feminist-inspired scholars drawing upon insights from psychoanalysis, philosophy, anthropology, history, political theory, postmodernism, and literary criticism, as well as their own life experiences. Fem-crits primarily challenge the ideology of patriarchy as underscoring the existence and identity of women. According to fem-crits, girls are socialized through a masculine way of understanding, and, thus, our knowledge of the feminine is limited by the cultural expectations and experiences of the masculine. Fem-crits argue that patriarchy is infused into our legal codes and statutes; our understanding of work and leisure; our notion of the body, sexuality, and identity; and our political economic system. Fem-crits not only identify where and how patriarchy encodes the reality of women, they seek to change this through constructive theory building, political action, and educational awareness.

**Femininity, Traditional:**  Traditional women view their role in life to center around the family: mother, homemaker, supportive wife, and caregiver to the handicapped and elderly in the extended family. Representing about 85 percent of all women in the United States, these women accept both biblical and scientific statements that these are the natural and indispensable roles special to their gender. Cf. "Feminism, Liberal," "Feminism, Separatist," and "Feminism, Socialist."

**Feminism:**  A movement and an awareness of the cultural sources of gender inequality. According to feminists, the absence of women's liberation and the experience of the continued injustices they confront are fundamentally linked to biology (i.e., the feminine sex).

The movement has many divisions. Several major divisions include: Marxist feminism, separatist feminism, liberal feminism, socialist feminism, postmodern feminism. These contrast to traditional femininity/gendering patterns in which men use four kinds of power to dominate women: social power, moral power, economic power, and, often, physical force. Feminism is opposed to biological interpretations of gender inequality, to most theological justifications, and to structural-functional views that hold that gender division of labor is essential to the functioning of all societies. See each form separately for a more detailed explanation. See "Feminist Theory" and "Subjectivity" for more.

**Feminism, Black:**    The theories pertaining to women who are also people of color. Black feminism emphasizes left-liberal, socialist-feminist, progressive, and critical dimensions in explaining the black woman's struggle in society.

Two broad divisions of black feminism are discernible. The first called for political partnerships and coalition building between women of color and progressive activists groups. This mobilization strategy was identified as the necessary mechanism to change the social condition and plight of black women. The second and more recent trend in black feminism examines the relationship between black women and other women of color in relation to white women. Black feminists contend that white feminists are not equipped to speak meaningfully about the problems of being female and black in society. Indeed, as bell hooks has argued, by metaphorically invoking and appropriating images of suffering black women to advance the plight of ALL women, white feminists have, knowingly or not, re-legitimized the exploitation, victimization, and racism embedded in Western culture and perpetrated against women of color.

Regardless of these divisions, black feminists generally do not subscribe to a "man-hater" philosophy. Women of color need to tell their own stories, speak their own truths, and establish their own contexts through which to engage in the political, social, and economic debates confronting society and affecting black women. See "Critical Race Theory," "Politics," "Truth, Sojourner" for more.

**Feminism, Liberal:**    Liberal feminists (formerly termed "bourgeois" feminists) advocate equal opportunity and equal rights for all women. They demand the right to compete fairly for all jobs and professions, including the top positions in public and private life. This position stands in contrast to traditional gendering patterns in which women are taught to defer to men in all public and most private spheres. Liberal feminism stands in contrast to socialist feminism, which argues for the elimination of class and bureaucracy rather than for equal opportunity to compete in what socialists call "structures of domination." It also contrasts with separatist feminism, which does not want to compete with men but to exclude them from social life. See "Femininity, Traditional," "Feminist Theory," and "Politics" for more.

**Feminism, Marxist:**   For Marxist feminists the critique of a woman's subjugated standing is traced to the sexual division of labor. The gendered economic barriers imposed on women in the division of labor are responsible for their victimization and oppression (i.e., women have economic value only in their capacity to reproduce and/or function as caregivers). In this capacity, women are no more than unpaid laborers. Thus, liberation is a function of economic change.

**Feminism, Postmodern:**   Postmodern feminists incorporate the insights of socialist and Marxist feminists and establish a radical critique. Postmodern feminists draw attention to oppression conveyed through language. In other words, economic and political oppression are not only gendered in construction and effect, they are primordially shaped this way through language (e.g., *his*tory, *man*kind). Postmodern feminists argue that the syntactic construction of words and speech (i.e., discourse) invalidates the voice of and way of knowing for women. It is this languaged reality that is reproduced and re-legitimized through economic, social, and political processes. See "Irigaray, Luce" and "Politics" for more.

**Feminism, Radical:**   A struggle against both capitalism and patriarchy. Central to radical feminism are the assumptions that socialist revolution does not automatically liberate women, that women should not trust men to "liberate" them "after the revolution," and that women should take responsibility for their own liberation. Part of the theory holds that the liberation of women liberates men in the same instance from their sexism.

**Feminism, Separatist:**   Separatist women want to build separate family systems, separate businesses, separate sports and recreation, and separate religious organizations. Separatist feminists argue from the data that men are irreconcilably violent, brutal, demanding, and dominating. Some separatist feminists reproduce role inequality in personal and public relationships; others advocate a much more democratic set of relationships. Separatist feminists constitute about 3 percent of the population. Cf. "Femininity, Traditional."

**Feminism, Socialist:**   Socialist feminists urge the elimination of all forms of inequality (e.g., race, gender, and class). Socialist feminists argue that liberal feminists and their call for equal opportunity to compete only changes the gender of the oppressor, not the oppression. They point out that not only must ownership of the means of production change (Marxist feminism) but so, too, must the social conditions and experiences that give rise to the sustainability of capitalism. Socialist feminists contend that capitalistic economic systems are patriarchal, excluding and dominating women. Thus, socialist feminists are keenly aware of the link between economic and gender oppression in their critique of the social order. Cf. "Femininity, Traditional." See "Feminist Theory" and "Politics" for more.

**Feminist Methodology:**   Feminist methodology has several major differences from modern science methodology. Feminist theory emphasizes "standpoint epistemology." This view holds that each major group in society has its own standpoint from which to understand and act upon social life. This view contrasts with the presumption of objectivity in which modernists assume that the researcher can stand apart from society and history and can make judgments and form theory without any cultural or political bias. Feminist methodology also values storytelling and poetry as sources of insight and understanding, whereas modern science tends to use standardized questions and statistical analysis. Finally, feminist methodology openly supports egalitarian gender relationships and a much wider status-role for women (and men).

**Feminist Standpoint Epistemology:**   A position developed by "second wave" feminists. Standpoint epistemology argues that the knowledge positions or points of view of those subjugated should be privileged as a way of promoting the possibility of greater knowledge for, by, and about those marginalized collectives. In order to better understand the experiences of women, gays, the homeless, juvenile gang members, addicts, and so on, the voices and languages of these groups need to be affirmed. This affirmation will liberate them and, in the process, contribute to an increased awareness of who they are as people and how they are excluded from the conforming culture. See "Womanism" for more.

**Feminist Theory:**   Feminist social theory argues that traditional gender roles are culturally determined and unnecessarily limiting to women. Instead of seeing the sources of gender inequality in biology or physiology, feminists hold that power inequalities reproduce gender inequalities. Feminists hold that patriarchy is a special historical family form, that there have been dozens of other family forms in human history, and that new family forms are emerging all the time, as social, technical, and economic conditions change. Most feminists accept gender divisions but do not want these extended to public office, high status jobs, middle-class professions, or sports. See "Feminism, Liberal," "Feminism, Socialist," and "Womanism" for more.

**Feral:**   It means wild. It refers to a child who has grown up with little or no social interaction (an isolate) and, in particular, to one allegedly raised by animals. This last condition is seldom claimed to have occurred and is not generally believed. Most if not all ferals are simply abandoned and/or grossly neglected children. This experience tends to confirm the importance of culture as the mediator of behavior. The Marxian position is that people create themselves as human beings when they create culture. When they are deprived of the right or power to create culture, they become "feral" at any age.

**Fetishism:**   This concept refers to any pathological interest in an object. People who work within a premodern religious sensibility invest sacred content into trees, mountains, rivers, and stars. In psychology, the word is used to refer to persons who invest erotic content into physical objects rather than into human beings. In Marxian thought, fetishism refers to the worship of material objects (e.g., cars, houses, gold, and other collectibles) in place of an allegiance to the social lifeworld in which these have human meaning.

**Feudalism:**   A social system composed of estates; each estate had its own customs, laws, and occupations based on rules of heritage. Feudal France had three estates: clergy, nobility, and crafts-people (merchants, serfs, and servants). Feudal Russia had four: nobility and gentry, clergy, townspeople, and serfs/peasants. Feudalism was a stratified system by which the surplus value of labor from workers, servants, serfs, and peasants was funneled to an elite, called the nobility, who in turn supported the clergy and bought from the townspeople. Feudalism grew out of a predatory warfare system wherein some victors stayed behind to rule and extract wealth to send to the royal court elsewhere. The third estate (merchants and crafts-people) is the origin of the capitalist class. This stratum led a series of revolutions in the seventeenth century, replacing feudalism with capitalism as the dominant system for funneling wealth to the few. See "Fifth Estate" for more.

**Feuerbach, Ludwig Andreas (1804–1872):**   A German materialist philosopher whose writings are crucial to an understanding of Karl Marx's Hegelian roots. Feuerbach charged that true socialist endeavors were about moving to praxis and responding to the problems of racism, sexism, elitism, and other forms of exploitation born out of capitalism. Marx claimed to have "stood Feuerbach on his head" in his Eleventh Thesis. This is a reference to Marx's concern for those who talk about revolutionary change but do little to bring it about.

**Fichte, Johann (1762–1814):**   German theologian/ethicist who followed Immanuel Kant but made practical reason superior to theoretical reason. Fichte, not G.W.F. Hegel, first posited the triadic conflict process called the dialectic and named the stages in this theory of change: thesis, antithesis, synthesis. Schilling later applied the dialectic to nature and to history. Fichte's ethical views held that human beings have duties to each other that lead to a world culture in which everyone has rights and freedoms. Fichte was dismissed from his position at Jena for his views on freedom and revelation. He ended his career as rector at the University of Berlin. (See the work of W. L. Reese.)

**Fifth Estate (Fifth Column):**   A social layer that did not fit into the three (or four) estates of feudalism. It is composed of journalists, critics, and intellectuals who do not celebrate existing social arrangements. In fascist Spain, the term became "fifth column" and was used as a term of derogation for those who sent reports to other countries about the brutalities of the Franco regime. See "Fourth Estate" and "Feudalism" for more.

**Fiscal Crisis:**   An economic crisis that develops when the state generates additional funds by printing excess money (thereby causing inflation) and by raising taxes on the middle class (thereby immiserating those who receive wages and salaries that can be taxed), or by engaging in deficit spending (thereby adding to inflation and to debt service). See "Disemployment" and "Kondratieff Cycles" for more.

**Flagrante delicto:**   Latin: *flagrant* = obvious; *delicto* = wrong. Caught in the commission of wrongful behavior. Some persons can be arrested only when caught committing a crime. Aside from this, a warrant from a judge is necessary, wherein the arresting office must then state "probable cause." In sexist societies, husbands are/were permitted to kill wives and their lovers if caught flagrante delicto (i.e., in the act of intercourse).
   More critical analysis questions the conditions (e.g., social, political, economic, and cultural) under which some behaviors are defined as obvious wrongs and others are not. Further, throughout history, similar behaviors have undergone considerable redefinition with regard to their wrongfulness. For example, homosexual intercourse was defined as a flagrant act of misbehavior up until the mid-1970s in most jurisdictions. Today, however, the same conduct is not generally regarded as criminal. What changes are the social forces through which we define the behavior as flagrante delicto or not.

**Floating Signifiers:**   A concept relevant to the social-psychoanalytic theory of Jacques Lacan. According to Lacan, the unconscious is structured much like a language. Thus, it embodies words or phrases (signifiers) charged with psychic energy that await articulation. These words/phrases float amidst a sea of other words and expressions that can be uttered in any given situation. According to Lacan, what is uttered is dependent upon one's internal conversation with oneself and one's external interactions with others. See "Decentered Subject," "Lacan, Jacques," "Semiotics," and "Sign" for more.

**Folk Society:**   A small intimate society in which a sense of community is provided. The members regard each other as having status by virtue of being born into the group. Solidarity is based upon "Dramas of the Holy" in which each member is sanctified as part of the group. Most production and distribution is shared, although there are often gender, age, and ethnic differences in social honor and wealth. Status honor continues as long as one stays within the norms and embodies the values of the society. Status honor in folk societies contrasts with capitalism, where status depends upon exchange for (and only for) profit. Modernists refer to folk societies as "primitive," "backward," "undeveloped," or "savage." They may be low-tech societies; however, solidarity and sharing are not lacking.

**Folkway:**  A customary way of behaving, the nonobservance of which is punished by only minor inconvenience; a weak norm. Folkways are hostile to the notion that behavior is genetically based, since they are learned and vary widely between cultures.

**Football, Ideology of:**  According to Marxist analysis, American football helps reproduce capitalist ideology through the character of the sport. Among the capitalist ideas and relationships found in commodity football are: (1) division of mental and physical labor: A special coaching cadre plans while the players execute; (2) objectification of football players: They are merely human capital to be used and discarded, bought and sold for profit; (3) the extraction of surplus value from fans through the market system and from players through the wage system; (4) militarism in training and games as well as in pregame shows; (5) emphasis in the game on possession; (6) emphasis on destructive competition; (7) emphasis on accumulation (of points) without purpose; (8) emphasis on the demand for respect for authority; (9) a labor elite of "stars"; and (10) passive consumption for fans.

A critical Freudian analysis would focus upon the center as the symbolic mother, the ball as a phallic symbol, and the opposing goal line as the hymen of a forbidden female.

A critical feminist assessment would note that it reproduces machismo and teaches young men to compete and to dominate other young men, encouraging semi-controlled violence as a legitimate form of recreation. Cf. "Baseball."

**Force:**  Latin: *fortis* = strong. This term is an exemplar of the poetics and politics of definition: It began as a word to refer to human effort, was adopted as metaphor into physics, and from physics made its way into sociology. It is so vague a concept that it can be defined only by reference to some set of actions that push or pull another object or person one way or another.

**Force, Structural:**  A system of social practices that fixes as permanent the unequal chance to satisfy needs. These include racism, sexism, class position, ethnocentrism, bureaucracy, and nationalism. One can neither criticize nor change such structures without facing a variety of formal and informal sanctions. Apart from a belief in the legitimacy of such norms due to childhood socialization, structural force is based upon fear of and submission to sanctions and upon the individual's recognition of his/her own powerlessness in the absence of realistic alternatives. Various forms of authority (charismatic, tradition, legal-rational) validate "structural" force.

**Fordism:**    A form of labor process with an extreme subdivision of labor, close control of the work process by supervisors, and the pace of work determined by the speed of the assembly line. Named after the Ford automobile factory system, which was itself modeled after meatpacking plants in Chicago. Cf. "Democratic Self-Management" and "Z Theory." See "McDonaldization of Society" and "Taylorism" for more.

**Formalism:**    The concept is relevant to the sociology of law and can, in part, be traced to the work of Max Weber. Formalism means the "rule of law." It is sometimes called legal formalism and formal rationality. Essentially the concept implies that the legal system and the rule of law exist in a highly autonomous state. In other words, formalism maintains that the law functions independent of intervening effects such as religion, politics, education, and the like. Moreover, formalism means that the rule of law, independent of influencing factors, possesses the potential to fulfill the desired social values of equality, individuality, community, and so on. Thus, according to the notion of formalism, the law produces a great deal of freedom for people while, at the same time, limiting its coercive impact in their lives. The often cited maxim for legal formalism is: "Similarly situated people should be identically treated."

When examining the extent of formalism in law, there are four possibilities: (1) *repressive formalism*—the autonomy of the legal order is high and the fulfillment of social values is low; (2) *instrumental Marxism*—the autonomy of the legal order is low and the fulfillment of social values is low; (3) *liberal legalism*—the autonomy of the legal order is high and the fulfillment of social values is high; and (4) *informalism*—the rule of law is low and the fulfillment of social values is high.

Critics of formalism claim that the doctrine is too narrow; that is, it can be oppressive (e.g., repressive formalism). People can be on an equal footing under the law but differentially experience its impact. For example, if I earn $10,000 a year and another person earns $100,000 per year, do we experience the same substantive justice when receiving $100 tickets for driving under the influence (DUI)? Formalism is an ideal of how the law should function in everyday practice. Because it is an ideal, it is not totally realizable. See "Ideal-Type" for more.

**Foucault, Michel (1926–1984):**    French historian and social theorist who examined such enduring questions as sexuality, mental illness, punishment, and the manner in which modern institutions exercise coercive power to discipline and regulate the behavior of individuals. Foucault resisted rigid categorizations. He believed that such labeling functioned to reduce the human subject to finite possibilities and to oppress it. Thus, Foucault renounced observations that he was a follower of Marx, Freud, or the poststructural/postmodernist luminaries of his time. His voluminous writings, however, wove together many of the insights from these orientations.

Foucault is credited with explaining how power and knowledge are interrelated. Regimes of power exert their will to normalize, de-pathologize, and homogenize individuals through inventive and technical disciplinary practices. For example, the madhouses and asylums of the eighteenth century were reconfigured as psychopathic public hygiene facilities designed to "treat" and "correct" disease. This reconfiguration, as an expression of knowledge, affirmed a certain truth: that objectivist and positivist science could address all the ills of society with sufficient faith in psychiatric medicine. Foucault contends that medical justice became a disciplinary mode of surveillance in which psychiatry/psychology socially policed difference understood as disease.

Foucault demonstrated how the function of the power/knowledge relationship denied individual and collective difference, plurality, and variation. Indeed, through his genealogical investigations, Foucault argued that disciplinary institutions (e.g., the hospital, the prison), as systematic articulations of circumscribed truth, were oppressive to the human condition. Foucault also pointed out how the language of these systems possessed the capacity to marginalize and victimize. Referring to a person as "braving" emotional difficulties conveys a different meaning and intent than if the same person is said to be "suffering" through psychiatric problems. Foucault was particularly interested in how language operates to affirm certain realities while discounting others. See "Baudrillard, Jean," "Discursive Formations," "Genealogy," "Panopticism," "Postmodernists/Postmodernism," and "Total Institution" for more. Cf. "Goffman, Erving."

**Foundationalism:**   A pejorative term applied to the effort to ground some set of principles upon pre-given facts. Postmodernists are generally opposed to foundationalism. Affirmative postmodernists, however, accept foundations as long as they are local, provisional, and relational, wherein responsibility is accepted. Thus, for example, it is possible to ground morality but only as a set of behaviors special to a given social lifeworld constructed by humans for particular, historical purposes. Cf. "Anti-Foundationalism."

**Fourier, Charles (1772–1837):**   A socialist who held that human beings had "appetites" that under capitalism became antisocial but that under socialism would become sources of happiness and assets to society. In his ideal society, the basic unit of social organization was the *Phalanstery* in which there would be prosperity, equality, and cooperation. A number of utopian communities were set up in Europe and in the United States based on these ideas. They had limited success. (See the work of W. L. Reese.) See "Phalanstery, Phalanx Socialism" for more.

**Fourth Estate:**   A term applied to the proletariat who did not fit into the three estates of feudalism. Marx thought it to be the carrier of the general interest and the source of progressive revolution. Sometimes applied to journalists. Cf. "Fifth Estate."

**Fractal/Fractal Geometry:**   A structure that occupies only a part of the space/time available to it. In Euclidean geometry and Newtonian physics, structures occupy one, two, three, or four dimensions and exhibit rational, linear behavior. In Chaos theory, complex natural and social systems have a different structure and behavior. Since the same set of variables can produce different sets of fractals (outcomes), most of the assumptions of modern science are reduced in epistemological value; that is, prediction, replication, falsification, and tight correlation are much less helpful in the knowledge process than had been thought. See "Chaos Theory" and "Hyperspace" for more.

**Francis of Assisi, St. (1182–1226):**   Son of a prosperous merchant, Francis disinherited himself from his father. He took vows of chastity, poverty, and obedience to the teachings of Christ and went among the poor, giving them both spiritual and material help. He founded the Franciscan Order of Monks, which split up when some observers found they could not follow his ardent rules. The Friars Minor observe these rules strictly as do the Capuchin monks. Friars Conventional hold property in common and use products for the poor. Because of his love of nature and animals, Francis is often shown holding a lamb or a bird.

**Frankfurt School:**   The Institute for Social Research founded in 1923 and located in Frankfurt, Germany. It brought concern for ideology, human intentionality, and reflexivity back into Marxist theory and sociology. It was Marxist, Freudian, Weberian and neo-Hegelian all at once. In World War I, the working class of each country joined the capitalist class to fight other capitalists and workers in other countries. The founders of the Frankfurt School thought that ideology was part of the answer to social, political, and economic marginalization and began work on the social sources of fascism and the authoritarian personality. They found this source in the patriarchal family, and in the racism, sexism, and fascism of art, cinema, magazines, and other mass cultural forms. Then, too, orthodox social science tended to adopt the model of objective "laws" that seemed to be beyond human reach. Radical sociology had been depoliticized by adopting a positivist style after American, French, and British philosophy of science. Led by Max Horkheimer, Theodor Adorno, Herbert Marcuse, Eric Fromm, Walter Benjamin, and others, the Marxian interest in alienated consciousness and the creative role of humans in constructing social forms was reasserted. Critical theorists, especially Marcuse, made a criticism of the obstacles to human praxis in both capitalist and socialist societies. See "Adorno, Theodor", and "Habermas, Jürgen" for more.

Also known as the School of Critical Theory or critical sociology, the Frankfurt School recognizes that structural Marxism leaves many questions unanswered. Critical theory seeks to remedy this by incorporating theory from Freudianism, phenomenology, existentialism, and, lately, from feminist and postmodern scholarship. See "Critical Theory" for more.

**Freedom:**   A political construct by which individuals under capitalism can escape the obligations of reciprocity in social relationships. In fact, no human being qua human is independent of others insofar as social reality is concerned. For a person to be a social being, s/he must present and be understood by others. It is not freedom that is liberating but rather the full right to participate (and the material resources to do so) in the creation of culture. It is this participation that is necessary to the human condition. Cf. "Existentialism."

**Free Enterprise:**   An economic system wherein capitalists are free to hire or fire, invest or disinvest, and produce or not produce. Social relationships are displaced by economic goals; production is based on profit rather than the needs of a society.

According to socialist theory, the term is misleading in that it refers to a situation in which the capitalist is free to do anything s/he wishes to increase profit. The "free world" is one in which capitalists are free to make profits and to move capital and jobs around the world. Modern business tries to reduce the place of both worker and consumer in the free enterprise system by a variety of techniques, including advertising, public relations, and, in the most extreme instances, price fixing, blacklisting, and bribery of elected officials.

**Free Love:**   Refers to the transfer of human sexuality from the bonds of marriage and of male collectives to the private concern of mutually consenting adults. Love, sex, and sensuality are not free in the liberal sense of market freedom but in the sense of being free from the rules of patriarchy and monogamy. It is supported by most socialists beginning especially with Saint-Simon and Fourier. Those advocating free love also condemn discrimination against illegitimate children and advocate abortion and the acceptance of consensual cohabitation as a marriage form. Conservatives condemn free love as group love or as the conversion of women from the property of one male to common property of all males.

**Free Will:**   The idea that people act as willful individuals and need not accept slavery, patriarchy, or any social form unless they so choose. Free will often signals a religious argument: If God knows and controls everything, how can mankind claim to be free? In a political context, it signals an argument against state control of the market. Whatever the case, people are socialized to a sociocultural world, are put into social roles, and are often coerced to pattern their behavior in conformity to norms and values. Still, they have more freedom than they sometimes think. In a totalitarian society free will is minimal. Dialectical theory suggests there is some changing relationship between private intentions and public policies. There always must be some constraints on human behavior. For example, we must use the rules of language if we are to construct social reality. However, such constraints can enable rather than defeat the human project. See "Management Science" and "Praxis/Practice" for more.

**Freire, Paulo (1922–1997):**   Brazilian educator and social philosopher. His work on education has been linked with both postmodernists concerned with the philosophy of language and with feminists interested in consciousness-raising strategies.

Freire's work centered on the liberation of oppressed groups (adult illiterates) through critical methods of education. He referred to this method as dialogical pedagogy. Dialogical pedagogy requires that one "speak true words." This is a moment when action and reflection are connected. To speak true words is to possess the capacity to change the world in which one finds oneself; that is, it is to become an active agent in the process of truly becoming liberated.

Freire further described this process of dialogical pedagogy as *conscientizacao*. This activity invites both the speaker and the one who is "spoken to" to develop a shared political vocabulary. This shared vocabulary is to be examined for its "generative themes." Generative themes embody the socioeconomic conditions that effectively discount, invalidate, or otherwise repress the subject's capacity to reflectively transform her/his environment. The aim of *conscientizacao* is to empower the oppressed and marginalized to participate meaningfully and actively in the transformation of their own society. For Freire, this is the moment when one, through language and action, is a cultural revolutionary. Through dialogical pedagogy, disenfranchised subjects decode the discourse of *conscientizacao* so that its connection to macro-sociopolitical forces can be unmasked and decentered. It is a process that requires one to systematically assess what is, through an "authentic process of abstraction," so that one can then envision what might be. See "Education, Revolutionary" and "Pedagogy" for more.

**French Revolution (1789–1799):**   A violent overthrow of feudalism that started out as a bourgeois revolution based upon calls for reason (rather than faith) and a free market (rather than a system in which merchants paid the nobility for the right to produce and trade). It developed into a democratic call for "liberty, equality, fraternity." The Revolution was subverted by Girondists and Jacobins; later Napoleon took state power and channeled French enthusiasm into an expansion of the French Empire. See "Jacobins" for more.

**French Student Movement of 1968:**  A series of antiestablishment protests by French students based at the Sorbonne in Paris. The students were joined by workers; the French government conceded to their demands; and the movement collapsed. It inspired student power movements in the United States and Japan. The movement was also instrumental to the work of poststructuralists, semioticians, and postmodernists of the time.

**Freud, Sigmund (1856–1939):**  An Austrian, Freud studied psychology under Charcot, a Frenchman appalled by the treatment of the mentally ill. Freud developed several important concepts: stages of psycho-sexual development, the unconscious, repression, and the geometry of the mind. The mind has, according to Freud, three parts: the id (primitive desires); the ego (personal wants, wishes, and urges); and the superego (the norms, values, and morality of society). The ego mediates between the internal desires of and the external demands on the individual in a semi-calculated fashion (i.e., how much one can get away with without being caught and punished).

The father is the source of the superego and is hated for repressing primitive desire. Since the mother is uncritical and nourishing of primitive desire, she is loved. There are three stages every normal person must pass through: the oral stage, in which sucking and biting give pleasure; the anal stage, in which urinating and defecating give pleasure (at least to the mother); and the genital stage, in which desire is transferred to an adult of the opposite sex.

When there is a conflict between deep desire and social demands, desire is repressed and embodied in disguised habits. This is called neurosis. The basic source of trouble is found in how the mother handles the movement through the three stages: She can help the child to move through them without trauma, or she can reward too much or punish too much. Unable to get through these infantile stages, the child becomes fixated or "stuck" in a stage and is condemned to reenact, in compulsive fashion, such childish desires (e.g., smoking is an oral fixation; a cigarette is a phallic symbol).

The role of Freudian psychology is to make these hidden and forbidden desires visible to the patient so they can be handled in a mature way. Freudian psychology is emancipatory in that it frees people from childhood fears and anxieties. Today, advertising and marketing firms utilize

Freud's insights to create ads that take advantage of neurotic compulsions by linking products to their resolution. For example, Virginia Slims cigarettes are false resolutions of penis envy on the part of girls. Critical theory and the Frankfurt School tried to retrieve the emancipatory aspect of Freudian theory. See "Condensation," "Displacement," "Dream Work," "Freudian Revisionism," "Marcuse, Herbert," and "Oedipal Complex" for more.

**Freudian Revisionism:**   The use of the principles of psychology to manage consciousness on behalf of an elite rather than to liberate humans from their inability to communicate with themselves and others honestly and openly. Undistorted communication was a central concern of Freud as was the ability to love and to affirm the "instincts of life." However, his vision was subverted by the use of sociology and psychology to sell commodities on television in a particularly despicable form of Freudian revisionism. For example, sexual insecurities are exploited as a way to subliminally sell automobiles, beer, hair spray, furniture, clothes, and so on. See "Freud, Sigmund" and "Marcuse, Herbert" for more.

**Friendship:**   A social form in which affection, mutual support, and association for its own sake are present. The quality and type of sharing found in families, collectives, and authentic neighborhoods is also found in friendships. Friendship is a parallel economic form in which goods and services are freely given. Thus, friendships help moderate the excesses of capitalism. See "Economic Forms, Parallel" for more.

**Froebel, Friedrich (1782–1852):**   A German educator, Froebel joined with Comenius and Pestalozzi to help ground a modern (really postmodern) philosophy of education. He established the kindergarten in 1837 and taught that students must want to learn and that it was a natural development of the human spirit rather than a chore or a coercive process.

**From Each According to His Abilities; to Each According to His Needs:**
A phrase attributed to Saint-Simon that Karl Marx adopted, popularized, and utilized as a basic ethic for establishing a socialist society. It means that people should do as much as their talent and skill permit and should get all that is necessary for a good and decent life. Thus, the rationalization of work and wages is set aside in favor of reason and justice. See "Needs Principles" for more.

**Full Employment:**   A public policy that tries to find work for any and all who want it. A full employment law was enacted during the Truman Administration. Today, however, economists report that 5 percent unemployment is best and that full employment leads to wage inflation (i.e., supply is low; demand is high). See "Disemployment" for more.

**Function/Functionalism:**    Latin: *fungi* = to perform. In math, the notation "y = f(x)" means that the value of *y* depends upon the value of *x*. In adopting this notation one adopts the idea of a dependent and independent variable, as well as the idea of directional causality.

In sociology, the term is used to justify existing structures in the claim that society would not function (survive) without those structures. The problem, however, is that functional theory supports poverty, inequality, hierarchy, gender differentiation, and class divisions as functional (healthy) for society. Purists also argue that crime, vice, and pollution are necessary to make the system work. See "Conflict Theory" and "Durkheim, Émile" for more.

**Functional Interchange:**    A process by which different institutions in a society produce and exchange in such a way as to complete and complement each other to make the whole system work. In the human body, the lungs, heart, stomach, and liver do different things and make possible a whole organism. Similarly, the market, banks, factories, the state, the church, the police/army, schools, and the family are the major institutions in modern society. A complex division of labor is regarded as more rational than centralizing the performance or regulation of such tasks into one institution.

Critical theorists challenge the legitimacy of functionalism. Trouble arises when people claim that class, race, gender, and authority hierarchies are "functionally necessary." Critics contend that functionalism is used to justify the social forms that exist, since they are the product of social evolution. See "Social Darwinism" and "Durkheim, Émile" for more.

**Functionary:**    A worker in a bureaucracy who is given a position and a narrow range of rules within which to work. S/he does what S/he is told to do and is held accountable for competent service. Functionaries are separated from their coworkers and from the larger society by rules that make them accountable to the top echelon in the bureaucracy or workplace.

# G

**Galileo, Galilei (1564–1642):**  An Italian astronomer and natural philosopher, Galileo was one of the central architects of modern science. In his *Dialogue Concerning the Two Chief World Systems*, he set forth the idea that the sun (rather than the earth) was the center of the universe. Forced to recant and forbidden to teach or talk about his views, Galileo is said to have muttered in the stillness of his room, "Still it turns," in reference to the rotation of the earth around the sun. Galileo decentered the earth and by extension all theology that holds that the earth and all the creatures on it were the result of a special act of creation.

**Gambling:**  Playing a game for money when winning depends more on luck than skill. In religious usage, gambling is a pathway to the holy. Gods or spirits affect the outcome of the fall of dice or cards and thus communicate favor or disfavor upon the one who throws the dice or holds the cards. Many gambling laws forbid the activity in order to prevent profanation of the divine. Gambling used to be a very profitable business for organized crime. Now the state runs most legal gambling operations and profits greatly, since the payoff is 20 percent or more. See "Corruption, Theory of" for more.

**Game Stage:**  One of two stages set forth by G. H. Mead for the social development of children. In the play stage, children take the role of significant others but are inventive. In the game stage, understanding and compliance with rules becomes important. Both kinds of activity are a prelude to adult social performance.

**Gandhi, Mohandas K. (1869–1949):**  An Indian lawyer trained in London who became central to the liberation of India from the British Empire. Gandhi, called Mahatma (great soul), advocated passive resistance to British tyranny and economic exploitation. Carrying on from Henry David Thoreau and Leo Tolstoy, Gandhi organized and politicized great numbers of Hindus. After India became autonomous, Gandhi called for the acceptance of the "untouchables" and for respect for Muslims in India. More militant Hindus objected; Gandhi was assassinated in 1949 but continues to be a symbol of peace, forgiveness, equality, and social justice. Martin Luther King adopted many of Gandhi's views and tactics in his effort to organize, politicize, and resist racism in the United States. (See the work of W. L. Reese.)

*Gemeinschaft:* A German word translated as "community," the central concept of which is attributed to Ferdinand Tönnies. It contrasts to mass society, wherein social relations are weak or missing. Cf. *"Gesellschaft."* See "Community" for more.

**Gender:** Gender refers to the psycho-social division of labor in a society, not to the biological and physiological differences between men and women. Gendering varies dramatically across cultures; biology and physiology vary little. (One uses the words "male" and "female" to refer to biology; one uses the words "men" and "women" to refer to the product of social gendering work.) Most societies socialize to two and only two genders, but some societies provide for three or more. Physiological differences permit the specification of many genders. Developmentally, gendering patterns begin early, as skills, beliefs, and attitudes are inculcated in young males and females. By age 3, most young people begin to embody a gender division of labor in household, play, school, and friendships. In such societies boys and girls form separate groups before puberty and begin to embody traditional patriarchal role relationships soon thereafter. In more egalitarian societies childhood is much less differentiated by gender. Adult relationships are much less stratified. See "Abuse, Spousal" and "Sexism" for more.

**Genealogy:** The practice of looking at history in order to reclaim forms of knowledge and being that have been omitted, excluded, or disqualified. Genealogy dismisses any history or science that is presented as accurate and complete. Genealogical practice is often attributed to Michel Foucault. Among other things, his work explored punishment, sexuality, and mental illness. See "Foucault, Michel" for more.

**Generalized Other:** Our overall impression of what we believe others will think about us and how they will respond to our behavior. On the basis of that understanding we modify our behavior—sometimes in compliance, sometimes in deception—depending upon the quality of the relationship. The ability of people to generalize over a wide variety of particular incidents is a remarkable human capacity and the basis of much "self-"government. See "Looking Glass Process" for more.

*Gesellschaft:* A German word translated as "business" but used to refer to a society in which there is a complex division of labor, anonymity, contractual relationships, and hierarchical bureaucratic relationships. It is the opposite of community. The concept is attributed to F. Tönnies. In such a society human beings are left to their own devices; in community, goods and services are produced to meet collective needs. Cf. *"Gemeinschaft."*

**Gestalt:**   German: form, shape, figure. A school in psychology founded by Friedrich Wertheimer and others that held that sense perceptions were not simple impressions that mirrored nature but rather psychological constructs interpreted by human beings within a whole. Thus, an event or an aspect of nature and/or society is not registered unless it is significant to the beholder in terms of some cultural theme or practice. The concept of gender is a case in point. Most of us "see" only two genders. In terms of the physiology and chemistry of actually existing human beings, however, any number of genders might be perceived. This view of the knowledge process is further developed by postmodernists and postmodern feminists.

**Gilligan, Carol:**   An American social scientist who noted that the voices of women were excluded by Lawrence Kohlberg in his work on the stages of moral development. Gilligan taught us that if these voices had been included, moral development would have put people and supportive social relations before the use of abstract principles as the basis for assigning moral standing to those who take such tests. See "Voice/Voices" for more. Cf. "Essentialism."

**Glossary:**   Greek: *glossa* = tongue, and by extension, speech or language. One gives a "gloss of meaning" to unusual words or unusual usages of words. In this case, a glossary is a book which defines/explains terms from points of view (e.g., Marxist, socialist, feminist, critical, etc.) not usually included in standard dictionaries.

**GNP (Gross National Product):**   The total dollar value of all goods and services produced for sale by U.S. firms both at home and abroad. However, it is not a measure of the useful and necessary things people do. For example, the unpaid work that women do in the household is not included in the calculation, whereas many forms of production are. It is a measure of the quantity not the quality of life in a state. Since capitalism depends on expansion, growth in GNP is closely monitored.

**Gobineau, Arthur (1816–1882):**   Gobineau was a French nobleman, diplomat, and philosopher best known for his views on Aryan supremacy. Aryans are said to possess higher capacities to appreciate beauty in art, music, and politics. "Racial" mixtures dilute Aryan superiority and is to be avoided. This view became part of the social philosophy of Nazism and led to the death of millions of people who did not conform to the ideal type of the Aryan. Eugenics devolved out of the same views. (See the work of W. L. Reese.) See "Eugenics" for more.

**God:**    A supernatural being with various powers to intervene in the social and natural world. For most believers today, the God concept has several components: (1) creator of all; (2) a plan for social life; (3) a monitoring/judging role; and (4) the ability to revise or suspend the laws of nature or society. Marx held that the God concept was the projection of social power onto fictional beings. Durkheim held that the God concept was society assembled in some drama of the holy; he called this social fact the super-organic. Postmodern theology suggests that the God concept and the sanctification/profanation processes are distinctly human processes that change as social circumstances change. See "Theology, Liberation" for more. Cf. "Agnosticism" and "Atheism."

**God, Death of:**    The claim by Mainländer, Friedrich Nietzsche, Jean-Paul Sartre, and others that belief in God was disappearing. For some, modern science killed off such beliefs, since natural explanations accounted for most of what was attributed to divine agency. For others, God died when people failed to live up to the "plan" attributed to that God. Marx argued that capitalism, the market system, and commodification destroy all that is holy and sacred. If God is dead, then there seem to be two choices: nihilism (and the license to do whatever one wishes) or a congenial and well-tempered social philosophy invented and adopted by human beings in collective public discourse.

In anthropological terms, the concept of "God" or "gods" embraces all that is valued in a given society—especially the common heritage and solidarity that mark an authentic community. In such a community there is a unity above and beyond the narrow self-interests of the individuals who compose that society. When this unity is destroyed by capitalism or other forms of elitism in which material possessions are emphasized, it is said that God is dead. As the technical and rational displace social and magical processes of creating culture, mystery and awe are lost and the world becomes more profane. See "Atheism." Cf. "Agnosticism."

**Gödel's Theorem:**    Kurt Gödel offered a mathematical model indicating that it is not possible to prove or disprove the extent of consistency, predictability, and stasis within a system, given the inherent instability of essential conditions emanating from the activity of all systems. Thus, Gödel's theory is a rejection of totalizing approaches to knowledge. Gödel's theorem is a principle of essential undecidability, incompleteness, and uncertainty. This principle is compatible with postmodern analysis dismissing foundationalist claims to truth. Both Gödel's theorem and postmodern science contend that there are no overarching, all-encompassing, self-contained, globalizing positions on the constitution of society, the function of law, the practice of religion, or any other question that goes to the essential structure of any system. See "Postmodernists/Postmodernism" for more.

**Goffman, Erving (1922–1983):**    American sociologist and social psychologist, Goffman is best known for his dramaturgical and Symbolic Interactionist analyses of situations and role performances. Goffman studied the "expressions given off" by people, particularly the more theatrical, gestural, and nonverbal dimensions of presenting the self in everyday life. These expressions can be distinguished from the "expressions people give," which relate much more to the verbal statements individuals communicate about themselves. See "Dramaturgical Analysis," "Dramaturgical Society," and "Symbolic Interaction" for more.

Goffman coined the terms "front stage" and "back stage" mannerisms. These refer to the dichotomy identified above. Front stage mannerisms are more socialized and more controlled role performances engaged in by people. Goffman invoked the metaphor of the actor to help illuminate the drama and mask-wearing implied in front stage behavior. Back stage mannerisms refer to the more informal, personal performances, when there are no "outsiders" to impress. When we are attending to some religious conviction, playing the role of a professional worker, disciplining our children, or participating in an athletic event, there are certain props, cues, ceremonies/rituals that are part of how we manage our front stage impression to others. These performances are not so austere when living the drama of back stage mannerisms. However, our "true" identities are not revealed with back stage performances either. As Goffman points out, our backstage impressions remain, and we promote the appearance of being a good teammate/role player.

Goffman also examined the effects of "total institutions." Total institutions refer to the demoralizing and debilitating effects that hospitals, prisons, the military complex, and other institutions or institutional practices have on the soma and psyche of human beings. Goffman wrote about the "identity stripping" that occurs under such indoctrination. Goffman's observations offer a critical context for understanding the social situation of persons placed in total institutions and the patterns of initiation that occur. Cf. "Foucault, Michel." See "Actor," "Back Stage," "Dramaturgy," "Impression Management," "Self, Social," and "Total Institution" for more.

**Golden Mean:**    A term from Aristotle and his theory of value (axiology). Aristotle held that happiness is the goal of human beings and is best achieved by embodying the Golden Mean. The mean lies between having/doing too much and not enough. This seems vague, but Aristotle set a specific mathematical solution that informs some ideas even to this day.

**Golden Rule:**    A guide to ethical behavior from Jesus: "Do unto others as you would have done unto yourself." It existed in reverse form for ages before Jesus: "What you do not want done to yourself, do not do to others" (Confucius). There is a problem with the Golden Rule: If one wants others to compete, be cruel, or engage in war, it justifies such behavior. See "Hammurabi, Code of," "Kant, Immanuel," "Kantian Imperative," "Praxis/Practice," and "Utility/Utilitarianism" for more.

**Government, Forms of:**   There are several forms of government: anarchy (no rulers); aristocracy (rule of the best); monarchy (rule of a king); oligarchy (rule of the few); democracy (rule of all adult persons via public discourse); totalitarianism (close control of all aspects of public policy by a dictator); fascism (close control of economics, politics, and the media by state officials); and neo-fascism (the use of high technology more so than the use of police, prisons, and military to control thought and behavior). Socialism comes in several forms: bureaucratic socialism (similar to fascism); democratic socialism (same as democracy but extends beyond politics to economics); and communism (worker control of production; distribution on the basis of need and/or merit). Patriarchy refers to a form of social life organized around a large family, band, or clan in which the senior male rules. Matriarchy refers to a set of sisters and their children in which the senior female rules. Seniority is based upon several factors: age, experience, wisdom, strength (for men), number of children, and personal style.

**Grace:**   Latin: *gratus* = beloved, agreeable. The term entered religion and theology from the three graces: fate, providence, and fortune. Grace now refers to a special spiritual quality in which a person turns from evil to prosocial behavior. Grace became a center piece in Christian theology. On the one hand, it requires a lasting commitment to the teachings of the Christian God; belief in the grace of God can convert the most violent and villainous thug or empower the weakest and most vulnerable person. On the other hand, it is used to ground the view that all judgments have already been made by that God and people are either blessed or condemned. Martin Luther took the latter view, as did John Calvin. Grace, in the latter sense, is used as an apology and as a powerful legitimating idea for great wealth and power among Christians who accept Luther's and Calvin's interpretations.

**Gramsci, Antonio (1891–1937):**   Founder of the Italian Communist Party and author of *Prison Notebooks*. In this book he added much to the role of intellectuals in helping or obstructing human emancipation. His concept of "organic" intellectuals emphasized the connection between the social location and the political understanding of intellectuals. His notion of "hegemony" explored how state mechanisms (e.g., the media, the schools, the police) perpetuate the class interests of ruling elites and how such power brokers govern with the active consent (knowing or not) of those who are oppressed. See "Civil Society" and "Hegemony, Ideological" for more.

**Great Man Theory (of History):**   Thomas Carlyle (1795–1881) argued that all of history is driven by the genius (or madness) of heroes. For Carlyle, the hope of humankind resides in the hero who offers a solution in which lesser people can find a place. Marxian/socialist theory argues that history is driven by conflict between groups: lord and peasant, master and slave, owner and worker. There are several choices about how history works. See "Heroic" and "Historiography" for more.

**Green Movement, The:**   An environmental movement in Europe (now in the United States) that embodies several progressive elements, including protection of the environment, social justice, and democratic participation.

**Gregory I, Pope (540–604):**   Pope Gregory sent the first missionaries to Britain. He is said to have specified the seven deadly sins and encouraged the plainsong chants that bear his name. Gregory is important to the history and sociology of religion in the United States. His efforts to spread Christianity greatly affected social norms, law, and justice in Britain and still shape everyday life in the English-speaking world.

**Grotius, Hugo (1583–1645):**   Dutch author and a founder of international law. In his work *On the Law of Booty* Grotius developed the concept that the oceans were free to all nations. He also began work on the rules of war and peace. His writings on the theory of law still resonate in sociology of law arguments. Grotius held that human beings were savages with the capacity to reason. This capacity led to a social contract set forth in writing or custom. The contract differs among societies but is binding upon all in that society. Natural law takes precedence over civil law, custom, and even divine law.

**Group:**   A set of status-roles (not persons per se) that requires intersubjective understanding, cooperation, intimacy, and a sense of "we-ness" in order to achieve a purpose within a social framework. A family or a ball team is a group, but a row of workers on an assembly line or a set of slaves or prisoners working at a task is not a group. In colleges, sororities and fraternities are organized as groups, whereas classes are often impersonal and interactively barren.

**Group Dynamics:**   Group dynamics are complex and continuously changing, but there are some patterns. There are engagement activities (Goffman calls these "clearance moves"), socio-emotional behaviors that address conflicts, and task-oriented actions. Central to all group activity is symbolic interaction, through which intersubjective understanding emerges. Groups often have status hierarchies that pre-shape the behavior of their members. There are also "disengagement" activities. These activities permit group members to set aside the claims each has on the other until the next group meeting.

**Group of Seven:**    There are seven nations that meet regularly to coordinate economic and political policy in the global economy: the United States, Great Britain, France, Italy, Germany, Canada, and Japan. In the global stratification system, these seven are joined by some twenty or so societies possessing advanced industrial capacity. Collectively, these nations are often accused of extracting wealth and food from some 120 or so "underdeveloped" countries. There are also a handful of socialist countries outside this stratification system. These include China, Cuba, Yemen, and Vietnam. See "National Security Managers" and "Stratification" for more.

**Group Think:**    A term used to ridicule the ability of people to individually effect thinking, feeling, and acting within a group setting. George Orwell (Eric Blair) coined the term when referring to the effects of coercion and authority on independent thought. Today, it is used to deride people whose opinions differ from right-wing and left-wing intellectuals.

**Guattari, Félix (1930–1992):**    A Lacanian trained psychoanalyst who worked at the experimental psychiatric clinic in La Borde, France, from the 1950s to the 1990s. Guattari remained politically active throughout his life, advocating for an "autonomy" movement: a politically-inspired, though non-party-based, revolution establishing more emancipatory rights for citizens in their daily lives and in their psychic existences. He also was an influential figure in the European Network for Alternatives to Psychiatry.

Guattari's work on the micro-politics of desire and psychoanalysis was linked with Gilles Deleuze's radical Nietzschean (anti-dialectic) philosophy of difference to produce a number of works. Most notable among these are: *Anti-Oedipus* (1983); *Kafka: Toward a Minor Literature* (1986); and *A Thousand Plateaus* (1987). These texts are significant to a postmodern assessment of capitalistic rationality, fascism of the soul (i.e., the desire to be led), and modernity's domination through normalizing discourses that invade all aspects of everyday social life. See "Baudrillard, Jean," "Deleuze, Gilles," and "Lyotard, Jean-François" for more. Cf. "Marxism."

**Guilt:**    A judgment on the part of others that one has done something legally prohibited or morally reprehensible. The word carries negative emotional content and prepares both the accused and the judge for severe punitive action. See "Shame" for more.

**Habermas, Jürgen (1929– ):**  German philosopher critical of many postmodern theories for their counter-Enlightenment critique of modernity. Habermas's work is an elaboration of the Frankfurt School and critical theory in general; however, his emphasis since the 1970s has been a more systematic application of the "linguistic turn" to issues relevant for social theory, cultural studies, and political action.

In sum, Habermas criticizes postmodern theory (particularly that of Lyotard, Derrida, and Foucault) for abandoning reason and rationality and for privileging, instead, an a-political and anti-ethical framework of difference and multiplicity. Habermas argues that a critique of Western rationality and metaphysics requires a normative foundation. This foundation provides a standpoint from which to analyze and promote social transformation. For Habermas, what is essential is a universalistic theory of communicative action that proceeds "rationally, unhistorically, and reconstructively" to point out the progressive and regressive features of modernity. This is dissimilar from the particularistic and deconstructive methodology utilized by many of his postmodern contemporaries. Habermas contends that his notion of communicative action preserves modern values of consensus, social rationality, solidarity, and emancipation and, thus, serves as a meaningful basis from which to engage in authentic and systematic social critique. See "Adorno, Theodor" and "Critical Theory" for more. Cf. "Derrida, Jacques," "Postmodernists/Postmodernism," and "Postmodernity."

**Hammurabi, Code of:**  A set of 282 laws drafted some 4,000 years ago. It is similar to the Mosaic Code. (See "Moses" for more.) The code was reportedly given to King Hammurabi by the god Shamash for the governing of the people. Many elements of the code still inform Roman and English law today. The Code of Hammurabi is reduced in most criminology books to a statement (i.e., "An eye for an eye; a tooth for a tooth"). The code was used to justify cruelty to people who offended or were found guilty of a crime. See "Golden Rule," "Kantian Imperative," "Moses," and "Utility/Utilitarianism" for more.

**Hand, Invisible:**   The idea, attributed to Adam Smith, that behind the seeming anarchy of capitalist production and distribution was an invisible hand that brought order and long-term progress to a free-market economy. The law of supply and demand was the means by which this hand worked. If owners set the price of goods too high, competitors were free to provide the goods at a lower price. If they set wages too low, workers were free to go to other, higher paying jobs.

According to socialists, the invisible hand law ignores several facts of economic life: (1) If it takes millions to enter a market, then the freedom to compete is seriously reduced. (2) If there is already a surplus labor force, then the freedom to take another job is seriously limited. (3) If six firms produce most beer, breakfast cereals, or automobiles, then they are free to fix prices and market share—they can have a price war and drive out any small firm that tries to lower prices or increase wages. Price fixing, conspiracies to divide up markets, blacklisting, and bribery are thus, metaphorically, fingers on an invisible hand.

**Hedonism:**   Greek: *hedone* = delight, pleasure. Epicureans held pleasure to be central to happiness, but for them its pursuit entailed spiritual values of prudence and restraint as well. The term now carries negative emotional content and refers to those who define happiness in terms of wealth and luxurious living. In capitalist cultures hedonism is grounded in the utilitarianism of Jeremy Bentham.

**Hegel, Georg Wilhelm Friedrich (1770–1831):**   A German philosopher whose work and its criticism advanced the understanding of the human condition. From Hegel, Karl Marx took much: the notion of alienation, the role of labor in creating human consciousness, the idea of a continuing "negation of the negation," and other less tangible contributions, including Hegel's great confidence in sweeping analysis and personal insight. To Hegel's thought, Marx added much: With his critique of Hegel, Marx brought an abstract Hegel into the real world of loving, struggling, overburdened workers who were growing increasingly miserable in capitalist societies; Marx thus created the theoretical basis for democratic self-government, community, and praxis. See "Marx, Karl" for more.

Hegel is used by some to justify fascism, since he held that what small rationality was possible in human affairs was to be found in the state. Hegel also charted 272 natural categories that are the grounding of modern phenomenology. Cf. "Phenomenology, Postmodern."

**Hegelian Dialectic:**   A view offered by Hegel that all *a* implies *not-a*, that *not-a* tends to negate *a*, and that a new *a* emerges out of the conflict between *a* and *not-a*. Hegel was concerned with showing how, in this way, one could approach absolute knowledge. Karl Marx's critique of this position was that knowledge was a product of creative human beings, not an absolute to be approached through a dialectic. Marx did, however, accept the principle of the dialectic to account for class conflict and social change.

**Hegelian Left:**   A student movement in Germany that extracted the liberal elements of Hegel's work and used it as a basis for social philosophy. In particular, the movement took Hegel's idea of a historical trend toward self-knowledge to locate progressive politics in education and the knowledge process. Marx was a member but abandoned the Hegelian Left because it lacked class analysis and gave too much credit to ideas and not enough to action. Marx located the general interest in workers and democracy more than in the state and science.

**Hegemony, Ideological:**   The use of law, religion, art, science, cinema, or literature to celebrate and legitimize one way of doing things to the discredit of alternative ways. It is often used in preference to direct force. Marx put it succinctly: "In every epoch, the ruling ideas have been the ideas of the ruling class." Through hegemony, the ruling class governs by the active consent, knowingly or not, of those who are oppressed. See "Gramsci, Antonio" for more.

**Heidegger, Martin (1884–1976):**   Heidegger was a founder of existentialism and important to postmodern theology and morality. He began with the concept of *dasein*, a German word meaning "being there." Once a human being is hurled (*geworfen*; *werfen* = to throw) into the world, the question becomes how to comport oneself. For Heidegger, the answer is based upon *Sorge*, the capacity to care. This capacity leads to "authenticity" and a genuine understanding of one's own self and the world in which one lives. The quest for authenticity is driven by *angst* (anxiety), which in turn arises from *das niches*, the nothingness that besets human beings without authenticity and concern for others. *Das niches* is a positive category because it gives us freedom and a motive for thought, action, and poetry. If there were something upon which all could agree, then freedom would be just that much more foreclosed. All this taken together leads us toward *Eksistenz*, the things and patterns of being that are. Thought and poetry complement each other: The thinker explains being and essence; the poet identifies the holy and the profane.

   Heidegger was identified as a Nazi sympathizer. His *dasein* philosophy, particularly in connection with authenticity and the meaning of being, appears consistent with Hitler's quest for a true Aryan race. See "'Me'" for more.

**Heisenberg, Werner (1901– ):**   A German physicist credited with the uncertainty principle, which claims that one can know either the position or momentum of a particle but not both at the same time. This view is now extended to call into question the entire knowledge process; the thought is that one changes a field by studying it. With the advent of Chaos theory there is empirical grounding for this view, but at the same time one can know with fair precision just what mixture of order and disorder exist in any given dynamical regime. See "Chaos Theory" for more.

**Heresy/Heretic:**    Greek: *hairesis* = a taking for oneself. In religion, science, and philosophy, a heretic is one who doubts that which is given as revealed truth (of God).

**Hermeneutics:**    Greek: *hermeneutikos* = interpretation. In religion, hermeneutics is the study of the meaning of holy writings. In literature, it is the search for the "true" meaning of a text. In critical theory, it is the study of how intersubjective understanding is possible and how it emerges through symbolic interaction. Jürgen Habermas holds that a good and decent society requires three forms of knowledge: positive knowledge, hermeneutical knowledge, and emancipatory knowledge.

Ordinarily we think that we reason all by ourselves. Yet we recognize that others understand us and that we understand them. This intersubjective understanding probably means that we work together to create meaning. Symbolic Interactional theory, ethnomethodology, phenomenology, and dramaturgical analysis all focus on how social reality is constructed by intending, insightful, cooperative humans. Hermeneutics examines this process in what one says and in what one writes. Cf. "Postmodernists/ Postmodernism."

**Heroic:**    Modern and premodern historians focus on one person and/or one event with which to account for qualitative changes in a historical narration. Postmodernists tend to reject such practice as celebratory, exclusionary, and/or self-limiting. Events such as the coming of the prophet, the discovery, or the incidence, when raised to singular causal efficacy, are rejected by postmodern sensibility; thus Jesus, Columbus, Hitler, and other such "heroic" figures are reduced to one of many possible representatives of a time or point of view. See "Great Man Theory (of History)" for more.

**Hierarch:**    Greek: *hier* = sacred; *arch* = ruler. A high priest or pope. The sociological term "hierarchy" refers to layers in a formal organization. The assumption is that the top layers are better than the bottom layers, as in the practice of calling deans and chairs "higher administration." We do this despite recognizing, for example, that students and teachers are the heart and soul of a college.

**Highlander:**    A radical, critical school in Tennessee in which workers, women, African-Americans, and others meet to learn how to organize and change the structures of domination that reduce the human spirit and harm the social process. Rosa Parks, the woman who sparked the Montgomery bus boycott in 1954, had just returned from such a gathering. Many union, civil rights, and antiwar people have attended and still attend Highlander programs.

**Hinduism:**   The complex, polytheistic, native religious system of India. In brief, Hinduism holds that there are cycles and stages of life, each of which is to be mastered in turn. If one fails in a stage, one may be reborn at a previous stage; if one succeeds, one is reborn into a higher, more demanding stage. For each male human being (Hinduism is a male-centered religion), there are four stages: the life of discipline; the life of a householder/worker; a period of retreat; and the life of a hermit, which leads to renunciation, the highest aspect of human awareness. Hinduism supports a "caste" system into which each person is born and must work all the days of his/her life: the *Brahmana*, a priestly caste; the *Kshatriya*, kings and warriors; the *Vaisya*, merchants and professionals; and the *Sudra*, farmers and workers. Then, too, there is an undercaste of "untouchables" who do the most degrading work. Similar to Christianity, there are three pathways to grace, salvation, and higher forms of being: the way of *Karma*, or good work; the way of *Jnana*, or meditation and knowledge; and the way of *Bhakti*, or devotion and faith. Buddhism arose out of Hinduism, accepting its spiritual qualities but rejecting the caste system.

**Historical Materialism:**   The use of the mode of production to explain all existing relationships and all changes in these relationships. According to this view, all analysis of state policy, ideology (including religion, political ideas, philosophy, art, and science), the military, and all other social institutions must occur through the mode of production of the society in which they take place. Qualitative changes in these social institutions must similarly be explained by changes in the mode of production or by contradictions between various elements of the superstructure and the mode of production.

With this concept, Karl Marx wanted to reject abstract idealism as a force that shaped human affairs. According to Marx, any system of explanation must be concerned with concretely existing factors and must be sensitive to the special history of each process that produces human activity. One cannot explain human events in terms of God, chance, destiny, history, fate, or probability. One must explain a society, a car, an individual, and so on by the process and means that produce it. Historical materialism does not reject the role of ideas in the productive process, as is often assumed. For Marx, human labor involved conscious shaping of nature after an idea. It is this ability to conceive of a purpose and to act on that purpose that distinguishes "the worst architect from the best of bees." See "Marx, Karl" for more.

**Historicism:**   A pejorative term used to reject the belief that there was pattern in history and that the future was determined by the past. The term was introduced by Karl Mannheim and adopted by Ernst Troeltsch to place more responsibility on humans and to open up the future to alternative, well-considered prospects. See "Prehistory" for more.

**Historicity:**   The particular combination of concretely existing social factors in which the interactive effect produces a unique event. Since humans create meaning through intention, the causality of an event thus can have a variable pattern. That varying pattern is what we call "history." This contrasts to ahistoricism, in which one seeks unchanging, universal laws with which to explain events. See "Stage Theory" for more.

**Historiography:**   One's approach to history and to its study is said to be a historiography. There are several theories about how to understand the sweep and pattern of history. These include: (1) Marxist thought and dialectical materialism; (2) the Great Man Theory; (3) the theological view (in which a god exists, has a plan for social life, and makes changes now and again for good reason); and (4) technological determinism (great inventions create turning points in history). Examples of the latter perspective are fire, the wheel, the alphabet, irrigated farming, metal working, the steam engine, automobiles, radio, television, and, now, computers. Each is given great emphasis in explaining the twists and turns in history.

The Marxist perspective is that "man makes history and that history has no independent causal power." Thus, "historical necessity" and "history decides" are mystifications in no way different from attributing such reified and deified powers to gods, nature, or absolutes: "History does nothing: it fights no battles, owns no riches, and does not use men for its purposes; it is nothing but the activity of man pursuing his ends." Real people set conditions in concert with other real people who limit the freedom of choice of other people. If the price of bread or milk is set by an agreement between suppliers and distributors, or if only one version of history is permitted, then there are "historical" conditions that "determine" behavior, but this is not the same as saying that history determines human affairs as some (including some Marxists) would have it. See "Great Man Theory (of History)" for more.

**History:**   Greek: *historia* = information, inquiry. That which deals with the unique, the private, or the non-recurring. It contrasts with "modernization theory," which studies the external, universal, and unchanging patterns of nature and society. In Chaos theory these distinctions are lost, since real systems display a mix of order and disorder, pattern and variation, change and renewal.

**HMO (Health Maintenance Organization):**   HMOs collect a flat fee per year from consumers in return for which they agree to provide whatever medical care one may require free or at a nominal charge. By contrast, under the familiar fee-for-service system, the physician and the hospital submit bills for what they did; the individual consumer or the consumer's insurance company then pays the bill. The attractive feature of HMOs is their ability to do away with apparently unnecessary treatment. The HMO makes more money when doctors prescribe fewer procedures. This is the opposite of the fee-for-service system. Studies consistently show that persons with ordinary health insurance submit to twice as much surgery as comparable persons enrolled in HMO-type plans. There are two major problems with HMOs: (1) Since profits are of concern, HMOs (may) limit service; and (2) the system does not deliver health and medical services to those in the surplus population.

**Hobbes, Thomas (1588–1679):**    Hobbes held that there was a war of each against all, that self-interest was a universal law of social psychology, and that in the natural state the life of man was solitary, poor, nasty, brutish, and short. This claim directs attention to the question of the sources of social organization. For Hobbes, these include: instinct (for gregariousness); power; consensus on values (produced by socialization); contract (among freely negotiating parties); and the will of God. Hobbes argued for a "civil order," one in which the best solution to the problem of order was a social contract that put all power in a monarch (a Leviathan).

The Marxist position is that social order in feudal and capitalist societies (or in elitist societies generally) is produced by coercion and control. On the other hand, social order should emerge from social justice.

Chaos theory suggests that order is not the central goal of a wise government. For chaologists, some mix of certainty and uncertainty best suits natural and social dynamics. See "Human Rights" for more.

**Homosexuality:**    Love of same sex persons; used to refer to males who engage in sexual behavior with other males. Homosexuality is forbidden in many societies and institutionalized in others. In recent times, homosexuality has been converted from a criminal act requiring punishment to a pathological act requiring treatment. In recent times, it has been de-criminalized and de-medicalized. There is a gay movement that advocates and demands recognition of homosexuality and homosexual partners. Many companies and states now specify that living partners are eligible for benefits, whereas before benefits were restricted to married couples of opposite sex. See "Lesbianism" for more. Cf. "Queer Theory."

**hooks, bell (1952– ):**    Also known as Gloria Watkins. hooks is a black feminist author of such works as *Ain't I a Woman: Black Women and Feminism*. She is best known for her critical stance toward white feminism. Specifically, hooks points out that the white feminists have, knowingly or not, victimized black women and, indeed, reproduced racist sentiments by making comparisons between the plight of women in general and blacks in particular. hooks contends that white women cannot usurp and ought not speak about the experience of being a women of color. Her prescription is for the establishment of a feminist theory that more systematically and completely articulates the experience of repression, marginalization, and de-legitimation that all (black) women embody and confront. This work is essential in order to develop a more honest appraisal of how to liberate (black) women and attend to their unique needs and sensibilities. See "Feminism, Black" for more.

**Hostile Contrast:**   Refers to the conflict between classes and elites/masses when one group enforces an exploitative set of rules upon another.

**Humanism:**   An ideology in which human dignity and the collective good is emphasized. Humanism usually employs science and logic to address problems rather than supernatural or mystical approaches. Freedom of the intellect, of criticism, and of association are highly valued as well. As such, humanism often opposes institutions that are coercive and/or exploitative. Sometimes humanists are criticized by Marxists as lacking a sociology (i.e., as not understanding the roots of oppression in the class struggle). See "Comte, Auguste" and "Theology, Postmodern" for more. Cf. "Marxism."

**Humanism, Abstract:**   The view that men and women are the measure of all things and that people should be the master of their own destiny and engineer their own social life through free and open political discussion. It was this abstract humanism (of Feuerbach) to which Marx objected. In Marx, human nature is a product of social conditions; rather than existing in a pure form that is then distorted by historical conditions, human nature is historically determined by concretely existing social relationships.

**Humanism, Socialist:**   The starting point of socialist/Marxist humanism is a militant struggle against "those conditions in which mankind is abased, enslaved, abandoned or rendered contemptible." This militancy goes beyond mere rhetoric to action for two reasons: (1) In struggle one transforms reality and thus satisfies the Marxian requirement that humanism must be real; and (2) militant struggle satisfies the Marxian requirement that "man makes history" (i.e., that the only hope of emancipation comes from the people themselves). This point emphasizes the value of autonomy in Marxian humanism. Socialist humanism also seeks the human fulfillment of the whole of mankind rather than of the isolated individual or of a single class. Marx does, however, invest hope in class struggle as the engine of progressive humanism. The goal of any Marxist humanism is to affirm the dignity and to support the promise of human beings. See "Theology, Postmodern" for more.

**Human Nature:**   In Marx, the mode of producing culture determines the being of people: "Production (in capitalism) does not merely produce man as a commodity, it produces him as a mentally and physically dehumanized being." The larger point is that human beings, unlike animals, have the rare gift and ability to create themselves in their full humanity if they act upon this radical anthropology. Marx's vision of human nature was that it became human in the process of creating culture (in the labor process). Here culture implies an ongoing process of intending humans joined in creating a rational mode of production. Just as language implies joint activity, the creation of all culture is collective activity. Art, science, medicine, knowledge, self, and society are collective productions that compose the nature of those who produce them.

**Human Rights:**   A set of rights that includes freedom of worship, assembly, association, speech, travel, and migration, as well as democratic self-government. The United Nations Universal Declaration of Human Rights includes these elements but also stresses cultural diversity and respect for national borders.

Many critics argue that there are human obligations that parallel these rights. Others claim the idea of human rights goes against human nature and that in any case such a belief is hopelessly utopian without great change in social institutions. Cf. "Hobbes, Thomas" for more.

**Husserl, Edmund (1859–1938):**   Husserl is noted for his work on modernist *phenomenology*. He developed a method for identifying the basic concepts with which people worked—it is called *eidetic reduction*. The process of discovering the *eidos* (essence) begins with a bracketing of all its nonessential elements. Space, form, weight, and time, for example, have an essence apart from what occupies the space, what takes the form, what gives the weight, or what happens in the time. The process of finding essence is called the *epoché*. *Noesis* is the process of intending to do, say, feel, make something; *noema* is the object intended; *phenomena* is the thing, act, or thought from the point of view of an outside party trying to understand internal psychological workings. Postmodern phenomenology takes the view that space, form, time and such exist only in the particular case; there is no preexisting ontology that answers to the concept. Without something having a form, there is no form. The concept of the cube is all abstract idealism with no concrete reality, since, in nature, there is no perfect cube. (See the work of W. L. Reese.)

**Hutterites:**   Inspired by their religion, Hutterites continue an agrarian way of life. They experience little crime, no poverty, no divorce, no drug abuse, and little gender violence. Hutterites live mostly in the Dakotas and in the prairie provinces of Canada. They have one of the highest birth rates and lowest infant mortality rates of any group in the United States.

**Hyperreality:**   A concept developed by the French postmodernist, Jean Baudrillard. Like most postmodernists, Baudrillard argues that objects (commodities) have more control over us then we do over them. In a consumer-driven society commodities acquire use-value so that we consume them for their "signs" and statements rather than for the exchange-value of their utility. Simulations constructed for us by technology (e.g., television, the Internet, the Web, CD-ROM) persuade us that the "real" no longer exists. When we cannot tell the difference between simulations and reality we have entered hyperreality. Our primary way of understanding people and human social interaction is to react (passively mostly) to simulations. Thus, we have no way to experience and appreciate relationships between people except as these relationships are defined (exchanged) through their sign values. The hyperreal, then, is a copy of a copy of a copy ad infinitum, such that no original can be found (e.g., Lyndon B. Johnson tried to present himself as a fictionalized Franklin D. Roosevelt, and Ronald Reagan tried to act like a president rather than like an actor portraying a president). See "Baudrillard, Jean," "Mass Media," "Sign," "Simulation," and "Value, Postmodern View of" for more.

**Hyperspace:**   Refers to the difficulty in locating firm and indisputable boundaries in social groups, nations, peoples, races, genders, universities, or even physical objects. The concept of "cyberspace" eliminates the concept of geographical space altogether. See "Fractal/Fractal Geometry" for more. Cf. "Cyberspace."

**Hypothesis:**   Greek: *Hypo* = below; *tithenai* = to put; place. That which lays underneath and grounds natural and social dynamics. For Plato, a hypothesis was the third rung in his ladder of truth. In modern science, it refers to a tentative statement that predicts a fairly stable relationship between two or more variables. The choice and investigation of a hypothesis always derives from human interests in prediction and control of the physical world and not from a detached quest for scientific truth. There are two kinds of hypotheses for which one searches: (1) H1 = a positive statement that one expects to find in a data set; and (2) H0 = a negative statement that one expects to find in a data set. See "Null Hypothesis" for more. See "Data" for more.

**"I":**   According to G. H. Mead, there are three levels of human behavior: (1) the level of impulse; (2) the level of sociocultural conditioning (learned behavior); and (3) the level of reflexive intelligence. For Mead, the "me" embodies the second level and represents the social self in which one internalizes and acts on the expectations of others. The "I" in Mead's model embodies the capacity for critical thought and for creative activity. Contemporary sociology emphasizes the "me" and tends to equate the "I" with selfish impulse. See "Act, Philosophy of," "Individual," "'Me'," and "Mead, George Herbert" for more.

**Idea/Idealism:**   Greek: *eidos* = vision, thought, form, shape. For Plato, an idea came from the essential structure/nature/form of a thing. One can see the seeds of Husserlian phenomenology in this usage. Leibniz used the term "idealism" to contrast with materialism. Idealism now refers to an emphasis on the role of ideas, gods, reason, and human will in the history of the world. Premodern thought took the view that there was a split between the ideal world and the rough approximation of it in "real" life. In everyday usage, idealism is a sustained effort to practice one's principles in problematic situations. The Marxian critique of idealism is that it is more a romantic gesture than an informed analysis. See "Utopia/Utopianism" for more.

**Ideal-Types:**   The concept refers to Max Weber's interest in how to examine various social phenomena. Ideal-types are theoretical and descriptive devices through which to better understand the complexity of events in society. Because ideal-types are instructive aids, they are only heuristic; that is, they are tools that lead to clarifying how a given process works or a particular system functions. Of particular significance is the application of Weber's concept to the study of law and legal decisionmaking.

   Weber identified four ideal-types relevant to law and legal thought. These include (1) formal rationality, (2) formal irrationality, (3) substantive rationality, and (4) substantive irrationality. These ideal-types are linked to a certain degree of formality (see "Formalism" for more) and rationality. The greater the degree of formalism, the greater the extent that the internal, established, formal rules of law will be applied in the analysis of a case. The greater the degree of rationality, the greater the extent that the process will be generalizable to all similarly situated people. *Formal rationality* as an ideal-type of lawmaking and law-finding exists in cultures where rules are identically applied to all persons who are similarly situated. This ideal-type promotes a high degree of predictability in decision-making. An example would be the bar against cruel and unusual punishment as contained in the Eighth Amendment of the U.S. Constitution. *Formal irrationality* as an ideal-type of legal decisionmaking exists in societies where magic, revelation, and prophecy govern the process. This ideal-type is prevalent in more primitive, mechanical societies. Formality is high but the generalizability of the decisionmaking to all identically situated people is low. *Substantive rationality* as an ideal-type of lawmaking exists in societies where a particular "external" legal principle is applied to a given case. For example, ethical mandates can, and do, at times take precedent over prevailing law, and decisions flow accordingly. Although there is a great degree of generalizability such that all persons are subjected to the same moral principle, the degree of formality is low. *Substantive irrationality* exists as an ideal-type of legal decisionmaking in societies where legal outcomes are situation specific and where there is low formality and low generalizability. In this instance, no norm governs the process. See "Weber, Max" for more.

**Identification:**    The process by which a young person internalizes a social identity into self-esteem. One "identifies" when one models one's behavior after another person. Identification always involves at least two parties: one who presents an identity and one who honors that presentation. In folk societies, identification is a complex rite and preempts the self-system for life. In mass society, it may involve only a ticket or a badge. In the latter case, identity is like a paper plate to be used and discarded.

**Identity, Social:**    The socially determined answer to the question, "Who am I?" One's social identity and self-system are composed of all of the roles (and associated social identities) that one occupies and enacts in the course of a given stage in life. In mass societies roles are so brief, superficial, and manipulative that an identity does not emerge as a stable, discernible pattern. Without social identity, behavior is often unstable, antisocial, and/or self-indulgent. In logic, identity denotes the absolute equality of one thing with another.

**Ideology:**    A generalized blueprint by which a given social lifeworld is created. Those things that give meaning and purpose to life—including art, music, poetry, prose, science, myth, joke, song, and religion—are an especially important part of an ideology. Sometimes ideology becomes reified into dogma and comes to be more than a general guide to the construction of social reality. Ideology can be a super-organic thing beyond the control of humans.

As a term, it is used to put down any social philosophy with which one disagrees. It was coined by Destutt de Tracy (*Idéologie* = the study of ideas) in opposition to the ideological hegemony of Napoleon. All social life requires a set of fairly comprehensive (but not necessarily compatible) ideas as the beginning point for the "self-fulfilling prophecy" in the construction of a social lifeworld. However, there are some important questions that follow: Which set of ideas are involved in the construction of the social lifeworld? How are these ideas to be transmitted to young people? And how much criticism is to be allowed? Marx held that ideology: (1) varies with the kind of political economy at hand; (2) varies with position, class, race, gender, and ethnicity; (3) is necessary for solidarity purposes; and (4) can be progressive or oppressive, depending on which ideas are valued most highly. See "Tracy, Destutt de" for more.

**Idiographic:**   Occurring uniquely from an unpredictable set of preconditions. Human behavior lends itself to idiographic processes, whereas physical objects behave nomothetically. Imagine a situation in which $f(a, b, c, d, e)$ sometimes produces $x$, sometimes produces $z$, and sometimes produces $\emptyset$? Think about five children at play or five scientists in a meeting. See "Nomothetic" for more.

**Idol:**   Greek: *eidos* = form, shape. In his foundational book about the new body of knowledge, *De Novum Organum*, Sir Francis Bacon took the view that science would chase four idols from the knowledge process: idols of the marketplace (*foria*); idols of the cave (*specus*); idols of the theater (*theatri*); and idols of the tribe (*tribus*). Postmodern critique holds that all research findings and theories are both a poetics and a politics. The question then becomes: Which idols are we to use and create in scientific investigation? See "Bacon, Francis" for more.

**Imagination, Sociological:**   A term coined by C. W. Mills to refer to the insights and empowerments produced by the study of social relations and social groups. With such an imagination one can begin to understand how the larger structures in society shape and pre-shape our own thoughts, feelings, and behavior. Racism, class position, ethnicity, and religious affiliation all exist prior to birth. Socialization and social role expectations often lead us to do things that, alone, we might not do. The social sources of both helpful and harmful behavior yield to the sociological imagination. See "Mills, C. Wright" for more.

**Immiseration:**   The process by which poverty and misery are produced by the ordinary operation of a social system. Marx held that the working class would be immiserated by the ordinary workings of capitalists because capitalism tended to disemploy workers and concentrate wealth and political power in the hands of a few. Then, too, capitalism tends toward cycles of boom and bust that periodically immiserate both workers and owners. Many argue, however, that capitalism tends to eliminate the lower and upper classes and point to the great improvement of workers in Europe and North America as proof. See "Embourgeoisiement " for more.

**Imperialism/Empire:**   A set of nations, countries, and peoples all controlled by a central nation that benefits therefrom. Imperialism includes: (1) expansion of production and distribution outside national borders; (2) central control of the money supply and finance; (3) export of finished goods to client nations; (4) division of labor (manual labor in the colonies and intellectual labor in the core country); and (5) restriction of human/civil rights in the periphery. Often direct military control is used until a "friendly" government can be installed. Capitalist countries, monarchies, dictatorships, and the former Soviet socialist system established empires. See "Indigenous Population" for more.

**Imperialism, Economic:**   A network of control methods (e.g., economic, political, military, cultural) that the dominant groups in one country use to subjugate and exploit people in other countries.

For Marx, imperialism had three major sources: (1) the search for markets to realize surplus value; (2) the export of surplus capital to other countries where interest and profits are higher; and (3) the search for cheaper labor, as workers in advanced nations make gains in wages and working conditions.

The euphemism "foreign aid" is used to convey the positive dimensions of economic imperialism. Economic imperialism does aid many in dominated countries but usually only large land owners, cooperative politicians, and small businesses. Often, this aid is temporary.

**Imperialism, Marxist-Leninist Theory of:**   Karl Marx, and later Vladimir Lenin, argued that the capitalist class must demand that the state help them obtain overseas markets and a dependable supply of cheap raw materials. Markets in other countries are necessary because the workers at home do not get paid 100 percent of the value of the goods they produce and therefore cannot buy them all back. Since capitalists in other countries want the same thing, the capitalist state has to go to war and/or bribe government officials in the target country. A cheap supply of raw materials is also necessary to keep production going and profits up.

**Implode/Implosion:**   Following Jean Baudrillard, the tendency of phenomenon in postmodern times to turn inward, thus destroying themselves and/or the assumptions that ground them. Thus, meaning "implodes" when special micro-languages are used in medicine, computer science, or religion.

**Impression Management:**  A term introduced by Erving Goffman that points to the efforts of individuals in a mass society to create dramaturgical images acceptable to bosses, fans, students, professors, and others with social or economic power. The concept directly challenges assumptions in Symbolic Interactionism about the shared-ness of symbols and the effort of people to work together for intersubjective understanding. See "Dramaturgy" and "Goffman, Erving" for more.

**Incest:**  Forbidden sexual behavior within close degrees of kinship. Incest usually involves sexual relations between fathers, uncles, or brothers and female kin over the age of 16. (Under that age sexual activity is generally defined as child abuse.) Stepfathers are more likely to be involved; mothers or aunts far less likely. Incest rules forbid such sexuality for three reasons: (1) It subverts the parental socialization process by putting the child in an adult status before she has been given such social status in a rite of passage; (2) the adult misuses the social power inherent in the parental status for personal purpose; and (3) it distorts all authority relations within a family. There is, as a consequence of shame and guilt, long-term psychological damage to those involved.

**Indeterminacy Principle:**  Also referred to as the "uncertainty" principle. A concept developed by the German physicist Werner Heisenberg. The principle is adapted from quantum mechanics. Essentially it states that it is not possible, with any degree of precision, to indicate concurrently the momentum (velocity) and the social location of an event. A painting is a good illustration of this principle. A painting tells us something about a moment in space and time. We do not know, with accuracy, what preceded it and what followed it. Both are significant to the moment represented on the canvas yet we are without this specificity. The painting cannot capture or embody fluid movement or continuous change. However, these are integral facets to the life of the painting and our existence.

Applying the logic of indeterminacy to science, we are led to conclude that every study or theory possesses some marginal utility based upon the restrictive parameters embedded and implied within the method of research or the conceptualization model itself. Science (knowledge), much like the painting described above, captures a moment in time and space. It can never be complete. Here, too, there is much that is overlooked or much that goes unstated (e.g., the assumptions of the theory, the position on causality, social structure, agency). The overlooked and unstated are the "before" and "after" of the painting and, when more closely examined, point out the layers of (conflicting) meaning(s) embedded with scientific truths. It is in this context that the Heisenberg indeterminacy thesis is relevant to critical inquiry. See "Longitudinal Analysis," "Postmodernists/Postmodernism," and "Ultrastability" for more.

**Index Crimes:**   Those crimes used by the FBI to measure how crime rates increase or decrease, including all Part One crimes: murder, manslaughter, rape, robbery, aggravated assault, burglary, larceny, and auto theft. Not included among index crimes are corporate, political, and white-collar crimes. Index crimes, while the most highly publicized and visible, are in fact a small percentage of all crime.

**Indigenous Population:**   Of or pertaining to the native or natural born citizens of a given society. Native American Indians are the indigenous population of North America. Indigenous populations are often exploited by those cultures seeking to advance their own imperialist objectives. This exploitation can assume several forms (e.g., cheap labor, ownership of peoples, the acquisition of land through force). See "Imperialism/Empire" for more.

**Individual:**   A unit of social existence whose boundaries are restricted to a single person. Social roles and social discourse suggest that the single individual is a fiction. If mind, self, and society are aspects of the same thing, then we are bound to others to the extent that we are social. Usually patterns of information flow mark the boundaries of the social entity. If people talk freely among themselves, then they compose a group rather than a set of individuals. See "'I'," "Individual, Theory of," and "Individualism (Possessive)" for more.

**Individual (and Socialism):**   According to Schaff, what matters most in socialism is the principle that the welfare of the human individual is the supreme good: "Socialism is by definition a system in which every individual is entitled to genuine, full development." Enmeshed in society, the real, concrete individual is the concern of revolution and the maker of history. According to Schaff and the humanist Marxism he embodies, social revolution is the protest of real humans against their isolation from community, and it is this protest that makes Marxism sensible. Without concern for the fate of the individual, all struggle loses its point.

This view opposes the focus on class, class conflict, and class struggle apart from the goal of relieving alienation and ensuring the possibility of praxis. An emphasis on the single individual has problems: It may encourage possessive individualism; it may deflect attention from social relationships; and it may endanger social revolution to the extent that privatized individuals find comfort and benefits from stratified societies. As Karl Marx proclaimed: "Man is an animal which can develop into an individual only in society."

**Individual, Theory of:**   The Marxian theory of the individual (sometimes called the Philosophy of Man) has three fundamental assumptions: (1) that the individual is a part of nature and not separate from it; (2) that the individual exists as a function of social relations; and (3) that the individual is a product of his/her own self-creation of labor within social relations. See "Individual" for more.

**Individualism:**   A social philosophy that sets the single person as the measure and repository of all judgment, wisdom, sin, folly, and morality. Adam Smith, Jeremy Bentham, John Stuart Mill, and Herbert Spencer provided the arguments for individualism. It is part of the Protestant ethic and the spirit of capitalism, since it justifies private interests above collective/public interests. It is progressive in that it opposes monarchy, church hierarchy, deadening collectivism, and suppression of human rights. Cf. "Praxis."

**Individualism (Possessive):**   There are several assumptions that are used to justify the private accumulation of wealth. These include: (1) To be human means to be free from dependence on the will of others; (2) the individual is free from any relations into which the individual does not voluntarily enter; (3) the individual is essentially the proprietor of her/his own person and capacities, for which the individual owes nothing to society; and (4) in a market society, one can sell one's capacities in exchange for fair remuneration.

Although each assumption could be criticized on a number of counts, the main points of rebuttal are as follows: (1) Being human involves the capacity to create culture; (2) culture cannot be produced apart from social relations; (3) a person learns to produce culture as a consequence of a labor-intensive process called socialization. One cannot socialize one's self; (4) in a market economy, one may sell labor only if some of the value of the labor is appropriated as profit by another who purchases it. See "Individual" for more.

**Induction:**   Latin: *in* = in; *ducere* = to lead in. A knowledge process by which one goes from observed data/facts to proposition and theory rather than from theory to hypothesis; the latter is called deduction. Empiricism relies on induction; rationality relies on deduction. There is a tension between the two in all scientific endeavor: Theories can never grasp the incredible complexity and ever-changing outcomes in natural and social reality but are instead convenient maps; facts by themselves give one no sense of the larger sweep of history nor of the probable future one faces in trying to survive, thrive, and control one's own destiny. C. S. Peirce argued for "abduction," a continuous going back and forth between data and theory. See "Peirce, Charles S." for more. Cf. "Abduction" and "Deduction/Deductive Logic."

**Inference:**   Latin: *in* + *ferre* = to carry something in. In Aristotelian logic, the process by which one reaches a conclusion from two or more premises/assumptions. See "Quantification Theory" for more.

**Information:**    Generally, the exchange of partly ordered structure between two systems. Anything that reduces mismatch between two systems (system and environment). In contrast, that which is completely known to both systems has no new content and thus is not technically information. Information must have some disorder (unknown data) as well as a set of rules by which to decode the new content. If there is too much disorder or if the signal cannot be decoded, then there is no information. If they are to be self-correcting and self-healing, all social systems require accurate, timely, decidable, relevant information about new and strange ways to do things. Thus, for example, such things as propaganda and secrecy are both obstacles to the ready flow of information.

**Infrastructure:**    The material base of a society and its method of producing goods and services. Infrastructure includes roads, bridges, dams, power stations, sewage and water purification systems, as well as all those lines leading into and out of offices, homes, and factories.

**Inquisition:**    Latin: *in + quirere* = to investigate. The word usually refers to an agency of the Catholic Church (still in operation) that looks into charges of individual heresy and the suitability of books and ideas. In the late Middle Ages the Inquisition burned, tortured, mutilated, and imprisoned thousands of "heretics." The Spanish Inquisition was the worst and lasted four hundred years (until 1834). Giordano Bruno was burned at the stake and Galileo was forced to recant his view that the earth was not the center of the universe. The Inquisition agency is now called the Congregation of the Doctrine of the Faith and publishes a list of prohibited books, movies, and theories.

**Instinct:**    A form of behavior programmed by genetic codes. Many people believe that some (or all) human behavior is pre-programmed as a result of countless generations of evolution, during which maladaptive behavior was eliminated in the struggle for survival. Most research suggests that human cerebral functioning can supplant and override any such predispositions. War, male dominance, stratification, mothering, and many other behavior patterns are often said to be instinctual. The concept of culture is used to emphasize the learned nature of these behaviors.

*Institutes, The*:    The elements of Roman law, codified in the reign of Justinian, that describe the law of nature (God's law), the people, and the state. These laws say who is a citizen, who is and is not free, how family law functions, and which children are under the control of which parents (i.e., children, grandchildren, and great-grandchildren). These laws regulate marriage (sanctioning only monogamous marriages between mentally competent and sexually mature members of the opposite sex not related by within three degrees of kin) and other property rights. They also permit, require, and regulate wills, fiduciary obligations, rights of passage, rights of way, usufruct (usury), weights and measures, inheritance, gifts, real estate sales, rights of slaves and animals, hiring and wage labor, partnerships, contracts, mandates, delicts (wrong-doing), contempt, security for claims until adjudicated, types of and qualifications for pleas, interdicts (what can be forbidden or required), penalties, and powers of judges. These topics are central to any legal system. See "Common Law" for more.

**Institution:**    A division within the larger social order that carries out a series of related tasks. An institution is composed of roles, actors, rules, objectives, and communication facilities. A given concrete instance of an institution is called an establishment. All institutions together should provide the resources (goods and services) by which a society survives and persons realize their human potential. Examples include education, religion, government, the economy, and family. Unless institutions are coordinated with each other there is a danger of imbalance.

**Institutional Racism:**    Those accepted practices that permit certain racially identified population categories to be excluded from the production of culture (usually political culture) and relegated to menial work. Since institutional racism involves rules, policies, and precedents, people who are not racists per se unknowingly continue the exclusion of others from access to housing, health care, the legal system, the political arena, and educational services by following ordinary procedures and recruiting from within kin, peer, and ethnic affiliations.

**Institutional Sexism:**    Practices in everyday life that presume women are less capable than men. These practices occur in law, religion, education, and business, where, generally, women are treated as if they do not have full adult standing. In the classroom, men are called before women, women are touched more frequently, and diminutives are used to refer to women (e.g., Jeannie instead of Jean; Susie instead of Susan; Betsy instead of Elizabeth). Men are more commonly called by their adult names (e.g., James instead of Jimmy; Robert instead of Bobby). Then too, professors more frequently respond to comments made by a men and pass over comments made by women.

**Instrumentalism:**    In philosophy, the position that experience or the utility of a thing determines its overall value. This logic can be applied to ideas and theories as well. For example, the value of a theory depends upon its (instrumental) usefulness. The social psychologist Kurt Lewin described this same concept as follows: "There's nothing so practical as a good theory."

**Instrumental Rationality:**    A system of organizing capital and labor to achieve a specific end with maximized efficiency. The political question is:

To what end is instrumental rationality employed? Cf. "Substantive Rationality."

**Intentionality:**    A mental act by which one participates in the organization of one's own behavior. The behavior of physical objects is "caused" (i.e., objects react to outside influence). A special character of humans is that they can act with judgment and insight and thereby act differently from what is "normal" or predictable. See "Act, Philosophy of" and "Management Science" for more.

**Interest:**    The price paid for the loan of money. Interest comes from surplus value. Sometimes interest is a fair return on investment; sometimes it comes from super-exploitation. Biblical law provided for usury; a fair charge for the wear and tear of loaned goods; and for a small payment for the loan of money. However, interest rates over 10 percent per year were defined as a violation of God's law. In addition, debts were forgiven entirely every seven years. (This is where we get the word "sabbatical.") In capitalist societies interest rates are supposed to be set by the free market, but there are two practices that ignore free-market ideology: (1) Banks get together and fix interests rates; and (2) the state sets interest rates up or down in order to stimulate or discourage consumption and investment. See "Corporate Crime," "Keynesian Economics," "Rent," and "Usury" for more.

**Internal Colonialism:**    A theory of poverty. Internal colonialism exists when: (1) one ethnic group dominates another; (2) there is territorial separation of subordinate ethnic groups into "homelands," "reservations," or "Native reserves"; (3) a special government created by the dominant group rules the subordinate group, using laws that differ from those of the dominant group but are fashioned by them; and (4) the dominant group systematically appropriates the surplus value of the subordinate group's labor.

**Internalization:**    The incorporation of social norms into the self or the personality, so that violations of norms will produce a sense of guilt. To the extent this happens, the notion that self and society are twinborn makes sense.

**International, First (1864–1876):**    An organization founded in London to coordinate the working-class movement around the world. The organizing committee included G. Odger, W. R. Cremer, and Karl Marx. It had modest success but was always limited by nationalism, conservative religion, racism, and gender privilege. See "Marx, Karl" for more.

**International, Socialist:**    There were four: (1) the International Workingmen's Association of 1864, organized by Karl Marx; (2) the Second International, organized in 1889, which collapsed when German, English, and

French workers opted for national interests rather than international class struggle; (3) the "Comintern," organized by Stalin; and (4) the Fourth International, organized in opposition to Stalin and Stalinism by Leon Trotsky in 1938. It continues, but without mass transnational support. Ernest Mandel is its best known leader.

**International Court of Justice:**   A court at The Hague, consisting of fifteen judges (elected for nine-year terms) who adjudicate disputes relating to international law. All members of the United Nations are automatically members of the court and subject to its rulings. However, nations may reject its jurisdiction in selected cases. The court may issue advisory rather than binding rulings. Many opponents on the right and left reject both the court and international law as intrusions into private matters.

**Internationalism:**   Refers to worker solidarity that reaches beyond national borders. One of the factors that divides workers and gets them engaged in destructive competition for jobs is nationalism, also called the alienation of patriotism. In the *Communist Manifesto*, it is clear that the proletariat has no homeland. Internationalism is an inseparable part of communism. The automobile, textile, or computer industry in the United States can move to South Korea, India, or Mexico and create animosities between workers there and in this country. By paying low wages in one country (South Korea: $.22 per hour; Hong Kong: $.57 per hour), capitalists can depress wages in other countries and thus increase the surplus value extracted from workers. Internationalism is a movement that represents the workers of the world as they unite to prevent this competition.

**International Law:**   A body of law negotiated and signed by some set of nations. These laws reduce the sovereignty of individual countries so that more powerful nations will not ignore less powerful ones in pursuing their national interests. International law deals with the formation of new nations, the acquisition of territory from other nations, human rights, warfare, the laws of the sea and of space, treaties, the treatment of aliens and refugees, and disputes between countries. The League of Nations and the United Nations were formed to deal with such problems and issues. Cf. "Grotius, Hugo."

**International Law, Private:**   Most states have a set of laws about how their citizens should behave or do business overseas. This is not binding on other nations but is binding on courts within the jurisdiction of the nation concerned.

**International Monetary Fund (IMF):**   The economic mechanism by which loans are arranged for developing countries. A more critical analysis identifies the IMF as the financial agency used by rich countries to force debtor nations to institute state policies that enable them to return both principle and interest to the banks that loan them money. Higher taxes, fewer programs of social justice, and a greater share of the gross national income in poor nations ensue as a result of the work of the IMF. The United States is the dominant power in the IMF.

**Interpellation:**   The process by which one speaks and is understood through language. All persons, in order to convey meaning, situate themselves and are inserted within the language system. For example, in order for a jailhouse lawyer to represent a fellow inmate's case during a trial, the jailhouse lawyer must situate himself within the language of the law. Indeed, this is what "good" lawyering is all about. The interpellated subject is, knowingly or not, an agent for the continued legitimacy of the language in operation.

**Interrogatory:**   In civil law, a discovery device consisting of formal written questions submitted by one party in a dispute to another party or witness, the answers to which are usually given under oath. It is a powerful legal weapon but the questions must be directly relevant to the case at hand.

**Intertextual:**   Infinitely complex interconnections between stories about nature, society, or history that do not allow for clear and identifiable beginnings, boundaries, endings, or binary oppositions. Absolute intertextuality presumes everything is connected.

**Intimacy:**   A form of social relatedness in which the boundaries between self and other are not clear and definite. Intimates share freely and give each other emotional support when needed. In stratified relationships, intimacy can work against a person, as a great many women have discovered when they depend too much on males for economic support and emotional comfort.

**Intuition:**   Latin: *in* + *tueri* = to look at. Refers to the idea that one can come to the truth of a thing by reflection and meditation. Socrates held that a person was part of the spirit world before birth and thus "knew" everything. The shock of birth suppressed the memories of ultimate truth, but in quiet moments these memories could come back as revelations. More likely, such intuitions are the result of the human brain organizing a lot of diverse data and putting them together in a new and insightful pattern.

**IQ:**   Intelligence Quotient. The ability to learn, remember, sort, and apply information, measured by problems given on a pencil-and-paper test. There is a lot of controversy about IQ tests. The main controversy is whether IQ is shaped more by genetics or environment. If it is genetics, then those who score highest can claim some superiority. Racism and sexism are both justified by pointing to IQ scores. However, if such tests are biased in favor of things white men are likely to do or know, then that argument loses its force. There are any number of unscaled informational flow systems in the human body. IQ tests measure only cognitive abilities. Muscle memory, blood chemistry, hormones, enzymes, and tissues all gather data. They store it, retrieve it, and apply it to survival problems not easily encoded in paper tests. Then, too, human beings live in a symbolic social lifeworld that may be stupid or intelligent apart from the ability of the person. The point is that intelligence is not just something located in the braincase of individuals. To set this ability as the final test of human merit is a political act rather than a scientific one. See "Cognitive Capacities" and "Consciousness" for more.

**Irigaray, Luce (1930– ):**    French feminist social theorist and philosopher who trained in psychoanalysis with Jacques Lacan. Irigaray was dismissed from the Lacanian school because of her radical and critical perspectives, which differed from those of Lacan. Cf. "Lacan, Jacques."

The essence of Irigaray's critique focuses on language, the body, and psychoanalysis. Irigaray contends that the discourse of Western culture and thought is saturated in masculine meanings; these are meanings that reduce difference and multiplicity to sameness and unity. However, the feminine voice and way of knowing is constituted by pluralities. She draws attention to this in her work, *This Sex Which Is Not One*. Irigaray demonstrates that masculine logic can be traced to "the phallic economy of sameness." The nexus of feminine sexuality, though, can be traced to a woman's two labia. These contrast with the unitary male penis. However, notwithstanding this difference that is constitutive of the feminine sex, women, through masculine language and sense-making, are repressed and denied their uniquely lived desires in language and action.

Irigaray endorses the figurative rather than biological condition described above for women as "other." Indeed, because of their otherness, women more authentically dwell in nonlinear modes of reason and understanding. This is women's *jouissance*: an excess grounded in plurisignificances, multiplicities, inconsistencies, and heterogeneities. Irigaray's prescription for the plight of women is a constant debunking of the texts that define Western culture and thought. This debunking or decentering is not a systematic, targeted, and vigilant dismantling and reconstitution of phallocentric language. These activities would unwittingly support the phallic economy of sameness. Rather, the deconstruction that Irigaray has in mind is one that is fluid, contingent, and positional. Similar to Michel Foucault, she resists a totalizing feminist methodology because it, too, possesses the power to oppress, victimize, and alienate alternative expressions of difference. This feminine fluidity, as a method of process, includes such techniques as reflexivity, mimetism, and semiotic analysis. See "*Ecriture feminine,"* "Feminism, Postmodern," "Phallogocentrism," and "Sexuality" for more. Cf. "Essentialism," *"Jouissance,"* and "Kristeva, Julia."

**Irrationality:** A mode of thinking in which a complete knowledge of all prior events and their interactions is inadequate to account for a final product. Behavior cannot be predicted because imagination and ingenuity create completely unique and unpredictable conduct. The human interest in change and renewal is served by irrational thinking, whereas the human interest in prediction and control is served by rational thinking.

**Irreversibility:** A situation in which a system is able to survive by transferring order from its environment. Since society depends upon its population base for order, all societies must see to the health of the population upon which they depend. The same is true of the physical base upon which both depend.

**Irreversible Socio-Dynamics, Theory of:** A set of principles that indicate how a social system may maintain itself as a stable "irreversible" entity (despite the second law of thermodynamics, which says that every system tends toward disorder). The major point of the theory is that a system must be organized to maintain its own boundaries, seek quality variety, use it to adapt to new conditions, and maintain the integrity of the environment from which it draws its order. Since a human population is the most important environment of a social system, human societies must first look to the well-being of the people. Chaos/Complexity theory expands this body of knowledge to include the importance of nonlinear feedback in producing self-similar structures.

**Issue:** A conflict situation in which there is no accepted solution for dealing with an exigency. Often two (or more) individuals or groups take differing positions on how to reduce mismatch between system and environment. Wisdom and judgment are required to resolve issues. The resolution of a "problem" entails consensus on how to deal with the mismatch; that is, only technical reason is necessary to solve a problem. Problems have solutions; issues require a political process in order for a solution to be generated. Cf. "Problem."

**Iteration:** A concept that has relevance both in philosophy and in the physical sciences. According to Jacques Derrida, when we speak there is always and already hidden away the trace of something else present. This something else is the absence (or negation) of what is said. For example, utter the word "white" and we are, at some level of thought, asked to be mindful of "not-white" and "black"; utter the word "straight" and we are, at some level of thought, asked to be mindful of "not-straight" and "gay." This effect is always present as the naming of phenomena proceeds, despite the iterative context in which it is discussed. Moreover, as we are engaged in different situations and speak of "white" or "straight" there are countless disproportional effects in meaning and understanding. For example, to speak about "White Pride" before a group of neo-Nazi youth does not have the same iterative effect when spoken before a group of NAACP (National Association for the Advancement of Colored People) members. Meaning slips, is unstable and uncertain, given that there is an absence (non-white and black) present in every expression—an absence that varies, depending on context. See "Derrida, Jacques" for more.

This same logic of instability through iteration is contained in Chaos theory. Chaos theory is interested in plotting the movement patterns of a physical system (e.g., the internal human body) or social system (e.g., the economy). Chaos theory posits that the initial conditions of a system always behave in a nonlinear (unpredictable) fashion. We do not exactly know how the system will move or in what direction it will gravitate. This essential and initial (dis)order is constant throughout various iterative investigations of the system. Thus, our understanding of any system is necessarily based upon a state of uncertainty, disequilibrium, instability.

# J

**Jacobins:** A left-wing group in the French Revolution that embodied a radical democracy and absolute equality. The Jacobins attacked the last remnants of the feudal system and the clergy. Maximilien Robespierre led the Jacobins; Denis Diderot gave the group its slogan: "Justice will come only when the last king is strung up with the guts of the last priest." They held power in France from May 1793 to July 1794. This was a time of terror during which many opponents of the revolution were guillotined. Composed of small businessmen, militant workers, and members of the lumpen-proletariat, the Jacobins were ruthless in destroying their opposition. They were named after St. Jacques Convent, where they met. Cf. "French Revolution."

**Jim Crow:** A series of laws by which blacks were denied social, political, and economic status in the south (and north) after the Civil War of 1860–1865 in the United States.

**John Birch Society:** A right-wing group founded by John Welch, a candy manufacturer, and named after an American soldier killed in the communist advance in China in 1945. Welch accused Presidents Roosevelt, Truman, and Eisenhower of being communist agents because they supported state intervention in the economy and state ownership of the post office, highways, and social services. The Society declined in the late 1960s but has recently gained new members.

*Jouissance:* A notion of profound significance in French postmodern theory. As developed by Jacques Lacan, *jouissance* (*jouis* + *sense*) refers to that enjoyment, excess, or fulfillment that is beyond words or expression. Its application to postmodern theory signals how, through discourse, we long to convey our needs, hopes, despairs, and aspirations—in short, our desire. However, words and phrases (whether spoken or written) are incomplete. They do not ensure us of our *jouissance*. Nonetheless, we struggle to ensure that our desire finds embodiment in discourse, through intersubjective communication. *Jouissance*, then, is that which is ineffable yet at the heart of our very being. See "Lacan, Jacques" and "Readerly (Versus Writerly) Text" for more. Cf. "Irigaray, Luce" and "Kristeva, Julia."

**Judaism:**   The religion of the Jewish people and the foundation of both Islam and Christianity. It began as a compact between God, Abraham, and the chosen people. The terms of the compact (covenant) are spelled out in Deuteronomy. The first five books of the Old Testament (Torah) compose the heart of Judaism; they are supplemented by the Talmud, which contains oral laws dating from the fifth century B.C.

**Judge:**   One who has the legal right to decide on guilt, lack of guilt, and the applicability of substantive, procedural, and evidentiary law.

**Judgment:**   A ruling by a judge that can be enforced by the power of the state. These rulings include fines, imprisonment, garnishment, divorce, commitment to asylums, custody of children, and orders to do or not do a specific act. Judges have a lot of social power that, in democratic societies, flows from the people to the state and then to the judge. In elitist societies, legal power loses its social character and becomes an alien force to be resisted.

**Junta:**   A ruling committee (often military) that controls the policy of a totalitarian or fascist state.

**Jurisdiction:**   The legal authority of a court to hear a case and render a judgment. Also, the geographic area in which a court has such authority.

**Jus:**   Latin: *ius* = right, law. There are four kinds of law: (1) *jus civile* = civil law; (2) *jus divinum* = divine or eternal law; (3) *jus gentium* = the law of nations or international law; and (4) *jus naturale* = natural law. Natural law usually means the same thing as *jus divinum*, whereas natural law means those regularities in nature (and maybe society) that can be teased out by the scientific method. *Jus civile* and *jus gentium* are clearly made by humans. There is considerable argument between premodern and modern thinkers about the reach, if any, of Natural law. Postmodernists tend to see all such laws as human work.

**Just Deserts:**   A criminal justice philosophy of punishment traced to Andrew Von Hirsch's 1976 work titled, *Doing Justice*. The just deserts doctrine holds that the degree and type of sanction a person should receive following the commission of a criminal act is proportionate to the seriousness of the crime itself. This theory purports to be based on equity. For example, if I kill someone, then I should be sentenced to death. The problem with just-deserts thinking is that it does not reduce harm as the goal of criminal justice; rather, it simply substitutes one harm (killing someone) with another harm (sentencing the person to death). It is a policy of repression and counter-harm that uses institutional harm to control crime, arguing that this will somehow make a difference in promoting and sustaining justice. See "Justice, Retributive," "Kant, Immanuel," "Punishment," and "Retribution" for more.

**Justice:**   Latin: *ius* = right, law. That which is right and proper in terms of a given set of principles or traditions. One must distinguish between justice stemming from the technical and rational application of a set of formally established rules, laws, or standards, and that justice that comes from social status, mercy, compassion, love, and reason. The latter transcends technical rationality. Often technical justice is used to defeat efforts to obtain more substantive justice in housing, jobs, health care, education, and social standing.

**Justice, Distributive:**   Those judgments that attempt to restore and repair the damage done by a criminal act. The idea is that justice and the general good are better served if a criminal is made to restore the original conditions of, or make some restitution to, the victim. In the case of wrongful death, for example, the perpetrator may have to provide for the family of the victim. Roman law is much more oriented toward distributive justice than is English common law. Cf. "Justice, Retributive."

**Justice, Retributive:**   Those judgments that inflict revenge upon the convicted criminal; that is, an eye for an eye, a tooth for a tooth, or a life for a life. In retributive systems of justice, pain and punishment have healing qualities for both the victim and the perpetrator. The victim (or victim's family) gains satisfaction from knowing that the perpetrator experiences an equivalent pain, shame, or loss; the perpetrator benefits by learning to avoid such behavior in the future. Cf. "Justice, Distributive." See "Just Deserts" and "Retribution" for more.

**Justice, Substantive:**   A form of ideological culture in which some set of principles are used to ground the judgment of right and wrong, guilt or innocence, and reward or punishment. A society cannot be called "just" until such principles honor and sustain dignity and productivity for every human being.

**Justice, Technical:**   A ruling or justification of an act from a set of established laws, rules, norms, or values. The problem is that rules, norms, values, and laws are often biased in favor of one group or another so that when justice is done, it may be irrational in terms of human rights or reason.

**Justify/Justification:**   To show a lawful reason why an act may be done. In this context "lawful" means a universally valid principle as well as a tight, logical rationale used to derive a judgment. There is a question, however, about the larger justice of the "lawful reason."

**Justinian:** Emperor of Constantinople who, in 537 A.D., "took on the cares of the people that they might live without care." Working through his appointed committee, Justinian had the body of Roman law codified and simplified. His *Institutes* (three great books) are the basis of civil law in modern Europe and the United States. Civil law is extended to all citizens *(civil)* and replaces common law and church law. The idea that one is a citizen and thus has legal rights is fundamental to contemporary law. Prior to Justinian, one had to be born into a tribe in order to qualify for both justice and legal protection. Roman citizenship gave protection to all conquered lands and began the process of universalizing both criminal and social justice.

The *Institutes* began with the words, "Justice is an unswerving and perpetual determination to acknowledge the rights of all men." The *Institutes* were the basis for legal proceedings in every colony of old Rome and remain so for modern Italy.

**Juvenile:** Latin: young person; one with less than full adult status. In law, persons 14 to 17 are generally tried in a special court. The court is instructed to work toward distributive, restorative justice rather than punitive, retributive justice. Juveniles are subject to juvenile law, including "status offenses" not binding on adults (e.g., truancy, underage drinking, curfew violation). See "Age Grades" and "Sociology of Youth" for more.

**Juvenile Delinquency:** Any act involving a person 14 to 17 years of age that violates a legal specification. Juveniles are processed by the juvenile justice system rather than the criminal justice system. In the United States and in other countries that adopt legal systems from England and northern Europe, distributive justice primarily informs this system, whereas retributive justice primarily informs the criminal justice system. Juveniles commit about one third of all serious crime (1995). In the United States, there is strong support to treat young persons as adults and subject them to pain and punishment.

Theories of juvenile delinquency are numerous. They broadly encompass six perspectives: (1) Delinquents make bad choices (classical criminology); (2) delinquents are born to be bad (genetics, socio-biological criminology); (3) delinquents are psychologically maladaptive; (4) juvenile delinquency results from poverty (social structural explanations); (5) certain juveniles are socialized to commit crime (social process theories); and (6) certain juveniles lack self-control (social control theory). See "Status Crimes" for more.

**Juvenile Justice System:** A complex and growing institution that handles the crimes and offenses of young persons. There are few constitutional protections for juveniles; however, the system is informed more by restitutive justice and restorative therapy than punishment and incarceration.

According to socialists, the system emerged to do two things essential to capitalism: keep children in school in order to have a more highly trained labor force and prevent children from competing with adult men for scarce jobs. See "Status Crimes" for more.

# K

**Kant, Immanuel (1724–1804):**   One of the more important contributors to the philosophy of science and a basic source for modern and postmodern sensibility. Kant worked and wrote at the University of Königsberg. He is best known for his work on analytic versus synthetic reasoning; a priori/a posteriori reasoning (before/after looking at data); and the categorical imperative.

In his *Critique of Pure Reason*, he made the postmodern point that all knowledge is a combination of how nature appears and of the nature of the observer. His imperative for ethical behavior and his formula for perpetual peace bear serious consideration. For example, the categorical imperative holds that if an act is wrong it must be so categorically; that is, in all instances. Thus, if killing is wrong, then so, too, is killing during time of war, killing to defend oneself, and killing to end one's suffering. Kant's categorical imperative is called a "deontological" approach to moral reasoning. In other words, in order to determine the morality of behavior you focus on the act and not the consequence of the act. The latter focus is termed "teleological." (Cf. "Golden Rule" and "Utility/Utilitarianism.") Kant's ideas were significant to the development of classical criminology and theories of punishment. See "Just Deserts" for more.

Modernist phenomenology owes to Kant the idea that there are some twelve "natural categories" that predate human thought. Postmodern phenomenologists would disagree.

**Kantian Imperative:**   A grounding for human behavior absent gods and natural law: "Act as if the maxim of thy act were to become thy will, a universal law of Nature." See "Golden Rule," "Hammurabi, Code of," "Kant, Immanuel," and "Utility/Utilitarianism" for more.

**Kerala:**   A small state in India, controlled by communists since 1957. Also, the first and only communist government ever elected in a free and open election. It sustained itself but was rejected by voters in 1959. The communists returned to power in 1967. Kerala has one of the highest literacy rates, lowest death rates, lowest crime rates, and the highest employment rate in India.

**Keynes, John Maynard (1883–1946):**   British economist who wrote *General Theory of Employment, Interest, and Money* (1930). It is the key text for saving capitalism from its cycles of boom and bust. He also did work on probability that continues to be used in mathematics. See "Keynesian Economics" and "Kondratieff Cycles" for more.

**Keynesian Economics:**   Named for John Maynard Keynes, a British economist who made the case in his classic text, *General Theory of Employment, Interest, and Money* (1930), that the ups and downs of capitalism can be eliminated or at least moderated in the short term by the fiscal policy of the capitalist state. When times are bad, the state stimulates demand with grants, low interest rates, subsidies, money supply, tax incentives, or by buying the "surplus" production and giving it away to needy people. When times get better, the state is supposed to increase taxes to pay for all the things it did during a depression. President Roosevelt first used Keynesian economics in the Great Depression of 1930. President Nixon said, "We are all Keynesians." President Reagan used the fiscal policy of the state to buy political legitimacy and left a huge national debt for the current generation to pay off. About nine out of ten dollars used by the state to stimulate growth go to the rich.

Keynesian economics works best if the credit is used wisely and is paid back by taxes when times are good. Depressions will be less serious and shorter but the long-term tendency of capitalism is to destroy itself by disemployment, concentration of wealth, and subversion of the political process. Keynesian economics can postpone or moderate these tendencies but not eliminate them. See "Credit," "Deficit Spending," "Expansion," "Interest," "Keynes, John Maynard," and "Mixed Economy" for more.

**Kibbutz:**   Agricultural communes in Israel in which workers share the planning of work, parenting, health care, education, and recreation. Kibbutzim apply the slogan "From each according to one's ability; to each according to one's need" and were founded by Jewish socialists from Europe after the founding of the Israeli state in 1949. One of the more successful Kibbutzim in Israel is Maagan Michael on the coast of the Mediterranean. It produces fish, fruits, and some market vegetables and uses drip irrigation technology. Housing is assigned free on the basis of seniority and need. It has its own collective nursery, but children go home at night. It has a senior center where elderly folk may work for wages or not. It provides free health care, free education up to high school, and pays for college tuition. Young men and women live in separate houses after age 16 and generally run their own lives. People may eat in the cafeteria free or they may buy their own food and prepare it at home. There is a theater that shows movies, plays, and concerts. It is one of 300 Kibbutzim; not all Kibbutzim are as successful as Maagan Michael. See "Co-Parenting," and "Phalanstery, Phalanx Socialism" for more.

**King, Martin Luther, Jr. (1929–1968):**   An African-American civil rights leader, Martin Luther King helped organize boycotts, sit-ins, and marches on behalf of black Americans. King was assassinated in Memphis in 1968. He became a threat to the power elites since he supported black workers in Memphis and opposed the war in Vietnam. King referred to the welfare system as an "evil system" that corrupts people and called for more sweeping reforms. The FBI engaged in secret and illegal efforts to discredit King. There is now a national holiday and a great many public honors given in his name.

**Knowledge:**   Greek: *gignoskein* = to decide upon, to determine, or to decree. Today it means sure and certain understanding of how nature and society works. There are many pathways to knowledge. In premodern times, one meditated or used psychogenics to connect with the infinite. Inspiration and revelation were also part of premodern knowledge. In modern science, there are two major pathways: (1) rational, logical deduction from formal theories and (2) statistical inference from data sets collected by observation and/or questionnaires. Plato contrasted opinion *(doxa)* with authentic knowledge *(episteme)*. The highest form of knowledge, according to Plato, was *sophia*, a knowledge of first principles from which all truth could be deduced. Postmodern views are that all knowledge sets are constructed within and for a given social lifeworld. Each culture uses different concepts to slice up the extraordinary complexity of nature to serve its own purposes. Each society creates social knowledge in the act of constructing the various social roles and relationships that compose social institutions and social life worlds.

**Knowledge, Democratization of:**   Socialist theory requires a system of production and distribution of knowledge involving those who are the subject of knowledge and those who are the users of knowledge. Thus, the subdivision of knowledge into experts and clients, where clients pay experts for their knowledge, is replaced. The democratization system makes all knowledge free to all persons based upon need and interests. Computer-based internets that charge a modest user fee could serve to democratize medical, political, religious, sexual, and economic knowledge. Cf. "Plato."

**Knowledge, Sociology of/Process of:**   There are three major pathways to human knowledge: (1) premodern knowledge that goes back to the earliest human beings; (2) modern science crystallized by the success of Newton, who found precise patterns of behavior in physics; and (3) postmodern knowledge that began in earnest in the 1960s. The first pathway gives the human enterprise the capacity to believe, to trust, to have faith, and to accept one's own inspiration as a pathway to knowledge. The second pathway emphasizes measurement, prediction, and observation as a way to ground truth claims. It has given us better agriculture, communication, transportation, health technology, and so on. The third pathway uses history, cross-cultural comparisons, and class or cultural interests to understand how truth claims are made and adopted. All three pathways are essential to the human project. See "Empiricism" for more.

**Kondratieff Cycles:**   Capitalism tends to exhibit regular cycles of boom and bust. There are three kinds of cycle. Long cycles with thirty- to fifty-year waves are called Kondratieff cycles, after the Russian economist who identified them in 1910. There have been several such cycles, going back to 1740, then 1790, 1840, 1873, 1890, 1930, and now, perhaps, the United States is on the downturn of such a wave. They are the outgrowth of capitalism's inability to sufficiently allocate profits for all, so that the wealth produced can then be bought in the marketplace. Workers do not get paid 100 percent of the value they produce; owners cannot use all the remainder. A surplus accumulates; workers are laid off; factories close; and the whole system tends to slow down.

After companies go bankrupt, products wear out, prices fall, new demand is generated, and there is an upswing. There are several "solutions" to these cycles, including,: Keynesian economics, wars, crime, welfare, and the inflow of foreign capital. Each solution renews demand and supply. Unemployment prevents both inflation and these economic cycles. There is considerable debate about whether these cycles exist. In recent work, Brian Berry reports that Kondratieff cycles are nonlinear. Thus, they may exist, though not in the regular, predictable form required by modern science. See "Capitalism, People's," "Expansion," "Fiscal Crisis," "Keynes, John Maynard," "Kutznets Cycles," and "Unemployment" for more.

**Koran:**   Arabic: *Qur'an,* from *qara'a* = to read. The holy book of Islam. The book contains the teachings of Mohammed and dates from about 622 A.D. The Koran is organized into *suras,* or chapters. Together, they provide the ceremonial, civil, and criminal laws of all of Islam. They teach faith, virtue, compassion, social justice, and battle for the faith. They contain condemnations of Jews, the delights of heaven, and the punishments to be expected in hell. Some 800 million or more Muslims take these *suras* seriously and, as a result, produce a low-crime society with mechanisms for redistribution of wealth to the poor, widows, and children.

**Kristeva, Julia (1941– ):**   A philosopher, psychoanalyst, and student of semiotics, Kristeva advances the postmodern feminist agenda in several ways. Her central critique addresses the question of sexual difference and how this difference is embodied in culture and human social behavior.

Kristeva is credited with developing and/or refining a number of important concepts. These include: (1) the *semiotic chora* (a woman's preverbal/psychic "pulsations" that primordially shape subjectivity and speech);

(2) the *thetic or symbolic* (masculine construction of logic); (3) the *mirror stage* (the nexus of the semiotic and the symbolic); and (4) *jouissance* (the joining of the semiotic and symbolic in the lived world; that which is beyond enjoyment or enjoyment in sense). See *"Jouissance"* for more. Cf. "Lacan, Jacques."

By examining the junctures among psychoanalysis, language, and culture, Krisetva argues that the feminine register (semiotic) is dismissed or subjugated by the male voice (symbolic). For Kristeva, there is a duality to the human subject: One side of this duality is pre-libidinal, preverbal, and semiotic (feminine); and the other side is instinctual, spoken, and symbolic (masculine). This duality influences all social life. Kristeva contends that society devalues, ignores, and/or rejects the feminine. What is needed is an *ecriture feminine* (a non-bastardized code and way of being) that more authentically speaks for and about women's ways of knowing. This code is critical to emancipating repressed feminine history, art, and literature and for establishing new cultural forms freed from masculine sensibilities. See *"Ecriture feminine"* for more. Cf. "Essentialism," and "Irigaray, Luce."

**Kropotkin, Peter Alekseyevich, Prince (1842–1921):**   Prince Kropotkin was a Russian army officer, naturalist, and politician best known for his seminal work on anarchy. Imprisoned for his efforts to aid farmers and workers, Kropotkin escaped to western Europe to write on mutual aid and anarchy. Left alone, he said, humans were naturally cooperative and could get along fine without a state to run things. He developed a communal form of anarchy in which he combined the absolute freedom of the individual with common ownership of the means of survival. He thought that, out of this social form, independent production units would form to respond to basic human needs. Cf. "Social Darwinism," "Struggle for Survival," and "Survival of the Fittest."

**Kuhn, Thomas (1922– ):**   American philosopher on the sociology of science. In his 1962 book, *On the Structure of Scientific Revolutions*, Kuhn identified and examined the politics that infuse officially accepted theories and worldviews. Science is a social product produced by a community of scientists. This community determines what shall be accepted as scientific orthodoxy and what shall be called "unscientific." Kuhn made the point that worldviews in a discipline, called "paradigms," are validated and taught as the truth until further research creates an intellectual revolution and new paradigms emerge to be treated as scientific orthodoxy. In a subsequent interview, Kuhn indicated that he thought that a final, comprehensive paradigm that would end the dialectics of knowledge was possible. Postmodern sensibility holds that nature and society are so complex that any number of paradigms are possible. Indeed, they dwell side by side in most disciplines. According to postmodern thought, a final, encompassing paradigm is not possible. All paradigms have limited, human usefulness, including premodern worldviews based upon trust, faith, hope, compassion, and belief.

**Kutznets Cycles:**    These cycles in capitalism are said to come along about every fifteen years. There is considerable controversy about them. See "Kondratieff Cycles" for more.

# L

**Labeling Theory:** A term introduced by Howard Becker to denote the feedback effects of formal control systems that police, judge, incarcerate, and discipline people. There is a complex feedback loop in which criminalized or deviant social identities (stigmas) become part of one's internalized identity as one is processed through social control systems. Labeling theory cannot be a theory of crime because labeling and the gradual incorporation of social identity into self-identity occurs in a wide variety of socialization processes. For example, one's identity as a doctor, lawyer, Catholic, and German all result from labeling processes. The concept is useful to counter theories that locate criminal behavior in and only in the psychology of crime and/or human conduct. See "Deviance, Primary" for more.

**Labor:** The concept of labor is important to Marxist and socialist theory. It refers to the process by which people create themselves as social entities by "appropriation of nature." Labor, thus, is not merely working but, rather, forming social relationships in which material culture is produced toward the end of creating collective life. "In labor, (wo)man as a species-being creates all his/her human characteristics." Some theorists prefer to use the concept "praxis" for unalienated labor and the term "work" as a neutral term for productive activity. "Toil" is a more pejorative term for alienated labor.

**Labor, Alienated:** Labor is alienated when it occurs within exploitative relationships: slavery, feudalism, colonialism, or capitalism. The solution to alienation in such frameworks is social change rather than psychological counseling.

**Labor, Contradictions in:** Karl Marx was quick to note that capitalism made the production of wealth relatively independent of labor power, but he still insisted on using labor-time as a measure for the giant social forces that were liberated. Capitalism sets the price of commodities based on the wages of those who produce them. Thus, a dollar, mark, or yen is a call upon a given amount of labor power from a given worker. Yet, industrial capitalism tends to disemploy people and thus reduces their ability to offer the labor power essential for the acquisition of money. This disemployment simultaneously creates inflation and makes it difficult for those who acquire surplus through capitalism to have sufficient capital to exchange for necessary goods and services (e.g., food, shelter, education, health care, communications, and transport). The state steps in to reconcile this contradiction and becomes an enemy to both worker and capitalist.

**Labor, Estranged:**   When labor is sold as a commodity, one's labor is no longer an affirmation of one's own essential being but the property of someone else. The worker feels free only when not working, and work ceases to be an end and becomes a means to an end. Its alien character is revealed in the fact that, if possible, work is shunned like the plague. As a result, the worker feels alive only in the exercise of his/her more primitive functions (e.g., eating, drinking, and procreating).

**Labor, International Division of:**   A global economic system in which most countries produce raw materials and food and provide cheap manual labor while rich, industrialized countries produce high-profit goods to sell abroad. Globalization of the economy began in the Middle Ages with the trade of clothing, ornaments, and small goods in exchange for spices, slaves, sugar, coffee, and precious metals. In today's modern global economy, rich and powerful countries sell cars, armaments, movies, knowledge, and luxury goods to nonindustrial countries in exchange for raw materials, tourist facilities (including prostitution), food, plasma, transplant organs, and an uncertain partnership.

**Labor, Surplus:**   The extra labor power used to produce more wealth than is required for the reproduction of labor power. The standard of living varies widely, and the amount of wealth allocated to the families of workers varies greatly, but there is an irreducible minimum standard of living below which family life and community life die out. See "Exploitation, Super" for more.

**Labor Discipline:**   A policy in which workers are "disciplined," such that the cost of their labor is competitive with the cheaper labor of workers in other countries. Opposition to unions and high wages, safe working conditions, and other benefits in America stem from the need to compete with other foreign workers (e.g., in South Korea people are paid $.22 per hour and less).

**Labor-Intensive Production:**   A system of production in which the labor capacities of human beings generate goods and services. It is indispensable to creating ideological and political culture. See "Exchange-Value," "Marx, Karl," "Surplus Labor," and "Value (Use-)" for more.

**Labor Market, Segmented:**   The United States has a labor market with three main parts. The primary or monopoly sector employs about one third of the workers in the United States and provides good wages and benefits and decent working conditions. The secondary sector is composed of those who work for small firms competing with each other for the trade of big business. In this sector wages are much lower, there is far less job security, and there are fewer prospects for advancement and benefits. About 40 percent of the workers work for these firms. The third sector is operated by the state. Although wages are a bit lower, it is a good place to work; that is, job security is higher and benefits are generally better.

**Labor Power:**   The capacity to produce wealth from raw materials as well as the capacity to use the material wealth thus produced to develop ideological culture. Ideological culture includes science, law, religion, art, music, drama, as well as all forms of family, intimacy, and friendship. It further encompasses prisons, warfare, patriarchy, and, on occasion, genocide. Karl Marx said, "Take the land and tools away from producers and all they have left is labor power." In capitalism, most people have to sell labor power to survive. However, there are several parallel economic systems that work within capitalism to provide goods and services. See "Economic Forms, Parallel" for more.

**Labor Power, Reproduction of:**   All humans beings have fundamental needs. These needs are material and spiritual. All societies have a set of common needs, an infrastructure, and culture (e.g., art, science, music, drama, religion, and recreation). Taken together, these factors constitute the minimal requirements for the reproduction of labor power. Any wealth produced above and beyond the satisfaction of these needs constitutes surplus value. See "Profit, Rate of" for more.

**Labor Theory of Value:**   A theory that says the value of an item is set by the labor-time required to produce that item. For Karl Marx and socialists, this implied that workers should receive the value added to nature by their labor and that the character of some of that added value by capitalists was exploitation. Marx took the concept from classical economics. Neo-classical economics used the concept of "marginal utility" and "diminishing returns" to set the source of value; thus moving it from the workers who produce it to the consumers who buy goods and services.

**Lacan, Jacques (1901–1981):**   The architect of postmodern psychoanalytic semiotics. Lacan was an unapologetic revisionist of Sigmund Freud's writings. He was influenced by Ferdinand de Saussure's posthumously published lectures on linguistics, the anthropological studies of Claude Lévi-Strauss, and Alexandre Kojève's lectures on G.W.F. Hegel, particularly in regard to the nature of desire *(desir)*. Lacan maintained that the unconscious was structured much like a language. Accordingly, in order to understand our interpersonal (intersubjective) and our internal (intrapsychic) experiences of self, others, community, and culture, Lacan claimed it was essential to identify and ponder the inner workings of that discourse located within the primary process region (i.e., the unconscious). For Lacan, this sphere was the repository of knowledge, power, agency, and desire. Lacan developed several elaborate schematizations on discourse, subjectivity, knowledge, and thought. In brief, however, Lacan argued that the speaking subject was not in control of what s/he said; rather, the discourse (languaged thoughts) of the speaking being spoke through the person; this is what Lacan meant when he claimed the subject was divided ($) or decentered. This theory was a direct assault on the rational, logocentrism implied in René Descartes' maxim "I think therefore I am." For Lacan, the subject could not be so purposive, in control, self-aware because the discourse of the unconscious was the crucial arbiter of all experience, knowing, and living. See "Decentered Subject," "Desire," "Floating Signifiers," "Irigaray, Luce," "*Jouissance*," "Lacan's Four Discourses," "Subjectivity," and "Topology" for more.

**Lacan's Four Discourses, Four Terms, and Four Positions:**  Jacques Lacan extends the ideas of constitutive theory to an intrapsychic dimension. (See "Constitutive Theory" for more.) Lacan's four discourses tell us something more about the relationship between intrasubjective (internal) and intersubjective (relational) understandings of social phenomena. In other words, the psychic component of the four discourses tells us how human development both constitutes and is constituted by institutional expressions of reality (e.g., religion, the family, education, law).

The four discourses include those of the *master, university, hysteric, and analyst*. These forms explain how desire (i.e., one's sense of being in language) does or does not find expression in speech. Lacan's four discourses also include four terms or factors. These terms are S1 (the master signifier); S2 (knowledge); $ (the desiring subject); and *a* representing *objet petit (a)* (or *le-plus-de-jouir*, i.e., the excess in enjoyment; that which is left out the lack).

*Master signifiers* (S1) represent key phenomenal forms—key signifiers (words or phrases)—that are developed in early childhood and that form the basis of one's subsequent development and are infused with specialized and idealized content. *Knowledge* (S2) is always and already self-referential. Meaning insists within a certain language (i.e., law = legalese; rap music = gangsta' rap). In order to know, one must situate oneself and be inserted within the language in use. *Desiring subject* ($) signifies the person who, through speech, disappears, is decentered, is divided. When we read an automobile sales agreement, for example, we understand that all of our enthusiasms, longings, dreams, and so on are cleansed in and are stripped from the words in the agreement. Our sense of being is not identified through the language of the agreement. The *a* in *Objet petit (a)* is that excess that is left out in the automobile agreement. It is the not all or the lack seeking affirmation, awaiting legitimacy through words yet unspoken or unwritten.

Lacan also identified four structural positions in the four discourses. These positions can be depicted as follows:

$$\frac{agent}{truth} \quad \frac{other}{production}$$

The left coupling represents the sender of a message. The right coupling represents the receiver or enactor of that message. The upper, left-hand corner represents the person sending the message *(the agent)*. The upper, right-hand corner *(the other)* represents the person to whom the message is sent. As above the bars, these positions are more conscious, overt, active, manifest. The lower, left-hand position *(truth)* represents the reality or identity of the person supporting the message sent by the agent to the other. The lower, right-hand corner *(production)* represents what results or is effected in the receiver's unconscious. Both positions below the bars are more repressed, covert, passive, latent.

The four discourses can be depicted as follows:

*Discourse of the Master*:
$$\frac{S1 \rightarrow S2}{\$ \leftarrow a}$$

The enactor of the message imposes his/her language/narrative on the other and endeavors to convince the other of this knowledge. The other, receptive to the message, experiences an incompleteness, a lack of self-valuation in the words/narrative. Despite this, the other reproduces the very knowledge that represses.

*Discourse of the University*:
$$\frac{S2 \rightarrow a}{S1 \leftarrow \$}$$

The *discourse of the university* is a more hidden form of the *discourse of the master*. Some governing entity or prevailing paradigm (e.g., the law, a patriarchal family, medicine), infused with its unique knowledge/truth, constitutes the other. In so doing, however, the other experiences psychic disequilibrium in this knowledge. That which is missing, left out, produces a lack.

*Discourse of the Hysteric*:
$$\frac{\$ \rightarrow S1}{a \leftarrow S2}$$

The despairing and alienated person realizes that their truth is not affirmed. Thus, the repressed subject endeavors to communicate this suffering and angst to the other. The other, however, interprets this suffering through only conventional master signifiers, through established norms, through existing knowledge. This response only contributes to the psychic despair and longing of the divided subject.

*Discourse of the Analyst:*

$$\frac{a \rightarrow \$}{S2 \leftarrow S1}$$

The "revolutionary" subject begins by offering to the other that which is left out *(pas tout)*. The other embodies this existence and forges new master signifiers, new awarenesses: desires more compatible with the despairing subject. This produces new truths or mythic knowledge. This knowledge, in turn, contributes to and affirms what is left out. Here, knowledge is positional and local. See "Lacan, Jacques" for more.

**Laissez-faire:**   French: let it be; let it alone. A slogan of those who believe there are economic laws regulating industry, trade, and banking that, if let completely alone, will drive the economy to better forms. It began as a reaction to state control of trade and was later used against state welfare and the central planning of socialist states. See "Liberalism," "Social Darwinism," and "Utility/Utilitarianism" for more.

**Lange, Oskar (1904–1965):**   A Polish economist in the left wing of the Socialist Party who moved first to England then to the United States and became professor of economics at the University of Chicago. He returned to Warsaw and worked on market socialism in order to retain its advantages while determining ways to share out surplus value to benefit direct producers and serve community needs. Lange made the case that market socialism fit within Marxist theory and practice.

**Language:**   Latin: *lingua* = tongue. In the sociology of knowledge, there is a question about the relationship of words to things. Most people assume words are verbal mirrors of that which "really" exists. Johann Gottfried von Herder held that words were imitations of nature. Wilhelm von Humboldt held that each language was a human invention containing a separate worldview. Ferdinand de Saussure also held that words were a result of creative human activity and that the naming of a thing was completely arbitrary. Franz Boaz held that each language had a special grammatical structure. Sapir held that language was poetic, metaphoric in nature, and helped people grasp some part of the realties around them. Carnap began the practice of inventing artificial languages using rules of logic; most computer languages follow his lead. Noam Chomsky argues that humans have an innate or deep structure that pre-shapes the use of words. Postmodern views usually hold that all languages are both a poetics and a politics; this view applies to scientific and sociological concepts, works, vocabularies. Semiotics is the study of language as "signs" and of their evolving meanings that are communicated at particular sociohistorical periods. See "Semiotics" and "Sign" for more.

**Language, Sexist/Racist:**   The everyday use of terms that degrade women and other minorities. Sexist language makes it appear that men are the only interesting part of the human species and that only they make history. Racist language makes it appear that one group is genetically superior to another group. Socialist feminist protocols offer non-sexist terms for use in writing and speech (e.g., "person" for man; "woman" for lady or girl).

**Large-Scale Organization (LSO):**   A formal organization controlled by a managerial cadre whose tasks (and rewards) are pointed toward the continuation of the LSO. Superimposed over the class system is another system of stratification in which LSOs are the dominant stratum of social organization and the mass base is the inferior stratum. This view suggests that orthodox class analysis is not enough to gauge the extent of human oppression and the target for social revolution: One must go beyond the stratification of owners and workers to that of organizations, nations, and blocs of nations in order to see the full picture.

**Law:**   Old English: *lag* = to lay down. (1) Any body of rules made by an authoritative body and enforced by a state. (2) A particular rule passed by a duly authorized body. (3) Tight connections between cause and effect that can be stated in precise mathematical terms; Newton's law of gravity is accurate to one part in $10^{27}$. Celsus defined law—number 1 above *(ius)*—as *"ars boni et aequi,"* the art of promoting that which is good and equitable. The idea of statutory law replaced both tribal norms, holy books, and commands of kings sometime around the fifth century, B.C. Both Cicero and Julian wrote that the law must be made with the consent of those governed by it. Cicero claimed that no one was above the law: neither kings nor rich nor powerful people. Both Greek law and Roman law provided for due process, as did the Mosaic Code.

We now think of law as a statute enacted by a competent lawmaking body that forbids/requires a certain act and that carries a penalty for violation. The socialist critique of law in this sense is that such legislation usually embodies the interests and aims of those in power. Reproduction of classist, racist, or sexist inequality requires the use of the monopoly of force claimed by the state. Most existing law helps do this. "The Law in all its majesty forbids equally the rich and the poor from sleeping under a bridge." See "Twelve Tables" for more.

**Law, Bourgeois:**   Capitalist law provides for the private ownership of the means to produce essential goods and services. Bourgeois law allows a fictitious entity, a corporation, to take blame for the crimes committed by the owners/stockholders. It also gives the state the legal authority to enforce the rights of owners, landlords, and banks over the rights of workers, people who rent homes, and people who borrow money.

**Law, Formal:**   With settled agriculture, new social forms arose, including empires. In Persia, the laws of diverse peoples were encoded into a formal set of state laws called the Code of Hammurabi. As new empires formed, new legal codes were developed. The most important codes are: (1) *Roman law* (Justinian code), which grounds the legal system throughout much of Europe and many its colonies in South America; (2) *Napoleonic law,* which grounds the present legal system in France and French colonies; (3) *the Constitution* (of the United States), which grounds law in the United States and in a number of newly independent nations around the world.

**Law, Natural:**   A set of commandments, given by one's God, that supersedes laws made by human beings. For those in the Jewish, Christian, and Islamic traditions, the laws set forth in Deuteronomy compose the core of natural law. Further, each religion has a set of interpretations and explanations that accompany the laws found in Deuteronomy and other biblical books.

**Law, natural:**   When spelled with a lower-case "n," natural law refers to those laws detected by scientists that describe regular and recurring patterns in physics, chemistry, physiology, biology, psychology, sociology, and economics. The new sciences of Chaos and Complexity teach us (1) that close connections between variables loosen as bifurcations increase in a dynamical regime and (2) that feedback loops displace the notion of causality.

**Law, Religious:**   For most of human history, law came from the various holy books of a people. Deuteronomy contained hundreds of laws, some of which protected the poor and the stranger. It served as the legal base for Jews, Christians, and Muslims. The first five books of the Torah are shared by all three religions.

**Law, Socialist:**   Socialist law guarantees equality before the law, eliminates the right of private persons to own the means of production of essential goods and services, guarantees access to health care, education, housing, and jobs, and provides for retirement with dignity.

**Law, Sociology of:**   The systematic study of the social origins of law, of the social context in which law operates, and of the social results of a given legal system. Law is a form of social control. Law arose in Persia, Rome, Britain, and France. The behaviors of these populations were regulated by elites; customs were set aside in favor of new rules about property, family, religion, work, and politics. There is reason to believe that formal law is found only in conflict situations.

**League of the Just:**   A secret socialist society active in the 1840s in Belgium, Britain, and France. Karl Marx and Friedrich Engels joined its Brussels branch in 1847 and reorganized and renamed it as the Communist League. Meeting in London that year, Marx and Engels were asked to draft the *Communist Manifesto.*

**Left:**   A noun and adjective that denotes those who hold liberal or radical political views. It was coined in 1789 after King Louis XVIII convened the Estates General to try to stop worker rebellions. The Third Estate (mostly business men) were put on the left of the king. The Second Estate (the nobility) were put on the right. The idea was to identify those who opposed the king with that which was sinister (Latin: left). Today the term refers to those who advocate reforms in politics, economics, and religion.

**Left Realism:**   A critical criminological orientation to the study of crime, law, justice, and community. The core of left realism is that street crime is real and that there is a fear of violence and victimization among the lower-class members of society. Further, left realists maintain that the victimization of the working class by street criminals who may be "ultimate capitalists" cannot be ignored at the expense of focusing upon upper-class crime. Left realists recognize that a socialist-oriented economy would go a long way in addressing the problem of street crime and the crime problem in general. However, controlling crime in the meantime, within the capitalistic system, is absolutely essential. The early model of left realism argued that the relative deprivation a person experienced in conjunction with an absence of political power to alter one's condition produced crime. To respond to this problem, left realists advocate for the adoption of more community-based solutions that reflect the needs, interests, and rights of local citizens.

**Left-Wing Marxism:**   That wing of Marxism that emphasizes human intersubjectivity, dialectic change, alienation, and historicism. It is criticized as being too idealistic (rather than materialistic), too subjective (rather than concerned with objective relations in capitalist societies), and, in the rejection of the "right-wing," an obstacle to the development of Marxist science. Left-wing Marxism raises important questions about the role of philosophy, about method, and about the necessity of cultural and ideological revolution as part of the total social revolution.

**Legal Aid:**   A program in which poor persons are provided legal services paid for by public funds. In criminal cases, attorneys are provided. In civil cases, advice and assistance is provided. Usually the court will decide eligibility for such legal aid, but the U.S. Congress provides for legal aid clinics in rural and poor areas. Recently, these clinics have been dismantled and/or underfunded. The rationale for such aid comes from the U.S. Constitution's Sixth Amendment, which provides for equal protection under the law, due process, and other rights.

**Legal Fiction:**   An assumption in law that something that does not exist or is false may be taken to be true by judge and jury if both parties agree to it. It is widely used in divorce cases and sometimes in criminal cases. There is also the legal fiction that a corporation is a "real person"; thus stockholders and officials are not responsible for corporate crime even though they select the corporate officers who then engineer the crime. The corporation is fined but never imprisoned. See "Crime, Corporate" for more.

**Legal-Rational Authority:**   In Max Weber's work, legal-rational authority refers to the authority of people who occupy offices in a bureaucracy. The authority is in the office not the person (a boss, a police officer, or a professor). It is said to be rational because goals are achieved by enforcement of rules. A variety of personal wants, desires, and goals are pushed aside in favor of the goals of the formal organization. Jürgen Habermas denies that legal-rational authority is rational, since it may not be oriented to human values. This failure sooner or later creates a legitimacy crisis because a belief in legality for its own sake creates a world without meaning. In principle, a formal rule is hostile to praxis and to historicity since the law exists prior to and apart from the situation in which human action is called forth. In everyday practice, law is interpreted and, thus, regains some historicity. In addition, laws are often disobeyed with impunity and/or rescinded. See "McDonaldization of Society" for more.

**Legitimation Crisis:**   As the economic crisis of capitalism grows (e.g., inflation, unemployment, obsolescence, loss of markets), the administrative branch of government expands into the realm of things usually handled by public discourse. The role of history and of tradition shrinks, and in reaction, public opinion politicizes settled items like the right to tax, the right to welfare, the right of the state to govern.

**Leibniz, Gottfried (1646–1716):**   German philosopher and mathematician who took a degree in law at Altdorf. He was the founder of the Prussian Academy of Science and the political adviser to the King of Prussia.

Leibniz invented a machine that could extract square roots and argued with Newton about who invented calculus first. His philosophy included the concept of the monad, a basic unit of reality that now seems strange. He argued that if God existed, He would create the best possible of all worlds.

**Lenin, Vladimir Ilyich (1870–1924):**    A Russian revolutionary who guided the first great socialist revolution, founded the Russian Communist party and the Comintern (Third International). Lenin made many contributions to socialist theory; perhaps two of the more important were his principles of organization for the revolution itself and his strategy to prevent counterrevolution after taking state power. Syzmanski has summarized Lenin's principles of organization for revolution as follows: (1) recruitment of energetic, hard-working, respected, and militant people into the vanguard party; (2) commitment and enthusiastic execution of party policy; (3) a thorough knowledge of existing social conditions in which the party must work and of the internal situation at all levels of the party; (4) coordination of all activities of all members; (5) full democracy within the party; (6) flexibility in strategy and tactics in advancing the revolution; (7) the proper mix of openness and secrecy; and (8) an appreciation of the role of leadership. Marxist-Leninist parties are to be disciplined, dedicated, and determined. After the seizure of state power, the major role of the socialist state is suppression of the former ruling strata and control over demoralized workers, the petite bourgeois, the peasantry, and the lumpen-proletariat. Lenin's theory of imperialism and of the conditions of colonial exploitation make Leninism widely accepted in third world liberation movements. See "Revolution, Theory of" for more.

**Lesbian/Lesbianism:**    Sexual activity between women. From the island Lesbos, where women who felt no great need for male company and intimacy resided. Sappho was a woman and poetess who lived on Lesbos and gave the name to any woman who refused to be dominated, sexually or otherwise, by males.

Lesbians were a vocal force during the women's rights movement of the 1970s. They advocated for a politics of women-to-women relationships, arguing that such bonds fostered greater intimacy, genuine egalitarianism, and an absence of patriarchal convictions.

**Lévi-Strauss, Claude (1908– ):**    French anthropologist who held that social structures are objective entities that exist independently of human consciousness. As such, human behavior is pre-shaped, and the individual human subject fades into an effect of structural dynamics. Human beings engage in activities designed to hide the difference between the actual reality and their ideal image of it. Myths hold together the image and the ideal. Marriage and kinship systems function as "languages" that permit the exchange of information. As women marry outside a kin grouping, they take with them much latent information that can be used, if necessary, to cope with changes. All structures can be seen as "grammars" in this view, and all can be studied as such. (See the work of W. L. Reese.)

**Lewin, Kurt (1890–1947):**    German psychologist who came to the United States to teach social psychology at the University of Iowa and elsewhere.

Lewin is one of the architects of postmodern social psychology. He argued that the totality of a "life-space" shaped human behavior. He argued that the single case was a better pathway to knowledge than were statistics from large research projects. His work on democratic interaction is important. In studying authoritarian and democratic youth groups (Boy Scouts in this case), Lewin reported that democratic practice is more disorderly at first but more productive in the end than are authoritarian forms. He is also noted for his work on attitude change through informationally and interactionally rich group dynamics. For example, in a classic experiment, he showed that women who talked openly and freely were more likely to adopt dietary practices helpful to the food shortage in World War II.

*Lex domicilii:*    The law of the land in which an offense occurs. In international law, *lex domicilii* holds unless there are diplomatic or other reasons to put it aside. For example, American soldiers who are stationed in Japan and Germany are not subject to *lex domicilii*. They may not be tried for rape, theft, murder, or assault in local courts; however, they may be court-martialed.

*Lex loci contractus:*    According to international law, contract law is governed by the place where the contract is made; however, contracts made in Mexico that are illegal in the United States can be set aside. Contracts made in Mexico that have no counterpart in the United States can be enforced via international law.

*Lex talionis:*    The law of retaliation. More broadly, it is the law of conflict and war that gives the right to define the law and conditions of life to the victor. This legal code still holds in warfare. Victors are seldom punished for the many crimes they do, nor are they usually required to return property and/or land taken in warfare. This practice is changing as American Indians turn to the courts for return of lands taken by the U.S. Army in violation of treaties. There is some effort to do the same for lands and property taken in warfare in other places. For example, England has been returning goods taken in colonial warfare.

**Liberal:**    Latin: free person. Liberal is one of the most confusing words in social discourse. It was used in English to refer to those with skills and trades that made them independent and gave them some status. The underlying meaning of "free" gradually worked into the political use of the term, such that it referred to liberty from all forms of oppression, including state oppression.

Today, it is often used as a pejorative term against workers and customers by corporate liberals who advocate a market unrestricted by law, and against women and minorities by those who believe in stratified social relations and demand freedom from state intervention on behalf of social justice. Shakespeare warned against "liberal villaine" as "vile encounters."

This kind of liberalism is set against all that is defined as sacred; that is, freedom from child pornography, incest, rape, and other forms of exploitation.

**Liberalism:**   There are two different uses of the term. First, it refers to an ideology that supports progressive and humane change within the rules set for a given social paradigm. Liberals stand for freedom of association, speech, religion, and residence. They use the state to moderate the worst inequalities or injustices in capitalism. Such liberals often defeat their purpose of a humane and just society by following the rules through which a stratified and exploitative society is created. Second, the term refers to those who want absolute freedom in the marketplace; the unrestricted right to own, use, abuse, or sell; the right to turn anything into a commodity if there is a demand; the right to move capital and jobs anywhere in the world where profits are higher or costs are lower. See "Laissez-faire" for more.

**Libertarianism:**   A theory of government that holds that the will of the state is under the control of the people; the interests of individuals are of greater value than the demands of society. Libertarianism can be as radical as anarchism, in which there is a rejection and dismantling of state control; or it can take on the more practical form of democracy in which the ideal is to promote individual rights. Libertarians reject state involvement or governmental intrusion, arguing that such involvement or intrusion is what has caused many of the social problems that afflict society (e.g., welfare dependency, joblessness, crime).

**Liebknecht, Karl (1826–1919):**   A German lawyer who helped found the Social-Democratic Party in Germany and the Socialist Youth International and who proclaimed the first German Socialist Republic in 1918. Along with Rosa Luxemburg, he inspired a whole generation of Germans to overthrow German capitalism. Along with Rosa, he was murdered by a police death squad, the *Freicorps*. A bridge in Berlin, adjacent to Karl Marx Platz, bears his name.

**Linear/Linearity:**   This concept refers to the case when a change produces an effect in perfect ratio to its cause. Thus, a one-pound push may move your car two feet; a two-pound push may move it four feet; a three-pound push may move it six feet, and so on. All modern predictive science relies upon linearity to yield the precision of predictions that is said to ground the highest, best theory. Chaos theory and nonlinear dynamics challenge these ideas. Most systems have turning points in which small change produces large, unpredictable changes. See "Chaos Theory" for more.

**Linguistic Code:**   See "Linguistic Coordinate System."

**Linguistic Coordinate System (LCS):**    In postmodern semiotics, all accurate communication is dependent on the language in use. The language in use is pre-configured by its own internal grammar. Precise sense-making cannot occur from outside the sphere of language in operation. Thus, for example, the juridical sphere (i.e., the legal system) is always and already coordinated by the language of law. Conveying precise legal meaning can occur only from within the linguistic parameters of "lawspeak." To illustrate further, in order to explain baseball's "infield fly rule" it is essential to rely upon baseball terminology (i.e., words or phrases). Without this specific reliance on the language of the sport, it is not possible to convey the precise meaning for the infield fly rule. Linguistic coordinate systems assume several forms: (1) *dominant linguistic coordinate systems* are those that promote and sustain capital logic, rational bureaucratic practices, and status quo power relations. These would include, among others, medicine, law, finance, and engineering. In their very syntactical construction, dominant linguistic coordinate systems deny access to those who are not specifically trained in or uniquely informed about the privileged discourse in use; (2) *oppositional linguistic coordinate systems* are those that resist, ignore, and/or work against the prevailing speech-thought-behavior patterns in use. All dominant LCSs psychically oppress and socially regulate those who fail to conform to the dominant code. Oppositional or insurgent codes would include the language of prison inmates, gangs, and the mentally disabled; (3) *pluralistic linguistic coordinate systems* refer to those discourses that are accessible to all citizens regardless of training or indoctrination. These systems would include the language of sports, popular culture, and media generated commercialism. See "Linguistic Relativity Principle" for more.

**Linguistic Relativity Principle:**    Developed by Benjamin Whorf and F. Rossi-Landi and known as the "Sapir-Whorf linguistic relativity principle." The principle states the following: "Users of markedly different grammars are pointed by their grammars toward different types of observations and different evaluations of externally similar acts of observations, and hence are not equivalent as observers but must arrive at somewhat different views of the world." What this principle suggests is that people embracing the language of one culture and other people embracing the language of a second culture will perceive and understand the same event differently. This difference in understanding is conditioned by the boundaries of their respective languages. The language habits of our culture color/encode our understanding of events much like the language habits of other cultures color/encode the understanding others have of the same events.

Whorf analyzed this principle in regard to the Hopi Indians in the southwest United States. He found that they do not have words that convey transitions in time (e.g., past, present, future). Instead, the Hopi speak about a continual and fluid state of becoming or of being in process. Clearly, this is different from how we understand time in relation to events. But it is this very distinction in language that informs how the Hopi (and how we) act, feel, think, intuit, know. What the linguistic relativity principle points out is the profound, independent effect that speech/language has on one's thought processes. See "Linguistic Coordinate System" for more.

**Locke, John (1632–1704):**    The author of a famous work on human understanding and the precursor of all modernist social psychologists. Locke held that the mind was a *tabla rasa*, or blank slate, upon which were written what we would now call software programs that processed sense data as they came in. The brain is the hardware and comes from biology and physiology. The mind is the software and comes from socialization and experience. Experience is made up of sensation and reflection. Complex relations are created in the mind through reflection on simple ideas derived from sense data. Universal ideas/concepts are thus constructed by human beings.

In his work on politics, Locke posits certain inalienable rights given by God and then argues that the state exists to guarantee these rights. Among these rights are life, liberty, and property (not happiness). Locke's views on property were built on the idea that there existed a benevolent God who gave humans the good earth as a source of wealth. The state embodies the pursuit of human rights, but if it fails, it can be and should be overthrown. These notions helped form the blueprint for the Declaration of Independence and the U.S. Constitution. Natural law underpins these rights; human law must conform to Natural (divine) law. See "Natural Law" for more.

Locke urged toleration of religious differences (again seen in the U.S. Constitution), except to atheists who "dissolve all" when they dismiss God. Locke also gave us direction for a philosophy of education: it should develop character, judgment, respect for evidence, and the value of work. Custom, tradition, despair, and indolence were enemies to this effort. (See the work of W. L. Reese.)

**Logic:**    One branch of philosophy that deals with rational thinking. Aristotle argued that formal logic was the bedrock of scientific knowledge and detailed the rules of valid inference. Aristotle set forth *syllogistic* reasoning in an "if-then" model. For example: (1) If all men are mortal, and (2) if Plato is a man, (3) then Plato is mortal. The truth value of (3) depends upon the truth value of (1)—*if* all men are, in fact, mortal—and (2)—if Plato is, indeed, a man: If (1) and (2) are true, then there is no escaping the fact that sometime Plato will die. This seems to be a fine pathway to truth, but note that it says nothing about the degree to which (1) and (2) are, in fact, true. Francis Bacon, in his work *De Novum Organum* (1620), described the rules of scientific inquiry upon which statements about the truth of (1) and (2) could be made. Karl Marx referred to syllogistic logic as the lower mathematics of reasoning and set "dialectics" as the higher mathematics of reasoning. See "Philosophy, The Discipline of" for more. Cf. "Dialectic" and "Science, Postmodern."

**Logic, Fuzzy:**    A term that refers to a form of computer programming or decisionmaking in which the boundaries of the sets (algorithms) used to guide decisions are permitted to change, sometimes in unpredictable ways. Cf. "Logic, Syllogistic."

**Logic, Syllogistic:**    There are three parts to syllogistic logic: (1) a major term, in which something is posited as true; (2) a middle term, in which another case is posited as true; (3) a minor term generated by a careful and rational combination of the first two terms. See "Fallacies" for some misuses of syllogistic logic. See "Aristotle" for more. Cf. "Logic, Fuzzy."

**Logocentric:**    A term describing systems of thought that claim legitimacy by reference to external, universally valid propositions. According to postmodernists, logocentric reasoning privileges certain terms (e.g., white, male, straight, objective) and subordinates their binary opposites (e.g., black, female, gay, subjective). Postmodernists are opposed to logocentricism and claim that all speech/writing unfolds this way. Logocentric reasoning produces a logic of unity or a logic of identity. Thus, logocentricism implicitly, though powerfully, dismisses difference. See "Derrida, Jacques" for more. Cf. "Phallocentric," "Phallogocentrism," and "Phonocentric."

**Longitudinal Analysis:**    A scientific method of analyzing social phenomena. Longitudinal studies examine events over time. The assumption is that by investigating a particular phenomenon over a period of years, more accurate information can be revealed about how that particular phenomenon operates. A research design based upon longitudinal analysis principles is suppose to eliminate or minimize biases that might otherwise not be accounted for in a more time-specific study (e.g., researcher bias, selection bias). Further, a longitudinal study is designed to capture the movement/behavior of a given phenomenon over time, such that it accounts for more subtle changes/fluctuations that, again, might not otherwise be detected in time-specific studies. The belief is that longitudinal analysis yields richer, more complete quantifiable data. This data enables the researcher to make more scientifically rigorous and robust truth statements. Cf. "Indeterminacy Principle," "Postmodernity," and "Postmodern Philosophy of Science."

**Looking Glass Process:**    Charles Horton Cooley set forth this idea about how human behavior is organized. It stands in opposition to the idea that behavior is grounded on instincts or inborn urges. The looking glass process says that we observe how others respond to our behavior and, being pleased or embarrassed by their reaction, we modify our own behavior. It is a simple way to refer to the fact that one's self is the product of many people working together. This principle is of limited validity in a stratified system, since those at the top do not worry about guilt, shame, or embarrassment. See "Generalized Other" for more.

**Luddite (also Neo-Luddite):**    A loose organization of workers in Leicester, Yorkshire, and Nottingham opposed to the introduction of textile machines because workers were disemployed and dispossessed by them. The Luddites destroyed machines in the early eighteenth century. The name comes from Ned Ludd, an idiot in Leicestershire, and was assigned as a term of opprobrium. Today, it refers to those who try to solve the problem of overproduction, disemployment, and the formation of a surplus population by opposing automation instead of capitalism. Luddite workers reason that machinery takes their jobs away so the solution is to resist machines. Socialist economics accepts both automation and increased productivity. The solution to disemployment is to appropriate some of the value of the increased products and to use it to support labor-intensive jobs, health care, child care, and education, as well as art, music, literature, and drama.

**Lukács, Georg (1885–1971):**    Hungarian Marxist theorist. He is noted for his work on the concepts of reification, totality, and the dialectics of subject and object. He is credited with being a forerunner for what today is called the sociology of knowledge. His work on culture and aesthetics, ideology and "true" consciousness, and objective knowledge and the privileged intellectual standpoint was significant for the creation of a more human and more humane socialism. See "Civil Society" and "Solidarity, Organic" for more.

**Lumpen-proletariat:**    The refuse of all classes. The lumpen-proletariat includes the unemployed and casually employed, discharged soldiers and prisoners, vagabonds, paupers, beggars, bandits, hustlers, brothel-keepers, servants, pimps, petty thieves and those who live off of them, male and female prostitutes, sons and daughters of the bourgeoisie too proud to work, and those surplus capitalists still dreaming of success. It does not include the dependent children, the discarded aged, the lame, the infirm, or those who accept welfare passively.

Marxists tend to view the lumpen-proletariat with contempt, since its members are too quick to steal or to sell themselves to those who have money. The lumpen-proletariat support themselves through various scams, hustles, and angles. Movies such as *Midnight Cowboy, The Sting,* and *New Jack City* give us a feel for this life. Actors such as Robert Redford, Paul Newman, Jane Fonda, Woody Allen, and Dustin Hoffman routinely play (and glamorize) the young hustler who is too proud to work at boring or menial tasks and yet who possesses too much talent to resign from life.

**Luther, Martin (1483–1546):**    Martin Luther is important in the sociology of religion. Luther taught theology at Wittenberg; he came to oppose the selling of indulgences by the Catholic Church. This opposition led to a more general critique of formal religious organization and to more individualist involvement in both religion and theology. In November 1517, Luther posted ninety-five theses on the castle church door. The theses made four points: (1) One cannot buy forgiveness from sin; (2) those in sin must pray for forgiveness; (3) the power of the pope to forgive is restricted to transgressions against the church and to its penalties in this life; (4) Christ requires true penance and cessation of sin; truly repentant sinners have already been forgiven and need not buy such. Luther also advocated a spiritual priesthood of all believers; one does not need the services of a priestly hierarchy to approach God. Luther translated the New Testament into German so people could read it themselves. Max Weber pointed out that, in doing so, Luther made a most important error. He translated "calling" into *berufen*, "labor," rather than into "invitation from God"; thus, work became a prime pathway to grace and salvation. Before the reversal, faith and meditation were the prime pathways to divine grace, with work being a poor third. The emphasis on hard work, thrift, and asceticism became, according to Weber, the spiritual basis for capitalism. Luther opposed the idea of free will, which also grounds capitalist market dynamics, but the wealth from free-market dynamics becomes, in other Protestant theology, clear proof of the "grace of God." Many princes took up the Protestant cause, since a great deal of church property came their way during the Reformation. Lutheran doxology accepts God as sovereign, Christ as mediator, salvation by work, and justification by faith—and rejects the mass, penance, saints, relics, and the pope as regent for God on earth. (See the work of W. L. Reese.)

**Luxemburg, Rosa (1870–1919):**   Born in Poland, the youngest child of a cultured Jewish family, Rosa Luxemburg grew up under the oppression of Czarist Russia. At 18, she was forced to flee to Switzerland because of her work with the Proletarian Party. Taking a doctorate in 1898, she wrote over 600 books, articles, letters, pamphlets, and essays. Luxemburg is best known for her case against Leninist centralism and against anarchist opposition to organization. Her position was that organization depends upon existing conditions of class struggle rather than upon a predetermined formula. She did original work on the role of military spending in domestic economy. Luxemburg worked actively as an organizer for revolutionary opposition to capitalism in Germany. On January 15, 1919, she was arrested and then murdered. Her skull was smashed in under a soldier's rifle-butt. At the time, she was urging young men not to enlist in World War I and kill other young men on behalf of German capitalists. See "Revolution, Theory of" for more.

**Lyotard, Jean-François (1924– ):**   Celebrated champion of postmodern theory as it relates to ethics, politics, art, and aesthetics. He studied philosophy and literature at the Sorbonne. He was influenced by Edmund Husserl, Karl Marx, and Sigmund Freud in his early works and then, momentarily, passionately examined the Nietszchean notion of a philosophy of affirmation. His latter works follow the linguistic turn and emphasize figure, form, and image ("energetics") over theory. He received his dissertation in 1971 and became a philosophy professor at Vincennes University. He was named professor emeritus in 1987.

His work *The Postmodern Condition* is acknowledged as providing the most strident rejection of modern theory and methods, as well as advancing the most ardent support for postmodern alternatives. Lyotard's most strongly held postmodern convictions center around "waging war on totalities." These sentiments metaphorically express his belief in variety, heterogeneity, and difference throughout all realms of social and intellectual life. Lyotard dismisses all foundational and universal claims to truth, knowledge, reason, and power. This "territoristic" line of analysis privileges the status of some perspectives while invalidating others. The problem with this "territoristic" and foundational method of understanding is that alternative ways of knowing are silenced, a plurality of discourses are denied articulation, and the multiplicity of being human is repressed.

Lyotard rejects the three conditions for modern knowledge: (1) the use of metanarratives to promote foundationalist views (i.e., the metanarrative of psychiatry regarding the mentally ill promotes the foundationalist view that modern science can solve all questions; (2) the effect of foundationalist claims, which is to spawn binary opposites wherein there is legitimation/de-legitimation and, thus, exclusion; and (3) a prescriptive economy of sameness in logic and behavior. Lyotard argues for a postmodern condition of knowledge that is positional, provisional, and relational. This is similar to Gilles Deleuze and Félix Guattari's call for a micro-politics of desire. See "Deleuze, Gilles," "Guattari, Félix," "Performativity," and "Postmodernists/Postmodernism" for more.

**Machiavelli, Niccolò (1469–1527):**   Author of *The Prince*, a text book on how to get power and keep it. Often misrepresented, Machiavelli argued that popular government is the most stable since it has the least problems of legitimacy; he suggested that princes, nobles, and the people each have enough power to keep the other two in check and prevent tyranny. The organization of the U.S. government into the presidency, the Senate, and the House of Representatives is modeled after that suggestion. Machiavelli held that liberty is important to the survival of a state and that the people are wiser than most princes. Cf. "Plato."

Machiavelli argued that when corruption is widespread, a strong king is useful. To keep power, the wise prince will respond to the people in good and gracious ways. But he will keep faith with the people only when it enables him to stay in power. The clever prince will use both love and fear to gain loyalty from the people. If force and terror are necessary, it is done ruthlessly and quickly in order to prevent opposition. Propaganda and religion are to be used to retain power; thus, order, stability, and obedience to state law can be guaranteed. Modern states and political leaders read Machiavelli differently; some focus on responsiveness to the people; some on the use of guile and force. (See the work of W. L. Reese.)

**Macho/Machismo:**   A set of values and behaviors that elicit respect and response to requests and commands by and for males. Some cultures require males to be controlling and competitive. These requirements produce male behavior that is "macho." Males fight with each other in order to define hierarchy; men beat women in order to elicit compliance to male demands. See "Abuse, Spousal" and "Crime, Male" for more.

**Macroeconomics:**   A field of study that looks at the larger sweep of history and the role played by different economic systems in history. The contributions of Adam Smith, Thomas Malthus, Karl Marx, Max Weber, David Ricardo, James O'Connor, Milton Friedman, and so on are important to one's ability to participate in a discussion of macroeconomics.

**Macro-Sociological Level of Analysis:**    Also known as the global or system level of analysis. This is the level at which one studies the overall structure or structural forces of a system and how the structure behaves or interacts in society. Thus, if one wanted to study the child welfare system at the macro-level, one would need to compare the interdependence of its various components (e.g., protective services, foster care division, adoption care services, juvenile probation division) in relation to such things as existing political, economic, educational, and social conditions. This comparison would enable one to make macro-level comments on the structural stability, efficiency, and effectiveness of the child welfare system. See "Macro-Theory" for more. Cf. "Micro-Sociological Level of Analysis."

**Macro-Theory:**    An attempt to describe how large systems work: the international capitalist market, a whole society, long-range patterns of social change, and so on. See "Macro-Sociological Level of Analysis" for more.

**Majority, Age of:**    The age at which a person is, in law, an adult. Usually this is age 18, but majority can be awarded earlier by a court. The age of majority has varied greatly with the mode of production. See "Age Grade" and "Sociology of Youth" for more.

*Mala in se:*    An act that is wrong in and of itself. *Mala in se* acts are tied to natural and positive law. Contemporary acts that are considered *mala in se* include such things as cannibalism, pedophilia, incest. The problem with *mala in se* laws is that if certain behaviors are wrong or illicit, they must be wrong and illicit because the act itself is harmful to society and its members. However, are there occasions when eating the flesh of another person is acceptable (e.g., eating dead people for survival)? When sleeping with children is practiced (e.g., National Man-Boy Love Association)? When sex with a family member has been endorsed (e.g., Greco-Roman culture)? If there are instances in which such actions are permitted and officially or unofficially endorsed, the question remains, Which acts are *mala in se*? Cf. *"Mala prohibita."*

*Mala prohibita:*    These are acts that are considered violations by custom, policy, statute. Crimes listed in the Uniform Crime Report are *mala prohibita* acts. However, one can reasonably ask if there might not be some behaviors that are wrong in and of themselves (e.g., rape, incest). These acts are called *mala in se*. Cf. *"Mala in se."*

**Malthus, Thomas (1726–1834):**    A population theorist who argued that food production increases arithmetically (1, 2, 3, 4), whereas population increases geometrically (1, 2, 4, 8, 16). These rates of growth mean that war, starvation, and disease are natural checks on population and should not be treated as social problems unless one wants to risk overpopulation. Malthus is also famous for the "law of diminishing returns." Together, these two ideas are used to blame the poor for their own poverty and thus to exculpate politics and economics. Malthus supported birth control for the masses. He opposed William Godwin, who blamed capitalism and the concentration of wealth for poverty.

Karl Marx pointed out that improvement in technology and in the technical division of labor could increase productivity to match and exceed population growth and that capitalism needed a better means of distribution to match its great improvement in the means of production. Marx called Malthus a "libel on the human race." See "Surplus Population" for more.

**Managed Society:**   A society in which social unrest due to capitalism or bureaucratic socialism is brought under control by technical (rather than coercive) means. Control of commercial media, electronic surveillance, counseling and chemotherapy techniques, as well as infiltration of radical (right-wing and left-wing) groups, are all technical measures by which an elite can control dissent with technicians and professionals instead of police.

**Management, Democratic Self-:**   In democratic self-management, workers own and operate the means of production. Management is spread broadly over the employees. Those who represent the plant, shop, farm, factory, mill, or mine are elected for a term and can be recalled for incompetence or abuse of office. There are many worker owned and operated firms around the world. They have limited success since they have to operate in a larger, globalized capitalist economy.

**Management Science:**   A set of principles and practices by which the consciousness (ways of thinking, ways of feeling, ways of acting) of workers is controlled by a small group of functionaries who specialize in learning as much as possible about psychology and sociology in order to reproduce capitalist relationships. Management science is a humane effort to replace coercion with persuasion and manipulation in the factories, offices, and schools. Its net effect, however, is to sustain elitism and to defeat praxis and community. It is also a technology by which prediction of and control of human behavior is perfected. This science is rational in that the behavior of workers is identical to the intention of managers. Cf. "Free Will," "Intentionality," and "Praxis/Practice."

**Managers:**   A special class positioned between capitalists and workers which preempts mental labor on behalf of the capitalist. Under socialism, the managerial stratum would disappear since mental labor would be reunited with physical labor. In some socialist countries, managers are in the service of a party elite who preempt mental labor to advance their careers.

**Mandamus, Writ of:**   Latin: *manu* = hand over. It now means we "demand." A legal order issued by a judge that demands that a person or property be handed over to a person named in the writ.

**Manslaughter:**   Homicide that is less than deliberate murder but more than mere accident. An intoxicated person who kills someone out of anger could be charged with the crime of manslaughter. Negligent homicide includes the death of a person in traffic when a driver is under the influence of alcohol or drugs.

**Mao Tse-Tung (1893–1976):**   A founder of the People's Republic of China and its first premier. Mao led the People's Liberation Army, which took state power in China in 1949. Mao was one of thirteen founding members of the Chinese Communist Party in 1921; he was a son of a middle peasant (land owner) and had little formal education, but learned about Marxism in 1919 from a well-educated professor of literature. Mao's major contributions to socialist theory include: (1) the possibility of peasant revolution (rather than industrial workers); (2) the advantages of guerrilla warfare (over formal military organizations); (3) the superiority of low tech warfare (over high tech weaponry) when soldiers are well trained, well educated, and well motivated to win; (4) the primacy of practice over theory; (5) the possibility of great leaps forward (over the idea that socialism must go through stages as in England, France, or Germany); (6) self-criticism; (7) opposition to the subdivision of labor as too divisive and too undemocratic; (8) the institution of the primacy of manual labor over intellectual labor (intellectuals had to do manual labor periodically in order to know first hand what they were talking about); (9) the primacy of politics over economics (see "Economic Determinism" for more); (10) self-reliance from foreign powers in both military and economic struggles; (11) the rejection of "peaceful coexistence" with capitalist powers; and (12) the cultural revolution in which young people were encouraged to criticize bureaucrats, "capital-roaders," and the cult of the individual.

**Marasmus:**   A wasting away of children who are without love and human stimulation. "Babies who are not loved don't live." Human beings without community become anxious, apprehensive, withdrawn, and self-centered.

**Marcuse, Herbert (1898–1979):**   Marcuse was part of the early Frankfurt School. He came to the United States when the Nazis took over Germany, and then taught at Columbia University, Harvard, and the University of California at San Diego. Marcuse made many contributions to emancipatory knowledge, beginning with his views on art (most of it squelched rebellion since it was too beautiful or too remote from everyday life) and ending with his views on sexuality in *Eros and Civilization*. In brief, he made the case that there was some justification for sexual repression in order to invest creative love in art, science, music, and politics. However, there was also "surplus" repression (the denial of love and compassion in classist, racist, or sexist societies). Marcuse also rejected the "heroic" theory of history in his work on Prometheus. But Marcuse agreed with Prometheus (and with Karl Marx), who said that he hated "the entire pack of gods" since they rob humans of freedom and agency. (Prometheus was chained to a rock by Zeus after he gave fire to people in spite of a command by Zeus not to do so.) Marcuse's interpretation of Prometheus and freedom spawned a student slogan of the 1960s, "The Great Refusal." One should say No! to sexual repression; No! to the investment of genius and craft in war; Yes! to the investment of joy, delight, and love in prosocial work; Yes! to erotic joy in friendships, marriage, and play. In *One Dimensional Man*, Marcuse spoke of "repressive toleration" in which the most contradictory works are found side by side in a false peace and mind-numbing harmony. Whereas Marx located the revolutionary leadership in the working class, Marcuse located it in marginalized groups in rich societies, liberation movements in poor countries, and free intellectuals everywhere.

Marcuse took funds from what came to be the Central Intelligence Agency (CIA) since he criticized Stalinism and bureaucratic socialism in the former USSR. His Great Refusal requires blind fate and a leap into liberation and whatever it brings. Along with Mao Tse-Tung and Marx, Marcuse inspired the New Left. Cf. "Freud, Sigmund" and "Freudian Revisionism."

**Marginal Cost:**   This is a theory of price. It says that price goes down as production goes up. For example, it costs less to produce the 10,000th shoe than the first 10, 100, or 1000 shoes because the machinery and labor is in place and has to be paid for whether they are working or not. It is an argument for big factories and against small business since small firms cannot produce 10,000 shoes a day/week/month/year. This law tends to support the concentration of wealth and the reduction of the middle class as inefficient producers. It also supports the exploitation and super-exploitation of labor power. To date, there is no good solution to the issues raised by the law of marginal cost: We do want to lower costs to machines, workers, the environment, and the general public; however, we do not want to see too much inequality and worker exploitation.

**Marginal Utility, Theory of:**   This is a theory of use-value based upon consumption rather than labor. It says that as one gets more of a certain good or service, the value of a good steadily declines. The first pair of shoes is valuable to the consumer; the second pair is still valuable, but less so; and as each new pair is bought, the margin between each subsequent use-value declines until the last pair of shoes has little value at all. Karl Marx discussed marginal utility in *Das Kapital*; Jevons, Menger, and Walras also wrote about it.

The central task of advertising is to defeat the law of marginal utility by assigning status value, sexual value, or other cherished values to shoes, cigarettes, beer, or any other good for which the law holds. Progressive economics has the task of figuring out how to match production and demand in order to distribute workers, raw materials, and capital goods in such a way as to meet legitimate needs and yet protect the environment and the general welfare.

**Market:**   A network of buying and selling usually based upon use-value, supply, and demand. Capitalists say a free market works best in the long run. Most socialists/Marxists hold that it should be replaced by collective planning so that production and distribution are based on need rather than profit. Some market socialists claim the market plays a vital role in any economy since it brings flexibility, creativity, and motivation to it.

**Markoviç, Svetozar (1846–1875):**   Serbian socialist who held that simple societies could go directly to socialism (instead of first to capitalism as most Marxists hold). He argued for a leading role by intellectuals (rather than the working class as Karl Marx held). (See the work of W. L. Reese.)

**Marriage:**   A union of two opposite-sex persons over the age of 16 that carries legal obligations for children, property, security, and mutual support. There are many forms of intimacy other than marriage as legally defined. New forms are emerging all the time as economic and social conditions render them attractive to people. See "Family" for more. Cf. "Common-Law Marriage."

**Marx, Early:**   The early writings of Karl Marx focused on the creative role of humans in producing social lifeworlds. The concepts of praxis and alienation were central to these works, and therefore Marx's writings were decidedly humanistic. The later Marx focused more on larger structural factors, especially capitalist relations and global analysis. There are those Marxists who are in either camp and some who are in both. The issue is whether those who look at Marx humanistically are too romantic to be useful in the hard task of making the revolution, since making it requires an understanding of and an opposition to the structural variables by which domination occurs. Critics of the "structuralists" say that a revolution that does not speak to the point of praxis and democratic self-management is a fraud. Thus, the older Marx without the early Marx is pointless. The nature of Marxism in some countries was settled before some of the early writings were available, and so the structural reading was dominant and often used to justify a dictatorship. See "Economic Determinism," "Marx, Karl," and "Vulgar Marxism" for more.

**Marx, Karl (1818–1883):**   Marx was born of a German-Jewish family and converted to Christianity. As a student at Bonn, Germany, he was first influenced by G.W.F. Hegel's ideas but came to reject idealist philosophy, preferring historical materialism instead. He related the problems in a society to the means of production and urged armed revolution by the proletariat in order to regain control over the means of production of culture without which human life (species-being) is impossible. Marx took a doctorate in philosophy from the University of Jena and went right to work in the sociology of law to explain why one set of laws replace another (to serve elite interests). In 1848, Marx and Friedrich Engels wrote the *Manifesto* of the Communist Party. In 1849, Marx went to England as a refugee from political oppression. Marx and his family lived in poverty while Marx spent years of research on *Capital;* the first volume was published in 1847.

Marx's humanism was tied to a critique of the forms of domination by which humans were alienated from their human potential. In the present age, capitalism and the class system are the major obstacles to human dignity, fellowship, and mutual aid. The class struggle is the means to overcome alienation, and communism is the social form in which one's full humanity is possible.

Marx helped organize, agitate, and analyze for social revolution. His sympathies were with the oppressed. His animosity was directed at the oppressive social form. Marx came to the conclusion that genuine human emancipation requires a radical transformation of capitalist (civil) society, such that a form of human labor is possible wherein people create themselves and each other as social entities. Marx held that this kind of human labor is possible only in a communist society since other forms of society (capitalism and feudalism), in their ordinary operation, alienate people.

Marxian theory rests upon the work of many predecessors, collaborators, and critics. There is much left to do to perfect both the theory and practice of human emancipation. The Marxian response to Marx is to transcend the limitations of his analysis and retain what is worthy of human emancipation as one base upon which to build. Cf. "Bourgeoisie," "Civil Society," "Engels, Friedrich," "Equivalence Principle," "Historical Materialism," "International, First," "Marx, Early," "Marxism," "Needs Principle," "Weber, Max."

**Marxism:**    A theory and method by which community is thought to be created or lost. The theory holds that collective production of culture creates community, whereas the loss of community arises from treating cultural products as commodities to be exchanged for private profit. The method of Marxism requires the "relentless criticism of everything existent" in terms of how praxis and community are affected.

Marxism also makes some important assumptions about how the acting subject participates in the creation of social facts and the interpretation of physical facts. Central to Marxist analysis are the concepts of class, class conflict, surplus value, surplus population, class interests, and social revolution. There are many forms of Marxism, including, among others, Marxist-humanism; Marxist-feminism; Marxist-Leninism. Cf. "Conflict Theory," "Guattari, Félix," "Humanism," and "Marx, Karl."

**Marxist-Leninism:**   A view that there are five basic principles upon which all Marxists worthy of the name agree:

1. the theory of surplus value
2. dialectic materialism
3. the class struggle
4. imperialism
5. the dictatorship of the proletariat

Serious challenges regarding the last two principles surround much of the discussion of Marxist meetings today.

**Marxist Methodology:**   Those practices by which science and philosophy are united with politics in the struggle for revolutionary change. Generally, any research effort that makes visible to workers the social sources of oppression, as well as any effort to make visible a world that might be conducive to praxis and community. Marxist research must enlighten, inspire, and politicize. It must be integrated into progressive social action oriented to praxis. As Marx said, the point is not to study the world but to change it.

**Masculinity Crisis:**   In a society where sexual activity is sublimated into aggressive competition, channeled into a narrow genital mode, or converted into a commodity to be sold only to those with discretionary income, one's essential sexuality is in crisis. For the male, working conditions further de-sexualize self and role: The division of labor strips the male worker of power and autonomy while it makes work machine-like in its practice. In such a society, sexual panic can be exploited to sell "macho" cars, cigars, sports, movies, magazines, and cosmetics. Sexual panic also can be harnessed and turned into moral outrage at the new, gentle pan-sexism of young people. Sexual panic can and is used to sell fascism and other political packages that emphasize strength, discipline, domination, and brutal enforcement of the normative structure.

**Maslow's Hierarchy:**   Abraham Maslow held that a pyramid of human needs exists. At the base are body needs; then the need for safety and security; then the need for love and self-esteem. At the pinnacle is the need for "self-actualization" or fulfillment. Although this analysis is useful, it does not necessarily follow that a good society emerges when all such needs are met for a part or most of the population.

**Mass/Masses:**   Latin: *massa* = a body of material that can be shaped or molded, as in kneading bread dough. In sociology, it means a collection of individuals with few if any social relationships: atomized individuals whose behavior is not mediated by roles, norms, values, or community. It is often used by elitists as a term of open contempt for the common people who are thought to be too ignorant, lazy, selfish, unstable, and easily per-suaded by democracy.

**Mass Action:**   According to Rosa Luxemburg, the objective roots of mass strikes and demonstrations are to be found in the soil of capitalist class re-lationships. She demanded that socialists treat the mass action of the work-ing class as the central focus of all revolutionary activity. This view tended to place Leninist theory of revolutionary organization in the context of class struggle. For Luxemburg, Leninism emphasized the political sphere at the expense of the total social process. As Luxemburg understood it, a revolutionary party structure takes its form and tactics from the larger so-cial struggle, not from the writings of Vladimir Lenin, who wrote about what needed to be done in Russia in 1917.

**Mass Base:**   A set of unrelated individuals who may, temporarily, be part of a public but not part of a solidarity. They have exchange power but not social power. Mass societies are composed of large bureaucracies in which most people work, go to school, get medical treatment, worship, or watch sports. Bureaucracies have three parts: (1) an elite that sets policy; (2) a cadre/staff that enforces the rules; and (3) a mass that is required to con-form to the rules. See "Moral Agency" and "Praxis/Practice" for more.

**Mass Communication:**   A system of organizing the flow of information such that it is unilaterally reproduced as "mass cult" rather than produced collectively as culture. Print, electronics, and cinema could be organized to provide for collective production (as is the case with CB radios, home movies, and typed correspondence). Electronics media need not be orga-nized to exclude communication. Mass communication systems exist when there is an interest in the unilateral control of consciousness or in the use of information sets as commodities.

**Mass Cult:**   A cultural item produced with capital-intensive means and sold as a commodity. Ordinarily, the production of culture requires inten-tion and social interaction. Machine production eliminates both. Mass vac-cination, mass produced sermons, mass produced editorials, and mass ed-ucation are mass cults in that the particular and concretely existing historical conditions of situated individuals and groups are not considered in the act of production. Mass cult is culture stripped of its social matrix and distributed as a commodity for private profit, power, or status.

**Mass Media:**   Any information flow system (radio, newsprint, television, journals, magazines) in which data and details are transmitted to a large audience of unknown others. This produces a mass society, in that there is no collective sharing or collaborative construction of the information sets in question. Often, a set of specialists is hired to tailor the information in such a way as to manage the consciousness of a population without the use of force, law, or face-to-face conflict. Cf. "Cyberspace," "Hyperreality," "Simulacrum," "Simulation," and "Symbol Sets."

**Mass Medicine:**   The practice of medicine without regard for social relationships or for individual differences in health, medication, age, or other significant factors. Mass medicine is cheap and thereby more profitable (or less costly to the state) than individually focused forms of therapy.

**Mass Movements:**   Political, religious, and economic protests involving large numbers of people who work outside of institutional politics largely because governments and political parties work against their interests and/or refuse to respond to collective needs and concerns.

**Masspol:**   The transformation of political culture (usually votes) into a commodity. Public relations firms, using dramaturgical technology, package and sell candidates and policies in the same way cereals and colas are sold. Advertising firms now deliver so many votes at so much cost per million (cpm), just as they deliver viewers for other commodities.

**Mass Society:**   A society of unrelated individuals passively consuming mass produced culture (mass cult). Since the end of the feudal system, there have been several factors at work to destroy social relationships. Capitalism destroys social relationships by producing for profit rather than for community. If one has nothing to exchange, then there is no relationship in the various delivery systems of the society. Bureaucracy destroys social relationships by treating all clients as objects to be processed in accordance with uniformly applied rules. The factory system removes fathers, children, and mothers from the home for eight to ten hours per day. The structure of mass, impersonal education takes children from both the family nexus and the peer group nexus and assigns them to groups convenient to administrative needs. The division of labor also progressively divides a population into a small elite that produces culture (for profit) and a large mass that consumes items as more or less fragmented others. This division is progressively true in medicine, sports, politics, and religion, as well as in drama and literature. C. Wright Mills viewed American society as twofold: an elite and a mass. The elite stratifies and maintains power and wealth using the technology of modern mass media.

**Materialism:**   A view that all knowledge comes from the senses, from careful observation, and from objective reporting of the dynamics of nature and society. Also, a philosophy that explains thought from being, mind from matter, and spirit from social organization. This approach is the opposite of classical philosophy. According to materialist philosophy, the "facts" of experience can be accounted for by the laws of physics.

Many folk theories and formal theories held that spirit tries to express itself in material form and the natural (imperfect) world results. Thus God (pure spirit) creates the world. Both Ludwig Feuerbach and Karl Marx reversed the relationship and argued that concretely existing social relationships determine thought, ideas, philosophy, and consciousness generally. This approach is known as the sociology of knowledge.

**Mathematical Sociology:**    An effort to transform all social relationships and all social change into precise mathematical formulae. These efforts ignore the qualitative transformations in politics, religion, speech, sports, and other human activities in which nonlinear transformations occur. It ignores the qualitative nature of the self-fulfilling prophecy in which people believe, trust, hope, and act on the expectation that social reality will emerge. See "Positivism" and "Quantification" for more. Cf. "Nonlinear Dynamics."

**Matriarchy:**    Literally, rule of mothers. This concept refers to a form of governance in which a set of sisters and their children live together. They occupy all the essential roles and perform a wide variety of labor. Authority resides in the most senior female, usually based upon age, experience, energy, personality, number of children, older daughters, and status of her mother. Men are usually absent or occasionally in residence when not engaged in hunting, warfare, male religious solidarity rituals, or other special activity. Matriarchy is thought to be the original form of governance of several premodern cultures. For the radical, critical, feminist, or liberal scholar, matriarchy is of interest since it speaks to the question of the gender division of labor esteemed in patriarchal societies.

Matriarchy was displaced by patriarchy with settled agriculture around 4,000 B.C. At that time, women became subordinated to and the property of men.

**McCarthyism (1950–1960):**    A form of political oppression in which only conservatives were held to be worthy of creating political or ideological culture. During the period of McCarthyism, any affiliation with anticapitalist, anticolonial, socialist liberation movements and/or with civil rights and antiracist organizations or causes subjected one to personal jeopardy. Senator Joseph McCarthy represented an era in American society and was not a single malevolent individual acting against the times.

**McDonaldization of Society:**    George Ritzer popularized the term. It refers to an effort to control all aspects of the production and distribution of goods via a highly organized set of rules. It embodies the bureaucracy that Max Weber called an "iron cage." All employees must wear the clothing specified, use the words rehearsed, work the hours set, and make the hamburgers exactly the same way in Moscow, London, Peoria, and Hong

Kong. This routinization of the labor process tends to destroy both variety and human agency. See "Fordism," "Legal-Rational Authority," and "Taylorism" for more.

**McDougall, William (1871–1938):**   English psychologist who taught at Harvard and Duke. He posited eighty-six instincts that account for human behavior and social forms: war, hierarchy, competition, and such. By the 1950s, these eighty-six instincts were reduced to four: the impulse toward sociability; new experience; security; and self-realization. By the 1960s, there was only one instinct: the sucking instinct. Now instincts are seldom used to explain human behavior. (See the work of W. L. Reese.)

**"Me":**   In the model of self laid out by George Herbert Mead (1934), the "Me" and the "I" exist in dialectic tension. The "Me" represents society-as-it-exists and as it involves a given individual. All of the social identities that key off of social roles compose the "Me." The response of the individual to symbolic interaction in which others shape behavior is also part of "me." Thus, "self" is a joint product of other persons—past, present, and, perhaps, future. In this context it makes sense to say that self and society are twin-born. The notion of the private, isolated autonomous self is a fiction. There could be no "me" without the social labor of thousands of others. Privatism and individual "freedom" thus tends to destroy both self and society. See "Heidegger, Martin," "'I,'" and "Phenomenology" for more.

**Mead, George Herbert (1863–1931):**   An architect of postmodern social psychology, Mead contributed much to a Constructionist view of social life (as against both divine and natural sources of social life). Mead held that mind, self, and society arose in the symbolic interactional process. Compare this to theories of mind, self, and behavior that treat them as individual and permanent sources of human behavior. He suggested that language arose in the *gesture*, that gestures are signs that point to existing objects/behaviors, but that speech is much more conventional and instrumental in the creation of social lifeforms; this orientation serves as grounding for Symbolic Interaction theory. Mead posited the "I" and the "Me" as components of the self that mediated behavior (which see). Shared meaning can arise if/when people take the perspective of others. (See the work of W. L. Reese.) See "'I,'" "Mind As a Social Product," "Psychology, Social," "Self, Social," "Social Psychology, Modern," and "Symbolic Interaction" for more.

**Medicalization:**   The practice of treating a forbidden behavior as an illness rather than a crime or a sin. Many forbidden activities have been de-sanctified and criminalized in the past 400 years. Currently there is a trend to decriminalize these activities and to medicalize them. These acts include alcoholism, drug addiction, homosexuality, gambling, homelessness. Cf. "Corruption, Theory of" and "Sanctification/De-sanctification."

*Mens rea:*    Latin: *mens* = mind; *rea* = competent. In law, it must be proven that a defendant had a "guilty mind." In law, the accused must be able to understand both the charges and the actions that lead to the charges, or s/he is *non compos mentis.*

**Mental Disorder:**    There are hundreds of forms of behavior that are interpreted as mental disorders. Generally, they are behaviors that are outside the traditional norms and values of a society. These disorders are classified into a diagnostic manual called the Diagnostic and Statistical Manual of Mental Disorders (DSM). A good deal of bizarre behaviors are treated as normal when they conform to normative expectations, especially those expectations in various religions. In law, when a psychiatrist, psychologist, or mental health clinician determines that a person is "suffering" from a mental disorder, adult decisionmaking capacity can be removed by a judge. Treatment, involuntary detention, or hospitalization, as well as the invasion of privacy, are then permitted. See "Psychopathic Disorder" for more.

**Meritocracy:**    Stratification systems based upon skill, knowledge, wisdom, effort, or personal genius. Meritocracy stands against inequality by accident of birth, race, wealth, use of force, or other less pertinent factors. In Western society, meritocracy is used to justify stratification by profession, bureaucratic echelon, or ownership. The socialist critique is that before merit comes class, gender, and ethnicity, which together form a social network to give those at the top a head start.

**Metaphysics:**    Beyond Physics. A branch of formal philosophy having to do with the ultimate nature of reality. It deals with the question of that which really exists (ontology) rather than that which seems to exist, that which we would like to exist, and that which exists for only the moment. Those in premodern modalities tend to argue that there is another, invisible world that takes precedence to this world in human affairs. Modern scientists tend to argue that there is only one reality and it has clear and sharp categories that can be measured and known through the scientific method. Postmodernists, in their more pessimistic moments, argue that one can never be sure of anything. More affirmative postmodernists argue that some limited, contingent, local, and relational truths can be asserted. See "Philosophy, The Discipline of" for more.

**Methodology, Theory of:**    In general, a methodology is a set of principles by which valid knowledge is obtained. Methodology is a subset of a larger domain having to do with the generation of information sets. Since all information sets are, technically, noise until translated into a concrete pattern of behavior by an insightful human, all information sets are part of a social lifeworld; thus, they are political. No methodology is outside the sphere of ideology. Scientific methodology is a special case in general and, where used, affects the social lifeworld under construction. Methodology is thus never value free.

There are several different kinds of scientific methodology. Broadly speaking, there are approaches that include principles from a quantitative perspective, and there are approaches that include principles from a qualitative perspective. Quantitative models argue that reality is essentially observable, retrievable, knowable, and controllable. Qualitative approaches agree with this point of view; however, they argue that grounding such analysis requires direct observation by or commentary from the participants or subjects of the study itself.

A more critical, postmodern analysis suggests that language functions as method. Discourse analysis is an approach in which evolving meanings pertaining to a social phenomenon are examined but are never complete. This incompleteness results because reality is fragmented, fuzzy, conditional, positional, and relational. Cf. "Critical Theory" and "Postmodernists/Postmodernism."

**Micro-Sociological Level of Analysis:**   Also known as the situational or local level of analysis. This is the level at which one studies particular localized aspects of how a system behaves, investigates specific interpersonal facets within an organizational structure, or examines daily practices, rituals, beliefs, customs of a given system or subsystem. If one wanted to engage in a micro-level of analysis regarding the child welfare system, one might study how a few individuals were processed through the system, investigate how the foster care unit of a particular jurisdiction functioned, or examine the routine encounters and daily life experiences within a local juvenile probation department. See "Micro-Theory" for more. Cf. "Macro-Sociological Level of Analysis."

**Micro-Theory:**   Any generalization based upon the observations of small-scale social phenomena. Usually, that which a given social scientist can grasp by his/her own direct experiences. Studies of group interaction, social occasions, asylums, churches, and so on are important, but often the larger content in which a given social phenomenon occurs is neglected and the total meaning is lost. For example, labeling theory makes sense on a micro-analytic level, but crime cannot be understood apart from the operation of the whole society. See "Micro-Sociological Level of Analysis" for more.

**Middle Class, Shrinking of:**   The middle class in the United States has been shrinking since 1970, as job opportunities disappear, wages decline, and programs of social justice are dismantled. Until 1970, the middle class was increasing and capitalism looked like it was fulfilling its promise to enrich all. As other capitalist countries took larger share of markets and as more restraints were put on corporate crime at home, American capitalists began to cut costs, automate, and to disinvest in the United States. The middle class has declined by about 15 percent in the past thirty years. Some 4 percent of the people who used to be in the middle class are richer and have more economic security. Some 11 percent have experienced downward mobility and a loss of social power and self-esteem.

**Middle Classes:**   The stratum in society that takes de facto control over the productive and reproductive process on behalf of the owners of capital for a salary, fee, commission, or royalty. Composed of managers, administrators, professionals, and technicians, the middle classes grow as the need for close control of the work force and the surplus population grows.

The term also includes those functionaries on salary or commission who administer to the needs of the labor force: lawyers, government officials, politicians, professors, salespersons, retailers, middlemen, public relation and advertising specialists.

**Migration:**   One of many solutions to alienated social relations. One packs up one's cherished belongings and moves to another, less hostile country. Other solutions include formation of underground structures, social revolution and social movements, and direct political action when institutional politics fail.

**Milgram, Stanley (1933–1984):**   A social psychologist who, in 1974, conducted an important experiment in which he showed the role of authority in producing harmful behavior. Milgram set up a phony electro-shock apparatus and collected data about the degree to which people would follow instructions even though they knew they were endangering the subjects. People were told that they would use electric shock to teach learners. Learners pretended to be not very bright and gave wrong answers. Teachers were then told to give them stronger and stronger shocks. They did. Of those told to do so, 65 percent gave the maximum 450 volts. Many objected and some cried, but still the teachers complied to the authority of the scientist. Milgram was staunchly criticized, and such experiments are now forbidden in most universities.

**Military-Industrial Complex:**   A phrase in a speech by President Eisenhower in which he warned against the expanding influence of the military in federal spending. Members of the House of Representatives and of the Senate try to bring military bases and weapons industry to their states in order to solve the problem of underemployment. A coalition builds up in which members of Congress and representatives from the military and the weapons industry exchange support. The same members of Congress are then hired by large corporations after they leave office. This results in an arms race that, in turn, is used to justify military solutions to foreign problems.

**Mill, John Stuart (1806–1873):**   A British philosopher noted for his contributions to a theory of free speech, women's liberation, and a well-accepted system of logic. His work on utilitarianism had liberal impulses. He asserted that the greatest good (utility) was the greatest happiness for the greatest number of people. See "Utility/Utilitarianism" for more.

**Millennium/Millenarianism:**   Latin: *mill* = thousand. A term in religion that refers to a prophecy in the New Testament and to a belief that a savior will appear one thousand years from the time of the last such savior, Jesus Christ. Prior to the year 1,000 A.D., many believed in the "coming of the end of days" and prepared by seeking spiritual comfort and guidance. As we approach the second millennium, one can expect widespread belief in and preparation for the advent of another savior who then, it is believed, will bring peace and justice to earth in a great upheaval. See "Eschatology" for more.

**Mills, C. Wright (1916–1962):**   Sociologist and controversial luminary in the social sciences. Mills believed that the role of the social scientist was one of concerned engagement with practical and intellectual life. Upon his death, he was professor of sociology at Columbia University. Mills found the macro-sociological writings of Karl Marx and Max Weber and the social psychological ideas of Sigmund Freud and George Herbert Mead to be immensely formative to his own knowledge base.

Prior to his death, Mills was developing a history of modern culture. Mills identified the division between the modern and postmodern age. The latter he termed the "Fourth Epoch." He is best known for developing the concepts of "the sociological imagination" and "the power elite." The former refers to one's capacity to understand social phenomena with historical specificity and with proper use of scientific knowledge. Through this process, one could attain and rediscover greater human freedom. The latter refers to the power exercised by members of the military complex, the industrial complex, and the governmental complex. According to Mills, free intellectuals need to assert their moral leadership. Failing this, other, less qualified, elites will do so.

In a sense, Mills was a utopian reformer. He argued that knowledge properly utilized could produce the good society. He did not believe it had quite arrived during his time and saw that this was the fault of individuals poorly exercising their knowledge. According to Mills, the sociological imagination was key to unlocking the potential for a more emancipatory existence. See "Imagination, Sociological" for more.

**Mind:**   The premodern understanding claimed that the mind was a separate part of the body that existed before and after birth. As such, it held that all the knowledge of the universe was and could be released by meditation or contemplation. Modern science generally held that the brain was a "black box": impossible to know. Only behavior was observable/knowable. Postmodern understanding accepts that there is a mind. According to postmodernists, the mind is the "software" and the brain is the "hardware" of human knowledge, feeling, and activity. Some of the software is preprogrammed by genetic inheritance. Noam Chomsky argues that language abilities are preprogrammed. Others claim that aggression, territoriality, domination, and acquisition are genetic. See "Self, Social" for more.

**Mind As a Social Product:**    In sociology, mind is a product of two or more persons in interaction. One's ways of thinking, feeling, and acting are, in Symbolic Interactional theory, constituted in part by one's culture, by one's status-role(s), and by role-others in a given definition of the situation. Mind is not something confined to the braincase of a single person, nor is it a stable, measurable entity. It is a fluid, emergent, collective product. See "Mead, George Herbert" for more.

**Mini-Cycles:**    Some economists hold that there are economic cycles of three to five years in duration. See "Kondratieff Cycles" for more.

**Minimum Wage:**    In law, the lowest hourly payment an employer can pay to a worker. As with welfare payments, minimum wages are always far below the cost of the reproduction of labor power; therefore, others must subsidize employees who are paid only minimum wages. Usually, it is the family of the worker (by giving free lodging, transport, clothing, food, and health care). In 1998, the minimum wage was $5.15 an hour. This amounts to $10,712/year for a forty-hour week/fifty-two weeks a year. The poverty line in 1998 was $19,100 for a family of four. In other words, at least three persons in the family must work to attain wages above the poverty line.

**Minor/Minority:**    In law, one who is not yet an adult. Minority ends and majority begins at 18, unless a court rules differently. See "Sociology of Youth " for more.

**Miranda Warning:**    A U.S. Supreme Court ruling that persons must be warned when they are subjected to custodial interrogation. The warning includes the right to remain silent and to have legal advice. It is necessary in order to protect the larger principle of due process and informed consent. The intent with Miranda is to offer some protection against coerced confessions. It was named after the 1966 case in which the police obtained information from Mr. Miranda while he was in custody and questioned.

**Miscarriage of Justice:**    A failure in law to achieve equity. Often the technical pursuit of law leads to a greater inequity than that meant to be discouraged by law. When this happens, judge, jury, appeals court, and the court of last resort may set aside the technicalities of law in order to prevent a miscarriage of justice.

**Mixed Economy:**   A basically capitalist market in which problems in the means of distribution are solved by welfare spending. Low profit lines of production are nationalized while long-term costs of production are socialized (e.g., pollution and occupational diseases). There is some central planning, subsidies, grants, wage/price controls, and periodic intervention in the economy through tax, interest, or money supply. See "Keynesian Economics" for more.

**Mobility, Downward:**   When one loses status, one is said to be downwardly mobile. There are lots of reasons why people lose social standing; capitalism tends to disemploy people; it moves high paying jobs to low wage countries and it tends to weaken ancient systems of status honor. Then, too, there are degradation routines that push people into low status situations. For example, divorce is harmful for women. All institutions have routines to disengage people. See "Degradation Routines" for more.

**Mobility, Intergenerational:**   The upward or downward occupational movement of a son (or set of men born in the same period) compared to the occupational status of his father. Notice the sexist bias in this definition; women are assumed to take the status of father, husband, or son. See "Intragenerational Mobility" for more.

**Mobility, Intragenerational:**   The upward or downward occupational movement of a single individual over his/her lifetime. See "Intergenerational Mobility" for more.

**Mobility, Social:**   A movement from one class status to another. Most mobility is a result of collective effort rather than individual effort, as implied in other definitions. For example, the difference in the social status of physicians in the United States today compared to 1900 is better explained by the power of the American Medical Association than by the increased success of private medicine in the United States. Most of the gain in longevity is the result of public health measures (e.g., sewage treatment, vaccination) rather than visits to a physician.

**Modern, Modernism, Modern Science:**   These words are used to refer to the kind of science and problem-solving approach modeled after Isaac Newton's most successful tracking of the movement of stars and falling objects. Modern science and modernity have given us a great many benefits; better communication, better transportation, better roads, buildings, bridges, sewer systems, and better housing. Modern science continues to improve the means of production of food, shelter, clothing, and medicine.

Yet, modern science has many problems, in that it dismisses complexity and mystery, relegates unexplainable objects to strict scrutiny, and is hostile to the emotions that expand the endpoints of human endeavor. It is a "magician's apprentice," with applications to war, to the exploitation of people and environment, and to the reproduction of its own approach to human knowledge and human frailty. Cf. "Postmodernists/Postmodernism."

**Modernization Theory:**  An economic theory in which science, technology, art, and all essential goods and services must be mass produced and mass marketed in order to maximize social well being. See "Development/Underdevelopment" for more.

**Mohammed (570–632):**  Founder of the Islamic religion. Mohammed began to receive divine revelations at age 40; these are collected in the Koran (Qur'an). He taught there was but one God and that Allah was his name. After failing to overthrow the idols at Mecca, he fled in what is now called the "great Hejira," which sets the beginning of the Islamic calendar. In Medina, he built a mosque and an army. Using the army, he brought Mecca into the Islamic fold and spread out from there to all Arabia. Over the centuries, Islam swept into eastern Europe, northern Africa, and east to Indonesia. Some 800 million people organize their lives according to the teachings of Mohammed: worship five times daily, make labor productive, care for the poor, and defend Islam with militancy.

Many progressives agree that the tenets of Islam are contrary to those of socialism. The rigid nature of the Islamic philosophy and way of life are in opposition with postmodernity. See "Koran" for more. (See the work of W. L. Reese.)

**Molestation:**  Generally used in law to refer to the act of an adult who harms a child either physically, as in the case of child abuse, or mentally, as in the case of sexual harassment. Often a polite term for rape and sexual abuse of a child.

**Money:**  Any commonly accepted medium of exchange (e.g., gold, letters of credit, government bills or currency, gems, silver). The socialist (nominalist) theory of money is that the value of it is always set by the amount of labor time that a monetary unit (dollar, mark, yen, pound, peso) can call forth from workers. Money thus has no intrinsic value; without the labor of others, money is only a name we give to metal, paper, or plastic. Those who hold large amounts of money try to increase the labor power it purchases. Those who have labor power try to decrease the amount of work represented in money. Karl Marx was critical of money, citing Shakespeare's poem: "Yellow glittering precious gold . . . gives title, knee, and approbation to the scoundrel, forces the wappened widow to wed again

[and] refreshes the hoar leper to the April Day." Socialists try to reduce/subordinate the role of money to common needs in determining who and what is bought and sold.

**Monks:**    An acronym for a form of social intimacy: men only, no kids. Two or more single men living together to enhance lifestyle and/or sexual pleasure. No kids and often no women are allowed to be part of this form of intimacy. There was a television series about such men called *The Odd Couple*. See "Dinks," "Swinks," and "Yuppie" for more. These are popular terms for those who refrain from traditional family and gender relations. See "Extended Family" and "Wonk/Wonks" for more.

**Monopoly:**    A monopoly is control of the terms of production and/or distribution by one or a few (oligopoly) large firms. It is a means by which costs can be lowered or prices can be increased without increasing the value of the goods or services produced. Sometimes monopolies (oligopolies) are effective when only a small portion of the market is controlled and a few large firms hold the line. If small firms increase wages or lower prices, big firms can use a wage/price war to eliminate them or simply buy them up. Anything that eliminates competition between suppliers creates an effective monopoly: Trade agreements, division of markets, mergers, union-busting, blacklisting, political bribery, as well as fair trade laws, conspiracies, bribes, subsidies, import duties, and so on are but a few of the devices by which monopolies are secured.

**Monopoly, International:**    According to the socialist critique, several lines of production controlled by a few firms that get together to fix prices and divide up the world market. Among these lines are: automobiles, oil products, chemicals, pharmaceuticals, breakfast cereals, nuclear energy systems, military goods, electronics, banking, light bulbs, sugar/sweeteners, coffee, plastics, book publishing, advertising and communications (including news services and entertainment). Coca Cola gets China; Pepsi Cola gets Russia.

**Monopoly Capitalism:**    A system of highly concentrated production and mass, unorganized consumers. Many isolated buyers compete against each other to purchase from a few large suppliers. A later stage of capitalism, monopoly capitalism creates serious problems of political legitimacy for capitalism by squeezing small entrepreneurs out of the class and, thus, eroding its own political base. Monopoly capitalism also undermines legitimacy by its inflationary practices and by corrupting the political process. Liberals think that the problem is monopoly, whereas Marxists think that capitalism, as an economic form, leads to bigger monopolies.

**Monopoly Sector:**    That part of the economic institution composed of big business: businesses with budgets up to several billion dollars, a work force of up to 300,000 and more, high wages, price agreements, employment stability, job security, good working conditions, pension plans, opportunity for advancement, and collective bargaining. The monopoly sector controls more than one third of the work force and is growing at the expense of the competitive sector.

**Moral Agency:**   The right to set policy and enforce rules. In authentically democratic societies, moral agency is widely dispersed among workers in school, medicine, religion, government, business, sports, and the arts. In bureaucratic or elitist societies, moral agency is vested in a few people, firms, or state offices. Moral agency is always a social product; one cannot be moral all by oneself, even if most tests and measures of moral development make it appear so. Even dictators cannot lead if no one follows. The politics of a society create different models of morality. See "Mass Base," "Moral Order," and "Motive" for more.

**Moral Development:**   The process by which the norms of a society are internalized into the self-system of the individual. Lawrence Kohlberg posited six stages of moral development. The first involves grudging obedience to the norms in fear of pain. The last is oriented to transcendent principles of ethical behavior. This sounds progressive, but there are problems. Carol Gilligan pointed out that women tend to put people before principles. Blind enforcement of principles can and does great harm to both interpersonal relationships and to situated judgment informed more by rational calculation than by wisdom. See "Moral Order" and "Praxis/Practice" for more.

**Moral Entrepreneurs:**   Popularized by the work of Howard Becker and other labeling theorists, moral entrepreneurs are rule makers. They are groups that create deviance or definitions of deviance "by making rules whose infractions constitute deviance, and by applying those rules to particular people and labeling them as outsiders." Deviance in this context is what people define it to be. Today homosexuality is permissible; twenty years ago it was not. Today rock 'n' roll music is mostly acceptable; forty years ago it mostly was not.

In popular culture, moral entrepreneurship is a term used to scorn those who wish to outlaw pornography, sexual/sexist lyrics in rock or rap music, gambling, drug use, abortion, homosexuality, and prostitution—as well as other efforts to control morals. As a pejorative term, it excludes open discussion.

**Morality:**   A term referring to the degree to which the norms, laws, values, customs, and mores of a society are embodied in the everyday life of a person. People of high moral standing take care to live in conformity to the normative structure. However, with morality, one must ask: (1) How do these norms and customs speak to exploitation, inequality, and oppression? (2) What is the social location of the norm/rule/lawmaking process? Moral agency resides in an elite in stratified societies. It is distributed broadly in richly democratic societies.

**Moral Order:**    A system of human obligation, rights, and relationships that patterns a system of human interaction. That which is "good" or "bad" is defined by the moral order. Many organizations involving people have no moral order other than narrow self-interest. Therefore, they cannot be said to be truly "social" organizations. Banks, supermarkets, factories, and such have little in the way of a moral order. They are economic not social systems. Notions of good and bad are not of interest. Profit, efficiency, and productivity drive the system. See "Moral Agency" and "Moral Development" for more.

**Moral Panic:**    A form of pre-theoretical response to bad times in which some group is demonized and treated as if it were the source of one or more social problems. Teenage crime, teenage pregnancy, witchcraft, and UFOs (unidentified flying objects) are among the more common "panics" in which people and the media create the dramaturgical facsimile of immorality in order to explain why things go wrong. See "Satanism" and "Witchcraft" for more.

**Mores:**    Latin, plural: manners, customs; singular = *mos*. Those rules of behavior that have the character of "must" rather than "should." Shame and repentance follow the failure to observe the mores of a society if an individual has internalized the rules. A form of ideological culture, an elite can tap into this form of social control by passing laws that bring shame and regret upon their violation.

**Morris, William (1834–1896):**    An English writer and poet who argued for guild socialism. His book *Useful Work and Useless Toil* called for a return to medieval craftsmanship and collective ownership of factories, plants, shops, and other means of production.

**Mortgage:**    French: death earnings. A term that referred to a loan on an estate that would be paid when an heir came into property upon the death of his father. It now refers to any financial interest in a property created as security for a loan. The law provides that a lender may retake a property when payments are not made on time, even if all but the last payment has been made.

**Mosaic Code:**    A set of biblical laws regulating family, community, and intertribal conduct. Generally, it sets a contract between the Hebrew God, Yahweh/Elohim, and the Jewish people. The sense of the code is that if Hebrews follow these laws, they will be rewarded in this life by the lands, herds, and slaves of several neighboring tribes. The laws themselves are patterned after the 282 laws of Hammurabi, a Persian king who established a unified legal code to replace a myriad of tribal codes in order to better govern his empire. The Ten Commandments, said to be received directly from God by Moses, are patterned after ten confessions set forth in the Book of the Dead in ancient Egypt.

Mosaic law had many provisions for social and criminal justice that appealed to the poor and the oppressed in a time of trouble. It was adopted during the early years of the Roman Empire and, after merging with Roman law, became the source of ethical behavior in those lands conquered by Rome. Since the Mosaic code is recorded in the first five books of the Bible, and since these books are considered sacred by Jews, Christians, and Muslims, the code is now a central social philosophy for billions of people.

**Moses:**   A biblical character; a Hebrew said to be born in Egypt. The word "Moses" means "son" or "boy" in Egyptian; it means something like "one who brings out" in Hebrew. Moses may be a composite of several people: There is an Egyptian story about Sargon, who, like Moses, was hidden in an ark amid bulrushes to protect him from danger. The Mosaic code, named after Moses, is the prime source of ethical and moral behavior for billions around the world. Based on the Code of Hammurabi, the Mosaic Code is better known as Deuteronomy (the second giving of the God's Law). The first giving of the Law included the Ten Commandments, which ground both family and community behavior. Moses is known as the herald of monotheism for his requirement that the laws in Deuteronomy be read aloud in public every seven years. See "Hammurabi, Code of" and "Mosaic Code" for more.

**Motivation:**   A process by which human behavior is linked to certain conditions. There are many ways to establish such links. Money is only one and by far the least desirable motivation. Status, values, and social relationships have motivated people to organize their behavior in social ways for centuries. However, one should note that much behavior is not motivated but rather mutually produced through symbolic interaction with significant others. As a result, people do things they might not want to do or think of doing. The notion of a motive is linked to the problem of controlling behavior by external means, apart from socialization, moral agency, or social interaction. See "Motive" for more.

**Motive:**   Imperatives for behavior. Jürgen Habermas, George Herbert Mead, Émile Durkheim, and Sigmund Freud agree that most motives are shaped through the socialization process and represent norms and values, as well as the general expectations of others (society, significant others, mother/father, the peer group, and so on). Motive contrasts with the concept of an order, command, or rule; these are external to the self-system and may bear no relationship to social values. Modern psychology and significant social analysis try to explain human behavior in terms of motives when, in the empirical case, the concept of the rule, order, or command is a better analytic device. Since the division of labor in bureaucracies gives "higher" authority a monopoly over decisions, neither motives nor normative discourse are helpful in seeking the sources of behavior. See "Moral Agency" and "Motivation" for more.

**Multinational Corporation (MNC):**   A firm that has no home base and many factories, offices, and outlets in a number of countries. MNCs can buy labor cheap one place, sell dear another, avoid taxes everywhere, escape criminal action by selling off or closing down in countries with an unfavorable business climate, and generally play one government against another for favors.

**Multi- Versus Mono-Causality:**   The issue of causality is central to how people understand what happens in their life and all around them. There are different types of causal relationships. The most relevant for critical thought is the distinction between multi- and mono-causality. The notion of causality holds that event "A" produces event "B." This view of causality has two forms: (1) "A" is the *necessary* condition for "B" to occur; that is, "B" cannot occur without "A"; and (2) "A" is the *sufficient* condition for "B" to occur; that is, "B" could occur without "A" and could occur because of "A."

*Mono-causality* is linear. It maintains that one event produces (necessarily or sufficiently) the next event, which produces (necessarily or sufficiently) the next event, and so on. This is a model of interdependence. The following illustrates this process:

> the articulation of religious beliefs at home→
> strong moral and ethical framework for children→
> commitment to education, work, and family→
> productive, law-abiding members of society.

*Multi-causality* assumes two forms. These include *many causes* and *combined causes*. The "many causes" model indicates that several events can occur independent of one another to produce an outcome. Thus, the "many causes" model is a sufficient model of causality. Why are teenagers having children at an increasingly alarming rate? Several causal factors include television's portrayal of sexuality, peer pressure, the discomfort with condom use, poverty and relative deprivation, the absence of parental supervision and monitoring, and so on. In this model each variable can produce teenage pregnancy, but no single factor is necessary since any of the other factors can also produce the event. The "combined causes" model indicates that several factors must be present at the same time for a certain outcome to occur. This is not linear causality because the sequencing of the events can vary. With combined causality each factor is necessary for the specific effect to occur, but none is sufficient. The interactive combination of variables produces the effect. Critical thought tends to focus upon a multi-factorial model of causality. It is nonlinear and much more open to the changing dynamics of cause and effect expressed over time.

**Mussolini, Benito (1883–1945):**    Mussolini was the governmental dictator or premier in Italy from 1922–1943. He is credited with developing and applying principles of fascism to all political aspects of the country. Together with Adolph Hitler of Germany, Mussolini posed a substantial threat to freedom and democracy throughout Europe during World War II. He was called *Il Duce* (the leader) among the peasants and noblemen until his ideological practices stripped Italy of its ability to thrive in Europe's declining economy. He was executed by his own people. See "Fascism" for more.

**Mutual Funds:**    A form of ownership in which people join together to buy stocks and bonds. More and more of these are owned by collectives of different sizes. For example, the California Teachers' Union owns several billion dollars of stocks and bonds, as do many other pension plans. Other examples include AARP, TIAA-CREF, Chrysler Workers, and so on. At some point, such collective ownership will affect both investment decisions and government policy. The development of global equity mutual funds is also of interest to political economists, though the impact of these funds is yet to be determined.

**Mysticism:**    Belief in the power of supernatural beings and the possibility of communication with them. The fact is that physical and social phenomena do not always behave with the precision and regularity assumed/required by modern science. The question is how to explain disorder, sudden transformations in people, social life, and nature, unusual events, and so on. Many people accept that invisible beings bring these changes about to reward or to punish those who fail to live up to the norms and values of a society. See "Chaos Theory" for more.

**Mystification:**    A process of information control by which a person or class cannot identify self-interests. The Marxian position is that whoever controls the means of production controls the means to produce ideological culture: art, literature, drama, and religion. Those who control ideological culture then use this control to mystify opposition. Mystification is also the process by which false consciousness is created. Usually coercion or repression underwrite false consciousness, but sometimes, in the United States especially, the authority of respected persons can mystify voters, customers, students, and children by asserting as true that which does not correspond to one's experience in a concrete situation. See "False Consciousness" and "Sociology of Fraud" for more.

# N

**NACLA:** The North American Congress on Latin America. It publishes a continuing analysis of the impact of U.S. capitalism on South America. It is full of hard data and devoid of the strident, overdone rhetoric of many socialist publications. NACLA is a resource for anyone interested in the present arena in which capitalism and U.S. interests combine to produce violence and/or liberation movements.

**Name:** The name given a person is important to his/her position in the social order. In the United States usually one is given the family name of the biological father. However, naming is both a religious and legal act that may not occur. If given, a name may be removed either by deed or by law. In the latter case, one loses all family rights and obligations. Traditionally, name changing has been more of an issue for women, since they are expected to do so upon marriage. There is a great deal at stake sociologically, financially, and emotionally when such name changes occur.

**Narrative:** French: *narritif.* A term that connotes doubt about the value of grand theories, universal truths, global explanations, totalizing practices, or master codes with which to understand everything. Mini-narratives, micro-histories, local codes, and traditional myths make fewer of these claims and, thus, are more acceptable in postmodern life. See "Postmodernists/Postmodernism," "Postmodernity," and "Totalizing" for more.

**National Insurance:** A program administered by the state in which illness, age, unemployment, and physical or emotional handicaps are provided for out of public funds. These programs provide a subsidy to the upper class since they cover the unpaid costs of labor and bodily injury done in pursuit of profits. The tax process that provides the funds is of considerable interest in this respect; if they are regressive to the working class or to the middle class, then the subsidies are higher and the profits greater. See "Socialized Medicine" for more.

**Nationalism:** Loyalty to one's own nation and the practice of putting the interests of that nation above all other nations. It is also one of the many sources of war, injustice, and exploitation. Nation-states have been around for some 300 years. They are just now beginning to merge into blocs or dissolve into ethnic or regional segments. See "State, Theory of" for more.

**Nationalization:**   A process by which ownership and control of specific firms is transferred from private ownership to a national government. The motive to produce may become service and/or quality rather than profit. The performance of nationalized firms depends upon the quality of the government that runs the firm. Most nationalization occurs when capitalism abandons a given line of production as unprofitable and the state is forced to supply the good or service. This circumstance is called "lemon socialism," since only the lemons are nationalized. The capitalists keep title to the profitable lines of production. Great Britain is in great difficulty because it nationalized expensive, labor-intensive sorts of production while letting private corporations retain title to high profit capital-intensive lines of production.

**National Security Managers:**   Those who control opposition to capitalism at home and abroad. They include the secretaries of state, defense, labor, education, the heads of the three armed services, the head of the FBI, the director of the CIA, and the chairman of the Nuclear Regulatory Commission. The owners and top executives of business and industry along with the national security managers make up the "ruling class." According to socialist theory, these are the real decision makers in the United States. See "Group of Seven" for more.

**Natural Child:**   A child born out of wedlock or one to whom a family name is refused. Natural children bear a great deal of blame for their situation; properly, the blame should go to parents or society for so categorizing them. See "Bastard" for more.

**Nature, Liberation of:**   In "Nature and Revolution," Herbert Marcuse notes that the liberation of nature is an important, related part of the liberation of society. Commercialized nature, polluted nature, and militarized nature reduce the life environment of society and prevent humans from finding themselves in nature. The liberation of nature requires: (1) treating nature as subject; (2) treating nature as life (rather than as material); (3) developing new categories by which the natural world is experienced; (4) supporting the ecological movement; and (5) emancipating the senses in order to appreciate nature.

**Necessary Labor:**   That amount of work needed to reproduce labor power: the power to live, to learn, to work with skill, as well as the capacity to think beyond the immediate job or problem. Any labor beyond the labor required for these things is "surplus labor." The question then becomes, How is the value produced by surplus labor to be shared and distributed? See "Capitalism," "Communism," "Exploitation, Super," and "Socialism" for more.

**Necessity:**   A legal defense referring to the circumstances that compel one to commit a crime. If the harm avoided is greater than the crime committed, then one may invoke the necessity defense. Examples of the necessity defense include: prisoners who escape from a burning jail; sailors who discard cargo belonging to others in order to save a ship; and a parent who kills an attacker to save a child.

**Necessity, The Realm of:**   This term refers to the eternal and unvarying laws of God or nature to which all good, wise, and sensible persons should bend. Heavily politicized in favor of any one of 3,000 or more different sociocultural formations, the realm of necessity is supported by both science, medicine, and a wide variety of social control systems. Postmodern thought greatly expands the realm of necessity. Some postmodernists reject it altogether.

**Needs, False:**   Those needs above and beyond that which is required to construct a good and decent social lifeworld. Herbert Marcuse said that capitalism must generate layer after layer of false needs in order to realize profit. Since most workers do not get paid enough to buy 100 percent of the goods they produce, it is necessary to convince others to buy more than they need. Advertising is used to create these needs and to realize the last 5, 10, or 15 percent of profits on that which is produced but, without the creation of need, lies unwanted and unused in warehouses. See "Realization, Problem of" for more.

**Needs Principle:**   Based on the economic philosophy of Karl Marx. The needs principle is a doctrine of justice and social life attained only when a society reaches a socialist political reality. The doctrine is, "From each according to his/her abilities; to each according to his/her needs." This condition recognizes that people have skills, competencies, and resources that are significant to the maintenance of society *and* that they also have needs, longings, desires that sustain them and that must be sustained if they are to maintain their contribution to the good of society. See "From Each According to His Abilities; to Each According to His Needs" and "Marx, Karl" for more.

**Negation:**   A method of analysis (and expansion of understanding) in which new ideas are derived from existing ideas. This requires one to explore one's limitations and contradictions, "negating" every idea until a more adequate one is reached. Developed by G.W.F. Hegel, the "negation" is part of a dialectic in which A includes and is negated by non-A, and out of that negation comes a clearer comprehension of A. Hegel's own example is not particularly helpful: "Out of being and nothing is the unity of the two, and this unity is becoming." It is hard to understand something all by itself. Thus the concept of "bourgeoisie" is made more understandable by the concept of the "proletariat." When we consider both concepts together, we have insight that helps move us toward sensible action.

**Negation (of the Negation):**    A concept introduced by G.W.F. Hegel. It refers to a change in which the old quality is canceled out and a new quality emerges; think of the addition of an acid to a base, which produces a salt (in chemistry); or of the theft from a bank that has been exploiting workers and/or customers. In Marxist thought, the central negation is the negation of human dignity, community, and praxis. In these times, an important sphere of negation lies in the liberal assumption that the essential freedom of men and women is to be found in the realm of mind, reason, consciousness, or pure thought. For liberal theorists, the negation of that negation was freedom of thought, speech, and consciousness. Soul and mind were thought to be sacred. This position negates the Marxist view that human dignity lies in the realm of production of human culture, not solely in the realm of thought and speech. Modern modes of production require an invasion into the sanctity of pure thought. Management science preempts thought in the work process, whereas advertising and public relations attempt to manage needs and understanding. These professions negate the last realm of liberal freedom. Critical theory and socialist revolution aim to negate this negation by restoring human control over the means of production (i.e., activity as well as thought).

**Negentropy:**    Order, structure, predictability. The opposite of entropy: chaos, chance, random contact. A society must solve its problems of order. Some societies use force and coercion, especially economic and legal coercion, to produce order. Others use collective interaction and socialization to solve the problem of order. The production of negentropy is a fundamental question for the survival of all systems. See "Systems Theory" for more.

**Neglect:**    A legal term referring to the failure of a parent or guardian to provide for the emotional, physical, and developmental needs of a child. It is also used to refer to some act a prudent person would have taken in order to prevent the death or injury of another person. Neglect is the basis for charging the crime of negligence.

**Neocolonialism:**    After African and Asian nations won political independence, they found that they were still dependent upon international capitalism in terms of what was produced and who benefited from production. In addition, they found that their governments either cooperated with or were subverted by developed capitalist states. In neocolonial states, domestic ruling classes replace colonial administrators and a police capacity is used to provide cheap labor to capitalist firms.

**Neo-Marxism:**   An attempt to renew Marxism with the spirit and focus of his early writings, some of which were not available to Marxist revolutionaries until after the nature of Marxism was settled. The first wave of new Marxist economics came with O. Lange, P. Sweezy, and Joan Robinson. Some of the more recent concerns of neo-Marxists include alienation, praxis, democratic self-management, and the role of subjectively creating humans in producing culture and, in the same moment, themselves as human beings. Neo-Marxists also incorporate the best of recent scholarship and theory into their own work, but the social philosophy remains grounded in Marxism.

**New Class:**   A term used by M. Djilas to refer to a layer of party bureaucrats, managers, and top professionals in state socialism who were using their position for personal advantage. This new class "froze" the revolution in the USSR and elsewhere and, in turn, caused the collapse of bureaucratic socialism in the late 1980s.

**New Left:**   A mixture of students, prisoners, blacks, women, older people, and neo-Marxists that emerged in the mid-1960s, partly in response to repression at home, partly in rejection of right-wing Marxism and economism, and partly in response to Vietnam. Mostly without a coherent Marxian analysis of the United States, the New Left nevertheless moved against capitalist military ventures. Many of these Marxists trace their roots to Herbert Marcuse, Jürgen Habermas, Georg Lukács, Korsch, and Max Horkheimer.

**News:**   Information about change. A communication act must contain some new, strange, or unexpected information bit or one does not learn from it. All systems must have the capacity to read out, store, and retrieve information about change in the environment or change in the internal structure, if the system is going to be able to survive (maintain irreversibility). Some critics claim that the greater part of the information disseminated by the mass media is not news but, rather, social opinion. Cf. "Social Opinion."

**Nietzsche, Friedrich (1844–1900):**   A student in Germany who was appointed professor before he finished his degree. He held, in *The Birth of Tragedy*, that both Apollonian calm and Dionysian passion were important to art and to life. In *Beyond Good and Evil*, Nietzsche reduced all moral systems to those that favored master morality or those that promoted slave morality. Master morality is superior and is based in social rules, but society needs both moralities. Nietzsche held that the "will to power" lay behind all human action and that slave mortality was a disease that infected both democracy and Christianity. Nietzsche argued that one should philosophize "with a hammer," breaking up old superstitions. He argued that modern science had resulted in the death of God and that out of that death could and should arise an *Übermensch*: a person of high integrity, without prejudice, an intellectual, proud of his/her reason and responsibility, and with a "greatness of soul." Nietzsche is seen as a progenitor of postmodern sensibility. (See the work of W. L. Reese.)

**Nominalism:**   Latin: name, naming. An idea from philosophy that the names we give objects in nature and society are mere convenience. The question is whether objects exist in and of themselves or are merely names we give to some vague and slippery aspect of reality. For example: Can we speak of a forest or only of individual trees? According to postmodern philosophy of science: (1) Such collectives become real when they begin to affect the behavior of other systems in the environment; (2) there is a reality-creating process in which the name of a thing calls it forth (e.g., as when we name someone a "friend," "wife," or "son"); and (3) in fractal geometry, systems occupy only part of the space available and thus have fractal facticity; naming then begins to be a poetic and a political act.

**Nomothetic:**   A nomothetic system is one in which the relationships are stable and a set of principles (theory) can be derived to describe how the system works. The term is important to those interested in how societies work, especially since people often argue that societies are by nature nomothetic. Some people claim that a society could be (and maybe should be) organized as a nomothetic system, but the "normal" state is one of instability and unpredictability in human affairs. The answer to this question determines the kind of science one uses. See "Idiographic" for more.

**Nonlinear Dynamics:**   A form of dynamics in which a small change in a key variable has a large effect on the behavior of a system. For example, think of the straw that broke the camel's back. Then, too, large changes can be absorbed without changing the behavior of a system. For example, Itzhak Perlman suffered polio as a child but still became a world-class violinist. In Chaos theory, there are five dynamical states; simple systems can display both linear and nonlinear dynamics; complex systems usually display nonlinearity. Given nonlinear dynamics, modern science's search for stable, universal, and eternal laws with tight causality is not possible. This impossibility opens space for human agency and for qualitative changes in causality. See "Chaos Theory" and "Mathematical Sociology" for more.

**Nonperson:**   An individual who is defined as having no status (standing) in the social occasion under construction, even when s/he is physically present. Racist, sexist, classist, and ageist rules define given persons as sociologically nonexistent. Cf. "Person."

**Non sequitur:**  Latin: it does not follow (from what has been said or proven so far). See "Fallacies (of Thinking)" for more.

**Non-Zero-Sum Game:**  A game in which all players can win something more than they risk. As used in economics, it means a form of production and distribution in which a division of labor enriches all without irreparable harm to the environment. Cf. "Zero-Sum Game."

**Norm:**  A rule that specifies appropriate and desirable behavior. Much of human behavior is mediated by various norms learned in socialization and emergent in everyday life. Some theories also ground human behavior in genes, instincts, personal desires, or the single individual. A norm is also a statistical description of what people actually do in a situation. A good bit of mischief accrues when statistical norms are held to be necessary social norms, as in the bell curve's normal distribution of test scores. Empiricism holds that all such curves must come from the actual behavior of persons; those who believe that these forms are natural insist that all rational persons must conform to the curve.

**Normative Order:**  Patterns of human activity created by intersubjective understanding. In contrast, Jürgen Habermas claims that purposive-rational order generates behavior via external stimuli involving direct application of sanctions or indirect control of mass media.

**Noumena:**  Greek: *noema* = thought. In modern philosophy, there is a question about whether thought can grasp that which really exists. The term "noumena" refers to that which exists and can be known. "Phenomenon" refers to that which we think exists, or to that which, if existent, cannot be known, or, more commonly, to that which seems to exist to our limited senses.

***Nulla poena sine lege:***  A Latin term that means that the state cannot punish one unless there is a law that forbids or demands an action.

**Null Hypothesis:**  A statement that a given relationship between two or more variables does not exist. One always tries to confirm a null hypothesis, so one will not be tempted to confirm a hypothesis that one thinks is or should be true. See "Hypothesis" for more.

***Nullum crimen sine lege:***  No crime exists without a law passed by a competent lawmaking body.

**O**

**Objectification:** The process of turning a subject into an object. Any process that tends to reduce intentionality and self-determination. People are objectified when they are treated as a means to an end. Power objectifies by forcing people to do things they judge to be inappropriate. People are also objectified when they are turned into commodities (football players, prostitutes, slaves, etc.) in a market.

**Objectivity:** A stance of impartiality and disinterest in the search for truth. This stance assumes that truth (social facts) exists apart from the subjective activity of intending human beings. Cf. "Subjectivity."

**Obscene:** Any deed or word that degrades or corrupts something sacred in a society. As used in everyday life, it refers to deeds and publications that tend to promote sexual behavior outside the norms of a given society. It carries considerable emotional content and, when used, degrades and demotes.

There is considerable debate about what constitutes obscenity. There are obscenity statutes in most jurisdictions. Often the determination of what is or is not obscene is determined by "community standards."

Critics of obscenity statutes contend that the state regulation of nonconformist behavior dangerously impinges on one's right to self-expression, protected under the First Amendment of the U.S. Constitution. Lyrics in music, photographs displayed in a gallery, and printed words in a work of fiction can be labeled obscene. Critics argue that these are all instances of artistic expression. Artistic expression is suppose to offend, incense, and outrage if progress in thought and culture are to be made.

**Oedipal Complex:** A Freudian idea that holds that boys are jealous of their fathers and wish to destroy them. Oedipus was the son of a Greek king who had been warned that his son would kill him. The father ordered a servant to take the boy and murder him. Instead the servant placed the boy with a peasant couple who raised him. He became a warrior and on meeting his father, unknown, killed him. As spoils of war, Oedipus wed, still unknowing, the king's wife, his mother, and had two daughters by her.

Presumably, social revolution is informed by an Oedipal desire buried deep in the psyche rather than by exploitation, injustice, or other good causes. There is a companion theory for young girls called the "Electra complex." See "Freud, Sigmund" for more. Cf. "Electra Complex."

**Offense:**    A criminological term referring to observable behavior in violation of a law. An offense is a crime. In criminology, there are different kinds of offenses: (1) crimes against persons (e.g., assault, rape, murder); (2) crimes against property "rights" (not against property)—for example, theft, conversion, fraud, arson, forgery, burglary, robbery, and blackmail. The latter contain elements of offenses against the body of persons; (3) crimes against the public order (e.g., obstruction of right of way, loud or offensive talk or rough behavior, vagrancy, homelessness, begging, sleeping in parks, and other behavior unseemly to the middle classes); and (4) violations against international law (e.g., piracy, hijacking, war crimes, genocide, and apartheid).

**Office:**    A position in a table of organization that carries duties and authority. The notion of an "office" is an invention by which humans can be separated from a status without too much trouble. The notion of an office is useful only when it is desirable to treat people as interchangeable.

**Oligarchy, Michel's Iron Law of:**    The word "oligarchy" means rule of the few. Michel's Iron Law of Oligarchy says that those in power use that power to retain control of people, wealth, and nations. The term is used to condemn union leaders, socialist bureaucrats, and government bureaucrats who put their own office and staff above the programs and policies they are charged to administer. See "Union Corruption" for more.

**Ombudsman:**    A Scandinavian term referring to a person who accepts complaints against public officials and inquires into them on behalf of the injured party. The ombudsman then attempts to work for equity in the case at hand. Most universities have such officers, who protect students and staff against professors and administrators who practice sexist, racist practices, and/or religious bigotry.

**One-Dimensional Society:**    A society in which intersubjective understanding is impaired and critical analysis is crippled. This leaves merely technical work to be done.

**Ontological Category:**    Significant to the phenomenology of Edmund Husserl and Martin Heidegger. The term refers to an aspect of the natural world that has facticity apart from human intentionality. Race, ethnicity, and who one's parents are, are all examples of facticity: They are conditions that can never change. The ontological category is also an epistemological category that is (temporarily) reified by human intention and behavior. We have knowledge about our race, ethnicity, and heritage through our various descriptions of such factical realities with others.

**Ontology:**    Greek: *ontos* = being; *logos* = word, study; literally, the study of being. The term refers to the examination of the essence of phenomena. In traditional Western thought, ontology is important for deciphering what is at the core of human existence (i.e., the essential nature of love, beauty, justice). A feminist critique of ontology posits that this approach misses the relational dimension of human existence, which is more consistent with the natural behavior of women. Thus, for example, the ontology of women is located in the interrelational dynamic of mothering, networking with peers, or family life.

**Onus:**    Guilt, responsibility, burden. In law, one who has the onus of proof has the burden to prove a charge or accusation. In everyday usage, the word carries a negative emotional charge that denotes shameful behavior.

**Operant Conditioning:**    A system of socialization in which behavior is modified by linking specific stimuli (controlled by another person) to given behavior patterns. A form of Freudian revisionism, operant conditioning defeats reflection, judgment, and intersubjective discourse. It establishes unilateral control of behavior via the use of appropriate principles of psychology. Sometimes this process is called "behavioral modification" and is used on prisoners, students, alcoholics, and others who do not respond to existing norms. See "Conditioning" for more.

**Oppression:**    The practice of crushing those who criticize or advocate a different social lifeworld. Oppression varies: from withholding rewards to beatings, jailings, assassinations, as well as the use of chemotherapy and psychological technology. Control over the means of violence by an elite is the major approach to oppression.

**Order(s):**    An imperative directing organized human behavior. In Max Weber's view, an order derives its legitimacy from traditional or legal (rational) authority. Because the reproduction of class societies is based upon the continued inequitable appropriation of social wealth, all such societies must solve the problem of the legitimacy of the orders to work, to obey, to desist, and to keep the peace. These societies solve this problem by structural force. All orders neutralize motives and impair the normative process.

**Organic Theory of Social Organization:**    A model of social organization that holds that all societies, much like plants or animals, have parts that are essential to the whole organism. The idea is attributed to Herbert Spencer and developed by A. Schaefle and Friedrich Nietzsche. The theory holds that there are three "organs" in society; workers, traders, and capitalists. They perform the functions of feeding, distributing, and digesting. Consequently, capitalism is a natural, valued, and essential mode of production. Just as some animals are simple and complex, so are some societies. The theory becomes political when it claims that complex societies are superior to simple ones since the division of labor is great. See "Durkheim, Émile" for more.

**Organization Theory:**    A set of sociological principles by which human beings can be managed in factories, offices, and schools. The term refers to the theory used to make complex organizations work better, rather than to how to construct a decent and rational community. Max Weber, Frederick Taylor, Talcott Parsons, C. Argyris, and others are the major figures in this form of commodity science.

**Orwell, George (1903–1950):**    The author of many works on radical politics, Orwell wrote scathing critiques of both capitalism and bureaucratic/statist socialism. *The Road to Wigan Pier* discussed worker issues, whereas *Homage to Catalonia* examined the issues in the Spanish Civil War. His two critiques of socialism are famous: *Animal Farm*, a satire on Stalin and the cult of the hero in the USSR; and *1984*, a bitter and horrifying fictional account of the role of the state in controlling both thought and action. Orwell is credited with several popular phrases: "Big Brother is watching you"; "some animals are more equal than others"; and "group think." George Orwell is the pen name of Eric Blair, who was a bureaucrat in the English government and saw too well the effort of government to manage public opinion.

**Overdetermination:**    A concept employed by structural Marxists. Overdetermination means that, at any given time, multiple factors (especially the political, the economic, and the ideological spheres of influence) exert different degrees of control to effect a particular outcome. In other words, the cause of something is always multiple; that is, many influencing forces work in combination to produce a certain end. This concept was originally developed by Sigmund Freud in his understanding of how psyche (the unconscious) influenced soma (the body and behavior). The reason why homosexuality, for example, is legal in most jurisdictions today, and is no longer classified as a form of mental disease, is related to the overdetermining effects of the political, economic, and ideological spheres of influence in society. These effects were vastly different some twenty-five years ago when homosexuality was both illegal and a diagnostic category of mental illness.

**Overpopulation:**    The idea from Thomas Malthus that population growth outruns the capacity to grow food. Natural checks (disease, famine, war, and infanticide) are desirable and not to be removed lightly. This fact is, in the long run, true enough. What is of interest is how many people could be supported in different political economies. There are now about 6 billion people on earth. Most experts say the world is now over-populated and people should have fewer or no children.

The Marxian position is that with a good means of production and distribution of food, shelter, clothing, education, jobs, and health care, the earth could support between 20 and 100 billion people; that is, 20 billion people with American standards of food and energy consumption and 100 billion people with Asian patterns of food usage and energy consumption. Population theory thus needs to be set in the context of the political economy in question. Cf. "Demographic Transition Theory." See "Abortion," "Birth Control," and "Underclass (Undermass)" for more.

**Over-Socialized Model of Self:**   Dennis Wrong, in reaction to the view of the individual as a passive occupant of social roles and rules, criticized structural sociology. In contrast to this over-socialized model of the self, he noted that people are creative in taking and making the roles in which they find themselves, that they can disengage and take other, more fulfilling social roles. Yet Wrong's over-psychologized model of being is also a political trap. Our ability to transcend our culture and act upon our own will is greatly limited in coercive, bureaucratic, and managed societies. Within the same society, power and circumstance produce widely varying degrees of self-determination.

**Owen, Robert (1771–1858):**   A Welsh industrialist and philanthropist who helped put together utopian communities. He adopted communist ideas; reduced the work day in his own textile mills from fourteen to ten hours a day; established a day care center and a model school for his workers; and reduced his share to 5 percent profit. In 1825, Owen established a model community at New Harmony, Indiana, which failed. He also tried to establish a Union of All Classes and All Nations. Although Owen was opposed to religion, today only the Hutterites embody the ideals to which he subscribed. (See the work of W. L. Reese.)

# P

**Pacifism:**   A social movement opposed to the use of war to settle problems between nations, as in a pacifist movement akin to that launched by Martin Luther King, Mohandas Gandhi, or Jesus Christ.

Pacifism can also be an individual belief unconnected to a movement. It is the opposition to the use of (physical) violence to settle problems. It is an internal resolve that, through peaceful, open, and frank discourse, resolutions can be found to interpersonal disputes.

Militant Marxists and expansionist capitalists oppose pacifism, albeit for different reasons. Marxists claim that pacifism often freezes the false peace of oppression. Sometimes war is necessary in order to negate a greater negation. Expansionists argue that evolution is driven by conflict. In the end, inferior societies will be eliminated and superior societies will survive, as warfare for markets, raw materials, and between modes of production work their way through history.

**Paganism:**   A form of religion in which people believe that all of nature is sacred. Rivers, clouds, mountains, animal species, and all natural events (e.g., thunder, lightning, fire, frost, earthquakes, tornadoes, the seasons, and the four winds) are moved by spirits within them. Believing all of nature to be sacred, pagans are careful to use only that which they need to survive and to pray to the spirit of the animal or plant that they use. See "Pantheism" and "Profanation" for more.

**Panopticism:**   This is a term developed by the French historian and social philosopher Michel Foucault. To speak of the Panopticon is to speak of the machinery, modes, and methods of surveillance that ensure asymmetrical power. We are always under the panoptic gaze: The will to inscribe power—to colonize disciplinary practices for the body, with our identities, in our institutions (e.g., prisons, psychiatric hospitals, churches)—is increasingly inventive and productive. This ingenuity is because power comes from everything and from everywhere. Thus, we can speak of the panoptic disciplinary society. The panoptic gaze is a conservative force; it produces a society that is technologically normalized, de-pathologized, homogenized, corrected. See "Bentham, Jeremy," "Discursive Formations" and "Foucault, Michel" for more.

**Pantheism:**   Greek: *pan* = all; *thea* = god. The belief that God is in everything and not a supreme being apart or prior to the world. Sometimes it is confused with paganism.

**Paradigm:**   In linguistic and semiotic analysis, there is both a paradigmatic and syntagmatic axis that interact, such that speech takes place and meaning occurs. The paradigm refers to the words/phrases functioning as signifiers in a chain or sequence of speech. In order for speech to occur, certain linguistic forms (words) must be selected from an available array of possible linguistic forms. These forms are paradigms. Paradigms are grouped together by their degree of similarity and dissimilarity—for example, cool, cold, freezing, frigid. There is a progression of meaning implied in these paradigms. In conversational speech, unconscious decisions are made regarding which paradigm will be employed to convey meaning, intended or not. Cf. "Syntagm."

**Paralogic:**   A term used to emphasize how very little we know about so much. Paralogic is that which is unknown, admittedly false, and admittedly a fictionalized account of history, persons, or events. As Jean-François Lyotard contends, paralogic points to how much we claim the "truth" of something when in fact the claim is really a linguistic contrivance or arbitrary convention. See "Discourse" for more.

**Parens patriae:**   A legal term meaning, literally, the state is the father of all children. The term emerged as the lawmaking system began to replace the family as the agent in control of the fate of children. This shift served the labor needs of industrial capitalism. See "Child Savers," "Delinquency," and "Status Crimes" for more.

**Pareto, Vilfredo (1848–1923):**   Italian sociologist who studied elites. Pareto said that all societies are ruled by elites. There are two kinds: risk-takers, who force change; and conservatives, who resist change. He argued that these elites tend to take turns in controlling the destiny of a society: a circulation of elites. (See the work of W. L. Reese.)

**Paris Commune:**   For three months in 1871, the workers in Paris took power, held elections, and formed the city into a workers' commune. It was the first such social experiment in history. The commune established a dictatorship of the proletariat and set up ten ministries. The French army, with the aid of German troops, attacked and defeated the communards.

**Parliamentarianism:**   A political system in which the largest party determines social policy. Members of parliament are elected, hold office for a variable term, and select the government that is responsible to parliament. Karl Marx was critical of parliamentarianism since it represented capitalism and selected only those policies that reproduced class privilege. Social democrats support it as a "road to socialism." It can be used on behalf of workers and the surplus population created through capitalist labor policy.

**Parlor Marxism:**   The practice of talking about exploitation, sexism, and praxis but doing little to change the world (in disregard of the Eleventh Thesis). See "Eleventh Thesis," "Utopia/Utopianism," and "Vulgar Marxism" for more.

**Parole:**   French: speech. The conditional release of a prisoner upon his/her promise to avoid the actions and/or persons involved in the offense for which s/he was sentenced. Parole usually runs for the duration of the original sentence to prison.

**Part I Offenses:**   Based on Uniform Crime Report (UCR) categories. Part I crimes are defined by the UCR as "major crimes" and include rape, murder, negligent manslaughter, aggravated assault, robbery, burglary, larceny, and arson.

A critical reading would question how these offenses, committed typically in the context of street crime, have come to be defined as "major crimes." Street crime makes up a small percentage of the total crime committed, particularly when one includes corporate, white-collar, and international crime. Cf. "Corporate Crime." See "Part II Offenses" for more.

**Part II Offenses:**   Based on Uniform Crime Report (UCR) categories. Part II crimes include all crimes other than Part I offenses. See "Part I Offenses" for more.

**Participation Theory:**   A set of principles that supports collective sharing in the creation of culture. The thought is that culture and society do not exist apart from the collective activity of intending humans.

**Participatory Sociology:**   A form of sociology that incorporates action into the research methodology and theory in response to the needs of the surplus population.

**Party/Party Discipline:**   A political structure representing a class, ethnic group, or religious faction in a society. Party discipline requires a liberal political form if each party is to play a part in social policy. Many Marxists value the Communist Party as the vehicle for the general interest of society and for social revolution. Party discipline varies; the more hierarchical and elitist the party, the stricter the discipline and the greater the onus/penalty for failing to follow the party line.

**Pascal, Blaise (1623–1662):**    Pascal was a mathematician in France who had a mystical conversion in midlife. He represents the tension between faith in rationality and faith in mystery. He argued that there were two pathways to knowledge: *l'esprit géométrique* (reason) and *l'esprit de finesse* (inspiration). His dictum, which captures the tension between these two pathways, was, "The heart has its reasons of which reason knows not." Pascal was, thus, torn between premodern sensibility and the promises of modern science. Cf. "Descartes, René." (See the work of W. L. Reese.)

**Passion:**    Latin: *passio* = experience of; *onis* = suffering. The term was used by Aristotle to refer to the accidental properties, rather than the essence, of a thing. René Descartes, opposed to accidentals and looking for an underlying elegant order in nature and society, treated those things not amenable to his analytic geometry as emotional dispositions.

Today, passion is treated as a source of bias in science; it is treated as a source of energy in religion. If well directed, passion can be valuable to emancipatory science. (See the work of W. L. Reese.)

**Pastiche:**    A postmodern term referring to a collage of ideas; a "crazy-quilt" of views; a hodgepodge or patchwork in which contradictory claims, stories, and views are put together. The use of pastiche denies the usefulness of symmetry, compatibility, or logic. It glorifies confusion and contradictions in music, art, architecture, explanation, and social life itself.

**Patent:**    A grant by a state to an individual or an institution for an exclusive right to benefit from an invention for a period of time (seventeen years is usual). The idea is that the person who invents a useful tool or device should benefit from it. It is always difficult to draw a line between the person who invents something and all those who made the invention possible by prior discovery, skill, or participation. See "Copyright" for more.

**Patriarchy:**    Latin: *Pater* = father; *archy* = rule. A system in which gender relations are highly stratified. Males are given a monopoly over economic power, social power, moral power, and the use of physical force. Women are held to be inferior in intellect and in moral capacities. Thus women are in need of control and guidance by putatively superior males.

The patriarchal family emerged after settled agriculture developed (4,000 B.C.). In order to hold property (e.g., land, herds, tools, buildings), it was necessary to have a rule for transferring it from one generation to another. In patriarchy, transfer is to the eldest son. Patriarchy is the source of much mischief, violence, and pretheoretical rebellion by men, women, and children alike. Anthropologists tell us that gender relations are highly variable across cultures and, thus, subvert patriarchy's claims of dominance in and across cultures.

Feminist theory is generally averse to patriarchal arrangements. Socialist feminists claim that patriarchy is expressed through all gender relationships and embodied in institutional expressions of culture and social living. Postmodern feminists contend that patriarchal arrangements are embedded and legitimized in the discourse and thought utilized in everyday speech and interaction. For example: "*man*kind" versus "society"; "*hi*story" versus "story". See "Demonization," "Government, Forms of," and "Phallogocentrism" for more.

**Pauper/Pauperism:**    A person and a condition caused by labor and market practices in and only in a capitalist economy. Capitalism is the only economic system that tends to disemploy people. It is the only economic system that withholds food, shelter, and clothing for profits. See "Surplus Population" and "Underclass" for more.

**Peasant:**    A farmer on a small piece of land. Peasants occupy an ambivalent position in a market economy. On the one hand, peasants are "free" and own property. On the other hand, they often must pay taxes to the nobility or buy equipment, fertilizer, and seeds from merchants. They often borrow money to purchase these supplies. They usually have to sell to merchants at prices below the costs of production. Peasants often organize into co-ops but still have many problems. In the United States, Congress gives small farmers many subsidies that enable them to survive. The present push to end farming subsidies threatens the last few million family farms still found. See "Farming, Modern," "Peonage," and "Serf" for more.

**Pedagogy:**    Greek: *paidos* = child. The art and science of teaching. The most critically inspired position on pedagogy comes from Paulo Freire and his assessment of education, social practice, and revolution. Freire developed a postmodern method of active engagement with those whose voices were oppressed as a way of liberating them from the culture of silence. His method emphasized both the action and reflection embodied in speech as a way to promote true words. See "Dialogical Pedagogy" and "Freire, Paulo" for more.

**Pedophilia/Pedophile:**    Literally, the love of/for children. A pedophile is one who both fantasizes (through aids such as magazines) about having sex with a juvenile and/or acts upon such fantasies. NMBLA or the National Man-Boy-Love Association takes the position that sex between two consenting people is a natural, wholesome act and should not be censured.
    The attempt to eliminate pedophilia/child pornography has become a demon hunt, resulting in repressive laws (e.g., Megan's Law, the Communications Decency Act, "Porn on the Internet" scares). This demonization has been fueled by the outcry of a misinformed public and supported by most politicians: You "can't do anything with child molesters." Thus, pe-

dophiles are regarded as moral and social outcasts. Intervention in the form of psychological treatment is regarded as an unnecessary and costly expense. Pedophiles are socially constructed as deviant predators unable to curb their sexual appetites.

**Peer:**   One who has the same position in society as another. In a stratified, differentiated society marked by cleavages in racial, ethnic, sexist, religious, occupational, and educational involvements, "peer" refers to the number of similarly situated persons in close enough contact to get organized.

**Peer Group:**   A set of similarly situated persons who use each other and the norms of the group as a basis for organizing individual behavior. If there are no cross-generational ties, the resultant behavior can be quite antisocial.

**Peirce, Charles S. (1839–1914):**   Acknowledged as the architect of modern semiotics in the United States. At about the turn of the twentieth century, Peirce, a philosopher, was investigating the elements of meaning (the semiotic word is "signification"). He considered semiotics to be a branch of logic. Peirce maintained that words were laden with multiple meanings and, thus, that communication was essentially unstable, indeterminate, incomplete, and uncertain. For Peirce this was a liberating realization. Situated within the center of this axiom was the possibility for discovering other or alternative realities about people and about the social order that remained repressed and silenced.

Peirce maintained that semiotics entailed the cooperation of three elements: the sign, the sign's interpretant, and the sign's object. Peirce's classic statement about the *sign* is as follows: The sign (or *representamen*) "stands to somebody for something in some respect or capacity." Think of a word (e.g., "dog," "house," "book"). Each of these signs represents something for each of us. For example, when we say "dog" we may be referring to our canine best friend, or we may be referring to the puppy that our daughter wants us to buy, or we may be referring to the movie that we just watched. The sign creates in the mind of the person identifying the representamen an equivalent sign, a more developed sign. This is what Peirce called the *interpretant*. When we say the words "dog," "house," and "book" we conjure, we envision, a mental picture of a dog, a house, a book. In other words, the mental image (the interpretant) created in us as observers is the effect of our observations. The sign also stands for a real, tangible thing. This is the sign's *object* (in Peircean terminology it is also called the "referent").

Peirce believed that the human subject, too, was a sign; that is, a sort of semiotic self immersed in a sea of signs, awaiting articulation and discovery. This notion was a direct challenge to Cartesian philosophy, which presupposed the subject as purposive, rational, self-aware, centered, in control, and a determiner of all events. Peirce's semiotics is significant to postmodern affirmative thought. See "Sign" for more. Cf. "Wittgenstein, Ludwig."

**Peonage:**   A form of labor servitude in which a "free" farmer or worker toils for a landowner until a debt is paid off. Used mostly in Mexico to refer to those who rent land and work on shares for large landholders. Many farmers in the United States are, in effect, peons. L. Frank Baum mocked these debt farmers in the *Wizard of Oz* by using the Scarecrow to represent those in debt bond to capitalists (the crows that ate his corn). Baum had the Scarecrow go to the Emerald City to get some brains so he would vote for progressive politicians. In this case, it was William Jennings Bryan. See "Peasant" for more.

**Performativity:**   A postmodern term referring to the use of successful performance as a test of truth, value, validity, or outcome. It centers around "capacity, efficiency, control." Postmodernists tend to reject the notion as a modernist effort to reject diversity, flexibility, openness, or autonomy. Jean-François Lyotard, for example, views performativity as relying too much on logic and reason. Judith Butler, an American scholar of gender identity, however, points to the importance of "performances" in constructing new, different, and divergent images of gender. These representations shatter and increase our awareness of how such constructs as "heterosexuality" are nothing more than political contrivances. See "Actor" and "Lyotard, Jean-François" for more.

**Perjury:**   Giving of false testimony or faking evidence in a legal proceeding. Punishable by imprisonment and/or fine if and only if the person in question was/is under oath to tell the truth.

**Person:**   In law, an individual who has legal standing and may claim protection or judgments from a court. In sociology, anyone who has social status and has the right to social power within specified status-role sets. See "Competence" and "Nonperson" for more.

**Personality:**   An attribute of a person. In his critique of G.W.F. Hegel, Karl Marx insisted that the personality did not exist apart from the individual. Thus, it did not have a separation from the everyday, concrete behavior of people. Theories of personality today that treat personality as a stable, trans-situational entity apart from behavior are mystifications; to hold such a theory is similar to having a theory of the shadow that is disassociated from the individual and given causal power in the dynamics of behavior.

For Marx, personality derived from social relations (wherein culture is and is produced). Social relations thus embody existing modes of production. Modes of production are the foundations of personality. If we do not like the antisocial behavior of people in our society, the solution lives more in changing the modes of production than in "changing the personality" through psychotherapy, drugs, or other means.

**Personal Property:**   The property one claims control and use of that is a result of one's share of labor. Personal property includes clothing, housing, tools, furniture, and appliances to be used in the day-to-day reproduction of labor power. It is not to be confused with "private" property. This concept involves the notion that one person can claim ownership of socially produced wealth; of social relationships; social organizations; of the arts, skills, crafts, and services of another human being. Marxist theory rejects as invalid claims to private property but accepts qualified claims to personal property. In general, material culture is to be used to help generate ideological culture. The concept of culture implies collective endeavor and, hence, collective use of material items. One cannot produce art, science, language, or community by oneself. See "Private Property" for more.

**Perversion:**   Each society appropriates the sexuality, pain, and pleasure of its members to help reproduce social relationships. The private, nonsocial use of one's own sexuality for and only for personal pleasure is said to be corrupt, perverted, sinful, or pathological. Among the more common acts defined as perverted are homosexuality, masturbation, lesbianism, sodomy (oral or anal sex), whipping (for pleasure), fetishism (e.g., feet or clothing), eating unpleasant things. In general, perversion refers to the profanation of things sanctified by tradition and practice. See "Corruption, Theory of" for more.

**Petty Bourgeoisie:**   A strata of small business persons who own the means of production and also actively work with them to extract surplus value by paying low wages and charging high prices (e.g., grocers; dentists; carpenters; restaurant owners; bar owners; small farmers; barbers; electricians; independent truckers; franchise owners in hardware, fast foods, television, automobiles, and other products). These are the lower middle classes. The petty bourgeoisie often express hostility toward big business but, in the end, join to preserve capitalism, even as every small business is squeezed out by "modern business theory."

**Petty Bourgeois Science:**   On the one hand, a view that assumes that sociologists, historians, psychologists, and economists have most of the objective characteristics of small business persons: These academics have control over labor, over tools of production, income, privileges, ability to create ideas, and over others (especially students). These conditions make social scientists a natural ally to the bourgeoisie.

On the other hand, social scientists usually sell their labor power and are restricted in the ideas they may produce to those that sell. Control over work conditions is being lost as "professional" administration slowly usurps traditional functions of academics. The question is, Whose side will academics join in a crisis? Most physical and social scientists are conservative. Those who are not may overestimate their role in social revolution.

**Phalanstery, Phalanx Socialism:**    A unit of an ideal society imagined by Charles Fourier. A phalanstery was about a square mile in area, shared farm buildings and machinery with other phalansteries on its borders, and had communal dining halls, schools, nurseries, and recreation buildings. It provided private dwellings for about 1,800 people—enough to provide all essential needs and amenities to the community. The phalanx was subdivided into ten Series; each Series consisted of fourteen to thirty groups; each group was seven persons or more. The aim was to obtain a balance between individual freedom and social solidarity. Karl Marx and Friedrich Engels dismissed phalansteries as hopelessly utopian. Some Israeli kibbutzim incorporate some features of Fourier's plan. See "Fourier, Charles," and "Kibbutz" for more. (See the work of W. L. Reese.)

**Phallocentric:**    A term developed by feminist theorists. Phallocentric thought refers to the masculine-based way by which all understanding unfolds. See "Phallogocentrism" for more. Cf. "Logocentric."

**Phallogocentrism:**    A termed originally developed by Jacques Derrida and appropriated by several postmodern feminists, especially Luce Irigaray. The term implies that privileged speech-thought-behavior patterns in Western society esteem only male-centered logic (i.e., phallocentrism + logocentrism). Postmodern feminists such as Irigaray are critical of that dominant desire communicated in and through language. Postmodern feminists claim that such communication and/or styles of interaction inadequately represent the non-misogynized voice of and ways of knowing for women. See "*Ecriture feminine*," "Irigaray, Luce," and "Patriarchy" for more. Cf. "Epistemology," "Logocentric," and "Phallocentric."

**Phenomenology:**    Greek: *phainomenon* = appearance; *ology* = study of. A theory of knowledge that stresses the primacy of consciousness and subjective meaning in that action that produces social facts (phenomena). Classic philosophy (Lambert, Immanuel Kant, G.W.F. Hegel) distinguished between "noumena," that which exists, and "phenomena," that which humans perceive to exist. The thought was that people look at nature and distort it, since they are imperfect creatures. The modern expression of phenomenology is found in the work Edmund Husserl, who held that human thought (phenomena) was structured by preexisting categories and could be studied by "bracketing" what really existed until one could establish the essence (*eidos*) of a category of thought. See "Entelechy," "Epoché," "Heidegger, Martin," "Husserl, Edmund," and "'Me'" for more.

**Phenomenology, Postmodern:**   The postmodern position is that humans create scientific categories and social facts. Social facts are created by first proclaiming the existence of some social form (phenomena) and then, through one's own efforts, creating that reality. Scientific categories are established by selecting just that part of incredibly complex and interconnected natural and social realities that fit/create the category and by then treating all other events/elements as observer error, faulty research design, chance, or poor reasoning. There are no noumena or objective social realities apart from or beyond the act of creating. There is no built-in tendency for a thing to move in any given direction, and the concept of perfection is, again, a political historical way to legitimate whatever exists or whatever one thinks should exist. In postmodern philosophy of science, forms of reality may have a fragile, fractal, and changing geometry. See "Entelechy" and "Hegel, G.W.F." for more.

**Philosophical Anthropology:**   A set of assumptions about how human nature arises. Some say it is built into genes; others say it is formed in infancy and childhood; still others say it is a social construct that can be variable (labile). Marxism assumes that humans create themselves as species-beings in the process of forming social relationships and, within those social relationships, create culture. Cf. "Anthropology."

**Philosophy:**   From the Greek, *philos* = love; *osophy* = study. Philosophy began as theology and evolved into the "science about science." Philosophy offers many rewards and moments of insight that come from thinking, knowing, and understanding the world around oneself. Anyone who thinks beyond the moment or beyond one's own immediate self-interest is a philosopher.

**Philosophy (of Life):**   (1) A coherent set of principles that guide the construction of a social lifeworld. (2) The study of human knowledge. (3) A style of response to the problems of life that interferes with action and change. All societies need a philosophy to imbue their members with purpose, hope, faith, and fellowship. Whether societies benefit from formal knowledge of how they operate is an open question. Some people say they do not. The Bible says that "knowledge maketh a man's face to shine" and that wisdom is good. But the scientific and formal theories that have replaced folk theories have not offered an end to pain, nor added to human dignity or to fellowship. It appears that whatever knowledge is produced in an oppressive society is filtered through the oppressive relationships and, thus, reinforces that oppression. Emancipatory knowledge and conflict methodology attempt to break through the rule that knowledge in an exploitative society is exploitative knowledge.

**Philosophy, The Discipline of:**   There are five branches to the formal study of human knowledge: (1) *Epistemology:* deals with the question, How do we know something and how do we know it to be true? (2) *Metaphysics:* ideas about the nature of reality; (3) *Aesthetics:* ideas about that which is beautiful; (4) *Ethics:* ideas about that which is good; and (5) *Logic:* the study of the forms and laws of rational thinking. See each entry separately.

**Phonocentric:**    According to Jacques Derrida, the view that modern science relies too much on the spoken word in creating truth claims. Instead, trust should be centered in written texts. See "Derrida, Jacques" and "Logocentric" for more.

**Physiocrats/Physiocracy:**    A French theory of political economy that held that all value begins with commercial agriculture. Founded by François Quesnay (1694–1774), physiocrats posited three classes: (1) the productive class: farmers; (2) the appropriating class: landlords, royalty, clergy, and officials engaged in unproductive labor; and (3) the sterile class: those in industry who depended upon the surplus generated by farmers. See "Smith, Adam" for more.

**Piaget, Jean (1896–1980):**    A Swiss psychologist, Piaget traced the development of concepts in a child: shape, size, space, time, causality, chance, velocity, and such. His work provides a basis for a postmodern phenomenology in which all such concepts are the work of human beings and do not exist as such prior to and apart from human thought and human interests in controlling nature. (See the work of W. L. Reese.)

**Picketing:**    The effort by employees, citizens, students, or customers to protest. This protest may include the use of signs and slow walks at or near a place of work, a store, a public agency, or an office that engages in unfair/illegal practices (e.g., sexual harassment, discrimination in hiring). The U.S. Constitution gives people the right of "peaceful assembly in protest of grievance."

**Plato (428–348 B.C.E.):**    Plato was a Greek philosopher who founded a famous academy that lasted for centuries, until it was destroyed in war. Two aspects of Plato's work are particularly important: His doctrine of Ideas and his account of the ideal society, or Republic. Plato's doctrine of ideas can be summarized with recourse to his analogy of the cave in which humans dwell and in which they can know only the shadows cast on its walls; they take these shadows to be reality, when in fact they are simply images cast by the light of a fire. In Plato's story, one of the people in the cave escapes out into the world and, via the light of the sun (the Ideas), encounters reality, which now stands in stark contrast to the shadowy images in the cave. This thinking bears a close resemblance to postmodern philosophy of science and knowledge. Plato did accept the idea of objective knowledge and assumed that humans could attain such knowledge if they proved capable of dividing knowledge using his famous two lines: One line separated reason and math from belief and imagination; the other line separated first principles from universal forms. The scholar had to cross both lines in order to attain complete knowledge.

Plato's account of the Republic, an ideal form of society and governance, still informs many ideas that people have about the good society, including those of elitists everywhere. He began with the claim that the object of government is the good of the people (rather than the embodiment of the laws of God or nature). This good of the people requires a just social order. However, justice requires that every person does the work for which s/he is fitted. Plato holds that good law thus orders everything according to its nature. There are three generic "natures" in which to fit men and women: (1) artisans; (2) soldiers; and (3) rulers. Soldiers require more education than artisans; rulers must master all the sciences and serve an apprenticeship of fifteen years. At age 50, wise men and women become philosopher kings and rule society. These rulers embody the four cardinal virtues: wisdom, courage, temperance, and justice. Plato provides for communism but does not make it clear whether it encompasses the whole society or the two upper classes (who own what Karl Marx would call the means of production, distributing it on the basis of need and merit). If it is confined to these classes, then artisans would be landless and propertyless producers. According to Plato, art is to be controlled by the rulers since they have knowledge of first principles and universal truths.

Critics of Plato's philosophy contend that it advocates elitist social systems, state regulation of all social life, and the subdivision of knowledge into experts and clients. See "Bacon, Francis," "Knowledge, Democratization of," and "Machiavelli, Niccolò" for more. (See the work of W. L. Reese.)

**Plea:**    A formal statement by a defendant to a court attesting to or denying guilt to a formal charge or accusation. These pleas include: guilty, not guilty, and nolo contendere (I do not dispute the charge but at the same time do not admit guilt). In criminal cases where there is a question about the mental state of the defendant during the commission of the illegal act, the plea entered can also be not guilty by reason of insanity (NGRI).

**Plea Bargaining:**    A process by which an agreement between the prosecutor of a case and a defendant is negotiated. Usually the defendant agrees to plead guilty to a lesser, sometimes different crime in exchange for a more lenient sentence. For example: A rapist is allowed to plead guilty to assault and go free on probation; a child molester is allowed to plead guilty to a charge of contributing to the delinquency of a minor. In the U.S. Federal Court System, these bargains have to be approved by a judge.

In high-crime societies, plea bargaining is pushed in order to reduce legal costs, dispose of cases rapidly, and/or avoid building more prisons.

**Plebe/Plebeian:**   Latin: *Plebs* = the common people. Used as a pejorative term by elites to refer to the masses as common or vulgar.

**Plebiscite:**   Latin: *Plebs* = common people; *scitum* = decree. A referendum held to find out what people think or want by a vote.

**Plekanov, George (1856–1918):**   An early collaborator with Vladimir Lenin, whom he influenced. Plekanov accepted dialectic materialism (Friedrich Engels) but took a postmodern view of material categories; they were "hieroglyphs" rather than mirror images of material reality. He also accepted the dominance of *mode of production* but, with Karl Marx, argued that reason and science could loosen the determinacy of economics. (See the work of W. L. Reese.)

**Pluralism:**   The view that all human cultures are to be honored and respected, that no one culture (or society) is superior to any others, and that each culture has much to contribute to the human process. There are an infinite set of adequate cultures. The Human Areas Files counts between 3,000 and 4,000 cultures in human history. Sometimes, pluralism is a claim that there is no inequality in power or social honor for different populations within the same society. See "Pluralist Thesis" for more.

**Pluralist Thesis:**   The thesis that social, economic, or political power is dispersed among a variety of roughly equal groups in a society. A corollary is that any group could solve its own problems if there were sufficient interest by forming a power bloc to pressure government or to elect its own candidates. This view ignores all those who do not have resources to form an effective lobby in the state or nation (e.g., children, the poor, migrants, and others defined as less than fully adult). See "Pluralism" for more.

**Police:**   A set of persons appointed by the state and given the power to enforce laws, observe behavior, arrest persons, collect evidence, and testify as to a defendant's guilt or lack of guilt.

**Police State:**   A country in which the state uses police to prevent change in governing officials, in government systems, or to prevent resistance to privileged classes, races, genders, or ethnic groups. In capitalist societies, the underclass is most heavily policed; the upper class is seldom policed. See "Authoritarianism," "Fascism,"and "Mussolini, Benito" for more.

**Policing:**   The process by which citizens, students, customers, and dissidents are watched in order to collect evidence that is then used in a court of law or for private systems of justice.

**Politburo:**   One of three parts of the Central Committee of the former USSR. It pre-decided all policy, which then was approved by the People's

Congress who were, after a fashion, elected. Vladimir Lenin planned for the Politburo to be a temporary structure acting on behalf of the whole working class until socialist consciousness could be instituted. At that time, the state was to "wither away." Joseph Stalin limited government to himself and a few advisors. This action reduced the emancipatory impulse in communism to a dictatorship.

**Political Correctness:** A term originally used by persons on the political left as a way of reminding society of its racist, classist, sexist, and homophobic tendencies. Ironically, however, political correctness, as a doctrine promoting civility between and among all people, has been staunchly criticized as unnecessarily brutal in its application. The expression the "PC Police" has been coined. It signals just how damaging the surveillance actions of politically correct advocates has become. To be politically correct today can mean to be excessively hostile toward other people and their points of view, regardless of how unenlightened they may be. Thus, some advocates of political correctness are charged with doing the very thing they claim everyone should avoid doing; namely, failing to be tolerant of differences.

**Political Culture:** Policies, programs, and solutions with which to serve or defeat the human interest in change and renewal. If the masses are excluded from the process of creating political culture, then they are "surplus" (i.e., that part of the surplus population not privy to such creation). This exclusion strips people of their status as species-being. This exclusion is usually forcibly made.

**Political Economy:** A generic name for a sociopolitical complex that uses a given economic form as a basis for production and distribution of goods and services. There have been five major political economies in human history: (1) primitive communism; (2) slavery; (3) feudalism; (4) capitalism; and (5) socialism. Communism is a sixth political economy yet to be instituted in any great degree. Karl Marx held that each political economy had its own relations and its own laws or tendencies.

Contemporary political economy studies the economic foundation of political decisions. Usually involving Marxist analysis, political economy stands in opposition to bourgeois economics (which tries to make capitalism work better) and in opposition to bourgeois political science (which attempts to resolve the incompatibility between capitalism and a managed society within the assumptions of democratic theory).

**Political Emancipation:** In his work "On the Jewish Question," Karl Marx distinguished between the narrow range of political rights (e.g., freedom of speech, secret ballots, freedom of movement, universal suffrage, and representation in government) and general human emancipation. These narrow political rights are fundamental but there are others equally essential to the human project: the right to pro-social jobs, preventative and therapeutic health care, critical education, and civility and dignity as one ages. See "Emancipation" for more.

**Political Science:**   The art and science that examines how government, and its subsystems, behave, interact, and are organized. Political science includes the study of municipal, city, county, state, and federal practices. There are many political forms studied by political scientists (and sociologists), for example, anarchy, aristocracy, democracy, oligarchy, theocracy, authoritarianism, dictatorship. Each of these forms of government is based upon a different set of principles.

**Political Sphere:**   Political sociology distinguishes between the public sphere and the private, civil sphere. In his critique of political rights and of political democracy (separate from social rights and social democracy), Karl Marx held that people lead a double life: a fictitious life of community in the political sphere and a private life in the civil sphere. The notion that communism requires the end of the political state does not mean the end of political activity and political culture. Rather, it means the unification of political spheres with the entire social lifeworld in which real people experience life and its problems.

**Politicization:**   The process of returning questions of public interest to collective discourse. Sexism, racism, foreign policy, and science (via abortion and euthanasia) have recently been politicized where formerly they were taken-for-granted aspects of human life. Cf. "Depoliticization."

**Politics:**   Refers to the manner in which power (e.g., physical or psychological) is utilized to bring about some desired outcome. Politics exists in all dimensions of civic life. Consensus theorists contend that this politics is true in many family relations, at work, at play, and in our interactions with others. Each of these examples represents aspects of "political socialization."

Some feminists contend that social politics privileges masculine ways of understanding. Thus, the feminine is subtended; that is, women's ways of understanding are relegated to second class statuses. Radical feminists argue that there is a need to reclaim the feminine. Indeed, this reclamation is about retrieving their bodies, their points of views, their identities, their uniquely felt experiences, and their interiorized realities. This observation has led various feminists—representing diverse political perspectives, including black feminists, socialist feminists, postmodern feminists, liberal feminists, and so on—to conclude that the personal is political. See "Feminism, Black," "Feminism, Liberal," "Feminism, Postmodern," and "Feminism, Socialist" for more.

**Polls, Surveys, Samples, Theory of:**   Any social system, after it exceeds a certain critical size, cannot be known or controlled directly by a central authority but must be researched and controlled by statistical means. Consensus sociology provides the surveys, polls, and samples to the state or to those who can afford commodity science. These samples yield indices that are used by an elite to form policy. Monitoring all social life in the United States, for example, would require a polling system larger and more complex than the social life of the United States itself.

**Polyandry:**   A marriage pattern in which women have two or more husbands. It is a way to get more labor out of fewer women in patriarchal but impoverished societies. Cf. "Polygamy" and "Polygyny."

**Polygamy:**   Marriage involving multiple spouses. A generic term that includes the forms known as polygyny (many wives) and polyandry (many husbands). There are a few societies that practice some form of polygamy. Many societies practice serial polygamy; one mate at a time but several in a series. Cf. "Polyandry" and "Polygyny."

**Polygyny:**   A marriage pattern in which men have two or more wives. The practice extracts the surplus value of several women to support each male in a male solidarity. Cf. "Polyandry" and "Polygamy."

**Population Base:**   All of the people who come under the control of a given society. Many people are in the population base but not in the social base (e.g., children, prisoners, some minority groups, the aged, patients in mental asylums, soldiers, and various kinds of "nonpersons"). The population base is a biological concept, whereas the social base is a cultural concept.

**Population Theory:**   There are two major theories about "overpopulation." Thomas Malthus theorized that overpopulation occurred because the poor were prone to irrational overbreeding. The Marxian rebuttal was that a portion of the population was rendered "surplus" when feudal lords became agricultural capitalists and forced the peasantry off the land. The land was then used to grow cash crops (wool, cotton, beef, tea, sugar, cocoa, coffee, etc.) rather than grains and vegetables for food. See "Birth Control" and "Surplus Population" for more. Cf. "Malthus, Thomas" and "Marx, Karl."

**Pornography:**   Greek: *pornos* = prostitute; *graphy* = writing; therefore, sexual writing and, by extension, sexual art. Sexual art and literature becomes degrading when human beings are: (1) reduced to body parts; (2) used as and only as sexual objects; or (3) used to affirm power in a relationship. It is sexist when women are the primary casualty. Cf. "Erotic/Eroticism."

**Pornoviolence:**   The use of sex and/or violence as a means to generate a public for a commodity on television or other mass media.

**Positive Law:**   That body of law enacted by a lawmaking body and enforced by a state. Cf. "Law, natural."

**Positivism:**   A philosophy of science that claims that, if something exists, it can be measured; if something can be measured, it can be modeled and predicted. Thus, all human behavior can be recorded in "facts." Nothing else of interest to science exists but these facts. Saint-Simon introduced the concept and Auguste Comte made it an article of faith in his sociology.

The major criticism of positivism is that it freezes events and makes of the moment the whole of history, since it deals with that which "is" rather than that which "could be." Emancipatory knowledge processes are concerned with change from what is to what could be in terms of praxis and human dignity.

A second criticism comes from the hermeneutical sciences. These sciences note that human imagination and human interpretation are important parts of the social process and are not recorded nor recordable in number systems. See "Comte, Auguste," "Mathematical Sociology," and Quantification" for more. Cf. "Postmodernists/Postmodernism."

**Post-Fordism:**   A loose label given to production/work/distribution in an age of information. Decentralized, flexible, and disposable units mark post-Fordist philosophy. Post-Fordist factories employ the latest computer controlled machines in both design and production. They monitor sales in shops around the world and, via satellite, change production, production schedules, and designs without benefit of advice/consent from the home office. In Taylorist/Fordist schemes, planning was separated from execution. In post-Fordist times, the division between brain and hand is reunited.

These new changes are held to be the salvations of capitalism and the democratization of the shop. But problems remain: production for profit rather than need; growth of a surplus population; greater inequality in wealth, status, and power; depletion of natural resources; degradation of the environment; and colonization of human consciousness by consumerism and possession.

**Postmodern, Affirmative:**   Many see postmodern inquiry as liberating. Old standards of truth and certainty are called into question. Traditional models of masculinity, femininity, and gender relations are reexamined for their alienating effects. Old claims of social development (and underdevelopment) are deconstructed to show their biases. Old models of governance and economics are given new life and more democracy when the modernist tendency to control and to manage everything in a factory, school, office, or church is challenged. Affirmative postmodern thought subscribes to deconstruction and "reconstruction." The latter process requires a careful consideration of how to include the voices and ways of knowing of previously excluded collectives in all institutional aspects of social living.

Affirmative postmodern sensibility offers human beings considerably more scope for understanding human agency than that found in either premodern or modern worldviews. Premodern views tend to locate agency and full capacities to know in Gods or abstract realms of nature. Modern science retains the view that valid knowledge is buried in the dynamics of nature and that human beings must bend to natural laws if they are to be rational. Affirmative postmodern thought seeks to reclaim knowledges that are often ignored, dismissed, or silenced by dominant groups and the language they employ. For affirmative postmodernists, knowledge is relational, provisional, and positional; that is, there are "contingent universalities" conditioned by sociohistorical events always and already mediated by language. Cf. "Baudrillard, Jean."

**Postmodern, Nihilistic:**   The view that the knowledge process is hopelessly contaminated by subjective desires and political objectives; that there can be no basis for objective standards of truth, beauty, ethics, or philosophies of life. Universal and comprehensive theories of nature or society are impossible since (a) they do not exist and (b) even if they did, the search for them is always bound to the lens of one's own limited cultural concepts and values. Some more nihilistic postmodernists take the view a step further and claim that since there is no objective bases for ethics, all is permitted; that is, all is possible if one has the will and resources to impose that will on others.

**Postmodernists/Postmodernism:**   Refers to a critical perspective through which culture, society, and human social interaction is understood. Postmodernists reject the modernist and positivist conviction that rationality, objective analysis, scientism, capital logic, rugged individualism, and so on produce a world that is discoverable: a world constituted by essential truths that tend toward progress, order, and predictability. Postmodernism, as a critical sociological lens, questions the strategies of exclusion embedded in the modernist agenda. According to postmodernists, women, minorities, the disenfranchised, the elderly, and other collectives unable to find a place or succeed in the modernist pursuit of progress were (are) subjected to the disciplinary practices and modes of domination enacted through the preferred discourse of "logocentrism." Postmodernism stands in opposition to the modernist framework. Postmodernism questions the manner in which reality is conceived and debunks the scientific method privileged as "the" mode of acceptable analysis and inquiry. Postmodernists reject any and all attempts to reduce life experiences to "deep structures" (i.e., essences) or to cause-effect relationships. As a heterodox perspective, postmodernism is concerned with knowledge as local, truth as positional, understanding as relational. In the postmodern attitude, all claim-making assertions are validated. There are no subordinated points of view. See "Adorno, Theodor," "Foucault, Michel," "Gödel's Theorem," "Habermas, Jürgen," "Hermeneutics," "Indeterminacy Principle," "Lyotard, Jean-François," "Narrative," "Privilege/Privileged," "Saussure, Ferdinand de," and "Story/Storytelling" for more. Cf. "Positivism" and "Quantification."

**Postmodernity:**   Refers to that epistemological and historical break from the post-Enlightenment world of modernity in which claims to a retrievable, reducible, knowable, certifiable, and controllable world were rejected. The postmodern historical period reflects a disenchantment with the limitations of the modernist agenda (e.g., the oppression of citizen groups via capitalist industrialization, the suffering and exploitation of those whose logos departed from the presumed superiority of rational logic). Postmodernity, then, marked the birth of a new aesthetic—one devoid of absolutist, positivist, essentialist notions of justice, peace, community, society, culture, and so on. The postmodern historical period is much more attune to the incommensurable fullness of living in the social order and being human; that is, the nonlinear dimensions of existence (e.g., its ironies, absurdities, inconsistencies, contradictions). See "Habermas, Jürgen," "Longitudinal Analysis," "Narrative," and "Story/Storytelling" for more.

**Postmodernity, Sources of:**   There are several sources, often independent of each other, in which the critique of modern knowledge and its tendency to totalize, simplify, and depoliticize the knowledge process are made. Women object to the tendency of modern science to adopt Euro-centered, masculine values of power, control, order, and hierarchy. Third world people criticize modern science's tendency to set European standards for excellence/perfection in art, music, literature, and poetry. Religious people criticize modern science for removing the mystery and magic of human life from its knowledge products. Homosexuals and lesbians criticize the confinement of human sexuality to patriarchal values and social forms. Deconstructionists put all this together to locate the knowledge process in the larger sociocultural context in which it arises and tends to be reproduced. Taken together, deconstructionists reveal the partisan nature of all knowledge claims.

   Postmodern scientists, informed by the new sciences of Chaos and Complexity, have objected to modern science's concern with and preference for order, prediction, and discrete categorization. Postmodern scientists see disorder and connectedness in most really existing systems. These sciences provide an elegant empirical grounding for variety, difference, contrariety, and change.

**Postmodern Philosophy of Science:**   Postmodern philosophy of science accepts variety, contrariety, difference, loose causal connections, and sudden reverses in causality in its discourse about natural and social dynamics. Whereas modern philosophy of science favors the search for order and for tight correlations between two or more variables, postmodern scientists hold that causality is first of all a political construct that favors control and stratification of power. Affirmative postmodern philosophy of science holds that valid statements can be made but that they are limited, and truth values change with changing dynamical regimes. Karl Marx held that each social formation had its own laws or tendencies; that which produced crime in one society might not in another. Premodern philosophies tend to be more closely aligned with postmodern philosophies. See "Longitudinal Analysis" and "Represent/Representation" for more.

**Poststructuralism:**   This is the radical application of structuralism to the social sciences. Poststructuralists maintain that no essential truths or postulates governing the social order and its institutional systems are discoverable because "the" mechanism through which such truths might be ascertained depends on language. Poststructuralists argue that since the task of assigning meaning to phenomena (i.e., speaking about or discoursing about them) is utterly dependent on language, and since the acts of naming, describing, interpreting, understanding, and so on are entirely subjective processes (i.e., they require that one occupy a certain language or system of communication and that others do the same), it follows that the task of assigning meaning to the deep, structural conditions of institutions and systems of a culture or society is nothing more than an arbitrary (subjective) process of selection; that is, the assignment depends only on people sharing similar meanings. Since people do not interact and communicate through one language system (people interact and communicate through many), no precise, definite meanings can ever be discoverable. Thus, no deep structural conditions can ever be ascertained. At best, there can be only approximations. These approximations are themselves subject to divergent interpretations, dependent on the multiple codes through which individuals interpret and understand social phenomena. See "Barthes, Roland" and "Saussure, Ferdinand de" for more.

**Poverty:**   People are poor when they do not have the material basis for sustaining social life and for the production of culture. The conservative position is that poverty is a result of the personal failings or weaknesses of individuals and groups. The liberal position is that special help can repair or compensate for those failings. The radical position is that poverty is a feature of the system of production, not a characteristic of individuals or groups.

Socialists claim that mercantile capitalism produced poverty by displacing people from the land to make way for cash exports: coffee, wool, cotton, tea, cocoa, and such. Industrial capitalism produces poverty by wage and labor policy, whereas financial capitalism diverts surplus value from social use to the use of a leisure class and to the corporation itself.

**Poverty, Subculture of:**   A view of poverty in which a group of people hand down poverty from one generation to the next. People in a culture of poverty are characterized by feelings of marginality, helplessness, dependency, and inferiority. Oscar Lewis identified some seventy traits of those in the culture of poverty. The problem with the subculture of poverty theory is that it ignores the class system and thus the fact that the unequal distribution of wealth is a consequence of the appropriation of social wealth. The theory emphasizes the harm a culture of poverty does to one's psyche or to a community. Thus, it focuses more on the (alleged) differences in hopes and aspirations of individuals.

**Power:**   The capacity to control another's behavior while escaping reciprocal influence. Stratified systems of power, by nature, interfere with the collective creation of culture. Power is said to be traditional (parents), legal-rational (bureaucracies), and charismatic (saints, prophets). Power is often brutally coercive. See "Acton, Lord" and "Power, Forms of" for more.

**Power, Alienation of:**   The practice of claiming and exercising social power by some class, party, or ethnic group. If social power emerges only through the cooperative efforts of all participants (including those who raise issues and criticize practices), then a claim by a small subset of those participants to make decisions excludes those who should be included and transforms them into objects rather than subjects, a transformation that runs against the requirements of Marxian principles. See "Acton, Lord" for more.

**Power, Forms of:**   There are four major forms of power used to reproduce inequality: social power, moral power, economic power, and physical violence or threat of violence. In addition, there are all the norms and values that legitimate inequality, as well as all the established practices in everyday life that require compliance to inequality. Direct use of power is seldom necessary in "well-socialized" persons or in "well-organized" societies. The forms of power can be defined as follows:

1. *Social Power:* the form of power that comes from social relationships, social roles, and social institutions. When everyone is in a role, one must respond to role-others or sanctions/re-socialization ensues. Social life cannot go on unless there is response to the requests and needs of others in a role-set: parent-child, teacher-student, husband-wife, doctor-patient, or boss-worker. The question then becomes just how much equality is necessary in such relationships.

2. *Moral Power:* the form of power that comes from shared values and religious teachings. Even without role relationships, one is expected to respond to the needs of unknown others who are defined as persons in law and have social status in a group. Conversely, one can rob, maim, murder, or ignore those who do not have social status in one's own religion or group.

3. *Economic Power:* the power of money. In societies that use money as the primary medium for the transfer of goods (rather than social status), money comes to have great power. As Shakespeare said, "Yellow glittering precious gold . . . gives title, knee, and approbation to the scoundrel, forces the wappened widow to wed again [and] refreshes the hoar leper to the April Day." When one has no other economic system within which to acquire the necessities and the desires of life, one must acquire money. In capitalism, the only legitimate way to do this is to sell one's labor power. When one cannot or will not sell it, one can turn to family, to charity, to crime, or to state welfare.

4. *Physical Power:* the form of power that comes from the fist, club, gun, or threat of force. It does not always depend upon size or skill in arms but often upon status; small men have the moral right to beat women; women do not have the moral right to beat large men or small children. States claim a monopoly over physical power. Racist, sexist, and class organized states often allow men, whites, the wealthy, or ethnic groups the right to use physical force. See "Power" and "Underground Structures" for more.

**Power-Elite Thesis:**   A view advanced by C. Wright Mills, G. William Domhoff, and others to the effect that power in the United States is concentrated in a relatively cohesive and cooperating elite. Big business, big government, and big military are held to constitute a power bloc wherein the basic political and economic decisions are made. Fiscal policy such as taxes, interest rates, money supply, unemployment, deficit spending, foreign policy, housing starts, energy policy, welfare policy, research policy, and much more are said to be set by the interests of the power elite. Many people would add big unions and a technological elite to the power elite.

**Power of Attorney:**   The power given by one person to another to act on behalf of the first person, usually by written letter and usually confined to a specific act or situation.

**Pragmatism:**   A theory of knowledge that holds that the truth value of an idea is to be found in its practical application in everyday life. Pragmatism rejects the idea of universal and eternally valid laws that explain all behavior and rejects the notion of objectivity as a correct unbiased image (or copy) of nature. Pragmatism holds that only through our interests and actions do we know the world since we construct it pragmatically as we act on those interests. Critics of pragmatism allege that it often reduces itself to a cheerful notion that one can do anything at all if it works. Pragmatism has been used to justify aggression, imperialism, and the expediencies of the moment. See "Dewey, John" for more.

**Praxis/Practice:**   A complex activity by which individuals, in collectivities, create culture, society, and create themselves as "species-beings" (i.e., as human beings). The moments of praxis include self-determination (in contrast to coercion); intentionality (in contrast to reaction); sociality (in contrast to privatism); creativity (in contrast to sameness); and rationality (in contrast to blind chance). See "Act, Philosophy of," "Emancipation of the Senses," "Free Will," "Golden Rule," "Individualism," "Management Science," "Mass Base," "Moral Development," and "Rationality" for more.

**Praxis, Christian:**   The practical approach that liberation theology took in announcing that the Gospel called for three kinds of action: (1) apprising the poor of their exploited condition; (2) denouncing the injustices of capitalism and international imperialism; and (3) publicizing the facts of oppression and exploitation. The worker-priests in the movement also give political education and organization to the working-class poor. They also lead protests, confrontations, and demonstrations. Some priests engaged in Christian praxis have been beaten, imprisoned, deported, and defrocked. See "Base Communities" and "Theology, Liberation" for more.

**Precedent:**   In law, a ruling in an earlier court case that serves as a guide to judgment in a present case. Usually precedents are recorded in law books and are referenced in court so a judge and the parties concerned can study them and decide on their applicability. As a way to make judgments, precedent is set against both technical law and substantive justice, in that precedents are recipes for settling cases regardless of many differences found in all cases.

   Precedent is linked to the concept *stare decisis*, which literally means to stand by things decided. These decisions are often U.S. Supreme Court rulings or other appellate court cases that withstand the test of time and remain governing law. Through the doctrine of *stare decisis*, courts are required to utilize the logic of these rulings and apply this legal reasoning to similarly situated individuals involved in similar sets of facts. Thus, cases such as *Brown vs. Board of Education; Ohio vs. Mapp; Jones vs. the U.S., In re Gault* are, and will always be, precedent-setting cases. However, if they are overturned by subsequent court decisions, they no longer are *stare decisis* cases because the court (and thus the law) no longer stands by the logic of these cases.

**Prediction:**   Latin: *pre* = before; *diction* = to speak. To proclaim or affirm the behavior of a variable or system before evidence is collected. One of several modernist ways to build social theory. Chaos theory restricts predictability to simple systems, but even simple systems composed of a variable and a constant are unpredictable over time. Thus, Chaos theorists contend that there is a certain simplicity to the linear causality implied in the modernist notion of predictability. Chaos/Complexity theory restricts predictability to small regions in an outcome basin and to short runs on a bifurcation map. See "Chaos Theory" and "Decidability" for more.

**Prehistory:**    According to Karl Marx, human beings pass through three stages if there is good theory and good politics. The first stage is prehistory, in which humans are at the mercy of the blind forces of nature; the second stage is history, in which science and theory begin to offer human beings some control over their future; and the third stage is post-history, in which knowledge and politics come together in democratic forms to allow human beings to build the social institutions that are supportive of praxis and "species-being."

**Premodern:**    An era in which human thought was oriented around the idea that there were two worlds: one in which people lived in the present; and one in which people lived in the past and will live again in the future. This second world is variously inhabited by gods, saints, devils, angels, and other invisible spirits. Modern science tends to dismiss these ideas and, at the same time, dismiss much that is valuable and indispensable to the human project. See "Psychology, Social" for more.

**Prestige:**    The honor attributed to a social position irrespective of the merits of the person who occupies it. Mr. Nixon occupied the presidency, which is defined as a highly prestigious office, when he himself, following Watergate, was held in low esteem as a person. Prestige, as a social invention, is a technique by which the behavior of others is controlled apart from their intentionality. It is a way to legitimate an information set that may raise little merit on its own, from the point of view of the lower classes or others who honor the prestige of office.

**Presumption of Innocence:**    Every person is innocent of a crime unless proven guilty in a court of law. The burden of proof is on the accuser, and the rules of evidence control what is admissible to judge the case at hand.

**Price:**    The cost in money of a good or service. In a perfectly free competitive economy, price would be set by the interactive play of supply and demand. Socialist theory holds that price should be set by the amount of labor power necessary to produce/provide the good or service. The question then becomes, how are skill, talent, craft, and aesthetics registered in the measurement of labor time? Functionalists note that some workers make sacrifices of time, money, and energy to learn a trade, craft, or profession. See "Value (Use-)" for more.

**Prima facie:**    Latin: first appearance. A body of evidence that, on the face of it, makes it reasonable to assume a crime has been committed and that a specific person is responsible or not responsible. Prima facie evidence is suggestive but not compelling.

**Primary Group:**   A set of people with strong social relationships, characterized by face-to-face interaction between known and valued others. Behavior is organized collectively within primary groups. Identity and purpose arise out of such groups.

**Primitive Capitalism:**   A system of small-scale production for private profit. The term also refers to circumstance when many small suppliers deal with many small consumers. A first stage in capitalism, primitive capitalism led to industrial capitalism, which led to finance capitalism, which led to monopoly capitalism. The latter is the current state of capitalism.

**Primogeniture:**   First born. A rule in patriarchal family law that transmits land, title, and property to the first born male.

**Private Enterprise:**   A system of production in which decisions are made privately. The thought is that supply, demand, quality, and inventiveness go up while costs and waste go down if private initiative is encouraged. There is much merit to these claims. However, there are problems. Loss of community, increase in the surplus population, increase in crime, imbalance in growth, ecological disaster, shoddy practices, and so on accrue from private decisions about production.

The Marxist position is that democratic and collective decisions are better than private decisions. In the United States, food coops, credit unions, and public utilities are well-run and generally produce at a lower cost than private enterprise. In private enterprise, the costs of production are often socialized while "profits" are privately used.

**Private Property:**   That which is owned, used, and/or abused by a single individual. In most socialist philosophy, private property comes in two forms: (1) the means of production, which is to be owned in common or at least regulated for the common good; and (2) personal property, which is to be owned and used by individuals, families, or private groups. Many simple cultures view the notion of private property as absurd when it is applied to land, lakes, rivers, oceans, or to forms of life. Private property as a concept is not to be confused with personal property. Here private property means that property used in the production process and does not refer to clothes, toothbrushes, and such. Cf. "Personal Property."

Karl Marx developed the proposition that private property is the product, the result, the necessary consequence of alienated labor. Capitalists expropriate surplus value and turn it into material wealth. They do that when they buy the labor power of others and take part of the value produced for private use. Part of this use includes buying up farm land from peasants or bribing governments to "sell" common lands. Aside from questions of fairness, the capitalist purchases the only process by which humans can create themselves as human beings. In the act of labor, humans can realize that they exist as conscious, intending entities and can reflect on their own existence. Animals cannot. Thus, to purchase labor power is to purchase human nature and to use the product for private purpose.

**Private Sector:**   In some political economic theory, there are two sectors, a private and a public sector. Each produces goods and services. The private sector is capitalist and produces for profit. The public sector is funded by taxes and distributes on the basis of need. James O'Connor divides the U.S. economy into three sectors that produce and/or distribute goods and services: the monopoly sector, the public sector, and the competitive sector. The family, the church, and many forms of crime are parallel economic forms outside the logic of either private capitalism or the public sector.

**Privilege/Privileged:**   A postmodern term that rejects the practice of assigning great importance to an argument, a principle, a person, an event, or to explanations in texts: man over woman; objective over subjective; substance over form. See "Postmodernists/Postmodernism" for more.

**Privileged Communication:**   Some social relationships are so intimate that what is said within them is protected by law. Persons in these relationships cannot be made to tell what was said. These relationships include wife/husband, client/lawyer, communicant/priest, and patient/doctor. Thus, a wife may testify against a husband but may not be forced to testify by a court. Child/parent, student/teacher, reporter/ source are other relationships partly protected by law and custom. Researchers often promise anonymity to people interviewed, but the confidentiality of such communication is in dispute. The assumption is that the social relationship is more sacred than law, justice, or the crime at hand.

**Problem:**   Technically, a problem is a contingency for which a solution does exist. An "issue," on the other hand, is a breakdown (exigency/breakdown) in the system for which there is no agreed-upon solution. Issues are often defined as "problems" in order to avoid the search for a resolution. Both problems and issues assume a mechanical model of society in which control and prediction are possible and desirable. A society could be organized such that "errors" in the system were tolerated. Cf. "Issue."

**Procedural Law:**   Those legal rules that define the ways in which courts must act when hearing a criminal or civil case. They deal with obtaining warrants to arrest, collecting evidence, introducing evidence, using force, sentencing, and appeals. Substantive law defines what is legal and illegal; procedural law deals with how substantive law is enforced.

**Production, Social Relations of:**   Refers to the forms of ownership and control of: the means of production; administration; political control and violence; the forms of exchange; distribution; patterns of consumption of the social product; the division of labor power; authority relations; institutionalized social relations; the law; and the state. According to Marxian theory, the emerging dialectic between social relations and the forces of production marks the basic contradiction in society; and it is this contradiction that produces change. For example, the factory system contains both forces of production and social relations that tend to produce insightful critiques on the part of workers and new social relations by which to deal with those contradictions.

**Productive Labor:**   The unity of mental and physical labor. The idea here is that workers, forbidden to participate in mental labor, become merely physical objects (i.e., the laws of the physical sciences apply to an understanding of their behavior). In order to be human, however, one must be productive (i.e., produce culture), and this requires mental labor. Mental labor does not lend itself to analysis by physical science but by hermeneutics: the science of understanding and knowing. See "Hermeneutics" for more.

**Product Liability:**   The responsibility assumed by the manufacturer of defective or dangerous goods and/or the seller of deficient services. A fairly new body of law that protects consumers and the environment.

**Profanation:**   The process by which some people or some parts of nature are treated as if they were objects to be used or abused without thought. Sociologists/anthropologists divide up society and nature into the "sacred" and the "profane." The sacred is respected, cherished, and preserved. The profane is used or ignored. See "Demonization," "Paganism," "Reification," and "Sanctification/De-sanctification" for more.

**Profit:**   A claim, usually backed by force of arms or law, that some part of the value of labor power belongs exclusively to one person who may or may not have played a constructive role in creating that social wealth. In modern times, sufficient surplus value is accumulated to pay nonactive "owners" a profit by transferring some of the costs of production to the state, to the workers, or to the environment. Research and development, water and sewage treatment, worker training, worker insurance, guaranteed profits, bill collection, and so on exemplify a few of the costs transferred to the state by legislators who come from business or serve business.

The Marxist view is that all social wealth is produced by a set of cooperating workers and that it is unsocial to use force to appropriate wealth. Moreover, the point of producing wealth is to insure that the people create themselves as species-beings through community and through praxis rather than through the private use of material resources.

Profit is also one of three ways by which surplus value is distributed. Rents and dividends are the other two. Capitalist economists claim that profit is a return on investment and on the skill, foresight, or sacrifice involved in investment. Socialist economists tend to view profit as a form of crime in which surplus value is appropriated from those who produce it. In their view, the skill, foresight, or sacrifice made in investment is a form of labor and has a specific value, which varies depending on the situation and context. This value should be distributed in the form of wages or salary rather than in the form of profit, since profit includes a lot more than the cost of the labor power involved in investment.

**Profit, Falling Rates of:**   Karl Marx held that it is a tendency in any capitalist system for profit rates to fall. As the role of machinery increases, workers are disemployed. All value comes from the labor power of workers, and, thus, profit rates eventually fall since the disemployed cannot produce more value to exchange for that which they already produced. The surplus piles up in warehouses; prices fall; and profits decline. Profit rates in a "free economy" can be increased by either restricting output (farmers could burn crops or kill cattle) or by generating new demand via temporary depressions (which give time for goods to wear out), new inventions (cars, refrigerators, computers), crime, war, advertising, state welfare, and so on.

**Profit, Rate of:**   Karl Marx defined the rate of profit as $P = S/C+V$, where $P$ = profit; $S$ = surplus value; $C$ = constant capital (machines); and $V$ = variable capital (labor costs). Capitalists can increase profits by either decreasing constant capital costs (via automation) or decreasing variable capital costs (racism, sexism, union-busting, moving jobs to third world countries, etc.). See "Labor Power, Reproduction of" for more.

**Profit Sharing:**   Generally, the sharing of profit by workers in a factory. This gives workers a motive for faster, better work and results in lower rates of absenteeism and worker turnover. Sometimes workers own a factory and share out profits to all workers, after a probationary period of employment. Profit sharing can be used to sweat out more labor or to shift, gradually, from outside to inside ownership. Sometimes workers invest their pension funds in company stock and, thus, have a proprietary interest in caring for machinery and improving quality and quantity of goods/services.

**Proletarianization:**   The process by which the middle classes (farmers, crafts-persons, small store owners, traders, doctors, office workers, professors, lawyers, clerks, and others) are gradually being reduced to wage labor (i.e., they no longer own the means of production but, rather, sell their labor power to the corporation or the state). See "Embourgeoisiement" for more.

**Proletariat:**   Latin: *proles* = offspring. It refers to the lowest class in ancient Rome, which served the Romans only by having children. The word was picked up during the time of the Paris Commune to refer to those who served the nobility and merchant class with their labor. Karl Marx then adopted it in his class analysis to mean those who have only their labor power to sell or those actively engaged in the production process. Georg Lukács held that the proletariat is the source of emancipation since it alone can directly experience the contradictions of capitalism. Cf. "Bourgeoisie."

**Proof:** The means by which facts are determined to be valid or invalid. (1) In empirical science, proof is based upon observed facts and corresponding rules for interpreting them. (2) In law, proof is based upon competent testimony and admissible evidence. (3) In math and logic, proof is based upon valid reasoning from first, indisputable assumptions.

**Propaganda:** Persuasive explanations that are designed to shape public opinion and, thus, social policy. It involves the use of language by which one social paradigm is celebrated and other, different social paradigms are degraded. Propaganda, in its positive mode, is necessary to create social reality, since social reality does not emerge unless there is conviction, belief, trust, and faith. Propaganda helps generate these aspects of social life. The more serious political question is, Which social paradigm is to be used as a guide to construct social reality? Sometimes the term is used maliciously within one social paradigm to neutralize the claims of superiority made by other social paradigms. See "Social Opinion" for more.

**Property:** In law, anything that can be owned. The tendency in market economies is to make every thing and every act a commodity that serves as property. Most societies in most of human history did not grant property rights to most natural things (e.g., lakes, forests, water, game, land, and space) or to any social good: love, honor, sex, or political office. See "Commodification" for more.

**Prophet (Prophetic Mode):** One who exhorts a society to change itself. A style of doing science that is critical and revolutionary rather than conservative and supportive of the existing scientific paradigm. The term is used in sociology to distinguish between those who administer to the existing (structural-functional) paradigm (i.e., priests) and those who challenge the assumptions of that science (the prophets).

**Proscription:** A written statement forbidding an act.

**Prosperity Theology:** A religious movement that holds that God wants believers to be rich. It cites several passages in the Christian Bible in support of this argument. Although the Protestant ethic argued that God appointed some people as custodians of fields, flocks, and nations, it also called for thrift and hard work. Prosperity theology permits/justifies a luxurious life style.

**Prostitution:**   The conversion of sex, intimacy, and sensuality into a commodity to be sold under market conditions. Today, prostitutes are called "sex workers" and prostitution is referred to as a "sex trade." Both changes in terminology underscore the economic dynamics implied in the concept of prostitution. See "Prostitution, Theory of" for more.

Female prostitution is common in patriarchal societies. Male prostitution increases in advanced monopoly capitalism since gender distinctions are lost and jobs move to cheap labor countries. Child prostitution is found in any society where male adults are alienated from social power advantages in their work and in their relationships.

As a metaphor, prostitution refers to the impersonal sale of any cherished cultural item (e.g., loyalty, friendship, honor, genius, trust, respect, or public office).

**Prostitution, Theory of:**   The socialist feminist theory of prostitution is that women enter sex business as a result of the separation of production from distribution. Those in the surplus population have only their bodies to sell. Women are more likely to be prostitutes than are men in a patriarchal society since men are more likely to have job advantages. Men turn to prostitution as an avenue for social power when alienated at work or in politics. They can buy the dramaturgical facsimile of power for a brief moment.

The liberal bourgeois defense of prostitution is that since there is demand for commodity sex, it should be supplied by the free market. The patriarchal defense of prostitution is that men have sexual needs that should be satisfied by unattached females, especially when women are scarce. See "Prostitution" for more.

**Protected Person:**   In international law, protected persons include those on diplomatic missions, such as ambassadors and their families and staff.

**Protestant/Protestantism:**   A religion and a practice that places no obstacles between believers and their God(s). Generally, there is an elected governing council that selects ministers and makes policy about how to raise funds and disburse them, as well as about which programs of the church to support. Protestantism as a social movement came along to accompany capitalism. It challenged feudalism and serfdom on behalf of trade and commerce and proclaimed the natural dignity of men (more so than women). It challenged Catholic support for kings and princes. Some denominations, like Methodism, began as a refuge and haven for the poor and oppressed and, over time, became conservative and elitist. See "Protestant Ethic, The" and "Theology, Liberation" for more.

**Protestant Ethic, The:**   A set of values and practices that includes thrift, hard work, individuality, and stewardship of wealth on behalf of one's God. This work ethic, inculcated by the needs of early capitalism and all low tech economic systems, had its foundation in the premise that the "way of work" is the way to a state of grace and salvation instead of the way of faith (as in Catholicism) or the way of meditation (as in Eastern religions). A second premise is that the ascetic life is spiritually superior to the way of fleshly pleasure. Combined with the notion of stewardship, one has the ingredients for capital accumulation; that is, hard work, frugal living, and a philosophy that asserts that being wealthy is a service to God, who appreciates those who look after His/Her vast domains. For John Calvin, possession of property and the means of production was presumptive proof of a state of grace. Protestantism is hostile to feudal hierarchy in church and state and, thus, has progressive tendencies. See "Protestant/Protestantism" and "Weber, Max" for more.

**Proudhon, Pierre Joseph (1809–1865):**   A French social philosopher who gave socialism many concepts and ideas, including anarchy, the bourgeoisie, mutual banks, and the aphorism, "Property is theft."

**Psychogenic Aids:**   Physical substances that alter consciousness when ingested. Usually that altered state is experienced as evidence of solidarity; that is, the oneness of the group. In order to use psychogens for sacred purposes, it is necessary to define their private use as obscene, corrupt, evil, and/or depravation. For example, alcohol promotes solidarity if used collectively and if defined as a solidarity mechanism, whereas the private use of alcohol is described as an illness or a crime irrespective of the amount consumed. Generally, if a society uses one kind of psychogenic (e.g., alcohol, marijuana, peyote, special foods, tobacco) solely or in combination, the use of psychogens from other cultures is defined as corrupt or criminal. Sex, dancing, fasting, whipping, and breath control also alter body chemistry and can be used as psychogens.

**Psychology:**   A science and a discipline that studies individuals and the sources of human behavior. There is much controversy within psychology. Some turn to genes and to physiology as foundations of behavior. Some look at the mind and how it works. Others look at early childhood experiences and socialization to explain/predict behavior. Social psychology adds social roles, institutions, and larger structures to the explanation. See "Emergence Theory" and "Reductionism" for more.

**Psychology, Radical:**   The radical movement in psychology links the best conditions for a development of the personality and for release of creative energies to a change in social relations and institutions. This change requires the overthrow of class and power relations through whatever means are appropriate in a given historical context. Psychopathy is more of a social issue than a personal failing or internal conflict. Therapy involves a concern with internal distortions and with relief of private anguish, but within the context of supportive social relationships rather than through chemotherapy or individual therapy.

**Psychology, Social:**    A branch of sociology that examines the process by which people, together, construct social realities and each other as distinct social beings. Symbolic Interactional theory is central to the discipline and inquires into the process by which mind, self, and society are, in the same moment, created. See "Mead, George Herbert" and "Premodern" for more.

**Psychopathic Disorder:**    Behavior in law and medicine that warrants confinement and/or treatment. It includes sex with inappropriate objects and persons; investment of desire in ordinary items such as clothing or artifacts; uncontrollable rage and violence directed at innocent or harmless persons or animals. Psychopathic disorder is used as both a reason to control a person and a justification for unusual behavior. Judgments about it are often political. See "Mental Disorder" for more.

**Psychosexual Development:**    In Freudian theory, the sequence by which the forces of life (sexuality generally) become linked to social activity. It includes the oral stage, the anal stage, a passive pre-genital phase, and a genital or adult stage. The assumption is that trauma at one stage can impair development. Freudian revisionists use these assumptions to help sell beer, razor blades, cars, and other products that are associated with sexual anxieties.

**Psycho-Technology:**    A wide variety of technical means exists by which to control behavior apart from cognitive processes, self-control, and transactions. Several of these techniques include chemotherapy, behavior modification, electric shock therapy, electronic implants, electronic surveillance, psychosurgery, aversion therapy, and counseling. All of these techniques work to obtain that behavior desired by a professional elite. Psycho-technology is presently used mostly on prisoners and students; however, the technology is spreading to workers. For example, in Chicago, every move of 450 workers is monitored via TV cameras. Time-study experts keep charts on workers who are observed talking, or working too slowly. Instant replay is used to analyze any employee's behavior. Behavior modification is then used to "shape" worker behavior. These technical means work, but the behavior produced is not social behavior. It is simply behavior.

**Public:**    Latin: *publicus* = of or pertaining to the people generally. In political theory, the public sphere is the venue for formation of social policy with which to settle issues. It contrasts to the civil (now private) sphere, which is the venue for pursuing private goals. In mass society, it has come to mean a set of unrelated individuals who share at least one thing in common. For example, all those who read *Doonesbury* or who drive a Datsun are said to compose a public. Some people hold that a communication system is also necessary for the formation of a public, but communication implies social relationships and joint coordinated effort to advance the interest(s) shared. These coordinated efforts would then be examples of voluntary associations (if membership were restricted to a single item) or collectives (if there were some solidarity).

**Public Good, The:**   That which makes it possible for people to live in peace and safety. The public good often includes programs of social justice, as well as security in home or person or in travel to and from places of business and dwelling.

**Public Morals:**   Sometimes the public good is used as a justification for defining and attempting to eliminate criminal actions, as in laws regarding vagrancy, loud noise, drunkenness, rowdy behavior, prostitution, and other activities that offend most persons, or most high status persons, in a community.

**Public Opinion:**   An information set that is pointed toward the resolution of an issue. Authentically produced public opinion requires undistorted communication in the public domain and effective participation by all relevant sectors of the population base (environment). For example, the managed opinion produced by the Reagan/Bush administration violated the public opinion policy process. See "Social Opinion" for more.

**Public Opinion Policy Process:**   A process by which quality variety is generated in order to reduce mismatch between a social system and its environment. Generally, several options are generated and several publics support each option. A process of collective deliberation is necessary to select the best option or to organize a dialectic by which qualitatively new options are produced.

**Public Place:**   A place where people in general have access (e.g., parks, restaurants, cinema, shops, streets, museums, and other places serving people defined as adults).

**Public Policy:**   Generally, policy made by and for the people. Usually it is made by elected representatives (as in the republican form of governance) or by direct voting (as in democratic procedures).

**Public Relations:**   An attempt to defuse and deflect the hostility generated by capitalist modes of production. Along with private security, public relations is the fastest growing industry in the United States.

**Punishment:**   The use of pain or fine to sanction the behavior of a person deemed guilty of a prohibited act. Theories of punishment are many: Seneca gave three justifications for punishment: (1) to reform the criminal; (2) to give warning to others; and (3) to remove the criminal from the community so others may live in safety.

In utilitarian legal theory, a person commits a crime when the benefits of the crime exceed the liabilities of getting caught. This theory therefore suggests the solution to crime is best achieved by raising the costs of crime. The certainty, swiftness, and severity of the penalty are therefore "morally tolerable." In older social theory, punishment and suffering are thought to purify a person. In addition, there is the idea that when one is alienated from God, mortification of the flesh helps reunite one with the Absolute. Others claim that punishment is just "retribution" for evil or disgraceful behavior. See "Just Deserts" and "Utilitarianism" for more.

Modern psychological findings suggest that the best combination for shaping behavior is a lot of reward mixed with a small amount of discomfort/pain. Some people violate legal codes even when punishment is harsh, as in revolutions and warfare. Most people reason punishment away calculating that they probably will not be caught.

The critical position is that punishment for crime and fear of pain is a primitive form of ethical rationality. Efforts at restoration, peacemaking, and economic justice are pro-social solutions opposed to the punitive response. See "Bentham, Jeremy" for more.

**Putative:**   That which is assumed about another person or thing. For example, a "putative father" is the male assumed to be the father of a child, absent proof to the contrary.

**Pygmalion Studies:**   Pygmalion was a Greek sculptor who created a statue so beautiful that he fell in love with it. His faith in it caused the statue to come alive. George Bernard Shaw wrote a play by the same name about women who were empowered or degraded by the men in their lives. The movies *My Fair Lady* and *Pretty Woman* are contemporary versions of the play in which speech, dress, and comportment are taught to lower-class girls who then are taken to be and feel like princesses.

In 1968, R. Rosenthal and L. Joacobson set up an experiment in which teachers were told that their students had scored high on an IQ test and that they would do well. Actually, the students were assigned to classes at random, but, given the teachers' belief that they had "good" students, the teachers behaved in such a way that the students did, in fact, greatly improve in test performance over the six grades in which the experiment was conducted.

Today, the term is used generically to refer to all such studies that teach us that behavior and self-worth are collective products rather than phenomena located in the psyche of a single individual. See "Self-Fulfilling Prophecy" and "Social Magic" for more.

**Pyrrho (ca. 360–270 B.C.E.):**   Greek philosopher who argued that it was impossible to know anything with certainty. Since no truth claim has any better grounds than any other truth claim, the best thing to do is to submit to *epoché*, a suspension of judgment. In our profound ignorance, we should practice *aphasia*, noncommittal silence. As a philosophy of life, we should practice *ataraxia*, imperturbable serenity and tranquillity.

Many postmodernists take the view of Pyrrho. Yet Chaos theory tells us that even in the most disorderly natural and social dynamics there is an order to be discovered and used to plan and to control our futures, if only in the short term. Since most social dynamics take the form of a 2, 4, 8 or 16n outcome field, there is sufficient order and sufficient variety to make knowledge claims and to make judgments based on them. (See the work of W. L. Reese.)

# Q

**Quality:** The distinguishing attribute of a thing; its essential character. In classic philosophy and modern science, size, shape, weight, pattern of movement, sound, smell, and taste are attributes inherent in a thing. Postmodern philosophy of science holds these attributes to be arbitrary categories invented and used by human beings in pursuit of cultural goals. Thus, in postmodern philosophy of science, the size of an object is a function of the degree to which people are willing to set the boundaries of a thing. In sociology, this view translates into boundary setting for class, race, gender, age, national origin, and so on. The same is true in psychology for such attributes as IQ. Since natural and social laws are founded upon quality and quantity, these, too, are called into question as human constructs.

**Quality of Life Variables:** Certain variables are a good measure of the degree to which a society is well-organized in terms of praxis and community. In general, participation rates and dropout rates in central institutions, as well as in family, school, church, politics, and pro-social labor, signal positive and negative features of a society. Together with "quantity of life variables" quality of life variables help serve emancipatory interests by enabling a people to reflect upon and, perhaps, change their own social organization. Crime rates, suicide rates, absentee rates, desertion and divorce rates, infant mortality rates, child abuse rates, turnover rates, morbidity rates, alcoholism and drug abuse rates all point to a poorly designed social lifeworld in school, family, work, and in church. Perhaps the most sensitive indicator of a good and decent society is found in infant mortality rates; the nine months of pregnancy and the first year after birth are crucial to the well-being of a child.

**Quantification:** The process of transforming human behavior into number systems. There are major political problems with this practice: One loses information as one transforms behavior into word systems; more information is lost when word systems are replaced by number systems, and still more when summary statistics are used to replace the original data. Quantification can also be described as a process by which undesirable information is discarded. The political question is, Who decides what is undesirable? A second problem is that numbers can be manipulated by arithmetic and algebraic rules, which are coherent, whereas human behavior may be incoherent (i.e., emergent). Further, there are several numbering systems (scales) using the same symbols. What is a 5 in one system (e.g., in a nominal scale) may not be the same thing in another system (e.g., an ordinal scale). When human beings are referred to or classified as numbers, they are stripped of their humanity. Quantification is an instrument of modern science. Postmodernists are skeptical about what this "science" tells us about society and about our humanity. See "Mathematical Sociology," "Positivism," and "Postmodernists/Postmodernism" for more.

**Quantification Theory:**   In quantification theory, the process by which one reveals the underlying causal connections in natural and social phenomena by comparing the characteristics of a data set with normal, expected, or chance distributions is called "inference." There are several of these characteristics that one can use in order to make guesses about whether causality is at work; one can, for instance: (1) look at the flatness of a curve when creating a distribution along a variable; (2) assume that different outcomes one sees when a new variable is introduced (or removed) prove causal connection; (3) look at deviations from a center point and conclude that some cause is at work. Quantification theory does not take into account the qualitative changes that occur in the *same* set of variables when one of them makes a slight curve as a critical *(feigenbaum)* point. See "Inference" and "Rational Thinking" for more.

**Quantity:**   An attribute of an object or an attribute that can be expressed in terms of a comparison (more or less) with another such object or thing. In modern philosophy, there are four scales with which to measure quantity: nominal, ordinal, interval, and rational. Nominal scales enable one to count how many objects/attributes are present regardless of size or kind. Ordinal scales enable one to rank objects/attributes in terms of size from smallest to largest. Interval scales enable one to say exactly how much larger or smaller one object/attribute is than another. Rational scales enable one to multiply or divide objects/attributes by each other. One can count a group of apples and oranges, but one cannot multiply six oranges by five apples and get thirty bananas, nor can one say that a person with 120 IQ points is twice as smart as a person with 60 IQ points.

There are several arguments about the utility of quantification for establishing truth claims. Some people claim that truth comes only from the use of these scales, especially rational scaling. Others argue that qualities exist that are immeasurable and incommensurate. See "Rational Thinking" for more.

**Quantity of Life Variables:**   Income, housing, transportation, clothing, and other material possessions give measure to the degree that the economic system is working well. If this wealth is spread broadly throughout a society, it speaks well to the social justice built into the economic system. If wealth is highly stratified, and the ratio of those with less to those with more wealth is high, then one can anticipate rebellion and revolution. However, quantity of life variables do not tell all the story. Great wealth can fail to bring great satisfaction and contentment.

**Queer Theory:**   Broadly speaking, a phrase referring to the organization, culture, and behavior of homosexual, lesbian, bisexual, and transgendered individuals. The term was developed out of a coalition of gay and lesbian activists in the United States and the United Kingdom. The popular slogan "We're queer, we're here, get used to it!" became the rallying cry for the queer theory movement.

Queer theory represents a major ideological split from the more conventional "gay" and "lesbian" terminology. Queer theory advocates contend that when homophobic categories of sense making are embraced there is greater likelihood for homosexual social formations to gain legitimacy. This "reverse discourse" phenomenon thus neutralizes and de-sexualizes the power that the more stereotypical categories exercise over gay and lesbian individuals, particularly in their everyday social interaction.

More recently, critics charge that little in the way of race and class dynamics have found their way into queer theory politics. In response, ACT UP (Aids Coalition to Unleash Power) groups have attempted to link the social activism and sexual politics of queer theory with the diverse economic interests of minority and poor citizens. See "Sexuality" for more.

*Quotidien, le*:   The practice of focusing upon everyday life in order to describe or explain. Local stories thus have greater validity than do global explanations, national samples, or generalizing statistics.

# R

**Race:**   There is only one human race: the species, Homo sapiens. However, many people award themselves social honor and the right to dominate others by claiming that there are several "inferior" races of human beings. Although the concept of race is a false one, it has real consequences in economics and politics.

**Racism:**   A complex set of beliefs that some subspecies of human beings (stocks) are held to be inferior to others in certain important ways. These ways usually deal with the capacity to create ideological culture (they are savages) or to create political culture (they cannot govern themselves yet). Racial theories are highly selective in choice of data for confirmation. They serve as post hoc rationales for exploiting people or for denying social status. Defining some races as superior and others as inferior is a political matter rather than a scientific one. Sometimes "whites" are used as slaves, sometimes "blacks." Ultimately, it is a question of power.

Capitalism tends to destroy racist privileges for a number of reasons: (1) Black labor is cheaper in a racist society; (2) markets can be expanded by selling "white" goods and services to "blacks"; (3) strikes can be broken by bringing in people desperate for work, regardless of their "color"; (4) to the extent that merit is used as a criterion for hiring, there is always some number of African-Americans who work harder, longer, and more skillfully than some number of Anglos. See "Anti-Semitism," "Demonization," and "Rebellion, Pre-Theoretical" for more.

**Radical:**   Latin: *radicalis* = having roots. One whose analysis suggests that a fundamental change in social paradigm is required in order to solve problems. Most Marxists/radicals believe that the roots of most social problems are to be found in the political economy; the problems of capitalism (contradictions) cannot be solved within the system. They can only be transferred to other parts of the system or to other countries. Feminists believe that patriarchy must be destroyed (not males but male prerogatives and female oppressions). Black power advocates insist that racism must be sent to the dustheap of history. Most right-wing radicals (liberals) believe that the government (the state) should abandon all attempts to regulate the economy, to solve social problems, or to provide services not available on the free market. Other right-wing radicals believe that the liberal state should be replaced by one supporting gender, class, religious, or ethnic privilege.

**Radical Theater/Cinema:**    The use of cinema to reflect upon social relationships in a critical mode—in contrast to the use of cinema as a commodity. There are three structural aspects to radical theater: (1) It creates an honest dialectic between two or more difficult choices; (2) it erases the line between actors and audience; and (3) it moves people toward human agency in real life. See "Dramaturgical Society" for more.

**Rank and File:**    The ordinary members in a union or other association. The term comes from the military and gives one an idea of how seriously democracy is taken in a union. It refers to soldiers standing in rows (ranks) and columns (files).

**Rape:**    The forcible invasion of the body of another person. Force includes both violence and threat of violence. Although physical power is the chief mode of committing rape, physical violence shades into the use of social power to threaten job security; into the use of moral power to justify male dominance; into the use of economic power to buy the services that would not be given freely and lovingly.

**Rape (As Metaphor):**    Rape is often used as a metaphor to convey the anger and disgust that arises when one person invades the mind and soul of another without mutuality and sociality. Thus, there are several metaphorical varieties of rape.

**Rape, Feminist Theories of:**    The feminist theories of rape contend that it is a power device by which male hegemony is embodied. In more general terms rape is a semi-public control tactic by which women are forced back into the home or, alternatively, allowed to venture into public only under the protection of a male with status.

The problem of rape is described in several authoritative texts, including Susan Brownmiller's *Against Our Will*, Susan Griffin's *Rape: The Power of Consciousness*, and Angela Davis's *Women, Race, and Class*. Each scholar utilizes a distinctive approach, including radical, socialist, and black feminist perspectives, respectively.

In predatory warfare, young men were given the right to rape women and children while the older men took possession of plunder and returned home with it to share it out among families in the clan, tribe, or band. In modern warfare and in slavery, all women defined as nonpersons could be raped without social onus or personal guilt. In all societies, sexual norms are strictly enforced in respect to women defined as daughters, wives, mothers, nuns, and other females within given degrees of kinship. This explanation contrasts to reductionist theories which explain rape as biologically driven, as personal pathology, or as faulty socialization.

**Rational Choice, Theory of:**    A theory of crime that takes into account the motivation, the situation, and the criminal to explain the overall crime event. The perspective emphasizes how individuals (including offenders) process information and evaluate alternatives to make decisions about criminal conduct. In this model, a person commits a crime after the person weighs the benefits of criminal behavior against the costs of getting caught.

Rational choice theory is a reworking of the classical criminological perspective in which offenders were thought to possess free will, to be morally blameworthy, and to function as pleasure seekers and pain avoiders. The major difference between the rational choice perspective and the classical criminological orientation is that the former more broadly focuses on the characteristics of crime than on the individual to explain criminality. Cf. "Routine Activities, Theory of."

A critical appraisal would question the degree to which macro-structural forces (e.g., unemployment, poverty, urban decay) are adequately examined in the rational choice model. These dimensions are not as evenly integrated into the crime theory equation of rational choice and are supplanted with more psychological and micro-sociological explanations. See "Criminology" for more.

**Rationality:**    There are two kinds of rationality: technical and substantive. Technical rationality considers whether the means one uses to pursue a goal are sensible/workable/successful. Substantive rationality considers whether the goals one pursues are wise/humane/helpful to others. See "Praxis/Practice" for more.

**Rationality (As a Moment of Praxis):**    The organization of resources such that predictable outcomes are possible. In praxis, rationality is actively linked to the achievement of human purpose. It is not mere technical rationality in which mechanical determinism decides whether the means are effective in reaching a goal. Rationality as a moment of praxis implies that the goals themselves are oriented to a general theory of human rights and dignity.

**Rationality Crises:**    Capitalism produces distortions in the economic system. In popular democracies, the state moves in to correct those distortions but cannot formulate policy that threatens either competitive or monopoly capitalism. Thus, planning is impossible. The state responds to crises by emergency measures, by pleas for cooperation. It cannot choose between contradictory steering imperatives.

**Rational-Purposive Institutions:**   Those institutions (e.g., bureaucracies, prisons, the welfare economy, the military) that effectively control the alienated elements of the population through the principles of management science.

**Rational Thinking:**   A mode of thinking in which a given thing is conceived in terms of a stable relationship to another thing. Thus one thing is conceived to be equal to one fourth or one fifth of another thing. Rational thinking helps solve problems, since complex equations can be worked out. This mode of thinking, when applied to human behavior, is a source of great concern: (1) It reifies relationship to a fixed ratio; (2) it objectifies human agency by restricting flexibility; and (3) it replaces interactional causality with mechanistic causality. The latter causality reduces the sum of human interaction to stimulus-response processes.

Rational thinking produces predictable behavior and is desired in a society where it is useful to be able to predict (and control) the behavior of students, workers, voters, customers, soldiers, and masses generally. See "Quantification Theory" and "Quantity" for more.

**Readerly (Versus Writerly) Text:**   In postmodern deconstructive analysis, all communication, whether written or spoken, is a text. The readerly versus writerly distinction was popularized by Roland Barthes in relationship to interpreting classic literary texts; however, several additional postmodern theorists have applied his insights to legal narratives (Dragan Milovanovic, Bruce Arrigo), to film theory (Caja Silverman), to semiotic critiques (MacCabe), and to psychoanalysis (Gilles Deleuze and Félix Guattari).

The *readerly approach* reproduces the classic text's ideals. The organizing principles of this reading (and viewing) are primarily noncontradiction, coherency, and consistency. The reader/viewer is encouraged to accept "as truth" the words themselves. Thus, there is nothing behind or underneath the words. What the text means is direct, without question, on the surface. Missing from the readerly approach is the sphere of the text's production; that is, its connection to the political economy and to cultural inequalities that remain concealed. The reader/viewer experiences fulfillment. (See "*Jouissance*" for more.) The text promises a coherent narrative, and the reader/viewer interprets the text accordingly. Thus in this reading, subjects reconstitute and revalidate the dominant understandings of reality embedded in the readerly approach to the text. Both children's stories and accounts from mythology are particularly instructive here. The readerly approach emphasizes the manifest content of the narrative. Missing from this rendition, however, is the deep structure of the text that often represents a more cloaked reality, affirming certain power relationships and a certain understanding of the person in the social order. See "Barthes, Roland" and "Text" for more. Cf. "Writerly (Versus Readerly) Text."

**Reading:**   Explanation, view, or theory. Postmodernists speak of "your reading" and "my reading" without speaking to the superiority or great validity of one over the other.

**Realization, Problem of:**   Capitalism is the finest system of production so far developed. It tends to improve the means of production until this capacity far outstrips the capacity of people to buy all the goods produced. As capitalism increases productivity, fewer and fewer people can enter the market. This represents a problem; namely, How to realize profit on the unsold part of production? There are several answers: (1) Advertising can create demand for more and more goods; (2) capitalist firms in one country can take markets away from capitalists in other countries; (3) the government can buy up "surplus" wheat, sugar, tobacco, corn, and so on and give it away to needy people or other countries; and (4) tariffs can be put on imported goods to protect markets. See "Needs, False" for more.

**Rebellion:**   A spontaneous uprising against exploitation and oppression. Often, rebellions are poorly organized, poorly led, and short-lived. Nonetheless, rebellions are a dramatic symptom of a failed politics or economics. A good bit of low-level reform ensues from rebellions. In the United States, the riots and looting of the 1960s led to the Great Society and the War on Poverty Programs. These were dismantled in the 1980s and 1990s, since the rebellion failed to change the basic politics of the country. The Los Angeles riots that followed the acquittal of officers accused of beating Rodney King produced some minor legal and civic (public opinion) reform. These reforms, however, have yet to demonstrate any significant economic impact on the community in which the violence, looting, and bloodshed occurred.

**Rebellion, Pre-Theoretical:**   Most rebellion is pre-theoretical, in that it lacks good theory, good organization, and good programs. Workers sometimes steal, sabotage, slow down, or use violence on "scabs" and management. Marxist theory argues that particular people are not the class enemy but that inequalities in social relationships are. Destruction and violence is thus pre-theoretical, in that it attacks the wrong targets and adopts the wrong tactics. See "Banditry, Social," "Crime," and "Racism" for more.

**Recession:**   A politically safe word ("depression" is not). The "official" definition of a recession is defined as a period of at least six months in which production declines. A lot of people can be out of work, but there is no cause for alarm since gross national product (GNP) is not falling.

**Recidivism:**   Repeated criminal behavior. Recidivism is measured by the number of crimes committed by persons under probation and by the number of crimes committed during a three-year period by persons released from prison. It can be used to judge the success rate of the criminal justice system. More often, however, it is used to justify longer terms and harsher punishments.

**Red:**   The color associated with communism and, by extension, any radical movement that pursues social justice for all. The term was first used in this way in the French Revolution (1789); the red flag became a symbol of defiance and militant struggle for human emancipation. In Russian, *Krasnyi* means both red and beautiful.

**Red Feather Institute:**   A radical independent think tank put together by Tim Lehmann, Tom Harblin, Wendall Ott, and T. R. Young on July 4, 1971. It took as its goal the sustenance of radical consciousness and politics in the Rocky Mountain region. The election of Richard M. Nixon signaled to the founders the use of state power to eradicate antiwar activity, the civil rights movement, student power, feminist actions, as well as antisocialist and anticommunist police action. The institute had four programs at its inception: (1) The Transforming Sociology Series; (2) alternative syllabi for graduate students; (3) regular conferences for Marxists, feminists, and other progressive activists, including Protestant and Catholic clergy in the area; and (4) support for lectures by leading radical scholars outside the Rocky Mountain region. Young and his family built the Red Feather Lodge and hosted many conferences until personal tragedy intervened. The institute continues on a much smaller scale and has moved to its present address in Michigan.

The name came from Red Feather Lake Village, a small mountain town named after Princess Red Feather, the leader of an operatic troupe that so appealed to the residents that they renamed the town to honor her. The first meetings of the institute were at the Young cabin on Lake Papoose in Red Feather Village. It also adopts the French logo of the red feather for radical scholarship.

**Redistribution:**   When wealth accumulates in the hands of a few persons, most societies have mechanisms for its redistribution. Many religions call for tithes to support the poor. Some religions call for sabbaticals where debts are forgiven. Among the Northwest Indian tribes, the potlatch redistributed wealth. Banditry, kidnapping, and other forms of crime redistribute wealth outside of established rules of distribution. Taxation can be used to provide a safety net, or it can be used to funnel wealth to the upper classes. In contrast to capitalist societies, the socialist economic system distributes on the bases of both need and merit. It therefore obviates the need for redistribution.

**Red Squad:**   The term is used generally to refer to activities in any political unit where police are used to suppress dissent. The policies of the Red

Squad include: (1) the search for compromising behavior (whether legal or not); (2) an exchange of information with other police, including the FBI; (3) a network of paid informers; (4) ties with private, right-wing organizations; and (5) the use of collected information to make it difficult for one to keep a job, get credit, get insurance, or to seek political office. Red Squad agents pose as reporters or members of a radical group and attempt to cultivate mistrust and agitation between subject, friends, family—and all without due process or public writ. FBI files suggest that thousands of liberal democrats (who pose a small danger to capitalism) were closely watched, as were supporters of the women's liberation and civil rights groups, in the 1960s and 1970s. A similar trend existed in the 1980s when Red Squads were identified in Los Angeles and other cities that maintained disruptive strategies. Presumption of innocence, due process, and rights to political dissent are ignored by such activities.

**Reductionism:**   The practice of attributing causality to parts of a system rather than the system as a complex interactive whole. Thus crime is said to be caused by individual psychological states or even biochemical factors such as blood chemistry, brain waves, genes, and so on. Sometimes reduction is appropriate, but when it is not, reduction is a cardinal error in scientific inference and explanation. See "Biological Reductionism" and "Psychology" for more.

**Reference Group Theory:**   The theory that behavior is organized when one uses the standards and values of people who are in the same social position as a guide to one's own behavior. Reference group theory contrasts with the use of more general, universal, and/or egalitarian claims for rights and responsibilities. Poor people, slaves, women, and other minorities use other poor people, slaves, women, and so on (rather than rich, white males) as references by which to judge their own well-being. Role theory assumes interaction between the various identified groups; reference group theory does not assume it as much.

**Reflection Theory:**   The materialist theory of psychology that holds that thinking, feeling, sensing, and doing are reflections of the existing social order. This view sometimes reduces the creative and emancipatory potential of human thought to those moments when contradictions are so great that revolution occurs. Karl Marx held that human consciousness did reflect historical existing material conditions but that the contradictions stimulated radical thought long before material conditions triggered outright rebellion.

**Reform:**   A movement that attempts to solve the contradictions of a social paradigm without changing its basic structure. The attempt to improve prison life or to get food stamps to the poor is, in effect, counterrevolutionary, in that the harsher aspects of capitalism are moderated without ending poverty or crime. Some think that reform may be additive and thus result in revolutionary change.

**Rehabilitation:**    A liberal philosophy of crime and justice. Rehabilitation refers to the conviction that people can be helped and restored. The justice system functions as a means for treating people who cannot manage for themselves. Criminals are viewed as victims of racism, poverty, alienation, and the brutalizing effects of the criminal justice apparatus. The emphasis of the rehabilitative model is on treating the offender rather than punishing the offender. Thus, the punishment one receives for criminal conduct should be fitted to the individual. Cf. "Retribution." See "Restorative Justice" for more.

**Reich, Wilhelm (1897–1957):**    An Austrian ardent leftist radical, social philosopher, and psychoanalyst who pushed the boundaries of psychoanalytic theory and social practice. Originating one of the dissident trends derived from Freudian psychoanalysis, Reich's early acclaim stemmed from his research on character analysis. Unlike his psychoanalytic contemporaries, Reich argued that attacking one's psychic resistances, rather than interpreting the contents of the unconscious, would help liberate people from their neuroses, inhibitions, and sexual anxieties. In the late 1920s, while a member of the Vienna Psychoanalytic Society and director of the Viennese Seminar for Psychotherapy, Reich identified a theory that he believed justified large-scale social action. As a radical interpreter of Freud's work, Reich contended that the suppression of sexual impulses in children and adolescents was responsible for neurosis. He claimed that this suppression was connected to authoritarian families and to authoritarian social structures. In order to foster liberation from this oppression, Reich encouraged young victims to resist and revolt against authoritarianism, thereby gaining sexual freedom and personal independence. His ideas were not well received outside Austria because his observations were a direct assault on the Nazi regime. His ideas were not well received inside Austria because he mixed psychoanalysis with politics. Both socialist and communist parties in Europe rejected his insights. He eventually emigrated to America, where a small but loyal following developed.

**Reification:**    Latin: *res* = thing. The process of treating some aspect of nature or society as a special thing in and of itself. The process of creating social reality. More generally, the process by which an epistemological category (an idea) becomes an ontological category (a thing, event, cause, god, team, family, or any other social category) via human action. When social relations are reified apart from human intentionality and human control, alienation occurs. Reification is necessary to create social lifeworlds but can be a serious problem if coerced and made permanent apart from changes in material conditions. Intentionality and sociality are necessary to construct a distinctly social lifeworld; that is, one that is not part of the natural world until human beings create it. The "self-fulfilling prophecy" is sometimes used to refer to the reification process. See "Demonization," "Profanation," "Sacred/Profane," and "Sanctification/De-Sanctification" for more.

**Relative Deprivation Theory:**    A theory that holds that people do not become outraged at injustice, inequality, or other deprivations as long as other people like them (to whom they compare themselves) are similarly exploited or deprived.

**Religion:**    Latin: *ligio* = I bind; *religio* = I bind back (together). Religion thus refers to any set of beliefs and/or practices that binds a people together. As most people use the word, it refers to a "theistic" religion. (See "Theology" for more.) There are billions of people who live in harmony with each other and with nature, absent a God concept. Buddhism, humanism, socialist humanism, and many forms of paganism "sanctify" but do not deify. (See "Sacred/Profane" and "Sanctification/De-Sanctification" for more.) In Marxian terms, religion is usually alienated self-consciousness. It is a situation in which people assign to a god or to a devil their own power for creating or destroying. More generally, religion is a set of principles by which human beings bring purpose and meaning into their own individual lives while guaranteeing (a sometimes limited) solidarity between individuals. See "Theology" for more.

**Rent:**    Land, as with labor, is treated as a commodity in capitalist systems. Rent is the price one pays to a nonproductive land owner for the land one occupies and for the space, fertility, location, and improvements on it.
    The notions of rent and a landlord's rights have their origins in feudal conquest. Lords claimed property rights to common land and began to charge people to live on and/or farm the land in question. In order for the farmer to use the land s/he worked a percentage (usually one third or so) must be paid out to a nonworking "owner." See "Dividends," "Exploitation, Super," and "Surplus Value" for more.

**Replacement Discourses:**    In postmodern sociology of knowledge, the pivotal task is to identify and validate discourses that more fully affirm those differences and ways of knowing that reflect our society, without invalidating those ways of knowing already in existence. In other words, the constitution of replacement discourses is not an attempt to privilege new, different, and oppositional approaches to knowledge at the expense of those that preceded them; rather, the humanistic project of articulating replacement discourses is to "widen the net" for knowing, experiencing, living, and being human. This project endeavors to validate the excluded voices of women, racial, and sexual minorities; the disabled and disenfranchised; and of all those collectives whose styles of existence, when spoken and embodied, encounter resistance, devaluation, and de-legitimacy. Theoretical efforts in this direction rely heavily on the contributions of Jacques Lacan, constitutive theory, feminist postmodern theory, Chaos and Complexity theory, and topology theory. See "Dialectical Pedagogy" for more.

**Replication:**   One of several methods to prove the truth value of a hypothesis that does not depend upon reason or rationality. If the repetition of a study yields the same results as a previous finding, the hypothesis is treated as if it were valid or more valid than before. This is an instance of conservative science, in that the eternalness of social relationships are assumed. When replication fails, the assumption is that the data are poorly measured rather than that social life is idiographic (in which case differing findings both could be valid). Chaos theory and nonlinear dynamics teach us that complex systems never exactly repeat themselves.

**Repression:**   The process by which unacceptable views and actions are excluded from a social lifeworld. A given social paradigm is constructed and maintained by law, religion, morality, and socialization and re-socialization. Authorities use a wide range of punishments (sanctions), from moral condemnation to editing, "correcting," ignoring, as well as the judicious use of rewards. Control over the means to produce meaning (the media) is a major approach in modern repressive technique.

**Repression, Surplus:**   In Freudian analysis, repression refers to the process by which some sexual energy is "sublimated" (transferred) in order to meet the demands of work, social, and intellectual life. Herbert Marcuse pointed out that in a society of alienating work, a surplus amount of repression, over and above that required to reproduce social life, had to be enforced in order to keep the worker doing the same boring, meaningless work in the service of private capital. Then, too, joy, delight, compassion, friendship, and community must be repressed if people are to be treated as faceless others in school, work, church, marketplace, or politics. See "Reproduction (of Society)" for more.

**Reproduction of Labor Power:**   See Labor Power, Reproduction of.

**Reproduction (of Society):**   The process by which existing social roles, role-sets, groups, institutions, and allied culture are renewed from generation to generation. Parents, teachers, priests/preachers, judges, and peers tend to reproduce the beliefs, feelings, and behaviors essential to a social lifeworld. Managers, technicians, professionals, and artists embody rules, use instruments, do science, and create art that tends to repeat existing social relationships. Similar to a printing press producing carbon copies of a given information set, those in the reproduction sector do not produce or circulate goods but do valuable work for the capitalist class by establishing systems of control, administering them, and justifying them to the masses. From the Marxist perspective, society should be produced by insightful competent humans rather than reproduced by specialists or by coercion. See "Repression, Surplus" for more.

**Represent/Representation:**    Modernists and premodernists assume that it is possible to treat one thing the same as another; that is, each thing "represents" the other without loss of meaning or quality. Postmodernists say this act is impossible. For example, each act of marriage is different from every other, such that one cannot use the idea of a given marriage as a standard to which all others must conform. Further, given the great variety of people in a congressional district, no one elected official can "represent" the public without violating the needs and interests of some or most of the residents. And finally, a theory cannot be precise enough to represent each and every instance of the events that the theory purports to explain/describe. See "Postmodern Philosophy of Science" for more.

**Republican, As a Form of Government:**    Republican forms of government require periodic elections of representatives who then decide all matters of public policy. It is not to be confused with democracy, which calls for direct participation in policymaking.

**Restorative Justice:**    A humanistic philosophy of crime and justice. Restorative justice seeks to restore the victim, the offender, and the community. Restorative justice models promote victim offender mediation and victim offender reconciliation programs. Restorative justice supports humanism and humanistic ideals by endeavoring to restore the dignity and integrity of all parties harmed through the criminal act. These parties include the victim, the offender, and the community. Victim offender mediation and victim offender reconciliation programs are healing dialogues in which all parties in a given dispute speak about what happened and move to some form of restitution with the assistance of a mediator. Cf. "Rehabilitation" and "Retribution."

**Retribution:**    A conservative philosophy of crime and justice. Retribution refers to the conviction that people act freely, knowingly, are blameworthy, and, thus, should be accountable for their criminal actions. Retributionists are skeptical that offenders can be rehabilitated. The justice system functions as a mechanism for ensuring that punishment is swift, sure, and, where necessary, severe. The emphasis of the retributive model is on punishing the offender. Thus, the punishment that one receives should fit the crime and its severity. See "Just Deserts" and "Justice, Retributive" for more. Cf. "Rehabilitation" and "Restorative Justice."

**Reversal of Hierarchies:**   See "Derrida, Jacques."

**Revisionism:**   A pejorative term used by the Right and the Left to denigrate theories, views, and analysis with which they disagree. When the Left rewrites the history of slavery, warfare, or gender relations to credit slaves, colonies, or women with positive qualities, the Right uses the term. When orthodox Marxism is challenged or modified, the Left uses the term as a way to discredit such work.

**Revisionism, Theory of:**   Rosa Luxemburg identifies three major elements in revisionist practice on the Left: (1) reformist programs defined by the limits of what is possible within capitalist ideology; (2) a subordination of socialist theory to tactics; and (3) opportunism and willingness to stop agitation in order to win concessions. Such an agreement eliminates the threat of militant opposition to capitalist control. Luxemburg's point is that practice must be guided by revolutionary theory or else it degenerates into liberalism. Revolutionary theory always includes an emphasis on class oppression, class struggle, social revolution, and communism.

**Revolution:**   In the context of Marxist thought, the term refers to a radical transformation of the totality of a society, not just a change in the political or economic sphere. A socialist revolution means a radical abolition of old social relations and their replacement by new and more humane relations supportive of praxis and community. The five great structures of domination are the targets of revolution. Changing only one of them is inadequate to the making of a socialist revolution. See "Class," "Gender," "Marxism," and "Racism" for more.

**Revolution, Theory of:**   In formal Marxian terms, revolution occurs: (1) when there is exploitation; (2) when the workers are concentrated in a mass; (3) when there is communication between workers; (4) when there is leadership; and (5) when there is a coherent analysis to guide action. There are two distinctly different pathways to revolution in Marxian writings. First, there is the "immiseration thesis"; it says that revolutions come along when things get bad. Second, there is the thesis that says the revolution will be led by skilled and competent workers who have enough education, energy, and free time to think and to act on their class interests. See "Lenin, Vladimir" and "Luxemburg, Rosa" for more.

**Revolutionary Base:**   Which group(s) will make the revolution is a question central to all socialist, feminist, and emancipatory strategy. Karl Marx held that the working class would be the social base of the revolution, for the following reasons: (1) It alone can stop production; (2) it makes up the majority of the population; (3) its existence is a negation of species-being; and (4) only the interests of the working class correspond to the general interest. Interests of other classes, represented as the general interest, lead to only "political" revolution; that is, a change in the elite that rules. At the Nineteenth Congress of the French Communist Party, changes in the structure of the working class were recognized. The working class also includes salaried employees such as researchers, engineers, lower-level bureaucratic functionaries, technicians, specialists, experts, and others who reproduce capital. There is debate in socialist circles today whether: (1) such people are workers or petty bourgeois; (2) whether they will play a decisive role in making the revolution; and (3) what is the proper organizational structure to use, given the proper analysis with which to make the revolution.

**Revolutionary Practice:**   It is a Marxist view that revolutionary practice emerged not only from political struggle but from the work process. In *Capital*, Karl Marx presented the idea of evolution in praxis: from laboring activity to revolutionary activity to self-managing activity in post-capitalist society. An important part of the revolutionary process is not only the destruction of capitalist relations but also the transformation of the human nature of the revolutionaries and workers themselves. In the "Third Thesis," Marx emphasizes that it is essential to educate the educator. One must change not only the material conditions of society but also human nature itself, in a complex process of advances and reverses.

**Rhetoric:**   The artful presentation of an idea using verbal symbols. This was the classical meaning of the term. In modern usage, it has come to mean artificial and empty explanations, to be contrasted with serious, rigorous scientific inquiry and findings. Postmodernists hold that all writings and talks are rhetoric in the classical sense. As such, all texts should be seen as open, personal, and incapable of imposing ideological hegemony.

**Rhizome:**   A concept developed by the social theory work of Gilles Deleuze and Félix Guattari. The rhizome is a continuous line of variation (logic). An ant colony, for example, is a rhizome, and so is a field of grass (as opposed to a tree). The term refers to the process of sense making in speech whereby desire seeks embodiment through and attachment to words reflecting one's unique understanding of the world. Thus, the rhizome is a line of flight. It functions as an indeterminate journey; it is one that is never fully complete. The flow of speech, following the rhizome, is nonlinear. The chain of speech is a semiotic flow of desire always insisting and making its presence felt, always awaiting anchorage amidst other lines of variation. See "Deleuze, Gilles" and "Guattari, Félix" for more.

**Ricardo, David (1772–1823):**   A British economist who presented the labor theory of value that Marx adopted and modified. A socialist movement, in which Ricardo, Robert Owen, and Jeremy Bentham are combined to critique capitalism and to suggest reorganization of production and distribution of wealth, bears his name.

**Right:**    Latin: *rectus* = straight. The term has two different meanings. First, it usually is associated with conservative or elitist partisans: the Right. Second, in philosophy, it refers to the basis for claiming/grounding a practice or policy. See "Right, Philosophy of" for more.

**Right, Philosophy of:**    St. Thomas Aquinas held that the meaning of the terms "right" and "wrong" were based upon both reason and eternally valid laws of nature and society. Both terms were given meaning by the Christian God. Jean-Jacques Rousseau held that the terms were conventional and that their meaning rested upon the consent of the people. G.W.F. Hegel held that the law of abstract right was that one should be a person and respect others as persons. According to Hegel, persons could not be possessed as property or treated as objects. "Right" does not allow one to pursue private goals that diminish others or that oppose what Hegel calls universal will. Hegel assumed that there is a universal tendency (or will) on the part of both the world and the plan (given by a watchmaker God concept) according to which the world unfolds to evolve toward perfect embodiment of rational understanding.

One of the most troublesome questions in affirmative postmodern social philosophy is how to define human rights without appealing to universal and absolute standards. The postmodern aim is to protect variety and difference on the one side while working toward social justice, basic equality in social processes, and resisting oppression of elitist, sexist, racist, cultural claims on the other. See "Right" for more.

**Right-Wing Communism:**    Those who tend to emphasize the inexorable movement toward the collapse of capitalism apart from intentionality. Critics charge right-wing communists with overestimating the role of material conditions in revolution and downplaying the role of bourgeois ideology in mystifying and repressing the masses.

**Rising Expectations, Revolution of:**    A thesis that political problems in capitalism originate from the increasing expectations of people who have been liberated from poverty—in contrast to the view that political discord arises from the faults of the system itself. It is the success of capitalism rather than its failing that is said to be the source of unrest. It follows that the solution to unrest is more capitalism (and less government interference) rather than less capitalism.

**Rite of Passage:**    A ceremony in which a given social status is assigned to a person or stripped away. In most societies, children do not have social standing until they are first accepted as part of the human population in some birthing ceremony and, later, as part of the social base in a ritual. Part of the reason community is lost in mass society is that there are no rites of passage for young people. Capitalism avoids social relationships, and therefore rites of passage are unnecessary.

**Role Dispossession:**   A process by which a social identity is erased from the self-system. Degradation, debasement, and demoralization are rough equivalents of this term.

**Role Distance:**   Behavior by which a person communicates his/her lack of full commitment to the status-role at hand. Role distance is most apparent when one is in a role that is oppressive but, for some reason, cannot walk away from it. The best place to observe role distance in everyday life is in a large classroom or in any mass institution.

**Role-Set:**   A shared social form created by the interaction of two or more persons. Each person actively creates the social identity as well as the role of all others by complex and subtle responses to the presentations of those defined as significant to the occasion at hand. Each role-set is composed of general guides to action that are publicly known or taught to new members. All role-sets are mediated by larger social structures (e.g., class, race, and legal structures). A given role-set may be simple (e.g., a friendship) or complex (e.g., a medical unit in a hospital).

**Role-Taking:**   The process of looking at things from the perspective of another human being in the process of organizing social facts. The basic human activity by which transaction and intersubjective knowledge develops, role-taking is often aborted in power relationships. The subordinate is expected to sense every nuance of intentionality of the more powerful, and the more powerful cares little about the subordinate's intentions and interests, in that some resistance to one's directives is expected. Role-taking produces a knowledge of the "inside" principles, values, and sensitivities of another person.

**Role Theory:**   A set of assumptions about how human behavior is generated and ordered. The basic assumption is that the role-sets in a society account for most human behavior, from sexual activity to crime, as well as the more ordinary forms of behavior seen in a society. This view stands in contrast to biological theories of behavior that locate the sources of human behavior in genes and/or physical needs. The radical implication is that unsocial forms of behavior can be modified by reorganizing society rather than by individual therapy or imprisonment. The role is composed of at least two parts: an actor and a role-other; sometimes called ego and alter-ego. The radical implication is that self and society are twinborn. People cease being purely individuals when actively taking a role, since role always implies role-other. For example, the notion of a professor without a student is absurd. See "Social Role" for more.

**Rousseau, Jean-Jacques (1712–1778):**   French social philosopher whose writings are credited with shaping the French Revolution and the U.S. Constitution. He argued that the natural differences between people are exaggerated as societies develop, since the lawmaking process is used by the powerful to increase power and wealth; that art and science become corrupted as inequality grows, since service to the powerful, and not virtue, commands all rewards; that the state of savagery is no better than the will of the powerful since humans have not achieved humanity. Humanity is achieved in simple community, via a social contract in which both personal will and community will are respected. The common will is not to be found in the sum of all individual wills but rather in the sovereign or in the state (a public body personified by either). (See the work of W. L. Reese.)

**Routine Activities, Theory of:**   A theory of crime that emphasizes the interaction of three dimensions: (1) likely and motivated offenders (e.g., drug-dependent welfare recipients); (2) suitable targets (e.g., accessible and easily moveable goods); and (3) a lack of mechanisms to prevent or inhibit the would-be offender from violating the law (e.g., an absence of positive role model peers). Crime rates increase depending on the type of consumable goods that are easily transferable and on the absence of individuals to prevent those targets from being taken. Cf. "Rational Choice, Theory of." See "Criminology" for more.

Critical assessment of routine activities theory argues that the theory too simplistically reduces crime to routine patterns of play, recreation, and work time that trigger, at their intersection, motivated offenders, worthwhile targets, and the lack of guardians. Critical attention is drawn to larger structural dynamics—including illiteracy, joblessness, underemployment, poverty, and so on—that are ignored or under-examined by routine activities theory. Chaos theory questions whether patterns of social living are as predictable as routine activity theorists contend. Chaos theory argues that unpredictability and disorder are very much a part of human social behavior. See "Chaos Theory" and "Rational Choice, Theory of" for more.

**Ruge, Arnold (1802–1880):**   A radical democrat who served six years in prison for his political views. Ruge published various radical journals and other periodicals in which the early writings of Karl Marx appeared. It was through Ruge's efforts that Marx laid the foundation for a critical sociology with the maxim, "Engage in the relentless criticism of everything existent."

**Ruling Class:**   Refers to a loose assortment of capitalists and state functionaries who make the basic decisions in capitalist countries. Industrialists, financiers, agribusiness executives, large retail interests, and mass media have many conflicting interests but they share a common understanding that low costs and high profits are the objectives of capitalism. They work together or in tacit agreement to oppose anything that threatens profit/cost structures. Sometimes the leading capitalists get together via the Committee on Economic Development, which meets yearly. Often, a few corporations that dominate a market will have agreements about price and regional market divisions. Many corporations try to eliminate competition between themselves and encourage it among their customers and opponents. In this context, a "free market" means that customers are unorganized, and a "free world" means that capitalists are free to seek profit. See "Power-Elite Thesis" for more.

# S

**Sacred/Profane:**   A dichotomy (two-fold concept) in which people sanctify, honor, esteem, cherish, and worship part of humanity and/or the natural world (sacred) while treating the rest of the population and/or nature as though it had nothing but exchange-value (profane). Thus, some people sanctify trees, animals, and/or rivers, whereas others see them only as objects to be used, abused, ignored, or destroyed. See "Commodification" "Reification," and "Religion" for more.

**Saint-Simon, Claude Henri, Count (1760–1825):**   Saint-Simon renounced his royal title and worked toward the elimination of poverty and empowerment of the masses. He introduced the concept of positivism (Auguste Comte was his secretary) and held science to be the vehicle for social justice and social peace. He suggested a tripartite governance system: (1) a Chamber of Invention consisting of artists and engineers who would draw up policy proposals; (2) a Chamber of Examination in which scientists would evaluate the proposals; and (3) a Chamber of Deputies composed of industrialists who would implement the policies for the common good. He called for a secular religion centered on ethics and brotherhood and stripped of its gods and dogmas. Comte took much from Saint-Simon. (See the work of W. L. Reese.)

**Sanctification/De-sanctification:**   Those who work out of a premodern religious framework treat some persons, places, or activities as holy. Others are de-sanctified or treated as profane. Modern sensibility tends to treat all efforts to sanctify or de-sanctify as primitive thinking. In postmodern theology, sanctification is a social process by which great value is assigned to a people, some part (or all) of nature, and/or a social process. There can be no social life at all without sanctification. To treat everything as profane is to destroy the very foundation of social life. Not even capitalism or modern science would be possible without a set of values to which the scientist or the worker gave her/his rare capacity for faith, belief, hope, and trust. See "Criminalization/De-Criminalization," "Medicalization," "Profanation," "Reification," "Religion," and "Theology" for more.

**Sanction:**   A positive or negative reward for behavior. It is a means by which behavior can be externally controlled. Sanctioning first requires that positive or negative content be given to the item used as a sanction. Rewards and most punishments are useful as sanctions only if people take them to be such. This definition is secured by a number of tactics in socialization activity, but ultimately it is grounded in belief, faith, and understanding. Jürgen Habermas holds that normative behavior is being displaced by such external stimuli: "Indirect control of the masses through fabricated stimuli has increased, especially in the areas of putative subjective freedom such as electoral, consumer, and leisure behavior."

**Sartre, Jean-Paul (1905–1980):**   A French postmodern philosopher best known for his work on existentialism. Sartre held that human beings had a much greater freedom than most believe and that it was bad faith and/or self-exculpation to refuse/fail to act on that freedom. Human beings invent a "human nature" for themselves and then act as if it were natural and inevitable (existence precedes essence). Human beings thus negate the nothingness of the world by acting (don't forget, they/we could act otherwise). Since God is dead, we must invent our own values and standards in life. God is a name for our desire to bring order and stability out of ceaseless change and the somethingness we create out of the nothingness we find. Sartre said to invent yourself and to do so "with all your heart." Sartre also said that when we choose, "we choose for all mankind." This dictum is akin to Immanuel Kant's notion of the moral imperative. (See the work of W. L. Reese.) See "Existentialism" for more.

**Satanism:**   A set of beliefs and practices in which opposition to the hegemony of the patriarchal God concept is embodied. As the story has it, some angels were jealous of the power of God and rose up against Him only to be cast out of heaven. Still active, these fallen angels are said to tempt people (especially women) into denial of and opposition to God and to God's plan.

Today, satanism refers to the activity of people in support of various cults. Many cults mock Christian ceremonies and icons in their own practices. Other cults—such as neo-Nazi groups, youth gangs, heavy metal followers—deliberately rely upon images of death, destruction, disease, and so on as part of their indoctrination ceremonies.

Critics argue that satanic cults inflict untold emotional and psychological trauma/abuse upon impressionable youth who run away or are otherwise abandoned until adopted and initiated into the cult by its loyal members. Cf. "Moral Panic" and "Witchcraft" for more.

**Saussure, Ferdinand de (1857–1913):**   Architect of structural linguistics. In his posthumously published text, *Course in General Linguistics*, Saussure demonstrated how language could be studied based on existing laws of reasoning, without reference to its historical properties or evolution.

For Saussure, the sign was interactively constituted by the acoustic-visual image (signifier) along with a conceptual or meaning-based component (the signified). Saussure argued that all language is a system of signs in which ideas (signifiers) receive content (signifiers) in the act of naming them. This activity, however, was viewed by Saussure as essentially arbitrary. In other words, given the signifier-signified relationship, there was no inherent link between the two other than what people assigned to them. For example, an object that contains liquid in it (signified) is termed a glass (signifier); however, one has no intrinsic relationship to the other. This naming is a cultural artifact and nothing more. Saussure did believe, however, that the signifier stood in a stable, anchored relationship to its signified counterpart. See "Semiotics" for more.

Saussure's work is significant to poststructuralists and postmodern theorists who argue that social reality in all its varied facets is known arbitrarily and conventionally. Thus, since they are mediated through language, identity, art, politics, body, culture, psyche, and so on are all arbitrary and convenient contrivances. See "Postmodernism" and "Poststructuralism" for more. Cf. "Structuralism."

**Scapegoat:**    In Marxist usage, it refers to that sector of society in which all sources of evil are said to arise (the Jews, the clergy, the nobility, the monopolists) so that emancipation from this sector appears as a general emancipation. For Karl Marx, social evil resides in the obstacles to praxis and community rather than in the person or in a sector of the population. One does not get rid of the class structure by hanging capitalists but by changing the system.

**Science:**    The word means "to know." It usually refers to the methods and the bodies of knowledge by which we come to know about the world. Scientific activity is a social activity in which all of the assumptions and conflicts of that society are present. See "Science, Modern," "Science, Premodern," and "Science, Postmodern" for more.

**Science, Modern:**    A body of knowledge that holds that there are abstract "laws" that describe the ways in which nature and society operate. Modern science (i.e., the knowledge developed in the tradition of Isaac Newton) presumes precise and objective dynamics. Modern science has helped improve diet, health, transportation, communication, and construction. However, it sets order and tight causality as the normal behavior of all social, economic, biological, and physical systems. See "Science" for more.

**Science, Postmodern:**    Postmodern philosophy of science makes a place for variety, difference, unpredictable change, and disorder generally. It argues that the knowledge process has many pathways to truth and wisdom, that only short-term truth statements are possible for complex systems.

Feminist standpoint epistemology teaches us that there are many different and valid standpoints from which to "know" how a system works and should work. Karl Marx made the point that one's consciousness varies with one's position in the social structure. Both feminist and Marxist epistemologies contribute to a postmodern philosophy of science. See "Chaos Theory," "Logic," and "Science" for more.

**Science, Premodern:**  Premodern knowledge processes use trust, belief, faith, and hope to engage the reality construction process. These social psychological activities convert prophecies into social practices, social relationships, and social institutions. Premodern knowledge processes are fundamental to all others, including modern and postmodern science. See "Science" for more.

**Second International:**  A socialist organization that advocated gradual evolution toward communism via social democracy. It replaced the First International in 1899 and lasted until 1991. It gave rise to the welfare policies found in many European states. Liebknecht, Bebel, and Bernstein were among its leaders.

**Second Law (of Thermodynamics):**  A statement that generalizes the tendency of all systems to decay. In formal terms the "law" specifies that all systems tend to their most probable state. The most probable state is disorder, entropy, chaos, or random rather than ordered relationship. It is an improbable event that six molecules or six people will be in the same place at the same time with one and only one pattern of organization relating them. The secret to order is that there are "segregating" mechanisms, each of which "constrain" or reduce part of the improbability. For human systems, those segregating mechanisms are rules, roles, values, goals, and social relationships.

**Sect:**  A voluntary religious association in which all members are expected to engage in the production of religious culture irrespective of age. The structure is seldom bureaucratic; leaders are usually lay persons, and often leadership is distributed broadly over the congregation. Sects arise in mass, depersonalized societies and in times of trouble. Often they are separatist and resist integration into mass society. Sects ordinarily are founded on spiritual rebirth and a renewed interest in community and praxis. The means of production are held (not "owned") in common, and production is used communally to produce culture (not profit). The Amish, the Branch Davidians (Adventists), the Hutterites, the Quakers, and the Unitarians are examples of a sect. Cf. "Church."

**Self, Social:**  The sum of all the social identities presented by an individual and validated by others in specific and differing social occasions. Self and society exist simultaneously. One has no "self" until one is socialized to a particular social identity; that is, until one presents that identity (by behavioral means) and until some other person defined as significant honors and responds to that presentation. Thus, the concept of the mother without the child or the professor without the student is a nonsense notion. This definition disagrees with the Anglo-Saxon concept of the self as a thing having its own, independent nature, such that there is a "true" self to be discovered and used to mediate one's own behavior. See "Goffman, Erving," "Mead, George Herbert," and "Mind" for more.

**Self-Determination:**   A moment of praxis wherein a person acts with purpose and insight, as opposed to coercion and necessity. Subjective participation is stressed, as opposed to objectifying subjects. Cf. "Agency, Human."

**Self-Estrangement:**   According to Karl Marx, commodity labor forced the worker to be concerned with him/herself to the exclusion of species-being, and the process by which humans grasp their own humanity as a collective (as a brother/sisterhood) is destroyed by wage labor. In capitalism, people take themselves as the object of their thought when they think of "self." However, the essence of social being is that the object of such thought is not the isolated individual but, rather, that collective humanity that one treats as one's own essential nature.

**Self-Fulfilling Prophecy:**   The process by which things defined as real become real. Labeling theory holds that identifying young people as criminals produces a social reaction in which they are treated as criminal by others, come to view themselves as criminals, and do all sorts of illicit things as a consequence. The same is true of priests, prostitutes, physicians, professors, lawyers, and mothers. The point is that belief in the truth of a thing does help it come true. Self-fulfilling prophecy is a remarkable characteristic of social reality not found in physical systems. See "Pygmalion Studies" and "Social Magic" for more.

**Self-Realization:**   In praxis, it is that experience in which one realizes the full wealth of one's human capacities. It is an event profoundly pleasurable for its own sake, no matter how much energy and effort it might require, no matter how great or small the secondary rewards, such as fame, wealth, or success. In self-realization, the labor of the individual in producing material, ideological, and/or political culture results in positive or negative response from others. Without that response, one has no way of knowing if one exists, nor the quality of that existence. Thus, self-realization requires sociality.

**Semantics:**   A science dealing with the sources of and vehicles for conveying meaning between two or more human beings. Some people claim that words have intrinsic and universal meaning. Others contend that they are conventional and are used loosely, that the exchange of information requires an open semantic system. Cf. "Semiotics."

**Semiotics:**   Greek: *sema* = a mark; *otikos* = study of. Semiotics is the study of language understood as "signs." All words, phrases, gestures, or cues—all communication spoken or written—are signs. All language systems are themselves various sign systems (e.g., engineering, computers, accounting, gangs, prison inmates). Semioticians study the evolving meanings communicated through speech or through a text. For example, the word "gay" refers to someone who is lively or animated or to someone who is homosexual. More specifically, however, the interpretation of "gay" as someone who is homosexual has itself undergone a significance, a change, of meaning. As recently as twenty years ago, referring to someone as gay was insulting, derisive, and, if true, would result in ostracism and social disgrace. Today, however, we speak of "Gay Pride" or "Gay Awareness," indicating that to be gay (i.e., homosexual) is something to feel good about, something to celebrate. Semioticians not only study how the meaning of words evolves (e.g., from "gay" meaning that someone is animated to meaning that someone is a homosexual) but also examine how the specific meanings have changed attitudinally over time (e.g., homosexuality as horrible versus homosexuality as wonderful). See "Accenting the Sign," "Barthes, Roland," "Code," "Encoding," "Floating Signifiers," "Saussure, Ferdinand de," "Sign," "Sign System," "Signifying Chain," "Trope," and "Wittgenstein, Ludwig" for more. Cf. "Semantics."

**Sensual/Sensuality:**   Sensualists place equal or prior value on the senses, vis-à-vis reason. Enjoyment of taste, touch, smell, and sexuality are to be encouraged rather than repressed in the name of God or in the effort to transform people into workers who do not feel, love, hate, or enjoy their work or their roles in life. Sigmund Freud held that some erotic drive should be suppressed and rechanneled into productive labor, else nothing would get done in the pursuit of pleasure. Others, such as Herbert Marcuse, have argued that the senses need emancipation as much as does reason.

**Serf:**   A member of a caste required to perform agricultural labor for a "nobility." In feudalism, serfs are bound to the land and are treated as property. People are created as serfs by a coercive legal system. Serfdom and slavery are precapitalist ways to support a leisure class by extracting the surplus value of labor from farm and craft workers. The modern version is the contract labor system in agribusiness, except that under the contract system there is no security if one is sick, crippled, or if there is no work to be done. See "Peasant" for more.

**Sexism:**   A complex set of assumptions holding that women are suited for a secondary role in the creation of culture. To keep women in their "place," men are given social power within the marriage relationship, economic power in the inheritance of property, moral power through religious ideas, and authority to use physical power to ensure compliance to male hegemony. Those who support patriarchy appeal to biological attributes, as well, in justifying sexist status-role ascription and, thus, claim that it is rational. Although individual differences may be relatively great, differences between men and women as categories are small in terms of strength, intelligence, creativity, assertiveness, and other crucial factors. One cannot judge the ability of one woman or man in terms of the averages of a group of men or women. See "Abuse, Spousal," "Anti-Semitism," "Demonization," and "Gender" for more.

**Sexism (and Capitalism):**    Capitalism tends to dismantle ancient structures of privilege in the quest for markets and lower wages; age, sex, and racial discrimination offer both. At the same time, the reproduction of gender inequality is helpful to capitalism since there is always a pool of cheaper labor with which to drive down the wages of all. In the *Communist Manifesto*, Karl Marx noted that differences in age and sex no longer have any distinctive social validity for the working class; all people are instruments of labor, more or less expensive to use. The call is for men and women, blacks and whites, young and old to unite and end the divisions that capitalists can and do use against them.

**Sexuality:**    The socialist position on sexuality is that sexual activity is a natural and important human activity. It is not to be treated casually or used as an instrument of manipulation or for private gain. It is to be used as an affirmation and definition of a cherished social relationship. People are not to be treated as objects, nor are they to be treated as property. Sexual caress and response are personal matters to be settled between individuals without coercion or anxious guilt. Sexual activity may occur within marriage as an institution or outside of it, but this does not mean that marriage is to be taken lightly or that there is no mutual responsibility involved in sexual activity.

The critical position is that sexual experimentation of young persons is to be encouraged; however, young people are vulnerable in their doubt over and concern for their sexuality. Therefore, they should not be exploited. Critical advocates promote gay and lesbian sexual orientation, bisexuality, transgendered sexuality, and so on and regard issues of sexual identity as significant to emancipating persons who are socially/economically marginalized.

In capitalist societies, the chief concern of socialists is commodity sex and the use of sex to dispose of surplus production. See "Emancipation of the Senses" for more.

Considerable debate centers around whether "sexual identity" is a matter of personal choice or whether it is biologically determined. In the former instance, some feminists argue that sexual identity is a function of cultural politics. See "Irigaray, Luce" for more. Cf. "Queer Theory."

**Sexual Psychopathy:**   There are many forms of harmful sexual behavior, from clothing fetishism to rape and the sexual exploitation of children. According to Sigmund Freud, pathologies arise from repression of sexuality, which, in turn, comes from the incest taboo. The incest taboo splits male sexuality into tenderness and affection (directed toward mother) and lust and carnality (directed toward objectified females: cunt, piece, ass, whore, etc.). Freud held the incest taboo to be necessary in order to channel some sexual energy into work.

Herbert Marcuse held that sexual repression and joyful sexuality vary with patriarchy and that if work were as creative and delightful as play, sexual repression would not be necessary, love and tenderness would be reunited with sensuality, and sexual activity would not be split into "higher" and "lower" modes.

**Shame:**   A internal psychological judgment that one has violated a basic value, rule, law, or more of the society in which that person lives and to which s/he has been socialized. Shame is a private psychological state, whereas guilt is a public, social judgment. Shame carries great negative emotional content and renders a person less likely to do that deed or say that thing again. See "Guilt" for more.

**Sign:**   In semiotic terminology, all words or phrases, whether written or spoken, are signs. A sign is that which stands for something other or something more than the word or phrase itself as perceived by an observer. The sign is composed of two elements: the "signifier" and the "signified." Signifiers are the words or phrases themselves (e.g., car, house, gravely disabled). The signified is the content of the signifier; that is, the meaning assigned to the signifier (e.g., a mode of transportation, a place in which to keep warm, a person who is homeless). Thus, the sign is the relationship between the signifier and the signified. See "Accenting the Sign," "Code," "Decode," "Floating Signifiers," "Hyperreality," "Semiotics," "Sign System," and "Trope" for more. Cf. "Barthes, Roland," "Peirce, Charles S.," "Saussure, Ferdinand de," and "Wittgenstein, Ludwig."

**Significant Others:**   Those persons who are defined as important and worthy of mutual influence in creating a given line of meaning and activity. Usually role-others are defined as situationally significant. One must permit those defined as significant to help shape self and consciousness. The concept of the nonperson helps one understand the term. Who is defined as a "significant other" is a political matter.

**Signifying Chain:**   In postmodern semiotic terminology, this is a reference to the speech act. Originally developed by the structural linguist, Ferdinand de Saussure, the speech chain identifies the process of what is communicated. The speech chain can be conceptualized on the basis of the interactive effects of the *paradigm* (individually selected words) *syntagm* (clustering of words as sentences) semiotic axis. On the vertical axis (paradigm), discourse (realm of *parole*) is chosen from a community of language (realm of *la langue*). The paradigmatic component of the axis provides a range of options from which we may select. For example, when describing the temperature outside we might invoke the descriptors "cool," "cold," "frigid," or "freezing." The syntagm represents the horizontal component of this semiotic axis. The syntagm is the grouping of words together (i.e., the actual speech chain as articulated). Thus, in ordinary intersubjective communication, we select words (paradigms) and arrange or order them into a particular phrase or series of sentences (syntagms). The overlapping and interdependent effect of the axis creates an ephemeral and imaginary space where meaning (much like a slow moving film) is constructed and conveyed to the receiver of the message. See "Semiotics" for more.

**Sign System:**   In semiotic terminology, not only are all words, phrases, gestures, and so on signs but entire fields of knowledge are themselves sign systems. The language of law is a sign system. The language of culinary art is a sign system. The language of mortuary science is a sign system. All grammars or systems of communication are themselves represented by words and phrases that, when taken as a whole, stand for something more or something other than the words or phrases themselves. See "Semiotics" and "Sign" for more.

**Simmel, Georg (1858–1918):**   German philosopher and sociologist. Simmel was the son of a Jewish businessman who became a Roman Catholic. His mother was of Jewish ancestry but a practicing Lutheran. Simmel studied folk psychology, the history of art, and philosophy at the University of Berlin. He experienced difficulty in academic circles, mostly due to his Jewish heritage, his "casual" brilliance, and his anti-professorial, though aristocratic, intellect. He nonetheless was offered and accepted a chair appointment at the University of Strassburg, which he held from 1914 until he died of cancer in 1918.

Some people claim that Simmel was the founder of modern sociology. Others contend that he developed no systematic sociological theory and, thus, was merely an insightful stylist. His contributions to the study of social forms and to the sociology of art represent a comprehensive and significant conceptual model.

Simmel argued that the principle of living represented a continual process of becoming: a creative engagement or flow with forms. The individual gives meaning to these forms (e.g., education, culture, religion). Thus, for Simmel, life takes on substance through objects or forms.

Simmel also developed a theory related to money. A money economy both directly and indirectly advances the growth of the individual. For example, through money, large groups or collectives can be formed with identified purposes. However, money also substitutes economic transactions for personal expressions. Simmel saw a close relationship between the money economy, rationality, and natural science. Each is driven by estimation, precision, and calculation.

Simmel studied group cohesion and social group formation. This study further advanced his sociology of interdependence or relationalism. Simmel argued that money, similar to groups, possessed no inherent value. The activity of exchanging objects or the material forms through which money was exchanged imbued money with value. Social groups have meaning not as existing structures or forms but through the interaction of their participants. Cf. "Functionalism" and "Marxism."

**Simulacrum:**   Following Jean Baudrillard and nihilistic postmodern theory, simulacra (plural of simulacrum) are the words or phrases that remain after the compression, conflation, and collapsing of illusion and reality. Simulacra simultaneously reject authentic representation and artificial contrivance. Both presume that phenomena "really" exist. Postmodern existence is a deliberate blurring of reality and appearance, form and image, authenticity and illusion. All that is left behind are the words or phrases (simulacra) themselves. They express social living. They are understood to be more real than the real itself. See "Baudrillard, Jean," "Cyberspace," "Mass Media," "Simulation," "Text," and "Value, Postmodern View of" for more.

**Simulation:**   A copy for which no original exists. Think of the perfect son, woman, student, or priest. There are no "originals" against which other sons, women, students, or priests might be compared and evaluated. Since there are no originals, there can be no "copies" either. Copies need some objective, authentic reality against which to be measured. We come to knowledge through representations of the "real." These are simulations. Our knowledge of the O. J. Simpson double-murder trial, for example, was based on a series of simulations: media-crafted images that constructed a portrait of a man (Simpson) whom we had no direct, tangible, tactile relationship to. He was not "real" to us, and, thus, the media images were not authentic copies either. See "Baudrillard, Jean," "Hyperreality," "Mass Media," "Simulacrum," and "Value, Postmodern View of" for more.

**Sin, Original:**   A story that says human beings were once innocent but tasted the fruit of the tree of knowledge and lost both innocence and the capacity to know of God's goodness, mercy, truth, justice, and compassion. In ancient Hebrew stories now recorded in the Bible, Havva (Eve) gave Adam the fruit, and he took it. They were then cast out of Eden, a primeval utopia. This story is important as an explanation of evil that has psychological rather than social origins and that represents a justification of male gender privilege. Original sin was part of the process by which female gods were degraded and replaced by male gods some 4,000 or more years ago. See "Theology, Feminist" for more.

**Site/Space:**   Not a definable/identifiable place but, rather, a concept with which to mark topics or problems studied, or, perhaps, an opportunity to think about things not yet imagined.

**Skepticism:**   A critical stance that holds that all existing ideas are open to discussion and revision. Some skeptics doubt the possibility of truth and thus join nihilistic postmodernity.

**Slavery:**   An economic system in which some people claim ownership to the person and labor of other people. They claim a right to use, abuse, and to take the fruits of that labor. Slavery is composed of two separate and un-equal strata; the slave-masters and the slaves. Force and ideology combine to maintain slavery. Color has little to do with this economic form. For ex-ample, Vikings took slaves back from England and France on their raids; the Chinese took slaves in war or bought children from poor Chinese to serve as slaves; the Cherokee nation held slaves long before Columbus helped transform slavery into a global market; and many kingdoms in Africa took people home to serve as slaves. Slavery is an economic rela-tionship, not a personal relationship dependent upon skin color or intelli-gence.

**Smith, Adam (1723–1790):**   Scottish economist and moral philosopher who located ethical behavior in "sympathy," an ability to enter into the sit-uation of others. Whereas sympathy leads to ethical behavior, self-interest leads each person to seek his/her own economic advantage directed by an "invisible hand," which, in turn, contributes to the general welfare. Smith advocated both productive labor and a free market as sources of the com-mon good. The idea of a free market was emancipatory at the time, since it was set against control of licenses and royalties demanded by kings from both manufacturers and merchants. Smith was influenced by Turgot, a French economist/physiocrat who tried to free commerce and industry from control by kings and guilds. (See "Physiocrats/Physiocracy" for more.) Most modern/capitalist economists focus more on the free market and the assumption of an "invisible hand," while neglecting Smith's con-cern with sympathy and productive labor. (See the work of W. L. Reese.)

**Social Base:**   That set of individuals who are accorded status and thus have the right to construct social reality. The social base refers to all those persons who enter into social discourse, irrespective of what resources they have. Children are born into a population base; if accepted by some kin group, they are socialized and, later, accepted into the social base via a rite of passage.

**Social Capital:**   Generally social capital is the product of people working together to achieve something unattainable to them without cooperation or to individuals alone. The self, the various forms of material culture, and society itself cannot be produced by people working as private individuals. Social capital includes material items but is much more than merely the physical base of culture.

**Social Change Theory:**   There are many theories of social change. Each theory has varying validity. Population theories emphasize increase in the number of people per square unit as the cause of divisions of labor and related social changes. Cultural diffusion theory points to the stimulating effects of ideas and practices brought into a society by migrants. Capitalism pushes changes in technology, knowledge systems, and class, race, and gender relations. Those in environmental studies emphasize degradation of soil, air, and water as leading factors in social change. Many people think that great men are crucial to social change. Others put religion and religious prophets in the forefront. All of these theories are deeply interconnected and variously important when explaining social change. The larger point is that change is endemic; that is, it is impossible to reproduce precisely a culture or a society in each new generation. Social conditions and social practices are continuously evolving. See "Chaos Theory" for more.

**Social Contract Theory:**   The view that all social relations—including political, religious, and economic relations—rest on an implicit contract made by people through word and/or deed. The Sophists held that society existed by convention rather than by divine or Natural law, as claimed by Stoics. Socrates accepted his death sentence as part of the social contract; he benefited from Athenian society, so he was morally obliged to accept its judgments. See "Law, natural" for more. Cf. "Law, Natural."

**Social Control:**   In any conflict situation, social control becomes a major problem. Racist/ethnocentric societies, slave societies, patriarchal societies, and class or bureaucratic societies have great problems of resistance and rebellion. There are two major forms of social control: ideological and coercive. Most advanced countries use both. See also "Fascism, Techno-" for more.

**Social Control, Parallel Systems of:**   Refers to systems of informal or private justice. The United States has eight or ten parallel systems of social control, which makes it one of the most repressive countries in the world. Most of these controls are in the private sector or are only loosely connected to the state, so it appears that the United States is the "land of the free." In addition to the criminal justice system, which now supervises over 4 million people (1995), the parallel systems of social control in the United States include: (1) the civil justice system, in which private parties sue each other; (2) the administrative justice system, in which a few government agencies try to regulate some 15 million businesses; (3) the medical control system, which uses chemicals and psychology to control children, women, and those behaviors labeled "perverse" (e.g., gambling, homosexuality, drug use, alcoholism); (4) the private security system, which is made up of security guards, private courts, private prisons, and private detectives and is larger and growing faster than the criminal justice system; (5) the social welfare system, which monitors the behavior of some 15 million people, mostly poor women and their children; it enforces middle-class values of housekeeping, shopping, child care, and sexual behavior; (6) the peer review system, which monitors the crimes/delicts of professors, lawyers, doctors, brokers, and so on; it is user-friendly; (7) a religious control system, which superintends 10–15 million people who come before their priest/minister, confess their sins, and accept penance and punishment. In addition to these control systems, there are also the secret armies of the far Right and Left, CIA surveillance, and covert military operations. See "Criminal Justice" for more.

**Social Darwinism:**   A theory of social change that holds that progress is inevitable if only people will cease their interference with nature. This means that if others stop interfering with the plans of private business, there will be progress. The implicit assumption is that whatever capitalism does is natural and whatever those opposed to capitalism (e.g., liberals, radicals) do is interference. Charles Darwin is said to have repudiated social Darwinism, which is itself a more formal version of laissez-faire (let it be) social philosophy cloaked in the language of science. See "Eugenics," "Evolution, Social," "Functional Interchange," "Kropotkin, Peter," "Laissez-Faire," and "Struggle for Survival" for more.

**Social Democracy:**   A liberal, parliamentary solution to the problems of capitalism. Social democracy works with capitalism in gradual reform. It entails the state sector picking up the costs of capitalism: welfare for the surplus population; medical care for underpaid workers; psychiatric care for the angry and depressed worker; and many forms of subsidy to capital. Social democracy socializes the costs but not the profits of capitalism. The problem with social democracy is that it does not work when capitalism is in crisis and people, thinking it is really socialism that has failed, come to wonder if fascism, racism, nationalism, or fundamentalist religion is the answer. Cf. "Market Socialism," and "Socialism, Democratic."

**Social Distance:**   The social gap separating individuals and groups of classes. Georg Simmel introduced the concept in his work on social differentiation; Emory Bogardus developed a social distance scale to compare the degree to which people accepted or rejected social relationships with other races, religions, and classes.

**Social Engineering:**   The use of social research to solve social problems, as set forth by those who control a political system of society or a private organization. Social "planning" is the word currently in vogue.

**Social Harness:**   Full and competent participation in organizing the flow of meaning, affect, and behavior observed in a social occasion.

**Social Inequality:**   Differences between groups, classes, and genders with regard to power, wealth, and social honor.

**Socialism:**   A system of production where the state holds title to the means of production and decisions are made by a central planning unit on behalf and to the advantage of the entire society. The term is often used as a convention (e.g., when one means communism one says socialism in order to deflect coercion and to avoid emotional resistance to a point). Since socialism is akin to state capitalism it is held in greater respect in the United States than is communism. The United States regards communism as a system of production that completely contradicts the economic philosophy of capitalism. See "Communism," "Government, Forms of," and "Necessary Labor" for more.

**Socialism, Bureaucratic:**   An economic system in which the state (not the workers, not the collective) own the means of production and set economic policy. Work is organized into formal organizations with hierarchy, chain of command, and differential rewards. Cf. "Communism."

**Socialism, Christian:**   A wide-spread socialist movement in Christianity in which the social justice of Deuteronomy and the compassion of the Christ figure were combined in a call for social justice for the poor and oppressed. Reinhold Niebuhr spent most of his career teaching Christian ethics and theology at Union Seminary in New York. He held that changes in social institutions were more important than changes in the heart as a way to reduce and redeem sin. He inspired a whole generation of American ministers to work for social justice. See "Buddhism, Mahayana," "Theology, Liberation," and "World Council of Churches" for more.

**Socialism, Democratic:**   In democratic socialism, interactively and informationally rich discussions and elections are used to set social policy. These processes are used in every domain of public life: politics, economics, religion, and education. Democratic socialism contrasts with a republican form of governance, in that the latter political system perpetuates a disinterested citizenry that votes once every two or four years without much discussion or information. Plato denounced this version of democracy. As Vladimir Lenin professed: "Socialism cannot be victorious unless it introduces complete democracy . . . unless it wages a many-sided consistent . . . struggle for democracy."

**Socialism, Lemon:**   A phrase that mocks the quandary in which liberals find themselves. Liberals support capitalism, but as the accumulation crisis worsens, the state assumes responsibility for producing labor-intensive, unprofitable goods and services while the private sector retains the right to produce high-profit, capital-intensive lines of production. Lemon socialism produces inflation and fiscal crises.

**Socialism, Market:**   A variety of economic system in which the wealth produced by the labor power of workers goes directly to them while a small portion goes to meet collective/community needs. Market socialism attempts to keep the flexibility, creativity, and productivity of the market along with the social and economic justice of collective ownership.

**Socialist Humanism:**   The view that the supreme goal in life is the welfare of the human individual. This welfare includes the idea of liberty, equality, social justice, brother-sisterhood, and access to the material bases for the production of culture. The principles of socialist humanism are guided by definite theoretical assumptions: (1) that the human individual is a social product; (2) that s/he exists only as an "ensemble of social relations"; (3) that human development rests upon and is realized only in the appropriate social conditions; and (4) that social conditions depend upon the material base and the relationship individuals have to the material base.

**Socialist Liberation Movements:**   A wide-ranging series of collective efforts to overthrow capitalism, especially colonial capitalism, by indigenous socialists. Until recently, the effort was coordinated from the former Soviet Union in Moscow.

**Socialist Revolution:**   The transformation of society to communism: democratic self-management by collectives in the production of culture, augmenting praxis and striving for community. Often socialist revolution requires violence. In Chile, socialist revolution was peaceful until the Nixon Administration and the CIA engineered and financed its violent end. In the various right-wing military dictatorships and police states around the world, violence will probably play a role in socialist revolution. In the United States, the growth of right-wing paramilitary groups and surveillance technology may work to provoke violence, resulting in a popular movement toward socialism.

**Sociality:**   A moment of praxis in which the needs of other human beings are met at the same time one achieves self-realization. In the work of Karl Marx (and later George Herbert Mead, Charles Horton Cooley, and others), "self" is to be found in social relationships, not in the person of the private individual. Self-affirmation necessarily implies sociality. In capitalism, work may not imply sociality since it is private accumulation, not human need, that drives the productive system.

**Socialization:** The process by which young people are taught to honor the values and embody the norms of a society. The term first appeared in 1828 and was used by George Herbert Mead and Charles Horton Cooley to explain the way in which human behavior is patterned by interaction within primary groups such as family, school, and play groups. After socialization is completed, a "rite of passage" confers adult status on a person. That status carries with it the rights and obligations to reproduce existing social relationships or to work within the system to change it.

**Socialization of the Means of Production:** The process by which the tools, factories, land, and other goods used to produce essential goods and services are appropriated by the state on behalf of workers as a class. Sometimes force is used, as in the Russian and Chinese Revolutions. Sometimes the state sets up its own agencies to produce collective services (e.g., school, mail delivery, roads).

**Socialized Medicine:** A system of preventative and therapeutic health care paid for by the general public and available to all persons meeting the legal requirements of citizen or visitor to a country. Socialized medicine can be contrasted with the "fee for service" approach used in market systems of health care. See "National Insurance" and "Social Security" for more.

**Social Justice:** Social justice refers to a set of policies and programs in which quality housing, health care, education, transportation, and recreation are distributed on the basis of social status rather than, or in addition to, profit. The idea of "justice" varies with the mode of production; that is, what is fair and right depends upon the social relationships considered normal in a given time. In patriarchal societies, men rule and women defer to them. In slave-based cultures, slave-masters appropriate the wealth produced by slaves. In the feudal period, it was right and proper that kings and nobles lived better than peasants and craft persons.

An integrated view of critical social justice is in its infancy in the United States. One model, developed by Bruce A. Arrigo, considers the contributions of various critical criminological perspectives (e.g., anarchist criminology, peacemaking criminology, Marxist criminology, socialist feminist criminology, postmodern criminology). In his typology, Arrigo examines both themes of convergence (e.g., the role of power, the source of crime, the goals of justice) and themes of divergence (e.g., the nature of crime/law, basic assumptions, the nature of social justice) to comment upon the form that social justice takes in society. Cf. "Criminal Justice."

**Social Lifeworld:** That world created by intending humans and which includes status roles and social relationships; that is, specific social occasions. Humans live in a symbolic universe as well as a physical universe. When they create such a world, it is called a social lifeworld.

**Social Magic:**    The folk process by which social reality is constructed. It entails faith, trust, innocence, naïveté, and hope. Social magic produces a wide range of social phenomena, including healing, love, community, self-systems, marriage, authority, and so on. Social magic has at least four parts: (1) an ideational process involving goals, purposes, and intents; (2) a reification process involving a ceremony or ritual; (3) a performance phase in which trusting humans organize their behavior "as-if" the magical ceremony had validity; and (4) a combinatory link of points 1 through 3 to some meaningful social enterprise (i.e., social magic is not mere make-believe, just pretend, or idle practice). Social magic gains its efficacy from the remarkable ability of people to understand, believe, and fulfill. It is a folk method for constructing social reality, in contrast to scientific methods and theories used to create an ordered society. Social magic is part of the legacy from premodern thought without which society would be impossible. See "Pygmalion Studies," "Self-Fulfilling Prophecy," and "Sociology of Fraud" for more.

**Social Mobility:**    There are two kinds of social mobility. The first kind includes two forms: "vertical mobility"—the movement up or down social class from one generation to the next (e.g., if a father is a farmer and a son is an engineer, the son is said to be upwardly mobile)—and "horizontal mobility," the movement from one job to another within the same class strata. Social mobility is a notion that, in its language, symbolically awards denial of one's kinship, ethnic, religious, and class origins.

The second kind of social mobility is that of whole societies. The center of power and wealth has moved several times in history, from Persia to Greece to Rome to England to the United States. Increasingly today, the center of power and wealth is directed toward Japan and the Pacific Rim nations.

**Social Opinion:**    An information set that is pointed toward the generation of solidarity and consensus. Public opinion, on the other hand, assumes conflict and discord. Social opinion tends to reproduce existing social relationships, whereas public opinion tends to transform social relationships. Conservative societies must control public opinion and the process by which publics arise, and one way to do so is to fill the newspapers and television news programs with social opinion instead of public opinion. Cf. "News," "Propaganda," and "Public Opinion."

**Social Power:**    The power embedded in all social relationships. There are many things a person cannot produce alone. Self, social lifeworlds, language, friendship, and society are collective processes. When people take each other into account and respond to expectations legitimate within a given role or role relationship, social power exists. This power can transform the physical and social world; it can also be used to cheat, harass, deceive, and betray those who respond to it. Social life is impossible without mutuality and reciprocity.

**Social Psychology:** A scientific specialty that attempts to investigate the social sources of human behavior. Of special interest is the self-system and how it arises. Communication is the product of shared social lifeworlds as well as the social source of anxiety, misery, and alienation.

Formal social psychology developed independently of Marxism. Some people claim that it originated in Europe in the experimental laboratories of William Wundt. Much early social psychology was a result of racists searching for explanations of "national character" and superiority. Social psychology became almost exclusively an American discipline until World War II and the extensive interest first in propaganda and then in advertising.

**Social Psychology, Macro:** A branch of psychology that uses the larger structures of society to explain, in part, how human behavior is shaped and pre-shaped. Racism, sexism, class status, and ethnic/national identification are studied to see how and to what degree the behavior of categories of peoples is affected or pre-shaped by such structures.

**Social Psychology, Modern:** A discipline and body of findings about the ways and degrees to which human beings shape each other's behavior within a given sociocultural lifeworld. See "Mead, George Herbert" for more.

**Social Psychology, Premodern:** Many important social psychological capacities were developed over the many hundreds of thousands of years humans evolved. These capacities are largely ignored in modernist social psychology and/or are taken for granted. They include the capacity to believe, to have faith, to trust, to suspend disbelief, to hope, and to act as if things not yet true were or will become true. These capacities also include the many forms of emotion that bind people together or produce negative responses to persons, places, or things.

**Social Psychology, Socialist:** Socialist social psychologists hold that ways of thinking, ways of feeling, and ways of acting vary markedly with one's position in the social order. If one changes class position, for example, one is likely to change ideas about profit, rent, dividends, and about the inequality of wealth. Additional changes present themselves when controlling for gender, race, and age. When putting oneself in the shoes of another person one sees the social world differently. It is not that people are weak or mindless but, rather, that they are embedded in a different set of expectations, obligations, and rewards. The political point is that if one wants to minimize or maximize some form of behavior or some way of thinking/feeling, one should work to change society.

**Social Realism:**    A form of art that takes ordinary people with ordinary problems as its focus rather than the rich or the beautiful. Bertholt Brecht wrote plays and Pablo Neruda wrote poetry in the social realist genre. Some of Goya's paintings, a good bit of 1960s music, and even contemporary folk music (e.g., Woody Guthrie and Tracey Chapman) embody the social realist tradition.

**Social Role:**    The particular set of expectations about feelings, activities, and thinking assigned to a given social position (status). The role of a mother or of a physician varies widely from culture to culture. See "Role Theory" for more.

**Social Security:**    In the United States, a system of social services sponsored and funded by the federal government that provides resources for the poor, the aged, and those who are otherwise unable to sell their labor power on the market for wages sufficient to meet life needs. Benefits may be in cash, in services, or in the form of goods: food, clothing, and so on.

In social democracies, social security is set at a level such that a decent standard of living is possible. In the United States, minimum standards of living are set; social workers are assigned to monitor the use of cash and other services of the poor.

In capitalist societies, social security programs embody principles of "distributive justice" and "equity" but, at the same time, give large subsidies to the capitalist class. Social security programs benefit the capitalist class because poverty, illness, disemployment, and changes in the labor market are directly connected to the pursuit of profit and, thus, are charged off as a cost of production rather than as public welfare. The tax system defines how great the subsidy will be. Regressive taxation allocates even more subsidies. See "Socialized Medicine" for more.

**Social Status:**    A person's place in society in relationship to others. Status may be awarded upon condition of birth (e.g., race, gender, class, ethnicity) or upon merit. If social status is granted on merit, the conditions for the merit award can vary, from military to occupational skill, to musical or poetic talent, to the capacity to accumulate wealth. Status can be stratified, or it can be widely distributed without definitions of superior or inferior; that is, it is possible for every one to be accorded status as a full human being.

**Social System:**    A series of directives (rules, laws, norms, folkways) and compatible behaviors by which a social structure is produced. Thus, the class system produced class strata. The rule that the poor pay more for money, housing, food, and clothing while the rich pay less (in either absolute terms or terms relative to income) creates a class structure. The rule that blue collar workers are paid less than professionals serves as another support for the class structure. A social system is a complex working whole in which human beings organize their own behavior and coordinate it with others to produce an infinite variety of social forms.

Sometimes the term is used to refer to one, fairly self-contained social activity such as a school system or a money system. These are more appropriately identified as subsystems, in that they do not make sense apart from the larger whole. For example: Who would study electrical engineering in a "school" if the society were one in which electrical appliances were not used?

**Society:**    A complex form of social life composed of a network of different social institutions, each with a division of labor and a hierarchy of governance. Cf. "Community."

**Sociobiology:**    Sociobiology tries to ascertain which patterns of behavior are preprogrammed by inheritance. There is a great deal of evidence that many animal species engage in unlearned, complex behavior, like building, fighting, mating, and the rearing of their young. The question is how much programmed behavior is also found in the human species: To what extent is it overridden by learned behavior and under what conditions of stress or panic is genetically based behavior activated? Often, sociobiology attempts to replace social theory with biological theory. This practice tends to eternalize one kind of behavior or another and, thus, remove it as a topic for political discourse.

Sociobiology started out as a set of assumptions about the degree to which social organization (the class system, sexism, fascism, etc.) and social problems (crime, war, alcoholism, etc.) are based upon genetics and gene pools (race).

The critical position is that, generally speaking, the development of the cerebral cortex and other structures make it possible for human beings to organize a wide variety of social forms and create quite enough social problems without blaming nature for it. As a political matter, sociobiology has been used to justify inequality in the name of science, as in R. Richard Hernstein and Charles Murray's analysis of race and IQ in *The Bell Curve* (1994).

**Socioeconomic Status:**    A depoliticized way to refer to one's class position (usually SES). SES is measured by education, income, ethnicity, gender, and religion. In the United States, people like to think that there are no upper or lower classes, and they employ safe, neutral terms like SES.

**Sociology:**    A termed coined by Auguste Comte. Sociology is a science that studies *relationships* between people in contexts (not people per se). Sociologists investigate how people become social animals and how forms of social reality are constructed. The usefulness of sociology is not yet settled. Some who practice sociology maintain that it is a liberating, exciting venture appropriate to all persons who purport to be educated. Critics of sociology such as e. e. cummings claim that it is "the naughty thumb of science prodding the beauty of sweet spontaneous life." Karl Marx called it a "bourgeois pseudo-science." Sociology is scarcely two hundred years old. The rule is that any science gets its meaning from the larger society in which it is found. Sociology can be used as an instrument of oppression as easily as a tool of critical inquiry.

**Sociology, Emancipatory:**   Emancipatory sociology provides a society with its own critical self-knowledge, endorsing or resisting change as the case might be. It uses conflict theory and conflict methodology in order to reveal the positive and negative features of a society in terms of some set of human rights and obligations. Emancipatory sociology involves the oppressed and exploited in setting research questions and in formulating conclusions. It sees its task as distributing knowledge broadly through the social order more so than in journals, books, or lectures. The larger goal is the creation of a praxis society where people come to know society by helping to build it as much as by studying it in college classrooms. Cf. "Consensus Theory."

**Sociology, Radical:**   A movement within bourgeois sociology that aims to use social science for human purpose rather than managerial purposes. The position of the radical sociologist is that the scientific theories and methods of constructing social reality at home, at work, in politics, and in education should be at least as decent and rational as the folk theories and methods that were displaced. A number of American sociologists view themselves to be radical and/or Marxist sociologists.

**Sociology of Development:**   The application of sociological principles by which a given social paradigm is improved and extended. Revolution, on the other hand, requires a change in the social paradigm presently in force. In capitalism, the sociology of development is funded by the state and used to manage social problems at home and to extend the system of capitalism (and markets) abroad.

**Sociology of Deviance:**   The study of human social behavior in which there is some question about the appropriateness of the conduct. There are two broad approaches to studying deviance. One approach argues that it is a function of norm violation. The other approach contends that deviance is a function of societal definition.

The first model links behavior with social rules and their violation. One is identified as deviant when the person deviates from established social markers: rules against harmful behavior (e.g., arson); rules against relatively harmless behavior (e.g., spitting in public); rules about occupational behavior (e.g., dress code for one's profession). With this approach norm violator rates are studied, as are the individuals who engage in norm violations.

A second approach links deviance with society's reaction to the behavior. Further, the individual experiences interpersonal or collective reaction ranging from isolation to punishment.

A person becomes deviant in relation to society's successful application of the deviant label. Thus, for example, a vigilante may be a criminal; however, if the person behaves something like a Robin Hood, society's reaction to the person may include not only the dismissal of the deviant label but also, in its place, the elevation of the person to the status of a hero.

**Sociology of Fraud:**   The deliberate attempt to create the impression of a social relationship for purposes of private gain. The creation of social reality requires trust, faith, belief, and innocence. The quest for profits often exploits these human capacities. When this occurs, the sociology of fraud obtains and the social process is put in jeopardy. See "Mystification" and "Social Magic" for more.

**Sociology of Knowledge:**   The Marxian premise is that human knowledge depends upon and varies with one's position in the social structure. However, there is a modifying clause that holds that, under conditions of stratification, the lower classes tend to embrace the views of the dominant class to the disadvantage of the former. One role of the radical social scientist is to oppose the mystification of dominant class knowledge as perpetuated by the lower classes.

**Sociology of Recreation:**   The Marxist position on capitalist forms of recreation is highly critical. In the United States and in the West, there is the assumption that the world of work is necessarily alienating. The evenings and weekends are to be used to repair (re-create) the harm done to the human spirit. In socialist philosophy, humans should create themselves as species-being while at work, not in the intervals between work. There is also the problem of mass sports and capital-intensive recreation. Mass sports turn us into a passive audience, and capital-intensive recreation (skiing, snowmobiling, auto vacations, jeeping, bowling, etc.) not only ties up a lot of valuable natural resources in trivial activity but is often harmful to the environment.

**Sociology of Youth:**   The discipline that studies the ways in which persons are placed into and removed from age grades from birth through age 18. The sociology of youth deals with the differences in socialization between boys and girls, patterns of authority and resistance to authority of parents, the character of the parenting process, and the identity and number of the people involved in parenting. Generally, individuals are accepted into a family, tribe, or society when they go through a rite of passage. Through the rite, children are given both name and status in a social base as a legal child in a family. In the absence of such a rite, the infant is a nonperson and may be killed, become a ward of a court, or be adopted by another parent. After passage into a social base, the young person is put through a rather long socialization process. Usually at the end of this process, s/he goes through another rite of passage and is accorded full adult status. See "Age Grades," "Consent," "Juvenile," "Majority, Age of," "Minor/Minority," "Rite of Passage," and "Status Crimes" for more.

**Solidarity:**   Social power in its final, most perfect state. Solidarity refers to the condition in which a group of people view each other as cherished co-workers achieving a common goal. Where solidarity exists, social bonds are strong, mutual support is unreserved, and the exploitation of social bonds for private gain unthinkable. The position of the socialist is that solidarity is desired for the entire society not for just a part of it. Émile Durkheim explained some of the sources of social solidarity.

**Solidarity, Mechanical:**   A solidarity that arises when people eat, drink, worship, or play together. Mechanical solidarity can elicit cooperation between persons and groups who have little in common or even have, objectively, cause for conflict. For example, religion can bind people into mutually affirming relationships and common endeavor. Religion can bind slaves and slave-masters, workers and owners, whites and blacks, and so on and, thus, generate social peace.

The Marxist critique asks whether such a form of solidarity masks oppression or exploitation. See "Division of Labor" for more. Cf. "Solidarity, Organic."

**Solidarity, Organic:**   This solidarity is said to arise from a division of labor in which specialized workers in each occupation depend upon skilled workers in other occupations. Electricians, carpenters, plumbers, masons, and bankers are all involved in the construction of a home, office building, or dam. Regardless of race, religion, or ethnic loyalties, they respond to each other because they need each other to get the job done. Looking at the larger society, bankers, farmers, priests, police, clerks, teachers, and industrial workers all do something the others need or think they need. Émile Durkheim argued that this kind of solidarity was proof of the super-organic nature of society and proof that mechanical solidarity alone was not sufficient to solve the problem of social order.

The Marxist critique raises the question of whether the organic whole that emerges from this division of labor is congenial to the human project understood as praxis. Further, the Marxist view holds that culture must be produced collectively rather than divided up to the exclusion of some. This criticism suggests the concept of organic solidarity is an elitist apology for a system devoid of human solidarity. Both lambs and lions have organs that are functionally interdependent but that produce different animals.

The Marxist position, then, is to look at the totality. See "Division of Labor" and "Lukács, Georg" for more. Cf. "Solidarity, Mechanical."

**Solidarity (the Union):**   *Solidarno* is the name of the Polish trade union, the only one, when it began in 1980, independent of the Communist Party in the Socialist Bloc. It began in a dispute over increases in the price of meat set by the Polish government, itself controlled by the Polish Communist Party. After a series of strikes, the government conceded to the demands of the union. The Polish Supreme Court ruled that the Communist Party had no legal control over *Solidarno*. *Solidarno* led to the collapse of bureaucratic, elitist communism in eastern Europe.

**Solution:**   A fractal system that has the unusual ability to maintain its structure while passing through another system. Think of a wave or of an ethnic group in a foreign land; both can survive as a structured entity under the right conditions. Generally, nonlinear feedback loops permit such survival, whereas positive or negative feedback tends to destroy structure. See "Chaos Theory" and "System" for more.

**Sorel, Georges (1847–1920):**   Sorel was a French engineer who became a militant socialist and who theorized about the use of violence to overthrow capitalism. He advocated anarchy and syndicalism. His major work was *Reflections on Violence,* in which he argued that violence is necessary to counter the monopoly of the capitalist state in the arenas of law, wealth, and violence. He posited two forms of violence: physical and psychological. He argued that widely held social myths were more powerful stimuli to social movements than were the utopias of single persons. He is also known for his defense of Dreyfus, a Jewish officer in the French army who was sent to prison to cover up the corruption of French generals and colonels. (See the work of W. L. Reese.)

**Soviet:**   A Russian word for "council" or "committee." The soviet was supposed to be the basic self-governing unit of the former USSR. Soviets became dominated by the Central Committee of the Soviet Communist Party and lost most of their meaning as democratic bodies. At one time, there were over 50,000 soviets in the USSR. See "Trotsky, Leon" for more.

**Spartacus League:**   A revolutionary Marxist group in Germany founded by Rosa Luxemburg, Karl Liebknetch, F. Mehring, and Clara Zetkin. It was named after Spartacus, the Roman slave who led a slave rebellion against Imperial Rome. His legions were defeated in 71 B.C., and 6,000 of the rebels were crucified. Luxemburg and Liebknetch were murdered by German secret police, but the League continues as a youth group affiliated with the Fourth International.

**Specialization:**   The performance of a narrowly defined task, usually relating to technical work. The thought is that one can do something efficiently if one does it all the time. Specialization often subdivides labor so much that purpose of and control over work is lost to the worker. Specialists can be useful in capitalism since they know little of the social meaning of their labor. They experience no guilt or shame as a result of their work.

**Species-Being:**   This term means about the same as human being. The idea is that people do not automatically realize their being as a human species but rather have the potential to become human if they work hard at it.

**Spencer, Herbert (1820–1903):**   Herbert Spencer was a self-taught engineer and editor who used Charles Darwin's theory of biological evolution (struggle for survival; survival of the fittest) to fashion a theory of *social* evolution. The theory holds that predatory capitalism, exploitation, and ruthless individualism is best in the long run since the fittest persons, firms, and societies survive.

The critical Marxist response is that there is no end to this "long run" and thus the "best" never includes the quest for social justice and social peace. Instead, there is continuous and ruthless conflict for domination in markets, politics, religion, and gender relations. Spencer lies buried across the path from Marx's grave in Highgate cemetery in London. (See the work of W. L. Reese.)

**Sports (and Sexism):**   Sports reproduces sexist relationships in a number of ways: (1) all-male solidarities are typically generated; (2) women are used to recruit players; (3) women are used to give a sexual flavor to activities surrounding a game; (4) women gain the habit of finding identity and life through their menfolk; and (5) women learn to believe that their exclusion from other "all-male" activities (e.g., politics, management, and war) is appropriate.

**Sports, Ideology of:**   According to the Marxist critique of U.S. sports, football, baseball, hockey, basketball, and so on become alienated work (rather than spontaneous enjoyment of physical grace) because players and fans are objectified and a small elite make a profit from them. Modern sports, in advanced monopoly capitalist forms, are responsible for hypercompetition and for authoritarian attitudes, converting spontaneous, sensuous play into a business. Through advertising campaigns that take advantage of consumer sexual anxiety, corporations turn athletes into sex objects in order to sell products for more profit. Capitalism instills brutality and violence into the games in order to generate markets for the various sports and consumer interest in the products advertised between play. This process diminishes or, worse, destroys the beauty, elegance, and creativity of a physical art form by commercializing it. In short, that which was used to create community and promote praxis is, under its monopoly capital form, a business venture, a tax write-off, and a means to extract more surplus value from those workers with money left after inflation, taxes, and credit payments.

**Stage Theory:**    There are many stage theories in the behavioral sciences. They tend to describe all of human history in two, three, or four simple stages or ages. Some of the more famous theorists/theories are: the Greek poet Hesiod, who saw four stages: a golden age now past, then a silver age, a brass age, and, finally, an iron age; Auguste Comte, who saw three stages in social evolution: theological; metaphysical; and finally scientific; Sir Henry Maine, who saw two major stages in social relations: society based upon status and then upon contract. There are also theories of the transition of human bonds from mechanical to organic solidarity (Émile Durkheim); from traditional to legal-rational authority (Max Weber); from sacred to secular social life (Howard Becker); from community to society (Frederich Tonnies); from the simple to the complex (Herbert Spencer); and from trial and error in social evolution to scientific self-control of society (Ward). Sigmund Freud posited three stages in psycho-sexual development: oral, anal, and genital. Lawrence Kohlberg posited six stages in moral development. Karl Marx held there were three evolutionary stages; pre-history, history, and post-history. In pre-history, people were subject to the blind laws of nature. In history, people were subject to social laws made by elites. In post-history, democratic and collective agency was used to build new social forms. See "Historicity" for more.

**Stalinism:**    A form of socialism in which the production of political culture is monopolized by a leader or leaders. While the means of production of material culture are owned by the state, the principle of collective self-management is forcibly suppressed. Stalinism is to socialism as a military dictatorship is to the "free" world. It is anti-Marxist to attribute great heroism or great malevolence to a single individual. Stalin happened to rise to party leadership in a given time and in a given cultural complex; however, his name is commonly used to describe this sociopolitical period.

**State:**    A social institution that claims sovereignty over all who live in a given geographical area. It comes with agencies to administer, to police, to judge, to imprison, and to punish people. In structural-functional theory the state is said to be a neutral organ coordinating the other institutions on behalf of all the people.

Those on the far Right and far Left consider the state to be a dangerous and unnecessary institution that should be dismantled. Those on the Right tend to think the market or the church is the proper institution for governance. Those on the Left tend to think that private citizens or self-governing groups, firms, churches, communities, and other social units should displace the state.

**State (and Class Struggle):**    Many socialists see the state routinely on the side of capital even when the state passes labor laws to protect workers from danger, from long hours, or from unrestricted firing, or when it protects consumers from price-fixing and dangerous additives. Some people claim that the state can be made to work on behalf of the workers and that socialists should take state power and use it to build a democratic and communist society. Karl Marx argued that state power would "wither away" under a competent socialist government and that the state should be retained to administer policy, provided that policy was democratically determined. See "State, Theory of" for more.

**State, Theory of:**    The nation-state appeared with the rise of capitalism; state power was taken away from monarchs and feudal lords through a series of revolutions and located in parliaments, councils, and congresses. Nations exist through written contracts in which certain rights and responsibilities are set forth for both the state and the citizens of the state. There are a large number of international laws, adopted by many nations, that further establish and regulate the authority of the state. Those on the Right and Left view the state as a dangerous organ that intrudes upon and usurps personal rights and class interests.

The Marxian theory of the state is that it is an organ created by society: (1) to safeguard its general interests against internal and external threat and (2) to help the capitalist class extract profit. After the state comes into being, it begins to make itself independent in regard to society. The more independent it becomes, the more it becomes the agent of a particular class. The fight against a ruling class or a bureaucratic elite thus becomes a fight against the state and its police and is regarded as treasonous (consider, for example, Leon Trotsky). For Karl Marx and Friedrich Engels, the state meant the machinery of coercion not of administration. Marx held that administrative government (e.g., health, education, labor) was necessary. See "Nationalism" and "State (and Class Struggle)" for more.

**State Capitalism:**    A form of capitalism in which the state guarantees the markets and profits of capitalists by maintaining military bases overseas and by subsidizing many of the costs of production. Corporate liberals like state capitalism because it solves problems of capital accumulation. Small businessmen and "hard-hats" do not like state capitalism because their taxes pay for "welfare to the rich" and they benefit little from it. Sometimes the economic system of the former Soviet Union was called "state capitalism" as a term of contempt.

**Statistical Significance:**   The point at which a person is willing to infer a causal relationship between two or more variables using a variety of mathematical procedures. The critical position is that there are better sources for inference than numerical values. However, for large processes, numbers are often helpful in making the structural features of a society visible. These causal inferences lose their power as dynamical regimes become more and more chaotic. See "Chaos Theory" for more.

**Status:**   The standing (state) of a person with respect to the degree to which s/he is treated as a significant social other. Without status, an individual is a nonperson. The term is sometimes used in a snobbish way. The Marxist position is that status differences are politically inspired, exploitative, and alien to the human condition. A socialist society requires everyone be accorded status with full rights in the production of culture. Persons without status are excluded from the process of creating culture and the process of constructing social reality. Usually a person occupies several statuses during a lifetime. A status is a social-structural concept; its social psychological homology is a social identity (e.g., mother, priest, nephew, doctor, etc.).

**Status Crimes:**   A variety of restrictions upon behavior that are not binding upon adults but that for juveniles are policed and enforced (e.g., smoking, curfew, drinking, truancy, sexual activity, offensive language, leaving home, refusing to obey parents, or other behaviors that defeat a youth's socialization routines). Usually status offenders are processed through the juvenile justice system. It is a large and expanding control system that parallels the criminal justice system but that is informed by more humane and therapeutic judgments. Status crimes have the twin effect of upgrading the labor market by keeping people in school for more and more years and, at the same time, reducing competition for jobs with adults. Many liberals, especially those on the far Right, view any effort to control/socialize anybody as an unwarranted infringement of privacy by the state. See "Juvenile Delinquency," "Juvenile Justice System," "*Parens patriae*," and "Sociology of Youth" for more.

**Status Honor/Differentiation:**   Many societies define and rank people according to status-roles. Thus gender, occupation, race, age, and ethnicity are divided and ranked according to some arbitrary system of honor. This ranking produces conflict and greatly distorts symbolic interaction.

**Status Inconsistency:**   A concept introduced by Gehard Lenski, who pointed out that some people rank low on some systems of status honor and high on others. Lenski reported that such inconsistency fueled several social problems and social movements. Other theorists have found little or no such impact.

**Stewardship:**   An important term and view in Protestantism; namely, that there is an elite chosen by God to care for the flocks and the fields on His behalf. In Christianity, a steward of God is required to manage wealth with humility and prudence and preserve it for future generations. See "Elite" for more.

**Stimulation (of the Economy):**   In a depression, the government must look for ways to encourage production and demand or it loses political legitimacy. It may use fiscal policy (buying things, giving tax rebates, or reducing taxes); it may use monetary policy (lowering interest rates, printing cheap money); or it may give businesses special subsidies to expand. These various efforts of stimulation are called Keynesian economics and have worked to save capitalism; however, the price of Keynesian economics is increasing federal debt. Interest on this debt now runs about 11 percent per year of all tax dollars.

**Stoic/Stoicism:**   A school of social philosophy founded by Zeno in Athens in 100 B.C.E. The name comes from the Greek word *stoa* (porch), where the Stoics met. They contributed much to modern social philosophy, for example, the idea that there is a natural law that orders all things according to universal reason *(logos)* and that can be understood by human beings. This view informed Roman law (see "Law, natural" for more), which, in turn, led to the Enlightenment and to modern fascism. Stoics held that control of social life by reason required one to enter public discourse and assume the duty/responsibility for social life. Human law was superseded by this natural law and led to the concept of the *cosmopolis:* a society in which people would know and live according to the laws of the cosmos. Stoicism takes its name from the capacity of Stoics to commit suicide when they failed in their public duty. G.W.F. Hegel elevated the idea of natural law to the theory that all rationality resided in the state sector, which was informed by natural law. This theory justifies state control of all aspects of social life and informs both fascism and neo-fascism.

**Story/Storytelling:**   An explanation or description of events that makes no claims of ultimate, exclusive truth but, rather, admits that the story is but the teller's view (and the reader's/listener's interpretation), based upon their respective knowledge and point of view. See "Postmodernists/Postmodernism," "Postmodernity," "Totalizing," and "Writerly (Versus Readerly) Text" for more.

**Strata Organizing:**   A tactic of social revolution in which "unrecognized" workers are organized, thus adding to the pressures experienced by the capitalist system. Developed by the National Labor Federation, self-expanding cadres canvass those who are not permitted by law to form the usual trade unions and help organize them into "mutual benefit societies."

Included in the strata of unrecognized workers are farm workers; domestic workers; independent contractors; workers in small shops, businesses, and the service sector; people on welfare; and the unemployed. Together, these people represent the "surplus population" of society.

**Stratification:**   A process by which some people in a society are channeled into an inferior (or superior) social position, perpetuating some form of class, race, and/or gender inequality. This inferiority affects one's capacity to create culture and to enter into social relationships. As a result it diminishes the human potential of those at the bottom and at the top. Usually a stratification system requires those defined as inferior to produce items of material culture while the upper strata claim a monopoly over the production of political and ideological culture. Stratification systems also funnel wealth and power to the top of a hierarchy. Some people claim stratification is necessary (functional). Others argue that it is a structure of domination and only necessary if one group is to be exploited by another. Some people allege stratification is natural since some animal societies are stratified. However, human biology may well be qualitatively different from those animals used to exemplify stratification processes (e.g., baboons, hyenas, cattle, and chickens).

Karl Marx emphasized class stratification, and Max Weber added the strata of power and social honor as important and separate stratification systems. Leon Trotsky and C. Wright Mills thought stratification was composed of elites and masses. Mills identified three dominant elites: big business, big government, and big military. Other elites include big unions, major universities, several popular ministers/ministries, some sports stars, and movie celebrities. There is now a global stratification in which some seven nations regulate the political economy of the world. See "Differentiation" and "Group of Seven" for more.

**Strike:**   A stoppage of work or of all public services by those whose demands are not met in the established political institutions or governing bodies. There have been employee strikes, consumer pickets, student boycotts, and player strikes. Each has been an effort to achieve greater equity between the owners of the means of production and the workers.

**Structural Analysis:**   A perspective in sociology in which it is thought that social structures (e.g., the race, gender, and class structures, the normative structure) mediate behavior. These structures are highly regular patterns of behavior generated by systems of coercion or social control rather than by judgment, interaction, and democratic self-government. The Interactionist view is that insightful human behavior creates norms, classes, roles, and other social forms. Structural analysis is anti-humanist, in that the role of the creative person is minimized. Most conservatives (and order theorists) hold that social structures are (and should be) hard to change (e.g., the percent rule in parliamentary procedure or the strict enforcement of rules in a school or factory). The Symbolic Interactionist view is often a highly romanticized view of social reality. Interactionism ignores the coercive means and other techniques used to defeat insight, judgment, reflection, and mutual influence in the marketplace, at school, in the shop, and in the home.

**Structural Functionalism:**   A sociological perspective that emphasizes order, harmony, and cooperation between the various segments of society. Functionalists assume that all of the various parts (structures) of society are more or less necessary and that the continued well-being of society depends upon the harmonious integration of all these parts; that is, each part must contribute its special goods/services. Radicals see this view as an implicit endorsement of the status quo, as inherently conservative, and as a masking of oppression.

There are other views of what society is and how it works. For instance, Marxists are conflict oriented; that is, they look at society and see conflict and struggle rather than order, harmony, cooperation, and integration. From a structural functionalist position, crime is necessary. From a Marxist position, crime consists of behavior that destroys community, culture, or praxis. Crime is not necessarily functional.

**Structuralism:**   In linguistics and the social sciences it refers to a belief that all systems or institutions (e.g., art, literature, psychology, religion, sports) are constituted by basic, essential, structural conditions of fixity and absoluteness. When these foundational conditions or "deep structures" are positively identified and articulated, they promote a certain ordering of the universe; a proof that all objects and events in the cosmos are essentially retrievable, reducible, predictable and, therefore, knowable. Language, then, is *the* vehicle through which the structuring of the universe is ascertained and made manifest. See "Barthes, Roland" and "Saussure, Ferdinand de" for more.

**Structure:**   (Order, improbability, negentropy.) An improbable event produced by rules that work to bring objects into ordered relationships. This ordering of relationships is called the "segregation of entropy" in systems theory language. Sometimes social structure is produced by systems using power and coercion, sometimes by solidarity and cooperation, and often by a combination of both. Since Mandelbrot, the concept of structure has expanded to include "fractal." See "Chaos Theory" for more.

**Struggle for Survival:**   A central point in Charles Darwin's theory of organic evolution, which holds that people, groups, and species compete for food, sex, and status. Those people, groups, species, and so on best suited to obtain these things survive and those that do not are eliminated directly by death or indirectly by inability to rear offspring. Since the concept assumes conflict to be the source of change, "struggle for survival" is regarded as a conflict theory. See "Social Darwinism" for more. Cf. "Kropotkin, Peter Alekseyevich."

**Students for a Democratic Society (SDS):**    A radical student movement founded at Port Huron in 1962 that produced the New Left. Its main activity was resistance against the war in Vietnam, but it informed student power movements all over the United States. It survives in ten or so splinter groups that continue to provide theory, leadership, and experience to progressive causes.

**Subjectivity:**    (1) A personal point of view seen to be partial and distorted (Cf. "Objectivity"); (2) postmodernists use the term to warn one away from treating a person as "subject"; that is, as the sole author of his/her own beliefs, intentions, actions, or understandings. The acting subject is lost in an age of images, appearances, simulations, and dramaturgical enactments. The subject is also lost in a bureaucratic, elitist, social arena since agency is concentrated in top echelons. In postmodern thinking, the subject is therefore a fiction for which no stable, original "real self" exists. See "Decentered Subject" and "Lacan, Jacques" for more. Cf. "Feminism."

**Substantive Rationality:**    A system of planning or decisionmaking that considers goals as well as means. In Max Weber's work, bureaucracies are said to be rational in "technical" terms; that is, bureaucracy is a rational means to achieve goals. However, those goals may be decidedly elitist and destructive. Weber wanted to encourage people to be less innocent about the desirability of rationality that had, since the Enlightenment, been the center point of all knowledge processes. In socialist theory, "substantive" rationality means organizing capital and labor to produce the material conditions under which people can create themselves as human beings in collective and democratic political dialogue. Cf. "Instrumental Rationality."

**Suicide:**    Self murder. Émile Durkheim, with keen insight, explained suicide in terms of the degree to which a person is integrated into social life. At the low end of social integration, there is anomic suicide in which people destroy themselves because social bonds dissolve and life becomes meaningless to them. When people are tightly integrated and when there is a threat to the social group, people may sacrifice themselves in order to protect the group. Elderly Eskimo men and women sometimes walk away to die quietly when food is short; pilots sometimes dive their plane into a target in order to protect their own military. There is also the effort to "die with dignity" and/or to end pain. Dr. Kevorkian in Michigan has helped people who are beyond medical help commit suicide. Suicide in this context is also called "mercy killing." In England, there is the Hemlock Society, which offers instruction to people on how to end their lives quickly and quietly.

**Super Max:**   Refers to the new, super maximum security prisons being built around the country (e.g., Pelican Bay in California, Temmes in Illinois). Super Max facilities are designed to house literally thousands of prisoners. Critical penal scholars contend that such facilities are no more than high rises that "warehouse" prisoners. Further, they question whether adequate services can be made available to inmates. Finally, critical scholars argue that super maximum facilities function as the most recent manifestation of race and class discrimination. The construction of prisons around the country is the fastest growing industry. Those incarcerated increasingly represent the poorest segments of society, and growing numbers of prisoners are persons of color.

**Superstructure:**   According to Karl Marx, that part of a social lifeworld shaped by the base (means of production). It includes art, science, music, politics, law, cinema, literature, and religion. Marx held that the ways in which people relate to each other in the production of material culture (the base) affect people's ways of thinking, feeling, and behaving (their consciousness). This consciousness shapes the superstructure. Marx held the material base to be determinate of the superstructure, whereas Max Weber argued that the superstructure (e.g., the Protestant ethic) shaped the base (i.e., the capitalist system).

Postmodern sensibility and Symbolic Interaction theory view the dichotomy as false; ideas are always central to human behavior and, at points in the historical process, produce great change. Then, too, law, religion, and science are also productive processes. Ideological and political culture are just as important as material culture. See "Constitutive Theory" for more. Cf. "Base."

**Supply and Demand, The Law of:**   There is a tendency for supply to increase or decrease when the demand for it increases or decreases. In capitalism, since demand is a function of wages and salaries, and since wages and salaries depend upon profits, there is another tendency for demand to go up or down apart from human need or desire. In communist or socialist economics, supply is supposed to be set according to the needs of persons and communities rather than profit.

**Surplus Labor:**   In the *Grundrisse*, Karl Marx asserted that capitalism creates a work ethic of strict discipline and industriousness that, when mere subsistence needs are satisfied, is surplus. This surplus labor is a major cause of the collapse of capitalism. When people have time, energy, and such an ethic, they begin to fight for their full humanity. They fight against domination, repressed sensuality, poor performance, and unnecessary products.

In vulgar Marxism, people are thought to revolt when material conditions are bad; revolt occurs when people have the material resources to assert their humanity. The implication is that the new working class of alienated professionals and technicians are also a revolutionary base; perhaps more so than the blue collar worker.

**Surplus Population:**    All those surplus to the production of culture. In capitalism, those individuals surplus to the human potential needs of capital-intensive production. The dynamics of capitalism produce a surplus population because one way to increase profits is to replace workers with machines. Machines do not get pregnant, have hangovers, go on strike, appeal to one's humanity, talk back, require pensions, or fall in love. People do and, consequently, they reduce profits. Without employment, people are irrelevant to the exchange process. In capitalism, only those with money are accorded status in the exchange process; the rest are surplus. This is one of the most important concepts in Marxist theory, along with, perhaps, community and praxis. The surplus population includes the poor, the unemployed, older persons, children without families, prisoners, the idle rich, and so on.

In racist societies, minorities are defined as surplus to the human process and are banished, confined, or murdered by one means or another. In sexist societies, female children are defined as surplus and are killed at birth, given less food or other resources, and generally treated as less than full adults if they survive. See "Malthus, Thomas," "Pauper/Pauperism," "Population Theory," and "Underclass (Undermass)" for more.

**Surplus Production:**    A major contradiction of capitalism arises when capital-intensive modes of production create a surplus of goods and, at the same time, lower wages and/or replace workers with machines in order to increase profits. In this situation there is no market (and therefore no surplus production) since unemployed persons have nothing to exchange for the commodity and underpaid workers must spend their wages for basics such as food, shelter, clothing, and medicine. With a huge surplus production and a large surplus population, many problems arise. The welfare state supports the surplus population, while the warfare state creates or protects markets at home and overseas for the surplus productive capacity unused by domestic markets.

**Surplus Value:**    That part of the value of production that is above and beyond the costs of reproducing the labor force. It can be increased by certain political acts: (1) by compensating workers with less than enough to produce a social lifeworld; (2) by replacing human labor with machine technology; or (3) by replacing a market with a monopoly, thereby increasing the price of the item in question. Surplus value is appropriated by means of profits, rents, and/or interest. See "Rent" for more.

**Survival of the Fittest:**    A principle of organic evolution developed by Charles Darwin. The principle holds that those species and species members that best fit into an ecological niche have a greater chance to live and to reproduce their genes. The principle does not claim that the fittest are those persons who are the richest or the most powerful. Peaceful cooperation may fit the conditions of the environment better than violence, rape, and/or destruction. See "Darwin, Charles" and "Kropotkin, Peter Alekseyevich" for more.

**Swinks:**    An acronym for a new family form: single women, including kids. As more and more older women become politicized about abuse and battering, they begin to form households in which two or more such women live together with their children; sexual intimacy may or may not be part of the living arrangements. Cf. "Dinks," "Extended Family," and "Monks."

**Symbol:**    An information set (voiced, acted, written, or encoded in some fashion) where shared and arbitrary meaning is assigned. Symbols carry three kinds of information that guide human behavior: (1) referential content that gives the meaning or the standard use of a word; (2) emotional content that orients one to shame or delight, avoidance or acceptance, reward or punishment; and (3) behavioral content that guides one toward or away from some action, person, or situation. Thus, symbols are more than just a "guide" to social reality. Without symbolic interaction, there would be no social lifeworld.

**Symbolic Interaction:**    A complex process by which ideas are converted into social facts. In a "self-fulfilling prophecy," the prophecy contains the idea of the role, the occasion, or the social institution under construction. Then, through a process using words, gestures, clothing, equipment, and architecture, forms of social reality are constructed by some set of persons. This view of reality formation contrasts to theories that locate human behavior in genes or purely psychological processes. It also calls into question the idea that "forms" of social reality exist independently of the people who construct them anew in each marriage, church service, class, or business act. See "Goffman, Erving" and "Mead, George Herbert" for more.

**Symbol Sets:**    People have four sets of symbols that can help them define a situation and construct a social lifeworld: (1) voiced symbols that use some eight variables upon which to encode meaning (tone, pitch, volume, pace, etc.); (2) face and body talk (e.g., hands, face, legs, and eyes are used extensively to transmit information); (3) clothing and body decorations are used to denote gender, age, authority, and other background information; and (4) props (e.g., keys, clip-boards, guns, hats). These are all "personal" media and cannot easily be alienated. Cf. "Mass Media."

**Syntagm:**    The syntagm is the spoken/written speech chain. It is the arrangement, ordering, and placement of paradigms (words/phrases) into a series of thoughts or sentences, creating some narrative coherence. The paradigmatic/syntagmatic axis of communication was developed by the French linguist, Ferdinand de Saussure. It is significant for understanding the arbitrary nature of language and the manner in which speech unfolds. The interactive effects of the syntagm with the paradigm are the most conscious level of speech production. Cf. "Paradigm."

**System:**   Generally, a set of entropy segregating mechanisms; any fairly structured entity that has a discernible boundary between it and its environment. Systems range from the layers of sand, gravel, and rocks created by a river to complex living things. The human body can segregate entropy (pick out amino acids, sugars, fats, and other things from what is ingested; it can pick out oxygen molecules from others in the air, and so on). The human body is a working system (it is alive) only if it segregates entropy and thus reproduces order.

Chaos/Complexity theory teaches us that the boundaries of most systems are open and fuzzy; their geometry is fractal; that is, systems do not occupy all the space available in a time/space region. If one changes the scale of observation, even a denser system can be seen to be loosely connected. For example, think of atoms, molecules, the human body, and the classes one attends at college. They seem solid and stable, but they are really quite open and unpredictable. See "Solution" for more.

**Systematically Distorted Communication:**   According to Jürgen Habermas, the barriers to communication that produce normative behavior are usually subjected to scrutiny and reduction through "discourse"; that is, a special kind of conversation about things we ordinarily assume. But some social worldviews prevent discourse and, thus, distort communication. When communication is distorted, human behavior ceases to be free and uncoerced. Elitism and mass media, as they are organized, do not permit discourse. Rules about secrecy, authority, expertise, and so on all protect the implicitly valid claims of one party and prevent those claims from being called into question. See "Validity Claims" for more.

**Systems Theory:**   A set of propositions about how order is produced across all levels of physical and social reality. Generally a system depends upon the transfer of order from its environment if it is to survive as an improbable arrangement of events. The radical aspect of systems theory is that, if a system is not able to draw order from its environment, either the environment must be changed or the system must change. If the environment is threatened by the transfer of order, then the system itself must change. Theories of society, family, bureaucracy, crime, deviance, or disorder that ignore the environment (human and physical) of a society are political obstacles to adequate understanding and to a search for adequate variety. See "Negentropy" for more.

# T

**Taboo:** A rule forbidding certain behavior usually grounded in a sacred belief. Any behavior that interferes with social magic is the subject of taboo.

**Taney, Roger Brooke (1777–1864):** Chief Justice on the U.S. Supreme Court from 1836 to 1864. Taney ruled in favor of states rights, slavery, restrictive voting rights for workers and women, and control on the presidency. At different times, Taney worked for mass suffrage and condemned slavery as a "blot on our national character." Taney embodied the struggles and conflicts of a changing society. Early in his tenure, he was generally progressive in local terms. As he aged (and had more social power), he became increasingly hostile to humanitarian causes. The Drew Scott decision, which he engineered, brought him savage public criticism.

**Taxation:** Public funds are raised by a number of methods, chief among which is taxation. Taxes can be placed upon goods and services, property and gifts. Generally tax policies reflect the degree to which distributive and redistributive justice is made real in a society. In 1995, subsidies to the capitalist class through grants, direct payments, and loopholes in the tax code were about ten times greater (and went to far fewer persons) than subsidies to poor people through welfare programs. Generally taxation policy is determined by those who have greater economic and social power.

**Taxation, Progressive:** Tax policies that increase the tax rate as income increases. A person making $20,000/year might pay taxes at a rate of 17 percent for any taxable income; a person making $30,000/year might pay 20 percent; and a person making $50,000/year might pay 25 percent. After-tax income is still greater for those in the higher tax brackets, even though they pay more tax. Cf. "Taxation, Regressive."

**Taxation, Regressive:** Any tax policy that puts greater burdens on poor people and fewer burdens on the rich. Generally, flat rate taxes, although appearing equal, take a greater share of personal income from the poor than from the rich. For example, if you pay $500 in tax a year out of an income of $20,000, it is one fortieth of your income, but you have only $19,500 left to meet all your other expenses. If you pay $5,000 dollars out of an income of $200,000, it is still one fortieth of your income, but you have $195,000 left to meet necessary expenses. Thus, in the second instance, your discretionary income is much higher.

**Taylorism:**   Frederick Taylor did time-motion studies as a way of maximizing worker productivity. Taylorism is a system by which a clear-cut division of mental and physical labor is established throughout a factory. It is based on the precise time and motion analysis of each job in isolation and relegates the entire mental part of the task to the managerial staff. Marxists reject Taylorism and scientific management. The Marxian position maintains that the production of culture requires the unity of mental and physical labor. Taylorism claims a monopoly over thinking for management. See "Fordism" and "McDonaldization of Society" for more.

*Techne:*   The application of scientific principles to the production of material items. In ancient Greece, *techne* was the activity of women and slaves and involved the satisfaction of mere physical needs using ordinary technical knowledge, whereas *praxis* relied upon wisdom and judgment and was concerned with civil matters and the activity of humans beings qua human beings. *Theoria* dealt with the eternal truths and was the province of the gods, but theory could be revealed by a variety of methods, all involving escape from the things of the flesh and things of the world. See "Technocracy" for more.

**Technocracy:**   The rule by experts, engineers, scientists, and specialists. The role and function of the politician is preempted by the expert. In the 1930s, many workers thought that technocracy would be better than the elitist version of politics that thrived everywhere. The prevailing thought was that there was a natural division of labor and that the experts should make decisions, since they alone knew what was right and natural. However, the use of experts to determine foreign policy, manage workers, generate publics, and set medical policy strips away important social values such as praxis and community. In a well-designed society, the knowledge process would be widely available; that is, professionals and lay persons would share the research process and the decisions about how to use knowledge gained from it. Under capitalism (and bureaucratic socialism), knowledge and technology become instruments of domination and contribute to the growth of the surplus population. See *"Techne"* and "Technology" for more.

**Technology:**   Social knowledge objectified in the form of machines and routines. Any system for the transformation of natural material into cultural goods and services. In systems theory, a means of segregating entropy. See "Technocracy" for more.

**Teleology:**   Greek: *teleos* = end; *logos* = discourse. A view that all systems have a natural destiny. The acorn is destined to become an oak tree; a nation is destined to kill off Native American Indians and take possession of the land from sea to sea; a person has a natural destiny that can be known by IQ, aptitude, and preference tests.

Chaos theory and postmodern philosophy of science contend this idea is of limited validity. As Stephen Jay Gould points out, organic evolution could have taken any number of paths at a great many points in the history of the earth. It was by no means certain that humans would evolve, nor is it certain that they will survive in their present form.

**Terrorism:**   Terrorism refers to the illegitimate use of force by those who oppose existing social, political, or economic arrangements. Terrorism has a built-in conservative bias since the terrorists who take state power are later defined by their own historians as freedom fighters or progressives. The Irish Republican Army (IRA) exemplifies this point. Its members stay together, claim responsibility (thus, the British know that resistance to their control of Northern Ireland is still staunchly opposed), and are repeatedly given terrorist or freedom-fighting tasks until one or more are caught.

There are three views/definitions of terrorism: (1) Terrorists are organized into small, secret cells and are given orders via a "cutout" from those who hire/use them; (2) terrorists are assembled to engineer a given act of murder or bombing and then quickly disperse back to their country (or countries) of origin without claiming responsibility, and often blaming other groups; and (3) terrorists destroy a false peace between otherwise warring factions or nations. Algeria, when under French rule, is a good illustration of point 3. Algerian freedom fighters had the goal of destroying the false peace between the French army and the mass of Algerians. They committed acts of terrorism against the French army, which led to greater repression by the army. Finally, a general Algerian uprising ensued.

**Text:**   A postmodern term that treats all theories, all events, all persons, places, or things as a special construction in a special sociocultural world. Everything is a text, including this definition of the term. See "Readerly (Versus Writerly) Text," "Simulacrum," and "Writerly (Versus Readerly) Text" for more.

**Theology:**   Greek: *theos* = god; *logos* = discourse. The study of the God concept. Most people believe (a) that there is a supreme being that (b) has a plan for social life and (c) rewards those who live in harmony with that plan. Most people believe that there is a life after death in which one is rewarded/punished for one's behavior in this world. Some believe in a hell to which those who fail to accept the plan are sent.

Karl Marx held that the God concept was the projection of the power of the people onto imaginary beings. Émile Durkheim held that the God concept embodied social power experienced when people came together. G.W.F. Hegel said that God embodied the slow movement toward full knowledge of the real world; Pierre Teilhard de Chardin said something similar. Socialist humanism is a religion but not a "theism." See "Religion" for more.

There are three major theistic religions: Judaism, Christianity, and Islam. There are three major "a-theistic" religions: Buddhism, Confucianism, and humanism. There are also many "poly-theistic" religions: Hinduism, Shintoism, and paganism; these religions may have hundreds, even thousands, of gods to which they turn for inspiration, guidance, and comfort in time of trouble. See "Alienation," "Sanctification/De-sanctification," and "Theology, Liberation" for more.

**Theology, Feminist:**   Feminist theology is complex and varies widely across theologians but generally accepts that there was a time when major gods were female. As such, these goddesses were nourishing, caring, compassionate, and mothering. With settled agriculture, especially irrigation, gods replaced goddesses; they became controlling, angry, punitive, and jealous of other gods. Zeus, Yahweh, and Elohim were the first such male gods. See "Sin, Original" for more.

**Theology, Liberation:**   This theology was developed by worker-priests in Latin America, France, Italy, Spain, and, later, Argentina in dialogue with Marxist thought. Liberation theology holds that announcing the Gospel is not merely a matter of preaching the word to individuals, but, rather, the church is obliged to work toward both liberation and salvation. Liberation in the world means opposition to "structural sin" that plagues this world. There is still concern for personal sin, which threatens salvation in the sacred realm. Those priests who embrace this theology enter the world as social critics. They attempt to identify structural sin and trace that sin to its source. The working assumption is that since all people are brothers and sisters in the sight of God, all enjoy an equal and inviolable dignity while alive. This reasoning calls all class, power, and honorific relations into question. Often, liberation theology leads to democratic and communistic social arrangements and organizations. See "Buddhism, Mahayana," "Divine Right (of Kings)," "God," "Praxis, Christian," "Protestant/Protestantism," "Socialism, Christian," and "Theology" for more.

**Theology, Postmodern:**   Durkheim argued that the experiences of extraordinary effects occur during religious activity and are taken to be proof of supernatural beings. Further, these effects of special acts and psychogens produce feelings of ecstasy and visions of the past and future that are, in turn, viewed as proof of the existence of a supernatural world. Theism is, thus, completely natural in this account.

There are two major postmodern views on religion: affirmative and nihilistic. Both forms of postmodern theology hold that the God concept is a human product rather than a supernatural being who created the universe and who gives all natural and social laws. Nihilistic postmodern views argue that since God is dead/non-existent, each person has an equal right to claim or do what s/he believes best for him/herself. Since there is no final authority nor any firm anchor point for moral/ethical behavior, one can do as one wishes. Affirmative postmodern theology asserts that, even without the God concept to endorse them, there are good reasons to act ethically and to embody many of the teachings of great spiritual leaders.

T. R. Young argues that dramas of the holy are progressive when they sanctify people and the good earth. The political question then revolves around the ways those who use different dramas of the holy are treated. Liberation theology requires that people be respected and honored in their own right. See "Agnosticism," "Aquinas, Thomas, St.," "Atheism," "Christian Right," "Humanism," and "Humanism, Socialist" for more.

**Theory:**   Greek: *Thea* = to view, to gaze upon. We get our words "theology," "theory," and "theater" from the same root word. In modern science, the word refers to the immutable essence of things or to the regular patterns of behavior of a system or set of systems. In critical theory, the word refers to that which deals with the changeable affairs of humans. In Greek social philosophy, *techne* was relegated to women and slaves, *praxis* was the work of men, and *theoria* was the province of the gods. See "Bacon, Francis" for more.

**Theory, Theory of:**   It questions the nature of theory building or conceptual analysis, as in the theory underpinning a particular methodology. The Marxian perspective is that the realm of ideas (theory included) does not become a material force until an idea (or theory) is apprehended by insightful, knowing humans and translated into overt behavior. This view contrasts with idealism and mysticism, in which the realm of ideas has a life and a causal effect apart from actions of intending humans. Karl Marx's famous Eleventh Thesis embodies the point. Ideas themselves do have a part to play in social revolution but will not, by themselves, move the world one step closer to a decent society. Cf. "Eleventh Thesis."

**Theory of the State:**   The liberal view is that the state exists to balance reciprocity between social institutions. The conservative view is that the state interferes with free enterprise. The Marxist view is that the state is the "executive committee" of capitalism (i.e., it exists to protect capitalism). The neo-Marxist view is that the state grows to solve the problems of capital accumulation and political legitimacy in capitalist/elitist societies.

**Thermidor:**   The eleventh month on the calendar of the French Revolution. It gave a name to the overthrow of the revolution by the right-wing in French politics. Today, it refers to the wave of repression after a revolution, the counterrevolution triggered by that wave, and the merciless execution of the revolutionaries when or if the counterrevolution succeeds. One could use it as a cautionary term to encourage the peaceful quest for and acceptance of social justice; that is, it is not clear who will win, but it is certain that whoever loses will suffer greatly after the revolution. There was no Thermidor after the Nicaraguan revolution; enemies were forgiven by the Sandinistas and, after a successful peaceful counterrevolution, the Sandinistas were forgiven. Liberation theology was important before, during, and after that revolution.

**Third World:**   Those states that are neither capitalist (first world) nor socialist (second world). Third world countries include all of Africa (except Rhodesia and the Union of South Africa), all of Latin America (except Cuba), most of the Near East, Middle East, and Far East countries, and Southeast Asia. The third world is a prize for capitalist countries: cheap and docile labor, access to markets, and availability of raw materials. In order to guarantee control of third world nations, capitalists invite the national bourgeoisie to share part of the profits; politicians are subsidized by the multinational corporation; military bases are established; and the local military is well-supplied and trained in the capitalist country. In order to control the class struggle and socialist agitation, right-wing dictatorships arise. These dictatorships are mostly sponsored by the United States. They combine massive political oppression with openness to foreign investment. The best examples are Argentina, Brazil, Chile, Indonesia, Greece, South Korea, and Taiwan.

**Topology:**   Also known as "rubber math" or "rubber sheet" geometry. Topology refers to the pulling, twisting, and contorting of shapes without tearing them or destroying their essential properties. Topology theory is important, in that it is a qualitative model for explaining how complex systems move/behave. Several topological constructs include the borromean knot, the cross-gap, the mobius band, and the klein bottle. Jacques Lacan made considerable use of topology theory as a way of explaining the operation of discourse and its link to human agency. Lacan used topology theory to graphically illustrate the flow and movement of discourse as something that embodied particular forms of desire and conveyed circumscribed knowledge. See "Desire" and "Lacan, Jacques" for more.

**Total Institution:**   A form of social organization in which: (1) one's behavior is prescribed in minute detail; (2) one is treated en bloc rather than as an individual; (3) one and only one social identity is permitted; and (4) one is socialized (or resocialized) to do difficult or dangerous work apart from material rewards. Some total institutions are mere holding tanks for the refuse of a poorly designed society (e.g., prisons, asylums, orphanages). See "Foucault, Michel" and "Goffman, Erving" for more.

**Totalitarianism:**    A form of government in which all significant aspects of social life are controlled by the state, which, itself, is in the hands of an elite. This concept is similar to authoritarianism except that authoritarianism permits limited freedoms, usually to males or small business persons in the civil (private) sector. American prisons or the American military are the closest contemporary examples of totalitarian social organizations in the United States.

As an ideology, totalitarianism sees in itself and its premises a total and complete explanation of everything, asserting the rightness of acting logically upon those premises irrespective of the horror, recklessness, or irresponsibility of that action. It vests the force to control dissent in a bureaucracy that claims a monopoly over the production of political culture. See "Authoritarianism," and "Government, Forms of" for more.

**Totality:**    According to Georg Lukács, bourgeois science cannot be a critical science since it takes the viewpoint of the individual (or a sample of individuals) and ignores the "totality" that gives meaning to individual acts. In order to understand poverty, one must understand the whole system. The term "totality" refers to the whole system that operates to produce the phenomena found within it.

**Totalizing:**    A postmodern term referring to theories that offer a way of understanding everything (i.e., globalizing) and, thus, reject other ways of understanding events in the world. Thus, Marxist theory, the Christian Bible, Islamic theology, and structural functionalism are totalizing theories and are to be suspected. Cf. "Narrative" and "Story/Storytelling."

**Tracy, Destutt de (1758–1836):**    Coined the term "ideology": the science of what we now call propaganda. De Tracy began his work when Napoleon, claiming that it was dangerous to religion, suppressed the school he was in. Thomas Jefferson translated his works and published them in Philadelphia. (See the work of W. L. Reese.). See "Ideology" for more.

**Trade Union:**    A form of worker organization in which the workers in a given industry join with the owners to extract surplus value from the rest of the workers and surplus population. The interests of workers as a class are put aside in return for job security, relatively good wages, good working conditions, pensions, petty grievance procedures, and a chance for advancement to middle echelon jobs. These benefits help drive inflation, but the big unions protect themselves against it, so it affects those in the competitive sector and those in the surplus population.

**Trade Union Congress (TUC):**    The most general coordinating organization of British labor unions, which includes some 170 unions. Founded in 1868, it gave rise to the Labour Party in Britain and retains connection with it. Delegates to the TUC are elected. The TUC works for the common good as well as for the welfare of its union members. See "Union" for more.

**Transaction:**   The term emphasizes the fact that knowledge is always a result of the mutual influence of the inquirer on what s/he observes. If the realm of inquiry is everyday life, then the inquirer is simply a human being seeking to produce with another human being what they are going to do. After that is decided and they both "know" it, then intersubjective understanding exists and a social "fact" (i.e., that which is validly known) is established. John Dewey and Eric Bentley used the term to avoid the subject-object split that is implicit in such terms, which are common in a scientific paradigm the point of which is to treat as natural the isolation of people from each other.

**Transpraxis:**   A concept developed through the work of Friedrich Nietzsche and his criticism of G.W.F. Hegel's master-slave dichotomy. Nietzsche argued that when a person or group reacts to perceived hierarchical power relations and seeks to repudiate or renounce them, the relations of production are reproduced. In the process of negation, relations of production are reconstituted by those persons who support them. For example, children who are bullied by other older children attempt to neutralize the power of the bullies by soliciting the help of their even older siblings. In so doing, the nature of the struggle (kids not getting along with one another) has not been altered. Transpraxis, however, is specifically concerned with the deconstructive and reconstructive effects inherent in any reaction-negation response. More particularly, transpraxis is about the dialectics of (linguistic) struggle. Transpraxis is an affirmative attempt to liberate the subject from the imprisonment of language during precisely those moments when there is reaction to oppression. The goal is not to reverse the hierarchies (e.g., younger children now in control of older children); rather, the aim is to affirm in the act of negating, to validate in the effort to resist. Thus, that which is resisted is the hierarchy itself (e.g., good/bad; objective/subjective; white/black). If successful, transpraxis is the vehicle by which to effect a more humanistic and just social order. It validates multiplicity, difference, and diversity without privileging any one manifestation of multiplicity, difference, or diversity. See "Dialogical Pedagogy" for more.

**Trope:**   Greek: *tropos* = a turning. It refers to the figurative use of a word or expression, as in the changing meaning of signs. All words are tropes because they convey hidden values and implicit assumptions that need to be decoded. Postmodernists employ the term to refer to the tissued or layered dimension of speech understood as a text. See "Decode," "Semiotics," "Sign," and "Writerly (Versus Readerly) Text" for more.

**Trotsky, Leon (1879–1940):**   Lev Davydovich Bronstein was born in 1879 in southern Russia of Jewish peasants. Sent to prison, he took the name of his prison guard in Odessa to confuse the police. Trotsky was a Bolshevist leader who joined Vladimir Lenin and helped put down the counterrevolution. Trotsky's ideas include the idea that simple societies could move directly to socialism without going through capitalism; that the world capitalist system required a strong Soviet state to protect itself from international capital; that local soviets should have real power (see "Soviet" for more); that there should be a permanent revolution even within socialism; that there was a place for limited markets; and that socialism required cooperation between workers in all industrial nations (rather than socialism in one state as Joseph Stalin urged).

Stalin expelled him from the USSR; Trotsky found refuge in Mexico, where he criticized both German and Russian fascism. For Trotsky, the new worker's enemy became bureaucracy. He urged its overthrow in a political (as opposed to an economic) revolution and called for a plurality of socialist political parties. Trotsky organized the Fourth Socialist International in 1938 in Paris, where he called for socialist democracy, the overthrow of bureaucracy, and the liberation of the third world. He was murdered in Mexico in 1940 by Ramón Mercader.

**Truth:**   Anglo-Saxon: *treowth* = fidelity. In modern science, the term refers to the goodness of fit between a set of words and the reality that it purports to describe, explain, or predict. In this knowledge process, truth mirrors/corresponds to reality. In analytic logic, truth is a set of coherent propositions. In pragmatism, truth resides in the efficacy of a statement—its usefulness in solving some problem. In semantic theories of truth, truth is a set of statements (a metalanguage) that is based upon statements from everyday language. In postmodern sensibility, truth is a social product; things defined as true may in fact become true if people believe and act in a way compatible with the definition of the situation. The assumptions of correspondence and coherence do not fit the nonlinear dynamics revealed in Chaos/Complexity research. Postmodern philosophy of science grounded on nonlinearity argues that truth is complex, contrary, and changeable, depending upon both natural and social dynamics; one then speaks of fractal truth values and contingent truth claims. Cf. "Chaos Theory."

**Truth, Sojourner (1797–1883):**   Black American feminist and former slave. Sojourner Truth actively spoke out in favor of women's suffrage, slave abolitionism, and creative nonviolence. Truth was a speaker at the Akron Women's Rights Convention in 1851, where she identified the double oppression experienced by black women. This theme has been renewed in the writings of contemporary black feminists who argue that feminist movements have perpetuated racist ideology and practices by arguing that the political and economic conditions of white women are similar to the sustained plight of women of color. See "Feminism, Black" for more.

**Twelve Tables:**   One of the first set of written laws that laid the basis for Roman law. Roman law is at the heart of U.S. law. Along with Deuteronomic law and British common law, most of us think about crime, punishment, and social justice in the terms specified by the Twelve Tables and their successors. See "Law" for more.

**Two-Party System:**   The radical view is that the function of the Republican Party is to maintain discipline within the ranks of capitalists, whereas the function of the Democratic Party is to maintain discipline within the ranks of organized labor and dissident groups. This view contrasts with the liberal view that the two-party system is a source of change and provides for the peaceful resolution of issues. Since members of both parties work within the capitalist paradigm, real options to the paradigm are unlikely.

# U

**Ultrastability:**  A characteristic of any system able to maintain itself in a changing environment without exceeding the ability of the environment to repair itself. In postmodern analysis, ultrastability is seen as limited, given the essential instability and uncertainty contained within the initial conditions of most dynamic or complex systems. See "Chaos Theory" and "Indeterminacy Principle" for more.

**Underclass (Undermass):**  Persons in a racist, sexist, or classist society not needed or wanted in the production of political and ideological culture. Often they are confined to the production of material wealth (to be used by the privileged), but in advanced monopoly capitalism, the underclass is entirely surplus to the production needs of industry and commerce. For the underclass, birth control, abortion, abstinence, and other population-limiting practices are encouraged. In racist societies, genocide is used. In some sexist societies, female infanticide is practiced in order to remove those defined as surplus. See "Overpopulation" for more.

The underclass are also those who bear no relationship to the means of production whatsoever. They represent the aged, those on welfare, the unemployed, petty criminals, the homeless, idle children, those without work in the rural or urban slums, prisoners, the mentally ill, and runaway youth. See "Class Structure," "Pauper/Pauperism," and "Surplus Population" for more.

**Underground Structures:**  Forbidden ways of life with low visibility. They include economic, political, religious, or sexual forms of behavior that are contrary to the normative way of behaving and that typically appear in repressive societies. Underground structures vary from liberation movements in elitist societies to elitist movements in democratic countries. See "Power, Forms of" for more.

**Unemployment:**  The term given to the inability or refusal of workers to find work. Unemployment may be cyclical, seasonal, or frictional. *Cyclical* unemployment comes with the ups and downs of capitalism (see "Kondratieff Cycles" for more). *Seasonal* unemployment varies with climate.

*Frictional* unemployment refers to the time lag between increase in demand and the renewal of actual production. It is not found in any other economic system other than capitalism.

Karl Marx argued that long-term unemployment is a result of the replacement of workers (labor power) with machines (organic capital). Further, he argued that capitalism needs a "reserve army of workers" in order to keep wages down and profits up. See "Disemployment" for more.

**Union:**   An association of workers who join together to bargain about wages and fringe benefits, conditions of work and the labor process (e.g., safety, division of labor, job assignment), and the kind and quality of goods and services produced. Some unions stay focused on the welfare of their members only. Some unions work for better working conditions for both union and nonunion workers. Some unions work for social justice for all citizens. See "Trade Union" and "Trade Union Congress" for more.

**Union Corruption:**   Many unions are subverted in their social justice programs by the leadership. In exchange for personal benefits, the union leaders may accept company rules, invest union funds in corrupt schemes, and use violence to prevent opposition from arising. See "Oligarchy, Michel's Iron Law of" for more.

**United Front:**   Also broad front, frontism, and front politics. The term given to a broad coalition of communists, socialists, feminists, minorities, liberals, Christian socialists, environmentalists, and young people who work together for social justice. Euro-communism uses united front tactics.

**Unproductive Labor:**   That part of the labor force that owns nothing, produces nothing, and adds no use value to production. Included are sales persons, advertising agents, lawyers, insurance agents, stock brokers, real estate agents, most police, the military, servants, consultants, and waste makers.

The socialist critique is that monopoly capital has produced a new variety of parasites that, together with the clergy and the aristocracy, consume the surplus of a society that might be put to better use.

**Upper Class:**   Those who "own" enough of the means of production such that they are free to enjoy a life of leisure. In the early stages of feudalism and capitalism, the thought was that the productive system should be organized such that a division of labor could be made. Those who were dull or insensitive would produce material culture. Those who were refined, of "higher" intellect or artistic capacity, would possess the free time to produce "higher culture." Art, science, political and economic theory, music, drama, literature, and the "finer" arts would be produced by the elite.

Lesser humans would benefit from that art, poetry, music, and nobility of the soul.

**URPE:**   The Union for Radical Political Economics. The union publishes information of value to socialist sociologists with hard data to support analyses of the current problems of American capitalism.

**Usury:**   Excessive interest charged by lenders to borrowers. In the United States, interest rates vary by class; wealthy people generally pay about 7 percent interest, middle-class people pay about 12 percent interest, poor people pay 18 percent or more. Pawn shops charge about 120 percent per year, and loan sharks on the street charge 20 percent per week. The Pentateuch (the first five books of the Jewish, Christian, and Islamic holy book) permits usury and defines it as a fair charge for wear and tear only. In that context, no money would exchange hands for the loan of a tool or land if it were returned in as good or better shape than when borrowed. In addition, this holy book provides for forgiveness of debts every seven years (the sabbatical). See "Interest" for more.

**Utility/Utilitarianism:**   A social philosophy in which human behavior is guided by the greatest good for the greatest number of people. It became the guiding philosophy of the enlightenment credited to Jeremy Bentham and John Stuart Mill. The everyday interpretation came to be a justification for capitalism and inequality when it was translated as "rational egoism" and "enlightened self-interest." See "Bentham, Jeremy" and "Mill, John Stuart" for more. Cf. "Golden Rule," "Hammurabi, Code of," "Kant, Immanuel," "Kantian Imperative," "Laissez-Faire," and "Punishment."

**Utopia/Utopianism:**   Greek: *u* = no; *topi* = place. An ideal (in both senses of the term—see "Idea/Idealism" for more) society in which people reach their potential and live happy and productive lives. Socialist theory identifies some problems with utopian thinking: (1) Often utopias are ideals that ignore the existing limits and, thus, have no bridge from reality; (2) utopian thinking often separates theory and action; and (3) many utopias are fascist states with drugs and sex to pacify the masses. See "Agitation" and "Parlor Marxism" for more.

# V

**Validity Claims:** According to Jürgen Habermas, there are four things we assume when we talk to someone: (1) that any utterance can be understood by both (all) parties; (2) that its propositional content is true (it is not a lie or mistake); (3) that the speaker is sincere in uttering it and; (4) that the speaker has a right to be talking. When there is some reason to doubt one of these implicit validity claims, we assume that the speaker can be called into account. However, there are obstacles to accountability that invalidate the assumption. See "Systematically Distorted Communication" for more.

**Value:** A cultural item in which positive emotional response is defined. Values help establish what is important and how to decide between competing claims. Values also circumvent reasoning processes and help solve the problem of motivation.

**Value (Exchange-):** Karl Marx distinguished between production for use and production for exchange. Exchange-value is the value of one good in terms of the value of another good. (For example, a carton of cigarettes is exchanged/worth two dozen eggs). The focus on exchange-value creates several problems: (1) It justifies the withholding of essential social goods (food, shelter, clothing, medicine, recreation) when the exchange does not provide profits; (2) it mystifies and stifles critique since it enables capitalist theorists to discuss rationalization in terms of an increase in exchange-value rather than in terms of use-value; (3) it masks the intrinsic worth of commodities when artificial equivalencies are created; and (4) it replaces all other motives for production and distribution. In Marxist theory, the central reason for production is tied to the creation of human culture. In capitalism, production is keyed to profit/loss benefits rather than human need as such. Cf. "Value (Use-)."

**Value, Labor Theory of:** Karl Marx emphasized the role of human labor as the sole creator of value. The use-value and exchange-value of all commodities (including labor itself) are determined by the labor time required to produce them. There are two main criticisms of this theory: (1) Price is set by supply and demand, not labor time; and (2) capital goods create value apart from the labor of workers. According to Marxist theory, the first argument is not relevant since Marx was discussing value not price. The second argument is questionable since Marx's point was to stress that it is through labor that humans create their cultural environment. Thus, capitalism becomes a barrier to value as the surplus population develops. See "Value (Use-)" for more.

**Value, Postmodern View of:**    In postmodern economic theory, art, music, cinema, and scripts are used together in advertising to create a "hyper-text" in which the value of a commodity is artificially enhanced by borrowing on the art and craft of singers, sports stars, esteemed persons, and deep anxieties. This artificial enhancement creates layer after layer of false need. In such a world, value and price bear little relationship to use-value. Both use-value and exchange-value are displaced by the use of psychology, sociology, mass communications, and dramaturgy to create false needs. See "Cyberspace," "Hyperreality," "Simulacrum," and "Simulation" for more.

**Value, Surplus:**    That which is left after the costs of production are met. These costs are land, labor, capital goods, and safe disposal of by-products. Capitalists set prices anywhere from 5 percent to 15 percent (sometimes even more) above these unavoidable costs. This is called the "profit margin." The economic question is how to use surplus value. Some part could go to basic research and development of better goods and equipment. Some could go to those who have special merit in the productive process (e.g., inventors, skilled reliable workers, effective administrators). Some could be used for low-profit, essential services. Some could go to those who own the stocks of the company.

**Value (Use-):**    Anything that satisfies a human want, desire, need, or anxiety. It is the intrinsic worth of a commodity determined by the subjective meaning assigned to it by the one who labors to make that product. Karl Marx held that use-value varied dramatically between people and cultures, so one needed to dig deeper to get at the final source of value. Thus, according to Marx, use-value was to be found in labor value; that is, the labor that is invested in producing the commodity. See "Value (Exchange-)" and "Value, Labor Theory of" for more.

**Vanguard/Vanguardism:**    A feature of militant Marxist-Leninist theory that holds that only a few Marxists understand the sources of and solutions to exploitation and that they should lead the revolution and keep power after the insurrection until a socialist psychology is developed among the common people. The vanguard seldom encourages this socialist model of being, thus justifying continual domination by a party elite.

See "Cadre," "Centralism, Democratic" and "Communism, Movement of" for more.

**Variety:**   In systems theory, variety is that which is not part of the operating components of a system or its environment. The term is used to denote some changed condition. The interest of radical sociologists is in Ashby's Law of Requisite Variety. Ashby's law justifies the school of critical theory in terms that even the most reactionary "hard" scientist can appreciate. According to Ashby's law, in order for social systems to survive they must have a capacity for change and renewal, which is a standard feature of any system in an unstable environment. See "Ashby's Law of Requisite Variety" for more.

**Vico, Giovanni Batista (1688–1744):**   The founder of history as a science and discipline. According to Vico, "history is everything." Vico opposed the idea that science and reason informed the knowledge process; all ideas arise in a given history of a society. There are three stages in history through which every society moves: (1) the Age of Gods; (2) the Age of Heroes; and (3) the Age of Man. Societies change from theocracies to monarchies to democracies informed by reason and rationality. (See the work of W. L. Reese.)

**Victimology:**   A criminological subdiscipline founded by Hans von Hentig. Victimology focuses on the victim in criminal activity, and in von Hentig's text, *The Criminal and His Victim*, he examined this process systematically during the post–World War II era. Today, victimologists gather detailed information about victims; that is, they assess characteristics of victims in their relationship to offenders through such instruments as victimization surveys.

A more critical appraisal of victimology considers how individuals or groups experience harm and/or oppression in society. Critical victimology emphasizes the political, social, economic, psychological, and historical dynamics inherent in how power is either structurally or interactionally wielded to victimize women, minorities, and the poor.

**Victims Without Crimes:**   The phrase points to the harm done to society by those who are powerful enough to control the process by which crimes are defined as such by legislative processes. In capitalist modes of exchange, surplus value is appropriated, social power is perverted, and humans are turned into commodities (e.g., through prostitution, wage labor, and mass advertising). However, no crime or victim is institutionally identified, nor is any criminal legitimately policed.

**Viet Cong (Viet Minh):**   A Marxist-Leninist revolutionary party founded by Ho Chi Minh in 1941 to oppose French and Japanese colonialism. The

Viet Cong defeated the French at Dien Bien Phu in May 1954. At the time, the United States led Australia, New Zealand, South Korea, Thailand, and the Philippines in a military effort to prevent the communist victory in the southern part of Vietnam. It was the first time in history that the United States lost a war.

**Violence, Gender:**   The gender division of labor gives men the moral right to use force to obtain compliance from the women in their lives. There are three major situations in which men assume they have the right to beat women: (1) when sexual favors are denied; (2) when domestic services are withheld; and (3) when women do not use language forms that embody deference and obedience to men. Most feminists maintain that rape is a more public social control tactic.

**Virtue:**   Latin: *virtus* = manly. Socrates identified virtue with knowledge. Plato listed four virtues: wisdom, courage, temperance, and justice. Aristotle set the Golden Mean as the pathway to virtue. Saint Paul listed faith, hope, and charity *(caritas)* as central to Christian life. Thomas Hobbes had his own list: justice, gratitude, modesty, equity, and mercy. Baruch Spinoza held that virtue required that one live by reason. Voltaire held that virtue is an attribute of societies, not of individuals. (See the work of W. L. Reese.)

**Voice/Voices:**   Postmodernists use the term to refer to the person who tells a story/narrative or offers a theory; the focus is on the voice of the teller rather than the content of the story. The term also points to those whose stories are omitted in the telling of a story. See "Writerly (Versus Readerly) Text" for more. Cf. *"Ecriture feminine"* and "Gilligan, Carol."

**Vulgar Marxism:**   A term used by Vladimir Lenin and others to heap contempt on those who used the work of Karl Marx for the only and final arbiter in every dispute over policy. Vulgar Marxism is also used to refer to those who do not include the early Marx in policy discussion. The term is used to reject the assumption that the means of production (the base) is everywhere and always determinative of culture (the superstructure). Friedrich Engels used the term to refer to those who try to use natural law to explain social behavior: people, for example, who claim that human thought is a secretion of the brain or that human beings are atoms that bind together through force. See "Marx, Early" and "Weber, Max" for more. Cf. "Parlor Marxism."

**Wage Labor:**   A term used by Karl Marx to describe the fact that capitalism converts labor from the human activity of producing culture into a commodity. The price of commodity labor is called wages. In a capitalist system, people have only labor power to sell to get the necessities of life. Wages are set by demand and supply. However, they can be reduced to below the level required for reproducing the labor force by cooperation among capitalists and enforced competition between workers, by recruiting from underdeveloped nations, and by a large surplus population. Wage labor is increased by unions, by internationalism, and/or by welfare programs. There are parallel economic systems used by people to reunite production and distribution outside of capitalist logic. See "Economic Forms, Parallel" for more.

**Wages, Iron Law of:**   An idea credited to Thomas Malthus that assumed that wages tend to oscillate around bare subsistence. According to Malthus, when wages are higher people are inclined to have more children, thus increasing the labor pool and driving wages down. Lasalle used the argument against raising wages, whereas Karl Marx used it against the capitalist system. The Iron Law of Wages is falsified by the fact that if women receive education and work, they limit the number of children they bear.

**Wages, Real:**   Wages are what one's money can buy. Real wages are not to be confused with the number of dollars one is paid. When taxes increase or firms raise prices, real wages can go down even if one is making more dollars. Real wages increased in the United States for most people from 1940 until the mid-1970s, but have since declined. Capitalist economists think the trend can be reversed. Marxist economists disagree.

**Wallace, Alfred (1823–1913):**   English naturalist who first set forth the idea of organic evolution after years of collecting plants around the world. Wallace sent Charles Darwin a paper in which he described the ideas of the struggle for existence and the survival of the fittest. Darwin thought so well of the idea that he had it read at a scholarly conference along with his own ideas. Both Darwin and Wallace helped replace premodern ideas of divine creation with natural explanations of the emergence of plant and animal species. Focusing upon competition and "survival" of the fittest, they essentially ignored cooperation and mutual aid as aspects of survival within and between species. Herbert Spencer and others took this partial theory and elevated it to a general theory of social evolution in politics, economics, and warfare. (See the work of W. L. Reese.)

**War, Sociology of:**    War is the organized use of force against another people or nation. There have been several varieties of warfare in human history:

1. *Predatory warfare:* one tribe or band attacks another in order to steal herds, tools, weapons, or to take slaves, as in the Viking raids along England and France.
2. *Wars for colonial empire:* one people invades the lands of another and imposes an exploitive system on a people (e.g., the Persian Empire, the Roman Empire, the Inca Empire). Rule is indirect through governors.
3. *Wars of feudal conquest:* one petty noble conquers and rules several other "kingdoms" in an area. Charlemagne consolidated the petty states of France into empire in the eleventh century. Rule is direct through succession by birth.
4. *Wars of bourgeois revolution:* the middle classes overthrow the nobility and take state power, as in England, France, the Americas, and elsewhere.
5. *Wars of capitalist expansion:* World Wars I and II can be understood as wars between capitalist states, as each tried to solve its own problems of surplus population and crises at the expense of other states.
6. *Wars of socialist liberation:* there is an attempt to overthrow the capitalist/feudal state and take power on behalf of workers, as in Russia (1917), China (1949), Cuba (1959), Nicaragua (1979), and South Africa (1991).

**War, Theory of:**    From a socialist perspective, war is best understood as the extraction of value from people by military force. Karl Marx's theory of war sets basic conflicts over the means of production as the center point. There are different conflicts between differing groups in different political economies. In primitive economies, one tribe wars with another over land, water, and herds. In slavery, armed groups from one country enslave captives. In feudalism, one prince will try to conquer another prince and expand both land and subjects. In capitalist societies, the basic conflict between nations is over markets, raw materials, and access to cheap labor. Socialists distinguish between unjust wars and just wars. Generally, any war to liberate people or nations from domination is just.

**War Crimes:**   Violations of the Geneva Convention dealing with the treatment of war prisoners, civilians, neutral countries, and with other areas in which the use of state violence is prohibited.

After World War II, the United States and its allies convened a special court to judge the behavior of the German army and Nazi Party members who engineered the death of millions of civilians (mostly Jews, communists, and socialists but, later on, any one who opposed the Nazi regime). The German army murdered thousands of Polish officers, communist resistance leaders, and antiwar sympathizers.

The critical assessment focuses on war criminals and the victors of war. The victors of wars seldom convene courts to judge their own crimes against humanity and human rights. Since the Vietnam conflict (and given the many crimes of the U.S. military that have been filmed and presented on national news), every new member of the armed forces is required to take several hours of instruction on war crimes and is told that s/he has the right to refuse to obey an illegal order. War crimes continue in public and in secret among the armies of all countries and rebels.

**Warfare State:**   A term used to denote the role of military force in solving the problems of capitalism. In particular: The problem of markets is solved (1) by using the military to resist socialist liberation movements in colonial countries and (2) by using the military to absorb much of the surplus productive capacity of capitalists at profit rates guaranteed by the state.

**Waste Production:**   In a class society, some people do not have enough income, and some have a lot of "discretionary" income. In order to keep machines running, it is necessary to generate demand in the second group. One way to do this is to design products that wear out fast. People then will have to buy more light bulbs, cars, toasters, or TVs than they really need. Another way to generate demand is to promote fashions in cars, clothes, houses, or appliances. A third way is to generate demand for useless products or for products that use a lot of resources to save a little labor, such as electric knives, tooth brushes, finger nail files, or can openers. The drug industry has been known to create "illnesses" in order to generate a public. A better way to organize production is on the basis of need within the limits of ecological integrity rather than on the basis of profit.

**Wave Theory:**   Drawn from the field of quantum mechanics and physics, wave theory identifies the dual nature of matter. Matter is made up both of whole, tangible substances (i.e., particles) and partial, floating substances (i.e., waves). This dichotomy is significant for understanding the complexity of dynamic (physical or social) systems. Chaos theory posits that complex systems behave nonlinearly because the behavior of a system is unpredictable. This unpredictability is a function of its fluid essential nature. The welfare, housing, education, mental health, and criminal justice systems are (dis)ordered systems because they tend toward uncertain, spontaneous, inconsistent states. Depending upon the inputs to these systems, their concrete/abstract dimensions will shift, producing unexpected outcomes. See "Chaos Theory" for more.

**Webb, Sidney James (1859–1947), and Beatrice Potter Webb (1858–1943):** English economists and socialist reformers. A British couple who led the movement for social justice in England. (See "Fabianism" for more.) They were at the center of a set of intellectuals who adopted socialism to democratic politics and state welfare. The modern British system of health care, housing, education, and child care owes much to this group. They were models for such American couples as the Scott Nearings, Alfred and Elizabeth Lee, Elise and Kenneth Boulding, as well as hundreds of others who join love and labor in the marriage form.

**Weber, Max (1864–1920):**   Weber contributed significantly to progressive sociology. His critique/analysis of bureaucracy, his concern with forms of stratification other than class, and his work on power and authority all help us understand the larger structures that defeat democracy and human agency. He is best noted for his work on the sociology of religion. In his work *The Protestant Ethic and the Spirit of Capitalism*, Weber makes the connection between the Protestant ethic of hard work, frugality, and stewardship of wealth (on behalf of God) and the spirit of capitalism. In methodology, he is known for his use of "ideal types" and for *verstehen* (understanding) as a pathway to knowledge. Along with Karl Marx and Émile Durkheim, Weber is regarded as one of the most productive and insightful social theorists. See "Authority," "Ideal-Types," and "Vulgar Marxism" for more. Cf. "Durkheim, Émile" and "Marx, Karl."

**Welfare State:**   A term used to refer to any capitalist or feudal country in which the state provides comprehensive social security from "cradle to grave." Health care, child care, housing allowance, education benefits, pensions, and food stamps are the major forms of welfare found in such states. Capitalism is the only economic system that separates production and distribution and that produces a surplus population unable to reunite them. Welfare provides political legitimacy to capitalism by carrying the costs of supporting the surplus population.

**Westphalen, Jenny von (1814–1881):**   Childhood friend and wife to Karl Marx. Her dowry and her life were given over to Karl's work. She bore six children, three of whom died in infancy. She died of malnutrition and cancer two years before Marx.

**White-Collar Crime:**   Acts of petty thievery or embezzlement by which the assets of a corporation are converted to the private use of a middle-class functionary. White-collar crime is greatly condemned by liberal criminologists. Also termed corporate crime, it represents in real dollars the larger crimes of business, industry, and finance perpetrated against society and community.

**Witchcraft:**   There are two usages of the word that are of interest to critical/feminist scholars: (1) a set of beliefs and practices in which the forces/spirits of nature and/or the Devil are invoked to accomplish objectives (Christians tend to set the Christ and the Anti-Christ in opposition); (2) a form of feminist theology in which "good witches" use their powers to heal, to comfort, and to protect those whom fate, chance, or the "forces of evil" threaten. Socialist feminists see witchcraft as a political tool used against women who challenge patriarchy and male hegemony. See "Moral Panic" and "Satanism" for more.

**Wittgenstein, Ludwig (1889–1951):**   Born into a wealthy Viennese family, Wittgenstein's father was one of the richest men in Austria at the time. Originally, Wittgenstein studied engineering, specifically aeronautical engineering. His engineering training led him to an interest in mathematics. This interest later contributed to his philosophical endeavors. Wittgenstein studied under Bertrand Russell in Cambridge, England. Russell was a logician and mathematician. Wittgenstein learned a great deal more about logic and mathematics, as it relates to philosophy, while in Cambridge. He died of cancer in 1951.

In 1921, Wittgenstein published one of his major works, *Tractatus Logico-Philosophicus*. In it, Wittgenstein endeavored to demonstrate how all the problems of philosophy could be understood through principles of language. Wittgenstein is noted for explicating what he termed "language games." Language games essentially indicate that there are multiple meanings that attach to language systems; however, in order to appreciate that particular language system and how it operates, one needs to understand the rules of the language game in use. This concept is significant for a postmodern philosophy of language and represents a major departure from the structural movement, which argued that meaning in language was reducible to finite, essential possibilities. See "Semiotics" and "Sign" for more.

In Wittgenstein's later life he felt that he had solved all the problems of philosophy and pursued a career as a school teacher (1920–1926). However, he was a failure at this profession. Complaints about his temper and his austere teaching methods resulted in his resignation. Wittgenstein returned to an academic career and became professor of philosophy at Cambridge in England where he renewed his investigations of logic, philosophy, and language. He resigned his chair in 1947. In 1949 he discovered that he had cancer. Wittgenstein's other major work, *Philosophical Investigations*, was published posthumously. See "Peirce, Charles S." for more.

*Wizard of Oz:*   A children's story wherein the problems of capitalism are presented in allegorical fashion and the objectives of socialist revolution are personified by the characters of Dorothy (the search for social relatedness), the tinman (a quest for love and compassion), the lion (a search for courage and dignity), and the straw man (the search for insight, understanding, and wisdom). The Wicked Witch of the East was meant to be capitalism; the yellow brick road was meant to symbolize the gold standard and tight money policies; the silver slippers (not ruby) were symbolic of loose money policy; and the Wizard of Oz symbolized any fraudulent politician who gave the people what they could already produce themselves.

**Womanism:**   This is one of the African-American responses to feminism. Some women of color argue that the standpoint epistemology identified by critical feminist theory ensures the stable relegitimization of Anglo women voices but does little to embody the voice of women representing non-white cultures. African-American feminists such as bell hooks claim that womanism is about reclaiming the standpoint epistemologies of a diversity of women, including those of color. See "Critical Race Theory" for more. Cf. "Feminist Standpoint Epistemology" and "Feminist Theory."

**Wonk/Wonks:**   Women only, no kids. A marriage form in which two or more women live together without kids. Personal comfort and sexual pleasure are central to this form of intimacy. Cf. "Dinks," "Monks," and "Yuppie."

**Worker:**   One who must sell his/her labor power to another. One who produces wealth but does not own it after it is produced. Under some forms of socialism, the working class is considered to be the sole repository of worth. See "Working Class" for more.

**Working Class:**   Those who have only their labor power to sell and/or those who produce wealth in industry, agriculture, mining, milling, fishing, transport, communications, and forestry. The working class include white-collar people who perform essential services (e.g., nurses, doctors, engineers, teachers, and inventors). These services are not performed on behalf of the capitalist class. Sometimes artists, musicians, painters, dramatists, poets, and architects are included when they produce emancipatory art. Otherwise, they are considered bourgeois functionaries. The aim of authentic socialist revolution is to transform the working class into the architect and agent of general social policy. See "Worker" for more.

**Working Day:**   The period in a day that is necessary to produce enough value to cover the costs of reproducing labor power as well as raw materials and capital costs (e.g., buildings, tools, machines). The First International called for an eight-hour work day to replace the work day set by owners. Owners based their work day upon the physical and psychological limits of the fastest, best, and hardest workers. Sometimes these work days reached sixteen hours in England.

**World Council of Churches:**　A coalition of Christian churches working around the world for social justice. Many conservative church leaders condemn it as communist and/or socialist. See "Socialism, Christian" for more.

**Writerly (Versus Readerly) Text:**　In postmodern deconstructive analysis, all communication, whether written or spoken, is a text. The writerly versus readerly distinction was popularized by Roland Barthes in relationship to interpreting classic literary texts; however, several additional postmodern theorists have applied his insights to legal narratives (Dragan Milovanovic, Bruce Arrigo), to film theory (Caja Silverman), to semiotic critiques (MacCabe), and to psychoanalysis (Gilles Deleuze and Félix Guattari).

*Writerly approach:* This is a subversive and insurgent approach to reading a text. It emphasizes a multitude of interpretations that validate a variety of truths and knowledges. Unlike the readerly approach, which tends toward closure or toward the text's finiteness, the writerly approach resists structure and a definable, singular product. Here, the process is central. The underlying structures of signification, of meaning, are unearthed. The text is understood to contain an explosion and scattering of meaning. Rather than privileging one interpretation, one voice, through the text, the reader/viewer is encouraged to discover the multiple and repressed voices embedded in the words. Familiarity and coherence, cornerstones of the readerly approach, are resisted and supplanted with displacement and ambivalence. This is an active deconstruction (i.e., decentering and destabilizing) of sedimented and privileged meanings. It is also an active reconstruction of alternative truths and replacement ways of knowing. See "Author," "Barthes, Roland," "Story/Storytelling," "Text," "Trope," and "Voice/Voices" for more.

**Wycliffe, John (1320–1384):**　An Oxford scholar whose doctrines helped bring about a great transformation of Christian religion. Wycliffe held that all dominion over land or people comes as a gift from God. The land has the form of a fief and can be removed if the person to whom the gift is given does not serve God. The church is to serve the spiritual needs of people; it is not to hold property; it is lawful for the state to take property from any monk, priest, bishop, or pope who is not doing the will of God. The king is God's vicar on earth and has superiority over priests in all earthly matters. Wycliffe held that the Bible is the "charter" for all Christians and helped translate it into English. Its prose was an elegant and powerful poetry that served as a base for the King James version, still used widely today. Wycliffe sent priests out to spread the word. In Bohemia, Huss helped institute the Protestant Reformation that Wycliffe designed. (See the work of W. L. Reese.)

**Y**

**Yankee-Cowboy Thesis:** A view that American capitalists are split into two segments as a result of government expenditures. These expenditures have created a new elite with interests and policies different from those of the corporate liberals of the East—the "Yankees." The "cowboys" benefit from government contracts in the defense, aerospace, and electronic industries. They are said to favor more violent police and state tactics in dealing with foreign and/or domestic opposition to capitalism. The underlying question is: Is the ruling class split and engaged in mutual destruction or are the differences in interest and policy contained such that capitalism still rules America?

**Yuppie:** This acronym stands for young, upwardly mobile persons who are concerned only with their own lifestyle and economic security. It is used derisively or as a form of amused teasing. The perfect person in a capitalist society is one who maximizes his/her own pleasure, who helps extract surplus value from working class people, and who spends discretionary money as fast as possible. See "Dinks," "Extended Family," "Monks," and "Wonk/Wonks" for more.

# Z

**Zeno of Elea (490–430 B.C.E.):**   Aristotle held Zeno to be the inventor of the dialectic, through his famous paradoxes: (1) one grain of millet makes no sound when it falls to earth; 10,000 grains make a noise. How can 10,000 noiseless things make a noise? (2) Space is a nonsense notion since if it exists, it can be divided; if divided, either it has finite or infinite parts. Space with finite parts has magnitude; space with infinite parts has no magnitude. How can space exist if it has no magnitude? (3) A flying arrow cannot be flying, since it must be either moving in a place where it is or moving in a space where it is not. It cannot be moving in a place where it is, since it would be there and not moving; it cannot be moving in a place where it is not since it is not there. These paradoxes are now understood to be language games that bear no connection to the dynamics of natural and social systems. However, at the time, they did present one with a dialectic of analytic categories and thus revealed the human role in creating categories with which nature and society are analyzed. (See the work of W. L. Reese.)

**Zenophobia:**   Fear of strangers.

**Zero-Sum Game:**   A form of competition in which one party (or several) must lose while one (or more) gains. Cf. "Non-Zero-Sum Game."

**Zimbardo, Philip (1933– ):**   Zimbardo set up a social psychological experiment at Stanford in which he took twenty-four bright, mature, emotionally stable men and, by flipping a coin, designated some as "prisoners" and some as "guards." The prisoners were picked up at their homes by a police officer, searched, handcuffed, fingerprinted, blindfolded, and taken to prison. The guards were told they could make their own rules. The experiment lasted two weeks. Some prisoners became depressed, confused, hysterical, and had to be released after a few days. The guards, otherwise nice people, became cruel and heartless. Eventually, Zimbardo had to end the experiment early. The sociology of it all become too, too real.

**Zionism:**    An international Jewish movement founded in Switzerland in 1897 and calling for a homeland in Palestine for Jews persecuted in all nations. It was instrumental in establishing the Jewish nation in 1948 in what is now Israel. Zionism as such is grounded upon the first five books of the Bible, called the Torah.

**Z Theory:**    A form of management in which workers are involved in the work process on the factory floor. Schedules, division of labor, work assignments, and other aspects of the labor process are given over to workers to do as they see best. Investment policies, wages, fringe benefits, and decisions about the kind of products produced are not given over to workers to decide. Workers only determine how best to do that which is decided by top management. See "Democratic Self-Management," "Deskilling," and "Fordism" for more.

# About the Authors

**T. R. Young,** Ph.D., is a cofounding member of The Red Feather Institute in Michigan. He has been a university professor and, most recently, a visiting lecturer at the University of Pittsburgh, the University of Colorado, Texas Women's University, and Vermont University. He has written extensively in the areas of sociology, social psychology, and philosophy of science. His recent books include *The Drama of Social Life: Essays in Post-Modern Social Psychology* (1990) and *Chaos Theory and the Drama of Social Change: Essays in Postmodern Philosophy of Science* (1992). With Bruce A. Arrigo he is completing a book on Chaos theory and postmodern criminology. Young is cofounder and general editor of the journal, *Postmodern Criminology*.

**Bruce A. Arrigo,** Ph.D., is Professor of Criminology and Social Psychology and Director of the Institute of Psychology, Law, and Public Policy at the California School of Professional Psychology–Fresno. He has written extensively in the areas of criminology, law, and justice studies. His recent books include *Madness, Language, and the Law* (1993), *The Contours of Psychiatric Justice: A Postmodern Critique of Mental Illness, Criminal Insanity, and the Law* (1996), and the anthology, *Social Justice/Criminal Justice: The Maturation of Critical Theory in Law, Crime, and Deviance* (1998). With T. R. Young, he is completing a book on Chaos theory and postmodern criminology. Dr. Arrigo is also the editor of the peer reviewed, social science quarterly, *Humanity and Society,* and the founding editor of the quarterly, *Journal of Forensic Psychology Practice.*